ALSO BY SCOTT WEIDENSAUL

Living on the Wind:
Across the Hemisphere with Migratory Birds

Mountains of the Heart:
A Natural History of the Appalachians

THE GHOST WITH
TREMBLING WINGS

THE GHOST WITH TREMBLING WINGS

Science, Wishful Thinking, and

the Search for Lost Species

SCOTT WEIDENSAUL

❧

North Point Press

A division of Farrar, Straus and Giroux

New York

North Point Press
A division of Farrar, Straus and Giroux
19 Union Square West, New York 10003

Copyright © 2002 by Scott Weidensaul
Distributed in Canada by Douglas & McIntyre Ltd.
Printed in the United States of America
First edition, 2002

Library of Congress Cataloging-in-Publication Data
Weidensaul, Scott.
   The ghost with trembling wings : science, wishful thinking, and the search for lost species /
Scott Weidensaul.— 1st ed.
      p.   cm.
   Includes bibliographical references (p.   ).
   ISBN 0-374-24664-5 (hc. : alk. paper)
    1. Rare animals.   2. Extinction (Biology)   I. Title.

QL82 .W45 2002
591.68—dc21

                                                                              2001054605

Designed by Jonathan D. Lippincott

www.fsgbooks.com

1 3 5 7 9 10 8 6 4 2

For SMG
because it will surprise the hell out of her
and
for Connor Callaghan
in the hope that there are still unexplored corners
of the world when he's ready to look for them

Contents

◆

1. The Ghost with Trembling Wings   3

2. Proving a Negative   38

3. Chance and Calculation   65

4. The Noble Living   93

5. The ABC's of Ghost Cats   123

6. Cruising the Crypto-fringe   151

7. The Brothers and the Bull   187

8. Test-tube Babies   214

9. The Tiger That Isn't   243

10. Sweat Bees Ate Our Earwax   280

Notes and Bibliography   311

Acknowledgments   323

Index   327

THE GHOST WITH
TREMBLING WINGS

The Ghost with Trembling Wings

The overnight rain had stopped, leaving the forest heavy with moisture and the trail slick with mud. I moved down the path in the dim green predawn light, beneath palms and tall mahogany trees hung with vines, keeping half an eye on the ground—mindful that a snake, one of the big, venomous fer-de-lances that blend so well with fallen leaves, might be returning late from a night of hunting.

The air was overflowing with bird songs, only a few of which I recognized; the clear, piercing whistles of rufous-throated solitaires, and the buzzy, hurry-up-and-wait melody of the tiny bananaquits, which flitted ahead of me like yellow insects. The path wound its way down into ravines, across small, clear jungle streams, and back up again, and wrapped around the base of sodden cliffs covered with ferns, from which choruses of tree frogs still called, unwilling to relinquish the night.

After an hour of hiking, I rounded a bend and the forest fell away suddenly into a deep gash. I could finally see what I'd already known —that I was high on the side of a steep mountain, overlooking narrow valleys enclosed by craggy, tree-covered hills, their summits made indistinct by ragged gray clouds that whipped across them on the strong breeze.

St. Lucia lies midway down the Windward Islands of the Lesser Antilles, where the chain crooks like a bent finger toward Venezuela, 400 miles to the south. It is a volcanic island, heavily mountainous and covered in forest—the very picture of a tropical paradise, known through history as "the Helen of the Caribbean" for its natural beauty. Tourist resorts rim the coasts, while the interior is largely protected in a series of government forest reserves; unlike many of its neighbors in the Caribbean, St. Lucia has maintained much of its native habitat, making it an emerging mecca for ecotourism.

The northeast trade winds, which blow almost constantly through the winter dry season, wicked the sweat from me as I settled down at the edge of the overlook for a rest, unslinging my binoculars. In 1994, when a hurricane swept the region, torrential rains loosened the soil, producing catastrophic landslides across the island. The damage was far less in the forest reserves, where the thick jungle held the soil in place better than farmland or scrub did, but this hillside had nevertheless torn loose, entombing hundred-foot-tall trees in a slurry of heavy mud that roared into the valley below. Now, years later, the dizzyingly steep wall of the old slide zone was covered with fresh green growth, edged by a few old canopy trees that somehow escaped the carnage and stood lonely and tall.

A pair of large parrots, growling and squawking like preschoolers, flew out of the mist and down into the valley, blue and yellow flashing on their wings before they were swallowed by the trees. A broad-winged hawk wheeled overhead, giving a high, thin scream, then landed near the top of one of the tall trees and began to meticulously preen its feathers.

Sometimes, in the forest, it pays to play a hunch. I don't know why, but as I watched the hawk, I froze, binoculars halfway to my eyes, then very slowly turned my head to look behind me. An agouti was emerging from the dark tunnel of the trail. It is hard to describe an agouti; to call it a rodent, however biologically accurate that may be, conveys an entirely inaccurate impression, for there was nothing at all furtive or slinky about it. It weighed about 10 pounds and was the size of a fox, and looked like a cross between a sleek guinea pig and a deer—slender legs, a solid, squared-off body with no visible tail, and large, dark eyes. It stopped and looked around, its Roman nose twitching, the low sun casting a green iridescence over its glossy brown fur.

I had seen agoutis before in the rain forests of Central and South America, but only as indistinct shapes hurtling across the trail in the twilight or scuffling in the dark just beyond my flashlight beam. The head had a rabbitish look despite the small ears, and the hair around the rump was coarser and longer than the fine pelt on its neck and shoulders; when an agouti is alarmed, it flares this corona of bristles like a grass skirt.

The agouti padded forward on its small pink feet until it was within a foot of the pack lying by my side. Only then did it seem to notice me, staring up with those luminous eyes. It did a graceful pirouette of a hop, stopping to look back as if in disbelief. It flared its rump hair, skittered a few more yards, and stopped once more to peer at me. Then it finally seemed to resolve things in its own mind, and trotted off with dignified deliberation.

The enchantment broke, and I turned back to stare at the valleys and mountains spread below me, gauging my next move. I wasn't in the Caribbean to commune with rodents—I was there to solve a mystery. Somewhere down in that intensely green, intensely vertical landscape, a lost soul had been hiding for more than half a century. I was trying to find it.

Biologists estimate there are between 10 and 30 million species of living things on our planet, only a fraction of which have been described and catalogued. New species come to light every day, from obscure beetles to unknown birds and even a few large mammals. The two centers of this biological diversity are tropical ecosystems, which support almost incomprehensible numbers of plants and animals, and islands, which by their isolation promote the rapid evolution of unique life forms. Tropical islands, like those of the Caribbean, are thus doubly blessed by nature.

Prior to European discovery, virtually every island in the Antilles held species that were found nowhere else in the world—endemics, as they are known. Hispaniola had to itself three species of shrew, two kinds of ground sloth (one of which weighed 150 pounds), seven species of chunky rodents called hutias, a squirrel-sized insectivore with a rat-like tail and an impossibly long, pointy snout known as a solenodon, as well as more than two dozen unique birds. Jamaica had roughly thirty endemic bird species, as well as a hutia, five endemic snakes, a unique tree frog, two species of endemic bats, an iguana, and several smaller lizards called galliwasps. Cuba, the biggest island in the Caribbean basin, had the greatest diversity of life, including half a dozen sloths, a 400-pounder among them, and more than two dozen endemic birds, one of which, the bee hummingbird, is, at a shade over 2 inches long, the world's smallest bird. (Cuba's natural wealth is a textbook example of the principles of biogeography, a main rule of which is that the larger an island, or the closer it lies to the mainland, the greater the diversity of life it will support. But the Antilles also showcase a corollary: The farther from the mainland an island is, the more uniquely evolved its flora and fauna tend to be.)

Unfortunately, island species tend to be a bit less adaptable than their mainland counterparts, especially when confronted with new predators, and because of their limited range and population size, they are all the more susceptible to extinction. At the end of the last ice age, the West Indies were populated with an assortment of animals that would appear bizarre to modern eyes: giant ground sloths; rodents the size of small bears; several species of flightless owls on Cuba that were 3 feet tall, with long, heronlike legs for running down their prey; and a condor rivaling today's Andean condor in size. Many of these became extinct after the end of the ice age, 10,000 years ago, an extinction wave that intensified after Amerindians settled the islands, starting between 7,000 and 4,500 years ago. Paleontologists call these "first-contact extinctions," on the assumption that human hunting drove the losses. (But if humans took away, they also gave: agoutis like the one I saw were not native to the Caribbean but were apparently brought from South America by natives as a food supply.)

The large, the flightless, the tasty, and the unwary winked out on island after island, a trend that repeated itself with smaller and fleeter species when Europeans began to colonize the region in the sixteenth century. For instance, at least fifteen or sixteen species of parrots, including eight species of large macaws, became extinct after 1600, most of them now known only from notations in the logbooks of early explorers, who found them as palatable in the pot as they were colorful in the air. One species, from St. Croix, is known from only a single bone. The Cuban macaw, a stunning bird nearly 2 feet long, with a red head and body and blue wings, lasted a bit longer, finally disappearing at the end of the nineteenth century.

St. Lucia is very small—only 27 miles long and, at its most expan-

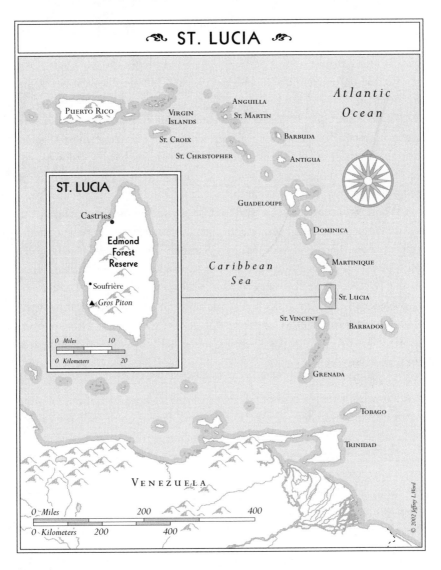

⚛ ST. LUCIA ⚛

ST. LUCIA

Castries

Edmond
Forest
Reserve

• Soufrière

▲ Gros Piton

0 Miles   10

0 Kilometers   20

PUERTO RICO

VIRGIN
ISLANDS

ANGUILLA

ST. MARTIN

ST. CROIX

BARBUDA

ST. CHRISTOPHER

ANTIGUA

Atlantic
Ocean

GUADELOUPE

DOMINICA

Caribbean
Sea

MARTINIQUE

ST. LUCIA

ST. VINCENT

BARBADOS

GRENADA

TOBAGO

TRINIDAD

VENEZUELA

0 Miles   200   400

0 Kilometers   200   400

© 2002 Jeffrey L. Ward

sive, just 14 wide, covering barely 240 square miles—and neighboring islands like St. Vincent and Martinique provided stepping-stones for colonizing wildlife. Consequently, its endemism rate is fairly low; there is a colorful ground lizard, a nonvenomous grass snake, a unique race of boa constrictor, and five species of endemic birds. The endangered St. Lucian parrot, or *jacquot*, which numbers barely five hundred individuals, is large and noisy, with a cobalt-blue face, a rich suffusion of red down the chest and belly, and splashes of blue, yellow, and red on the wings. There is the St. Lucian pewee, a species of flycatcher with a cinnamon breast, and a black-finch with bubblegum-pink legs. The St. Lucian oriole is vivid orange and black; like the parrot, it epitomizes the dazzle we expect from tropical birds.

There is precious little dazzle to the fifth species on St. Lucia's list of endemic birds, the Semper's warbler, which may be the dullest tropical bird on Earth. It is notable not for its plumage (which is the color of oatmeal, and as exciting) or its song (which no one has ever described or recorded), but solely for its rarity.

When the French and English first began squabbling over who got to keep St. Lucia—a disagreement that would last 150 years and see the island change hands fourteen times—Semper's warbler was fairly common in the lush mountain rain forests. It was first collected for science in the 1870s by a St. Lucian clergyman, the Reverend John E. Semper, and eventually named in his honor, though the Creole inhabitants of the island knew it long before as the *pied blanc*, or "white foot," because of its large, pale legs. The bird's scientific name acknowledges the same feature, merging the Greek words for "white feet" to create its genus name, *Leucopeza*.

Semper's warbler is about 5 inches long and gray—dishwater gray, battleship gray, old-movie gray. Dull, bland, flat: even the adjectives that best describe it are monosyllabic and boring. It is the kind of creature that birders dismiss as an LBJ, a "little brown jobbie," but even that suggests too much pizzazz. And yet, despite its lackluster appearance, birders have been combing St. Lucia's forests in search of it for years —drawn not by looks, but by the cachet of extinction. For within a few decades following its discovery, Semper's warbler went from common to kaput.

Judging by the number of specimens found in collections from the late nineteenth and early twentieth centuries, Semper's warbler must have been widespread, but by the late 1920s, the Caribbean ornithologist James Bond spent weeks looking for it without success. (This was the same James Bond whose name was later appropriated, with his permission, for Ian Fleming's fictional secret agent.) Some worried that the species was extinct, but kept on hunting. A single female was located in 1934 and promptly shot; at that time, stuffing a specimen for a collec-

All that may remain of Reverend Semper's dull little warbler are skin specimens like these at the American Museum of Natural History, collected on St. Lucia between 1880 and 1901. (Scott Weidensaul)

tion was sometimes considered more important than preserving the living species.

Stanley John, the St. Lucian who collected the 1934 specimen, spent further decades searching for the bird, which vanished for another twenty-seven years. On May 21, 1961, John spotted another—left alive this time—along the eastern coast near the village of Louvet. Like all the other recorded sightings, it was found in virgin forest with a heavy understory of ferns; John and other hunters said the species made a "soft tuck-tick-tick-tuck" call, pumped its tail up and down when perched, and sometimes quivered its wings when flushed.

Since then, Semper's warbler has been a cipher. Nothing is known of where, when, or how it built its nest, how many eggs it laid or what markings they bore, what the juvenile plumage looked like, or even what the male's song sounded like. Most important, nothing is known of its status—whether it is alive or dead. It has been written off on many occasions, only to pop up again in tantalizing but unsubstantiated reports.

One sighting came in 1969, another in 1972, still others in 1989 and

1995. The trouble with sight records, of course, is the lack of any form of objective proof. The 1972 sighting, for instance, is largely dismissed by experts because the two people who claimed to have seen Semper's warbler were inexperienced with Caribbean birds in general and the area in which they said they saw it was completely unlike the habitat in which it had always been found. By contrast, the 1989 sighting was made by Donald Anthony, an experienced wildlife biologist in the St. Lucian Forestry Department, who was hiking on Gros Piton, a high, sharp spike of a mountain along the southeast coast. On the face of it, this would seem good proof of the species' survival—yet it was a quick, fleeting glimpse, and despite another twenty-six ascents of Gros Piton in the years that followed, Anthony has never seen another Semper's warbler, leaving some to wonder if his brief original sighting was a mistake.

Why all the fuss over a dull little bird? Like a relative who isn't appreciated until she's gone, many creatures that were ignored, even vilified, in life become icons in the grand death of extinction. In the nineteenth century, mountain lions (also known as cougars or panthers) were hunted down with such vigor that they were exterminated in every state east of the Mississippi, except for a small population in Florida and perhaps some in the wilderness of New Brunswick. Within a generation of their extinction in the Appalachians, however, people began to report lion sightings in places like New York, Pennsylvania, and the southern highlands of Virginia, North Carolina, and Tennessee—reporting them not with the hatred once reserved for a large predator but with barely contained excitement.

The question of whether or not cougars survive in the East illustrates many of the difficulties and subtle allure that go with such mysteries. The subspecies of the cougar that originally inhabited the Northeast, *Puma concolor cougar*, has been considered extinct since the early 1900s, even though it is officially listed as "endangered" under both the federal Endangered Species Act and CITES, the international treaty that covers threatened plants and animals; this status provides protection should a cougar miraculously reappear. And reappear they do—private organizations that track lion sightings in the East say they get hundreds of reports every year, some from people like foresters, game wardens, and biologists who are hard to dismiss as crackpots. Yet outside of New England, where Canadian cougars may have recolonized, there has been almost no physical evidence, like warm road-killed bodies or indisputable photo-graphs. (There have been a few cougars that have been shot over the years, but close examination usually shows them to be of the Latin American subspecies common in captivity.)

I live in the Appalachians, and I know people who claim to have seen cougars here. Some are friends of mine, sturdy, reliable people. The idea is incredibly seductive—the notion that these gentle mountains, long settled and so badly misused by people for centuries, could have re-claimed such a potent symbol of wilderness as the mountain lion. Some-times, I think, we need to believe such things even when the evidence (or its absence) suggests we are deluding ourselves. Deep down in our overcivilized hearts, we need the world to be bigger, and more mysteri-ous, and more exciting than it appears to be in the cold light of day—especially in this age, when the planet shrinks daily and no place seems truly remote or unknown. People keep looking for the long-extinct Bachman's warbler or the marsupial Tasmanian "tiger" for the same rea-sons that they go to mediums in hope of contacting dear, departed Aunt Louise. We're unwilling to accept that there isn't more to the world than what we can see.

When it comes to charismatic wildlife, science, too, sometimes blurs into wishful thinking. Nor is this a recent phenomenon; even in the nineteenth century, when wonders were being found around every bend, explorers often hoped to rediscover survivors of an even more glorious past. Thomas Jefferson suspected that the Lewis and Clark ex-pedition would encounter giant ground sloths in the West, or mam-moths like those whose fossilized bones he had unearthed in Virginia. And Arthur Conan Doyle's *The Lost World*, about explorers who find di-nosaurs on a remote South American plateau, was merely a fictionalized account of a situation Victorian naturalists still thought possible, though unlikely—that in the deepest parts of the unexplored tropics, Creta-ceous reptiles still lived. Indeed, to this day some people hold out this hope, and mount expeditions to the heart of the Congo to look for Mokele-mbembe, a legendary dinosaur-like monster of the swamps.

We paint the blank spots on maps with our deepest fears and secret longings, and today we still grasp at straws, unwilling to admit that we've wrung most of the mystery out of the world. Sure, there are still a few new species of large mammals coming out of Laos, Vietnam, and

Cambodia, where decades of war kept scientists at bay until now, but for many people, that's not enough. So they comb the wilds of Cornwall, looking for tracks from the big cat known as the Beast of Bodmin Moor, or spend their vacations scouting the Cascades for Sasquatch. When a surprisingly credible report of ivory-billed woodpeckers—surprising because the species had been written off as extinct in the United States forty years ago—came out of the swamps of Louisiana recently, people immediately descended on the area, a strange mix of the skeptical, the curious, the methodical, and the overly credulous. One of the searchers was certain the birds were there, she said, because a friend was channeling their spirits, telling her they were at last ready to reveal themselves.

John Burroughs, the great nineteenth-century naturalist, said, "You must have the bird in your heart before you can find it in the bush." I was not channeling the spirit of Semper's warbler, but for months I had been combing through the scientific literature, talking to experts, visiting museums, and looking at maps until my eyes teared. I had it in my mind, at least; the only way to see if it was in my heart was to go to St. Lucia and find out.

The Edmond Forest Reserve lies in the snaggle-toothed mountains east of the town of Soufrière. You drive down the narrow streets, jammed with pedestrians, and make a left at the central square, where grass and trees grow now but where guillotines thumped during the French Revolution, spreading its bloodshed to even this remote corner of the empire.

At the little village of Fond St. Jacques, you turn off the main road and onto a track that deteriorates as it climbs into the hills, the roadway having long since eroded into deep craters surrounding small plateaus of black asphalt. Soon even this is gone, and the ramshackle four-wheel-drive is skidding and bucking over loose rock, past cows tethered in the shade of big trees so they can graze, past fields tucked on impossibly steep hillsides. Mount Gimie, at 3,000 feet the highest point on the island, looms over you, its peak wreathed in clouds. After an hour of driving, and just as you're casting a nervous eye on the temperature gauge on the rented car (before realizing that, like much of the instrumentation, it's broken), you top out at a little wooden lean-to that serves as the welcome center for the forest reserve. This is the jump-off point for the many people who come to hike the cross-island Rain Forest Walk, a popular trail that threads its way through part of Edmond.

I drove past the welcome center and down the road, stopping to unlock a cable gate. Amy, a friend from New Jersey, waited in the vehicle, which idled unevenly; her presence on the trip was an object lesson in the dangers of speaking too quickly. Some months earlier, when I was outlining my plans to look for lost species, she had said, "Well, if you ever need someone to help carry your bags, let me know."

People make this comment to me all the time, but usually I know they aren't serious—and besides, I ordinarily prefer to travel solo. But Amy, a tall, slender environmental educator, was quite serious. Since I knew that I'd need help with much of the fieldwork involved in looking for Semper's warbler, like stringing nets through the forest to capture unwary birds, and because I had a hunch I wouldn't be able to count on assistance from the St. Lucian authorities, I accepted her offer before she could change her mind.

Although Amy had worked in the swamps of south Florida and had lived for a time in a tipi in the mountains of North Carolina, I tried to be clear that this wouldn't be the standard Caribbean jaunt; she'd never been to the tropics, and I painted as accurate a picture as I could of what she should expect. Bugs. Mud. Heat and humidity. Venomous snakes. Poor food. Dicey accomodations.

On this last count, it looked as though we had lucked out. We were heading for a field station owned by the St. Lucian Forestry Department, which controls the reserves and oversees wildlife conservation on the island; for a small fee, we had been given permission to use the site, and for a much heftier price, a forestry worker would act as a guide. The offer was a godsend, since it spared us from making predawn drives to and from Soufrière on the long, bone-rattling road. The day before, Donald Anthony—the wildlife officer who had made the last credible sighting of a Semper's warbler—had shown us the place, a small cinder-block building painted pale blue, with a discolored rim of algae growing around the base of the walls, set in the woods surrounded by hundreds of blooming anthuriums grown for the floral trade. The metal slat blinds covering the windows were closed, giving the building a sleepy appearance.

Anthony, a muscular man with a pair of waterproof binoculars slung around his neck, rattled the door of the field station, but it was locked and he didn't have the key. It was fully equipped, he assured us, with everything from a generator to fresh bedding. All we needed to bring the following day was canned food.

Now we were back, and Theodore, one of the local forest officers, pulled up in his truck and unlocked the station for us. The front room was an office, though long unused, by the look and smell of it; the posters on the wall were curling and everything was covered with a layer of sticky dirt. Around the corner was a small kitchen—the counter had a number of large dead roaches glued to a thick coating of old grease, their legs folded up in a fuzz of white fungus; the dishes and flatware were sitting out in a drying rack, liberally speckled with mouse and roach droppings. There were two sleeping rooms, one with bunk beds and the other with a single, all the beds with nothing more than stained, smelly foam pads. Cracks in the ceiling had allowed a steady rain of brown bat droppings to filter down over time, but Theodore flipped the mattresses with a cheerful grin, exposing a side equally stained and smelly but without fresh guano. No, he said, there was no bedding; didn't we know we had to bring our own? The generator, he explained, was defunct, but there was a candle—he smiled brightly at our luck— and the toilet, sink, and shower were connected to clean well water, though when he tried the faucet a connection outside at the wellhead blew, sending a geyser spraying into the air until he patched it up.

It was, by a long shot, not the worst place I'd ever stayed in, but then I remembered that this was Amy's first trip outside the United States. None of the guidebooks had pictures of anything that looked remotely like this, and I wondered how this jibed with her plans for a Caribbean adventure. I was pretty sure, when I'd outlined potential unpleasantries months before, I hadn't said anything about bat guano.

"You okay with this?" I asked quietly.

"Please," she said, laughing and rolling her eyes. "I'm the one who lived in a tipi, remember?" And that was the end of that—though I did give her the room with the bunk bed, so she'd have something to deflect the nightly shower of bat droppings. Chivalry is not dead.

I lit the gas stove, boiled a huge kettle of water, and set about cleaning the kitchen as best I could. I opened one of the sagging cupboards to reveal a skittering host of roaches before I remembered my hard-learned credo that it's best not to pry into dark corners while traveling in the tropics. After we'd finished eating, there was time for a quick walk down the trail.

To an untrained eye like mine, blind to the nuances of tropical botany, the woods looked like many of the rain forests I'd been in across Latin America and the Caribbean. Anthony had pointed out that most of the trees near camp weren't native to St. Lucia, however, but were a mix of blue mahoe, a valuable hardwood from Jamaica, and Honduran mahogany, planted by the government in the 1970s to provide timber and to stabilize cleared areas in the mountains.

We couldn't really expect to find Semper's warbler here; the forest had little understory, and all the old records agreed that the bird was found in virgin native forest where there were lots of low ferns for cover. Once our guide arrived, our search would be directed deeper into the reserve, where there was still some native forest remaining. But the evening walk gave me a chance to get a feel for the place and make sure my equipment was in good order. Over one shoulder I'd slung the strap of a heavy tape recorder, with a pair of earphones attached by a long cord and a shotgun microphone—a long, foam-covered wand—riding in a holster on my hip. It was, I'm sure, a remarkably silly-looking getup, but the recorder could prove crucial in our search.

Seeing birds in the rain forest is tricky—the thick vegetation and a bird's natural shyness conspire to make a good, clear look a relative rarity. This is especially true of a timid ground-dweller, as Semper's warbler is thought to have been. Tropical ornithologists use a technique called tape-playback to great advantage in overcoming this hurdle. One makes a quick, on-the-spot recording of a singing bird, then immediately plays it back; the bird, hearing what it thinks is an intruder in its territory, comes charging in, spoiling for a fight. Several experts on Caribbean birds told me that they felt tape-playback offered the best shot at finding Semper's warbler.

There is an obvious drawback to this neat plan: No one, least of all me, had the slightest clue what a Semper's warbler song sounds like. "Though the voice and nest of this species are unknown, it probably breeds in the spring, and its voice could be insect-like," wrote the author of a checklist of St. Lucian birds. Walking through the evening twilight,

I realized there were also a lot of insectlike *insect* calls reverberating through the damp woods; picking out a nondescript buzzy trill from this cacophony would be a challenge. That said, the low diversity of birdlife on St. Lucia—especially compared with, say, a New England forest in May—was a point in our favor; I was hoping that eventually we'd be able to sort through the common bird songs and call notes, and zero in on the ones we didn't recognize. Maybe. No one said finding an extinct species would be easy.

When does an organism become extinct? The answer is at once self-evident and surprisingly complex. Extinction can occur in degrees—local extinction, in which a species is extirpated from one part of its range but not others; extinction in the wild, in which only captive populations remain; or functional extinction, in which perhaps only aged, nonbreeding individuals are left, or populations become so small and isolated that they will inevitably succumb to random fluctuations over time and die out: the "walking dead," as biologists sometimes call them. Perhaps the most vivid example is a palm, *Hyophorbe amaricaulis*, which has no common name and is found only on the Indian Ocean island of Mauritius, once home to the dodo. Just a single tree remains, and though it produces both male and female flowers, it does so at different times, and thus has never set fruit.

True extinction—final and irrevocable extinction—comes when the last individual of a species dies, leaving no viable offspring. Plants and animals can come perilously close to this juncture and still pull back; the Laysan duck, a species endemic to that coral atoll in the Hawaiian chain, was reduced to just seven birds in 1912, the result of defoliation of the island by introduced rabbits. The rabbits subsequently starved, and while three other kinds of Laysan birds became extinct, today there are several hundred of the ducks. By 1974, the Mauritius kestrel was down to only six birds, including two pairs in the wild; a redux of the dodo seemed inevitable. Thanks to inspired captive breeding, though, the birds now also number several hundred in the wild.

It is rare that humans can mark the exact day and hour of a species' extermination; often we know when the last captive specimens die, but uncertainty remains about when, or whether, the plant or animal vanished from the wild. The last captive Carolina parakeet, orange and green and so thoroughly tropical in appearance that it is hard to believe that this native parrot wintered as far north as New York and Illinois, died on February 21, 1918, in the Cincinnati Zoo, which just four years previous had seen the death of the last passenger pigeon. The last wild parakeet is believed to have been shot between 1901 and 1904, although the exact date and place are mired in speculative and unconfirmed reports. In fact, rumors of parakeet sightings continued to dribble out of the deep swamps of the Southeast, the last refuge for the species, through the 1920s and 1930s. A flock of parrots was even captured on movie film by a guide in the Okefenokee Swamp in Georgia in 1937, though no one who saw the short clip could say with certainty if they were Carolina parakeets or escaped exotic cage birds.

It's a big world out there, and proving a negative—the absence of a creature—is a tall order. The American Ornithologists' Union declared the Carolina parakeet extinct in 1939, despite the sporadic reports, but hope lingers long after logic gives up, and even the most hard-bitten scientist is usually reluctant to say with certainty that this animal or that one is well and truly gone. Bachman's warbler, a lovely songbird of the Southeast that dwindled when farmers cleared the native bamboo stands it apparently used for nesting, is a case in point. The last specimen was collected in Mississippi in 1949, the same year that the last known breeding pair was seen in South Carolina. A male—a pretty yellow bird with a black bib—was photographed on May 15, 1958, near Charleston, S.C., where sightings continued through 1961. The final time that a Bachman's warbler was sighted by reliable observers whose report was widely accepted was April 1962, in the I'On Swamp of South Carolina.

Yet despite a dearth of evidence, no one's willing to abandon this particular ship quite yet. Paul Hamel, the ornithologist who has spent the most time researching the demise of the species, and who has searched unsuccessfully for it through the Southeast and Cuba for almost thirty years, hedges his bets by saying it is "nearly, or perhaps already, extinct." Other experts adopt similarly vague language. One reason for the hesitation is a slow drip of reports over the years—a series of photographs from Florida in 1977 that appear to show an immature female Bachman's warbler, though not all experts agree with that identification; a report from Louisiana in 1988 that some ornithologists deemed credible; a series of unconfirmed reports from Georgia, the Gulf Coast,

South Carolina, and the Cuban wintering grounds in the late 1970s and 1980s.

Hamel, who lavished thousands of hours in the field without ever catching a glimpse of his quarry, has at least kept his sense of humor about the whole thing. At the end of a technical summation of what little is known of the species, he noted that "any detailed observations of the Bachman's warbler would be worth the bird's weight in gold. How much does one weigh? I predict 9.2g, and patiently wait to be corrected."

There is a procedural end run around making these pronouncements of death. One criterion often used is a cousin to the legal device of declaring a missing person dead after seven years—just wait fifty years after the last generally accepted sighting in the wild. This is the benchmark used, for example, by the international CITES treaty, and it is widely accepted by other agencies and scientists. But it is far from an iron-clad rule; the last Kauai 'akialoa, a Hawaiian honeycreeper with an impossibly long, curved bill, was seen as recently as 1965, but the bird is considered extinct because intensive searches have failed to turn up any sign of it and its lowland habitat has been altered beyond any realistic hope of survival.

Yet naturalists have learned to be cautious with their pronouncements of doom, because animals and plants have a way of proving them wrong. The showy Indian clover, a pretty pink annual that was once common on grasslands north of San Francisco Bay, was declared extinct in 1984 after repeated searches over the preceding fifteen years failed to turn it up. Acknowledging its demise seemed a safe bet; this was a plant, after all, not a rodent that could scurry down a hole to hide, or a whale capable of losing itself in the sea. Yet in 1993, Dr. Peter G. Connors, a scientist at the University of California's Bodega Marine Reserve, found a single clover plant growing near the town of Occidental; it pollinated itself (a trick, as we've seen, that not all plants can manage) and produced 92 seeds, 18 of which sprouted. Three years later, another patch—more than 200 plants this time, on a coastal bluff in Marin County—was found. Today, progeny of those plants, representing two unique local varieties, produce thousands of seeds a year, and new stands are being created.

In fact, while animal rediscoveries get the most attention, lost plants resurface almost as often, and frequently along even stranger paths. In 1909, a French botanist working in Madagascar collected the leaves and flowers of a weird little tree he couldn't identify. The pressed specimens of the unnamed plant were stored away in an herbarium and forgotten until 1963, when another French scientist going through the collections found them and named the species *Takhtajania perrieri*. Now the tree had a name, but no future, because no other specimen had turned up in the wild following the first collection—an especially frustrating situation for botanists, because the family to which the tree belonged, the Winteraceae, had been thought extinct in Africa for 30 million years.

Finally, thirty years after its christening and eighty-five years since its last sighting in the wild, a stand of live *Takhtajania* was found by a Malagasy forest worker, 90 miles from its original location. DNA tests suggest the species is one of the most primitive flowering plants in the world, a true living fossil that has provided scientists with remarkable insights into plant evolution.

While a few rediscoveries make the evening news or the pages of major newspapers—like the Javan rhinos found recently in Vietnam, or the captive lions seized from an itinerant circus in Africa, which appear to be a subspecies thought extinct since the 1920s—most of these recaptured gems merit hardly a mention outside the world of conservation biology. Yet regardless of the natural charisma of the animal or plant involved, each case represents a rare bit of good news in a world awash with environmental destruction—and it happens far more often than most people realize. Here's a fairly random list of lost species that, thanks to recent discoveries, are officially back in the fold of the living:

- Gilbert's potoroo, an endearing little marsupial the size of a rabbit from western Australia, which was discovered in 1840, seen a few times in the 1860s, and considered extinct for 125 years. What's more, it is one of four marsupials rediscovered in western Australia in recent years, thanks to more intensive live-trapping by scientists.
- The rufous-throated white-eye and streaky-breasted jungle-flycatcher, two birds native to the Indonesian island of Buru, where they had not been seen since the 1920s.
- The pale-headed brush-finch of southern Ecuador. Last seen in

1969, and evading several expeditions that searched for it, a tiny population was rediscovered in 1998; at most, biologists believe, the few acres of remaining natural habitat can support about fifteen pairs. Only five days after the species was rediscovered, a large fire threatened to sweep through this minute patch of arid scrub, but local landowners, alerted to the bird's presence, stopped the blaze, and conservation groups have purchased some of the area as a reserve.

• The large Jamaican iguana, thought extinct for nearly half a century, which was rediscovered in 1990, when a pig hunter's dog killed one in the hot, rugged Hellshire Hills. The population is estimated at between 50 and 200, making it for a time the world's most endangered lizard. But the 1999 discovery of six 18-inch-long lizards in the Canary Islands—a species, *Galliota gomerana*, thought extinct for more than five centuries—eclipses the iguana in terms of both rarity and sheer surprise value.

• The Congo bay owl, known only from a single specimen collected in 1951 in eastern Zaire and not seen again despite a number of intensive searches through the 1970s. In 1996, an expedition to study gorillas and birds in the region mist-netted one of the owls, which resembles a barn owl but has a deep cinnamon color.

• The giant woolly flying squirrel of the Pakistan Himalayas, a woodchuck-sized creature with a 2-foot-long tail and thick gray fur. Several specimens were collected in the late nineteenth century, but the last record of a live one was in 1924, and by the end of the twentieth century it was generally considered extinct. But in 1994, Wildlife Conservation Society researcher Peter Zahler and New York math teacher Chantal Dietemann relocated the legendary animal—though they needed help to do it.

Zahler's previous fieldwork in 1992 had been a bust, and the pair had wasted a month in 1994 trying to live-trap the animals, whose screaming calls they'd heard. Finally, they were approached by two elderly men who said they made their living by rappelling down the sides of cliffs at elevations of nearly 11,000 feet and collecting *salajit*, a local aphrodisiac believed to be the hardened urine of the flying squirrels. For a price, they would catch a squirrel.

"I sent them off with one of our empty food sacks, thinking I would never see them again, and went back to trying to decide what bait to use next to lure an animal whose diet remained a mystery," Zahler recounted. "Hours later, the two men returned and deposited a woolly flying squirrel at my feet."

Zahler's experience points up an important caveat in all this talk about "lost" species—they are usually lost only to the world at large, not to the people who share their environment. Just as a spectacular ruined city in the jungle may just be part of the neighborhood scenery to an indigenous hunter, so too an extraordinary zoological discovery to a Western scientist is often only the makings of dinner—or the aphrodisiac trade—to a local family. No doubt, those two Pakistani *salajit* collectors wondered what all the fuss was about, since they'd been living with the giant flying squirrel for generations.

Still, the notion of finding a lost species is a seductive one. I can't tell you how many times I've sifted through old newspaper clippings, or stared at faded black-and-white photographs—maybe Jim Tanner's famous photos from the 1940s of the last nesting ivory-billed woodpeckers in Louisiana, the birds as big as ducks, with their ludicrous white beaks and pointy crests; or the grainy snapshot from the 1920s of a thylacine, the marsupial "tiger" that had the body shape of a wolf and a set of zebra stripes on its hindquarters—an otherworldly beast, which the Australians exterminated to defend their all-too-pedestrian sheep.

Time and again—against logic, against sense—I would start to imagine. I could see the striped pelt of the thylacine moving through the Tasmanian bush, or summon up in my mind the manic call of an ivorybill echoing off ancient tupelos deep in some soggy forest. As I said, it's a big world; the swamps are trackless, the trees are thick. We humans are omnipresent but not omniscient; we can overlook the secretive and skittish. How easy, I would tell myself in daydreams, for a little thing like Semper's warbler to avoid our clumsy passage, in its rugged, wet redoubt in the Quillesse Range of central St. Lucia.

Imagining leads to a germ of hope, and hope sometimes leads to belief, to obsession and piles of old maps, to fruitless expeditions and squandered life savings. All of which would seem a sad and farcical pathology, except that just often enough, some lucky searcher hits pay dirt, and the world stands surprised and delighted with the discovery.

When the Europeans first landed on Bermuda, for example, they found an abundance of "a webbe-footed Fowle . . . of the bigness of an English greene Plover," which they named the cahow for its "strange hollow and harsh howling." The Spanish discovered that the cahow, which was actually a pelagic seabird known as a petrel, tasted good, and the English colonists that followed tucked in with gusto. Cahows had no innate fear of humans and were easy to pluck from their nest burrows— and not only by humans. Introduced pigs, rats, cats, and dogs ate the nesting birds, their eggs and chicks, and the island's natural vegetation was cleared and burned off, robbing them of cover. Within the space of a quarter-century the colonists ate the cahow out of existence, and by the 1620s it was considered extinct.

In 1906, however, a seabird was collected on Castle Island just off Bermuda. For the next ten years, the specimen was erroneously identified as a mottled petrel, a bird of the South Pacific, and not until 1916 did anyone realize that the Castle Island bird was, in fact, a cahow—the first seen in three centuries, a singular, tantalizing proof of survival. If the wraith of Blackbeard the pirate had walked down the main street in Hamilton, scientists couldn't have been more shocked. Another specimen surfaced in 1935, having collided with a lighthouse, and a third, which flew into a telephone line, in 1941. Four years later, one washed up on a beach, the victim of a fight with another seabird.

Obviously, the cahows were still breeding somewhere—but where? Until the nesting grounds were located, it would be impossible to gauge the size or security of the population. It wasn't until 1951 that an obsessive Bermuda naturalist named David Wingate located the breeding grounds—a mere eighteen pairs nesting on an offshore islet. Even today, with extraordinary attention and protection still spearheaded by the aged Wingate, there are barely forty pairs.

The cahow also points up the flip side of finding a lost species—what to do with it once it's been found. The general assumption is that the machinery of conservation law will step in and rescue the survivors, but the truth is that most of these ghost animals live in parts of the world with little or no functional wildlife protection. The black-footed ferret, considered extinct on several occasions but now the subject of intensive captive breeding, benefits from the federal Endangered Species Act, but that law applies to wildlife only in the United States and its territories. (Species from around the world, like elephants or gorillas, may be listed under the ESA, but that designation only affects their status in the United States, such as through imports of skins or live specimens.) The Convention on International Trade in Endangered Species, or CITES, is the dominant global law on rare plants and animals, but again, it is limited in scope—it covers only international commerce, and only those species specifically listed in its appendices, which rarely include species considered to be extinct. If someone were to try, say, to market cahow meat in the United States, CITES and the ESA could be brought to bear, but otherwise, protection of a rediscovered species is left entirely to local regulation, which in most of the developing world is scant or nonexistent.

Accounts of lost species like the cahow first caught my interest many years ago, and eventually sent me wandering around the globe to search for some of them myself. In the process, I found the subject is a good deal more subtle and complicated than I'd originally realized; what I'd assumed was mostly a tale of biology and science was actually enmeshed with human psychology, deep-seated desires, and the ways—accurate or imagined—in which we view our world. In a sense, the story I have to tell unfolds in three parts. We begin with the process of rediscovery, the many ways in which the lost come back from the grave, and what that means for the science and policy of conservation. Then the focus shifts to what it is that drives our search for lost animals, why we hunger for mystery and drama in even the most mundane of settings—and how wishful thinking sometimes warps our ability to distinguish between reasonable hope and delusion. Finally, it ends with the promise of resurrection—not just rediscovery of what has long been hidden, but the promise that emerging technology may allow us to literally raise the dead.

We are, at our core, an optimistic species; like the White Queen whom Alice met through the looking-glass, we can believe six impossible things before breakfast. The thought of cougars slipping through the hardwood forests of the Appalachians, or golden toads shining like embers in some hidden puddle on a Costa Rican mountain, adds luster to an ever-dimmer planet. And for those of us who treasure wild places and wild things, for whom the death of a species is a personal loss, we also need to believe the world is more complete than the catalogue of vanishing ecosystems would indicate.

And of course, rediscovery happens for real just often enough to keep the hope alive.

We quickly settled into a routine at the field station—waking up just as the frogs were ending their nighttime concerto and heading out into the forest before it was fully light. It would be chilly enough for long sleeves, often with the misty undersides of clouds dragging through the trees on the ever-present trade wind, or with the last dregs of a rain shower dripping around us. Sometimes I went out alone, other times Amy and I worked in tandem, especially if I was trying to record bird songs—the Library of Natural Sounds at Cornell University had asked me to try to tape the calls and songs of St. Lucian birds, especially the *jacquot*, the endangered parrot, of which there were almost no recordings available. I found it helpful for us to work as a team; wearing the headphones, I could hear only what the highly directional microphone picked up, while Amy could scan the surroundings and point me toward new or suspicious calls.

At other times I simply prowled the reserve alone, sitting for long periods wherever I found habitat that resembled the old descriptions of that of Semper's warbler—watching for furtive movements in the undergrowth, or trying (with increasing success) to filter out the mundane bird songs of a St. Lucian morning and zero in on the ones that were new or odd. Our guide, a tall, rail-thin man nearing sixty named Augustine, finally arrived one morning, after a string of frustrating delays, and led us deep into the reserve on barely visible tracks. We threaded our way among tall trees, on a few occasions crawling on our knees beneath fallen trunks, our packs scraping on the bark and the mud squishing between our fingers. We dropped down lower and lower, eventually creeping out onto a long, narrow ridge with a sharp slope to either side, which dipped into a saddle and began to rise again.

This looked like a good place for a line of mist nets; I figured that birds crossing from one side of the ridge to the other would take the shortcut through this pass. As Augustine cut saplings to use as poles, Amy and I cleared away the brush and fallen branches from a long corridor beneath the trees, so that within an hour or two, we had erected a line of half a dozen 40-foot nets, each 10 feet high and almost invisible against the leafy background.

We were sodden with sweat, our legs smeared with mud from the thighs down, and hordes of mosquitoes were starting to swarm, but at least we finally had the nets up. Even though it was already midmorning, and the hot sun had damped the birds' activity a bit, the spot we'd picked was proving to be a good one. Every ten minutes I walked the length of the nets, carefully untangling the songbirds that were hanging from them, birds that no doubt wondered why they'd never encountered such a big spider's web before.

The methods of scientific inquiry have changed somewhat over the years. A century or more ago, I'd have been roaming these woods with a shotgun loaded with very fine bird shot, taking measurements from dead specimens that would later be skinned and stuffed for the collection drawer. (Such collecting is still carried out on occasion, though only for specific purposes and always under strict government control.) In the late nineteenth and early twentieth centuries, collecting for the sake of collecting was all the rage, both by institutions with legitimate reasons and by private individuals with a fancy for natural history. Some people even made a modest living shooting, stuffing, and selling the birds and animals of the world's exotic backwaters, to fill the curio cabinets of collectors in Boston, Philadelphia, or London.

That was the case in St. Lucia, where a few colonials and natives peddled bits and pieces of paradise, including Semper's warbler. Today, those early specimens are priceless. More than a month earlier, we had followed Paul Sweet, the ornithology collections manager for the American Museum of Natural History in Manhattan, down long corridors that smelled faintly of mothballs and into one of many tile-lined rooms to either side of the hall, lit with fluorescent lights and filled with tall gray-white cabinets, each comprised of a dozen or more flat drawers. Going to one marked PARULIDAE: LEUCOPEZA, Sweet unlocked the cabinet and rolled out a tray with small gray bodies lined up neatly in a row.

"My, that's a dull bird," Amy said quietly, peering over my shoulder.

Sweet carried the tray to one of the long worktables that ran along the outer wall of the room, beneath high windows looking out on an un-seasonably mild March day in Central Park. The tabletop was slightly gritty under my fingers, and it took a moment to realize it was probably arsenic that I was feeling, used liberally in years past to preserve bird skins. He wished us well and hurried back to his other responsibilities, leaving us alone.

Of the mere thirty-four specimens of Semper's warbler known to exist, the AMNH holds seven, all of which were before us. These were not taxidermy mounts, stuffed to appear alive, but standard museum specimens made for scientific study—flat on their backs, wings closed, heads stretched stiffly out like lance points, legs demurely crossed and tied with the threads holding the labels. The eyes were simply puffs of cotton peeking out from inside the skin. Most were not especially well prepared. A few heads were crooked, bills agape and dribbling cotton; one was missing a leg, which lay disembodied in a corner of the tray.

Reading the spidery, archaic penmanship on the stained labels, we found that the oldest of the lot was collected on February 18, 1880, by the Reverend Semper himself, and originally presented to the Museum of Comparative Zoology at Harvard. Another dated from 1886, and the tag noted that it had been purchased from a local collector. One label had no collection data, while the rest of the birds were all shot within a three-day period in February 1901—a series, in the jargon of collectors.

The birds were about 5¼ inches long, a smooth, gun-metal blue-gray on the back, fading to pale silver below, with faint eyebrows. The only hint of color was a touch of sienna along the division between the darker flanks and the lighter belly, giving the undersides a curious tritone ef-fect. The bill was strikingly long and thick for such a small bird, with a noticeable curve to the upper mandible; nothing is known about the warbler's feeding habits, but ornithologists believe, based on the shape of the bill, that it fed on large invertebrates pulled out of leaf litter and undergrowth. The legs were also remarkably robust, though with age they were no longer pale but withered and dull.

I went to work with calipers and a ruler, taking measurements from the old skins. I photographed them from every conceivable angle, then put the camera down, feeling a little silly. It was busy work. The long trip into the city had been mostly to hold the skins in my hands, to get a mental image of the real bird, one independent of field guides, paintings, or written descriptions. If we caught a live Semper's, the measurements would be a valuable comparison, of course, and the photos would certainly help to confirm the identification, but I felt as though I were stopping at a shrine before setting out on a quest.

Amy and I sat for a long time looking silently at the skins, handling them with exaggerated delicacy, always aware of their fragility and rarity, turning them over, each of us lost in thought. "You know, they really are quite lovely, when you stop to look at them," she said. I'd been thinking the same thing, that the birds had an understated beauty that poor preparation and a century in dark drawers could not entirely dim. But I had to hope—if only for the dignity of Semper's warbler—that this wasn't all that was left, that there still was more to this species than these sorry, tatty remains.

We talked for quite a while, speculating on the bird's feeding habits, trying to deduce from the clues of its physique and appearance how it had lived. This started in a dry, scientific way, but as we both got into the exercise, I could feel the excitement building. Semper's warbler, which had for so long been an abstraction to me, was taking on life. The tone of our conversation changed, and without our realizing it, we were speaking of the warbler in the present tense, not the past. Somehow, in that room of quiet, neatly preserved death, I think we conjured a ghost.

Now we were in the humid mountains, trying to bring that ghost to life. Augustine had left as suddenly as he had arrived, but by now we knew our way around, and we kept working. The wind was blowing, rocking the big trees above us, setting the vines to gentle swaying motion; the palms that made up much of the understory rustled and murmured with a dry hiss. The canopy blocked most of the wind, but we tried to sit or stand facing into what little breeze reached us, fanning the worst of the mosquitoes away from our faces. During one lull, as I worked to extract a bird from the net, I glanced down and saw that both my pants legs were furry with the tiny gray insects.

We worked into the afternoon, wolfing down squashed peanut-butter-and-jelly sandwiches and swigs of tepid water between checking the nets and processing the catch, quickly taking a series of measurements from each bird. As the day wore on, we caught more and more species, and Amy filled pages in her notebook with neatly transcribed data, but none of them even resembled Semper's warbler, and I never had that jolt of adrenaline and the jerky misstep of the heart that would come with a small gray bird hanging in a net.

It was late in the day when, over the incessant sound of the wind soughing through the canopy, we suddenly heard a great approaching roar, like a train. Moments later, as we were still trying to figure out where the sound was coming from, a crashing wall of rain hit; I jammed my cameras and the expensive tape recorder inside a garbage bag and stuffed them into my pack as Amy scooped up the rest of the gear. Then, wriggling into our rain jackets, we both ran for the nets, as the rain began to work its way down through the layers of vegetation in big, splashy dollops.

The first bird, a bananaquit, was badly tangled, and with water pouring down my hands it took a minute or two to free it and release it into the storm. Amy, meanwhile, was holding a hummingbird and shielding it with her body; this one was easy to remove, as was another bananaquit, now quite sodden, hanging a few nets farther along. By the time the last bird was loose, the storm was passing, the roar fading down the valley, but we decided to roll up the dripping nets and call it a day.

The alarm went off at 4:30 the next morning, and I fumbled in the dark for my headlamp, shaking a few dry bat droppings off the rain jacket I was using for a blanket as I got up. I slept fully clothed, with my pants legs tucked inside my socks to keep out any hungry or curious bugs, and I thumped my boots sharply against the concrete floor a few times to make sure nothing nasty was hiding up in the toes before lacing them up. I shuffled groggily into the bathroom, where large brown snails were crawling on the damp walls and a single treefrog no bigger than my thumbnail was calling from the windowsill. I splashed some cold water on my face, and finally came fully awake, but the light and movement convinced the frog it was time to stop his serenade.

Amy was already up, sitting outside in the cool, breezy twilight eating a little breakfast, her long hair pulled back in a dark braid and a bandanna tied over her head. We soon had our packs loaded and shouldered, and headed down the trail in the near-dark, the rumbling coos of scaly-naped doves echoing through the forest. By the time we reached the

nets, it was fully light and there was lots of bird activity in the surrounding forest. Before we even had the nets completely open, I could
see small, twitching lumps hanging in the pockets we'd already un-
furled.

I tied a canvas carpenter's apron around my waist, stuffed a dozen
cotton drawstring bags in the pockets, and started back up the line, removing birds as I went. Most were bananaquits, among the most common of Caribbean birds—each one a little mite barely 5 inches long,
with a lemon-yellow breast, black body, and white eyebrows. The race
found here on St. Lucia has a black throat, not white as on most of the
Antilles; many animals and plants show a similar range of shape and
color between the islands, each place an ark of divergent evolution, patiently reworking the same raw material. The bill was thin and down-
curved, with a spot of red, puffy flesh at the corners of the mouth, like
a kid who's been sucking on a cherry lollipop. The tongue of one of the
bananaquits was sticking out as though in insult, and I could see a fringe
of slender filaments along its edges—the perfect sop for nectar, the
species' main food.

Each bananaquit went into its own bag, which hung by its long drawstring around my left forearm. More birds, more bags: a scaly-breasted
thrasher, big and aggressive, squawking and kicking; a tiny Antillean
crested hummingbird no larger than the last joint of my index finger,
black in the dim light, though in sunshine I knew it would glimmer with
iridescent green and gold; and several purple-throated caribs, a much
larger type of hummingbird, with a long, decurved bill and a plum-
colored gorget.

As I approached, the caribs would buzz in the nets, trying to escape,
their wings rattling like cicadas, but when I gently reached out to remove them, they invariably gave the most heartbreaking little cry—a
plaintive, descending whine, like that of a small, hopeless child. The first
time it happened, the sound stopped me in my tracks, and I had to shake
my head for a moment before getting back to the chore at hand. The
hummingbirds would continue to whimper in the bags, a diminutive
chorus of pity, and though I am usually relatively immune to anthropo-
morphism, I always made a point of finishing the caribs first so I could
release them as quickly as possible.

The main reason for the nets, of course, was the hope that a Semper's warbler would blunder into one of them, but in the meantime, there was other, albeit less exciting, work to be done. The fundamentals of Caribbean bird biology and ecology are still largely a mystery; the breeding seasons and nesting habits of many resident birds, for example, are at best only sketchily understood, and apparently vary from island to island. What we were doing was obviously haphazard and incomplete, but while we were waiting for Semper's warbler to make an appearance, I was determined to get as much information as possible from the other species we caught.

Squatting on the damp ground amid a cloud of mosquitoes, the bagged birds hanging from a stick that leaned out from my pack, Amy and I set to work. Using a thin, sensitive spring scale, I weighed each bird, still in the bag, then slipped my left hand inside and caught it with its head between my index and middle finger and my hand wrapped around its body. After weighing the empty bag, I measured the bird's tail, the length of the main leg bone, the wing, and the bill (this last was tricky on the caribs, with their long, strongly curved beaks), then used a soda straw to blow away the feathers around the vent and belly, which gave us a clue as to breeding condition. Males usually had a swollen cloaca, which serves in birds (as testes do in mammals) to keep the sperm away from the dangerously high internal body temperature. Females usually showed a brood patch, a large area of featherless, slightly swollen skin on the belly that acts like a hot-water bottle during incubation.

I released a bananaquit, which flew off with a series of indignant chirps, weighed the next bag, and reached in to extract a Lesser Antillean bullfinch, an inky black, sparrowlike bird with a chestnut patch on its throat. Bullfinches are common throughout the Windward Islands, and are amazingly trusting around humans; a few days earlier, while we were eating breakfast at a guest house up in Castries, a bullfinch had flown in through the window, landed on the table, and nonchalantly hopped up to my plate to steal a few fragments of scrambled egg. This one was less sanguine, and was chomping diligently on my finger with its heavy, seed-cracking bill. Amy flipped a page in a waterproof notebook—the humidity that morning was oceanic—and jotted down the measurements as I took them with a millimeter rule.

"Lesser Antillean bullfinch, male," I said. "Tail 47, tarsus 18, wing

66.5, and the bill"—the bird chomped again, catching the tender skin at the edge of the nail as I tried to lay the ruler along the upper surface of the beak—"the bill is 10 millimeters," I said, wincing. I rolled the bullfinch on its back and shot a blast of air through the straw to its vent—perhaps more strongly than was strictly necessary, but the bird instantly released my finger and glared up at me. "Cloacal protruberance is a 2," I said, and to our mutual relief I was finally able to release the bird.

Each round of the nets brought a few more tropical gems, birds that remain common in the forests of modern St. Lucia. So what is the difference between a Semper's warbler and a bullfinch or a thrasher? Why have so many species thrived when this one has dwindled, perhaps to the vanishing point? Semper's wasn't always a rare bird; the early collectors who worked in the Windward Islands were able to find it with little difficulty, skulking in the deep, shady mountain forests where the soil is slick and wet. While many were collected, the numbers shot for museum drawers cannot account for the decline.

It seems likely that the bird would have remained common, but for an early and, as it turned out, horribly misguided attempt at biological pest control. Isolated and tiny, the islands of the West Indies originally had few native mammals, so when the early sailing vessels docked and their stowaway rats jumped ship, they found a paradise. Black and Norway rats exploded in number, becoming serious agricultural pests—and also attacking the native fauna, including ground-nesting birds. But the rats also provided food for some of St. Lucia's indigenous wildlife, especially snakes. The island has only four species, three of them (including a subspecies of the boa constrictor) nonvenomous and quite harmless. The fourth, though, is another matter entirely—the fer-de-lance, one of a large group of closely related pit vipers found throughout the Caribbean and tropical Latin America. The St. Lucian fer-de-lance reaches lengths of 8 feet and, like its brethren, has a well-deserved reputation as one of the Western Hemisphere's most dangerous wild animals—not because it is particularly aggressive, but because it is often found in disturbed habitats near human dwellings, where its small mammalian prey is common.

The plague of rats and the danger from fer-de-lance prompted European colonists to try a little ecological rejiggering. British nationals in India knew that the mongoose was a ferocious predator of both rats and snakes, so the weasel-like animals were imported in the mid-nineteenth century and released on almost all the Antilles. The results were catastrophic. As hard as the rats had been on native wildlife, the rapacious mongooses were far worse; the myth of Rikki-Tikki-Tavi aside, mongooses prefer to focus on less dangerous or less cagey prey, and the birds of the islands—animals that had evolved in the absence of such relentless ground predators—were easy meat.

The toll was gruesome; in all, dozens of species of birds, lizards, small mammals, and a few snakes were driven to extinction in the century following the introduction of mongooses, though some may have succumbed to the combined effects of predation, habitat loss, and other pressures. Therein lies one reason why bullfinches, bananaquits, hummingbirds, and the rest of the species we were netting remain common: all nest in trees, safely out of reach of the largely terrestrial mongooses. Semper's warbler, presumably, nested on the ground, where it also foraged in dense cover perfect for an ambush attack, making it doubly vulnerable to the new predators. Yet it isn't the only ground-nesting bird in the West Indies, and others have managed to survive the mongoose onslaught, even on St. Lucia. Perhaps there was some unique vulnerability inherent in Semper's warbler, something that made it especially susceptible to mongooses—or to some other aspect of European colonization. Perhaps the loss of native forest, to which it seems particularly attached, reduced its population to the level where a single bad nesting season, or a severe hurricane, wiped out the tiny raft of survivors. Perhaps it, and it alone, had a weakness for an introduced disease or parasite. Without live birds to study, there is no way to tell.

Let me do away with the messiness of suspense: We did not find Semper's warbler, though for one glorious moment I had hope. Checking the nets on our final day in the forest reserve, I saw a small gray bird dart out of the undergrowth and hit the mesh a few dozen yards away, just as I was walking up. Nothing we'd caught thus far resembled this little, colorless creature, and my stomach lurched; I leaped forward, certain the bird would wriggle out before I could reach it. My hands were trembling as I fumbled at the netting, but it wasn't a lost species back from the dead—only a Caribbean elaenia, an olive-gray flycatcher usually found not down in the low brush of the understory but up on higher perches. As I pulled it from the net, it flared the feathers of its head, revealing a long, thin streak of yellow down its crown, and hammered at my fingers once or twice with its bill in indignation and fear.

A short while later, Amy and I began to fold up the nets and pack away the gear for our last hike back to camp; a few days later we were on our way home. So I cannot say whether Semper's warbler still creeps through the ferns of St. Lucia, whether it still trembles its wings when a hungry mongoose flushes it from the dim shadows, whether there are still quiet, hidden places unknown to people where its never-seen nests are still built and its never-heard song still echoes. For a long time before I came to the island, and through all my time there, I wanted to believe this was so, but I was never certain. I suppose I didn't really have the bird in my heart, so perhaps it isn't surprising that we didn't find it in the tree.

But as the plane rose over the blue Caribbean water and the small island faded to gray in the haze, I made a conscious decision, simply choosing to believe that Rev. Semper's dull little bird was still alive. It was a declaration of faith in the absence of proof, but the effect on me was surprisingly powerful. The world can be a dismal-enough place for a conservationist without adding a grief before its time.

In the 3.5-billion-year history of life on this planet, there have been five episodes of mass extinction in which the great majority of species vanished in a relatively short period of time. There has been an even larger number of smaller, less sweeping die-offs. The extinction that marked the end of the Cretaceous Period 65 million years ago, with the demise of the last dinosaurs and the loss of more than half the other species that shared their world, is the most famous, but was not the most devastating—that dubious honor goes to the great dying at the end of the Permian Period 230 million years ago, when an estimated 95 percent of all organisms then alive were killed in a catastrophic wave of extermination. (It was also very nearly the end of human history, in a way, because the protomammals, a group of reptilian offshoots from which true mammals later evolved, escaped the wave of death by a whisker; paleontologists have found the fossils of just two species of protomammal that survived the mass extinction, compared to a score that lived before the Permian event.)

It has become clear that the Cretaceous extinction was caused, or at least exacerbated, by the impact of an asteroid, whose crater was finally located off the Yucatán Peninsula in 1991, and there is some evidence that a cosmic collision also caused the great Permian death. But we are witness to the gathering pace of what ecologists have labeled the Sixth Extinction, and this time we are the asteroid, blistering the world with our appetites, our habitat destruction and climate change, all driven by the crushing weight of our population. By conservative reckoning, the planet loses three or four species an hour, eighty or more a day, thirty thousand a year—the highest extinction rate in 65 million years.

Extinction, paleontologists tell us, is natural. Since multicelled life first appeared, an estimated 30 billion unique species have inhabited the Earth, from bacteria and algae to mammoths and coneflowers. Today, in round numbers, some 30 million or so are alive—only one-tenth of 1 percent of all the kinds of organisms that ever lived. Judging from the fossil record, each species of marine life, like clams, averages about 5 million years on life's stage, while we less-tenacious mammals hang around for 1 or 2 million years.

So why become overwrought about extinction, if it is a natural and seemingly inevitable process? Because the pace today far surpasses that of natural extinction, commonly referred to as the "background extinction rate," down through history. While the fossil record is admittedly spotty, there is a fairly stable trend evident through the geologic epochs, in which roughly one species per year vanishes for every million species on the planet, a rate slightly less than the evolution of new species and thus a net gain for global diversity. "Human activity has increased extinction between 1,000 and 10,000 times over this level," Harvard ecologist E. O. Wilson has written. "Clearly we are in the midst of one of the great extinction spasms of geological history."

Thirty thousand species a year driven to extinction; most of these are invertebrates, plants, and fungi—the little things that make the world work, as Wilson likes to say. If that pace continues, by the end of the current millennium most of the plant and animal species on Earth today will be gone, and our ecosystems will be vastly different, much less stable places.

Of course, evolution will not stop; as long as there's something left alive, plants and animals will eventually diverge, splitting off into new species at an exponential rate, until the losses are once again made good. But it is cold comfort to know that natural selection will refashion new species from the dregs that survive a mass extinction. For one thing, we can't expect the newly minted forms to be anything like what we have now, any more than the mammalian fauna of the Paleocene resembled the dinosaur salad days of the Cretaceous just before it. There will be no more Bali tigers or black paradise flycatchers, never another small-whorled pogonia orchid or a gastric-brooding frog. "The beauty and genius of a work of art may be reconceived, though its first material expression be destroyed; a vanished harmony may yet again inspire the composer," the biologist William Beebe famously mused in 1906, "but when the last individual of a race of living things breathes no more, another heaven and another earth must pass before such a one can be again."

Yet even if I didn't think there was an inherent value in the plants and animals of today, representing as they do a lineage stretching back billions of years, the time scales involved in recovery from a mass extinction are almost incomprehensible. Looking at the fossil record, paleobiologists have found that biotic recovery—the return to the same level of diversity as before the extinction event—takes about 10 million years, a remarkably consistent period that seems to hold regardless of the magnitude of the extinction. To put that in perspective, 10 million years is *twenty times* longer than modern humans have existed, and even the most optimistic scientist expects we will be gone long before that 10-million-year penalty phase ends, most likely as a result of the ecological calamity we ourselves are perpetrating. This, then, will be humanity's most significant, enduring, and ultimately self-defeating legacy: a pauperization of our home that will persist long after we're nothing more than bones and dirt. At least you can't accuse a meteor of premeditated stupidity.

Except that not every apparent loss is irrevocable. Once in a very great while, a species that had been thought extinct is rediscovered, long before another heaven and another earth have passed. Sometimes it is utter serendipity, as when a biologist in the middle of the trackless Australian desert looks down at his feet and finds he's standing on a parrot missing for more than a century. Other discoveries are the result of careful planning, by scientists who plunge into poorly explored regions, often following little more than rumors, to seek creatures considered long gone. By contrast, not long ago naturalists in the Seychelles Islands of the Indian Ocean rediscovered eight geriatric individuals of two species of giant tortoises thought extinct since the 1840s—not in some remote valley, but in captivity, on the grounds of old hotels where they were kept as pets for more than a century. The tortoises had been mistakenly identified all those years; they have now been moved to small offshore islets in the hope that they aren't too old to breed.

Whatever the circumstances, there is a prodigal-son quality to these findings—the sense of snatching back something precious from the void. Those who find lost species sometimes speak in reverential, almost religious, tones of having performed some small yet splendid service to the planet.

Years ago, when I was just getting my start as a writer, I worked for the local newspaper doing general assignment reporting—soup to nuts, crooked politicians to local disasters. One day the police scanner on the managing editor's desk crackled just as I was finishing lunch, and since I was the only one in the deserted office, I yelled upstairs for a photographer and headed for the door.

It was a house fire, and a bad one, as fires in the anthracite region of eastern Pennsylvania often are. The old wood-frame homes, cheaply built cheek-to-jowl by the coal companies a century ago, flare up like paper, and they usually burn a block at a time, half a dozen houses up in flames in a heartbeat.

We could see the roiling smoke miles out of town, and the row homes were an inferno when we arrived, with arcs of water pouring in from the trucks of volunteer fire companies. It was cold—late winter, if I remember correctly, but in any case, I recall that the newly homeless were standing around under blankets, some of them disheveled and soot-smeared. Most were elderly, for a midday fire rarely catches the employed at home.

I made the usual rounds—the fire chief, who said no one was dead or missing, a few of the firefighters for comment on the hard work of killing a ravenous row-home fire, then some of the victims. I always hated this part of the job, knowing how little I would want to talk to a stranger in such circumstances, but several of the people seemed almost relieved to share their grief.

One was an older housewife, in whose home the blaze had apparently begun. She'd only had time to grab a few things from the living room before neighbors pulled her out and wouldn't let her back in, probably saving her life. The possessions she'd rescued lay on an afghan in the street beside her. There was a photo album and a motley, random assortment of things, including a large serving platter with a farm scene painted on it in a clumsy style.

We spoke for a few minutes; she wept quietly as she explained how she had discovered the flames, tried to get water to put them out as she screamed for help, then saw them erupting up her staircase and knew it was a lost cause. That's when she started racing around the living room, snatching up knickknacks, dropping them, changing her mind, clutching objects awkwardly in her arms until a burly neighbor had physically pulled her out of the smoke-filled room.

The importance of the photo album was obvious, but what, I asked, was the significance of the painted dish, which I assumed was some family heirloom.

"I dunno," she said, her voice steady for a moment, "I never cared all that much for that plate before. Picked it up at a yard sale. But now it's about all I have left."

At the time, I thought little about the quote, which never made it into the story. But these days, the world itself is on fire; sometimes literally, like the conflagration of Indonesian wildfires consuming rain forest, sometimes with the slow and nearly invisible erosion of habitat that everywhere diminishes the fabric of functioning natural systems. More than once, talking with biologists who have rediscovered lost species, they've made the same analogy—that they felt they'd rescued something from the bonfire of global extinction. Like that woman's nondescript plate, what may once have been considered commonplace becomes extraordinary, by the simple expedience of survival.

The stories I have to tell are about endurance against the odds, about faith and longing and hubris, of grief averted and grief confirmed. They are tales about animals, but really they're about people, about how our species is, at long last, coming to grips with the consequences of its actions—scrambling in the embers of a global biological holocaust, hoping against hope to save something priceless.

TWO

Proving a Negative

❧✿❧

Imagine a jewelry maker setting out to create a bangle in the shape of an amphibian—crafting a mold, perfect in every detail, from the pointed snout to the long, tapered toes; pouring in the hot, molten metal; burnishing and polishing the cooling cast until it glows with its own internal fire.

And if the result were suddenly to come to life, it would look just like the golden toad, without question the most dazzling amphibian in the world—a standout even among an order that includes psychedelically colored poison-dart frogs and other eye-popping wonders. Barely 2 inches long, with a slightly cobbled skin and obsidian eyes, the tiny toads are not gold but an intense, almost fluorescent orange—the kind of color you'd expect to see on plastic highway cones, not a living animal's skin. In fact, when scientist Jay M. Savage found the first male golden toads in 1964, in the cloud forests of Monteverde, Costa Rica, he thought the creatures were a hoax, some commonplace species that had been dyed or painted. They were not, and the sight of a breeding aggregation—a puddle containing hundreds of males, all waiting for the yellow-, black-, and red-blotched females to arrive—looked as though someone had spilled a pile of shiny Spanish doubloons onto the wet jungle floor.

Golden toads, known locally as *sapo dorado*, are as rare as they are spectacular, for they inhabit just a single ridge (known appropriately as Brillante, or brilliant) in the Monteverde Rain Forest Preserve, a range comprising barely 4 square miles. Or perhaps I should say "inhabited," because no one has seen this dramatic little amphibian since 1989. In the space of slightly more than twenty years, it went from wholly unknown to world-famous—its image marketed to tourists and its presence a driving reason for the protection of its mountain home—to missing and presumed extinct, amid lingering mystery and nagging guilt.

But if the golden toad is gone (and some people, at least, refuse to give up hope), it is surely not forgotten. Such is the case with many lost species, from grizzly bears in the southern Rockies to one of the largest woodpeckers in the world. The more dramatic, colorful, or formidable an animal is—the longer a shadow it cast upon its environment and the bigger the psychic hole left by its absence—the less likely we are to accept its loss, and the more apt we are to keep hunting and hoping, even when the evidence is pretty grim.

Most of the year, it seems, golden toads dug themselves down out of sight, pursuing a subterranean life. Only when conditions were exactly right, during the wet season that drenches Monteverde beginning in March or April, did the males emerge, gathering at shallow pools of rainwater—temporary puddles formed between tree roots, which held no fish that would eat their eggs. The females were intercepted as they arrived, ferociously fought over, fiercely competed for; a lucky male clamped a female in the hold known as amplexus, his forelimbs wrapped tightly around her middle for hours at a stretch, until she expelled her gelatinous eggs for fertilization. The annual breeding frenzy was explosive, concluding in just a matter of weeks, and if the tadpoles were lucky, they would complete their development before the dry season evaporated their homes a few months later.

All that I know of golden toads comes secondhand; I have never seen one, but I have several friends who encountered them in Costa Rica in the 1980s, and even years later the impressions were still vivid. "You're walking along a ridge in the cloud forest and suddenly you see all these Day-Glo orange things on the ground," one of them recalled. "And they'd just sit out there in broad daylight, unlike other toads." During the breeding season, the toads could be incredibly abundant; two scientists described counting almost a thousand in a single day in the 1970s, gathered in several large spawning aggregations.

Most of what we know about golden toad ecology we owe to Dr. Martha Crump, an expert on tropical frogs who happened to be in Monteverde in 1987 when the golden toads emerged. Although she was there to study tree frogs, Crump spent weeks observing the toads, noting their behavior, weighing and measuring them—all for no more urgent reason than scientific curiosity; taking data is what a biologist does. Marty Crump had no way of knowing that she was documenting the last orgy.

The next year, armed with a grant to study the unique toads, Crump returned to Monteverde and was puzzled to see no large breeding aggregations; in fact, only ten toads were observed that year, none breeding. The following spring, in 1989, Crump and her helpers found only a single golden toad. That was the last time, so far as is known, that anyone has seen *sapo dorado*.

At first, Crump and other researchers were only mildly concerned. Tropical amphibians like frogs and toads can be cyclical in their abundance, and the golden toad's subterranean habits would keep it out of sight unless breeding conditions were just right—though until that point, the toads hadn't missed a breeding season since their discovery in the 1960s. But as year after year passed without a sighting, the truth sank in, and by the early 1990s, the worried consensus was growing that the toads had, inexplicably, vanished.

No one knows exactly why the golden toad disappeared, but it wasn't alone. The harlequin frog, a once-common species, also disappeared from the reserve in the 1980s, and surveys in the 1990s found that more than twenty species of frogs and toads once found in Monteverde were missing. (Unlike the golden toad, these species are still found in other locales.) In fact, a large number of anurans (as frogs and toads are collectively known) have become extinct worldwide in the past twenty years, including the bizarre gastric-brooding frog of Australia, females of which swallowed their fertilized eggs and allowed the young to hatch in the stomach before disgorging them. The extinctions have flowed from pervasive and rapid die-offs of anurans in many parts of the world, including otherwise pristine wilderness reserves like the mountains of Costa Rica. Scientists were at first baffled, then frantic in their attempts to understand the massive declines; culprits from ultraviolet radiation and pesticides to introduced predators were identified, though none could adequately explain the phenomenon.

For Marty Crump and her research colleague J. Alan Pounds, the only factor that made much sense was weather change—Monteverde experienced two El Niño drought years in the 1980s, including one in 1987, the last year big numbers of toads were seen. They concluded that a gradual warming of the overall climate, peaking in those years, stressed the toad population to the breaking point. It seemed, at best, a partial answer. But then, in 1998, came conclusive evidence linking the worst die-offs, in the rain forests of Central America and Australia, with a fungal infection known as chytridiomycosis—"chytrid" for short, a parasite that had never before been known to attack vertebrates. Herpetologists finally had a plausible agent for the extinctions, though they acknowledge the "wave of death" rolling through world anuran populations is probably the result of several factors reinforcing one another.

"I don't think there's any question but that the drought had negative effects on the golden toads," Crump told me. "But now that we know about the chytrid fungus, I think it's entirely possible that the drought may have stressed the toads, making them more vulnerable to the fungus—if indeed it was present at Monteverde at that time."

It is possible that chytrid had always been present in the tropics and only became a problem when anurans were beset by environmental challenges like climate change. But there's another, far more depressing possibility, one suggested by the discovery of the fungus on healthy North American frogs—that chytrid is actually native to the temperate zone and was carried to the tropics by a human, like one of the many ecotourists that visit Monteverde. Or maybe the agent was a researcher; this is perhaps even more likely, since who better to serve as the carrier of a frog disease than a frog scientist? Herpetologists had to confront the fact that their boots or dip nets might inadvertently have introduced the very disease that is surging through the tropics, killing the animals they love.

But did the chytrid infection really wipe out the golden toad, or simply make a rare species even rarer—so rare, perhaps, that it was possible to overlook? It's impossible to prove a negative; anyone with an optimistic nature could choose to believe there are a few *sapos* still hidden in the Costa Rican jungle, and no one can say they're wrong. Only time, after a fashion, can answer the question of extinction, and then you still have to hedge any pronouncement of doom with qualifiers and weasel words. Hence, even herpetologists like Marty Crump speak of the "apparent" extinction of the golden toad.

I possess no oracle that can tell me whether or not the optimists are right about the *sapo*—I can only hope that, one day, someone hiking the damp, slippery trails at Monteverde will, against all odds, find a toad the color of sunset. But if it is impossible to prove the disappearance of a flamboyantly colored amphibian that lived on a single well-studied mountain range, how much harder to state with any certainty the fates of other more cryptic, more secretive, or wider-ranging species, especially one with a wary nature? Size is of little importance here; the animal need only be adept at staying out of human sight to "disappear."

For contrast, there may be no creature less similar to an inoffensive toad than a grizzly bear, one of the largest and most aggressive predators on the planet. No one would describe grizzlies as secretive or cryptic; their touchy nature got them in trouble with white settlers from the very beginning. Grizzlies were abundant in the Great Plains east to the borders of Minnesota and Iowa, but were eventually driven back to the northern Rockies, with Yellowstone their southernmost outpost. This was a local extinction, more accurately referred to as extirpation, but the process is the same as when an entire species dies. In either case, the legend sometimes lives on long after the animal is gone.

A big, potentially dangerous animal like a grizzly leaves its mark on the land. It makes its presence felt in many ways—ecologically, by exerting pressures and checks on prey species and lesser competitors, or (and this is a weak, misleading word, but I find myself at a loss for a better one) spiritually. There is an almost palpable completeness to the few remaining wild places that still have their apex predators, a sense of *presence* that I've never felt when the capstone animals are missing. This may just be self-deceit, but I don't think so; too often I felt that prickling of mingled excitement and danger, only to find out later that a big cat or bear or wolf had been in the area, unbeknownst to me. No doubt this is a holdover from our days as runty, stick-wielding hominids, when we were easy meat for hyenas, leopards, and cave bears. Our nerves remember, even if our waking minds do not. When wild country loses its pinnacle predator, that loss leaves a hole, and it's one that we notice, if only subconsciously.

The 1890s and early 1900s were bad days for grizzlies. Ranchers shot them when they could, and government trappers sprinkled the high country with the "Great Bear Tamer," the No. 6 leghold trap, a double-springed monster that weighed 42 pounds and worked wonders when set near a cow or deer carcass (usually with warning signs posted nearby, so some unlucky passerby wouldn't stumble into it). Sometimes they used poison or "set guns" rigged in trees, with trip strings stretched across game trails and tied to their triggers, but mostly the professionals relied on trained packs of blue tick hounds. The mighty bears vanished in state after state. Texas lost its grizzlies in 1890, Washington in 1913. California, whose state flag carries the golden grizzly of the Sierras, had exterminated them by 1924. They vanished from Oregon in 1931, New Mexico in 1933, and Arizona in 1935. In Utah, the last bear killed was "Old Ephraim," a half-ton boar known for stock-killing that was trapped in 1923; there is now a memorial to that grizzly in Logan Canyon.

In Colorado the story was much the same, but the endgame dragged out quite a bit longer. Some of the grizzlies there achieved legendary status, like "Old Mose" of Black Mountain, up in the Elk Range, which was said to have killed between three and nine men and 800 head of live-stock before his thirty-four-year career was ended in 1904. Government hunters were still killing a few griz through World War II in the deep, wild ranges of southern Colorado. The last one anyone killed was a baby in 1954, but one of those government hunters—a fellow who should have known a grizzly if anyone did—reported seeing a sow and cubs as late as 1967.

By the mid-1970s, even reliable sightings had ended, and the Colorado Division of Wildlife had officially chiseled R.I.P. on the grizzly's tombstone. Then, in a bizarre twist, the great bear made one last appearance in the Centennial State—in the fall of 1979, a hunting outfitter named Ed Wiseman and his client claimed to have surprised a bear while hunting in the San Juan Mountains, the rugged country in southwest Colorado. The bear attacked Wiseman, mauling him badly. Grabbing an arrow, the guide said he stabbed the animal in the neck and chest several times, after which the bear released him, ran off, and died.

To everyone's shock, it was a grizzly—an old female which, from the condition of its teats, may have once nursed cubs. The state mounted a two-year search to see if any more could be found or live-trapped, and while they discovered some suggestive clues like old dens, nothing substantive turned up. As one of the biologists involved in the search said, "Failure to catch a grizzly does not mean a definite absence of bears"— in other words, an absence of evidence is not evidence of absence. As the years lengthened again without any concrete proof, however, the Colorado grizzly was once more written off.

But not by everyone. Looking for the San Juan grizzlies has become almost a cottage industry in southern Colorado, the subject of a couple of books and an ongoing search by several grizzly experts and their students. What they've found is tantalizing but not convincing. Brown bears (of which the interior grizzly of the Rockies is but one race) are big, bold animals with an almost mythic disregard for humans, an in-your-face creature in both a figurative and a literal sense. I recall the times I've crossed paths with brown bears—the shock of seeing that shaggy mountain of a beast rear up from the willows, nose twitching, eyes boring into me, the almost tangible disdain for a meager thing like a person—and I can think of no creature less likely to be overlooked. But bears are also quite intelligent and adaptable, and some grizzly experts like Doug Peacock, who has spent years drifting through the San Juans looking for them, believe that the Colorado bears have survived by becoming the antithesis of the aggressive grizzly. The San Juan bears, Peacock and others argue, survived a century of ferocious artificial selection, in which only the meekest, quietest, most secretive grizzlies made it. They became almost wholly nocturnal, immensely shy, and almost supernaturally wary around people, and they have learned to get by on a lot less land, sticking to small home ranges instead of wandering all over creation.

(There may be precedent for this. Early encounters with black bears in the East, recorded by travelers in the seventeenth and eighteenth centuries, suggest that this species may once have been more consistently aggressive than is now the case—but after centuries of shooting and trapping, in which the most defiant and dangerous were shot, the species as a whole became more timid and retiring, and where it is hunted it remains almost completely nocturnal.)

I'm not sure what to think. A friend of mine, a serious bear nut who lives here in Pennsylvania but who keeps a cabin in southwest Colorado, saw a large bear there a few years ago, climbing among fallen timber at the edge of a mountain meadow. It was brown, but the color doesn't mean much—brown-phase black bears, known as cinnamon bears, are actually the most common color in much of the West. But this bear, Bob says, was different—bigger, humpbacked, with a dished-out face, not the smooth shoulder and flat profile of a black bear. This is a man who is not a biologist but who sees black bears on a weekly, at times almost daily, basis at a feeding station he maintains at his house; what's more, he photographed the mystery bear and collected a few strands of hair that snagged on one of the logs.

I've seen the picture; the bear is climbing over a downed tree, rather far from the camera and thus smaller than you'd like the image to be, but there is a pronounced bulge to its shoulder, and the face looks dished. To my untrained eye, it sure looks like a grizzly, but bear experts are divided. The hump could be just an accident, they say, a result of the bear climbing over the tree, its shoulder blade poking up in mid-stride and giving the appearance of a grizzly's characteristic mound of muscle. Bob sent the hairs to Colorado's wildlife agency, which conducted a microscopic examination of them, then forwarded them to a federal wildlife forensics lab for DNA tests. Though both labs concluded the hair had characteristics unique to grizzlies, the state's official line is that the animal Bob saw was a cinnamon black bear—a politically cautious decision, he suspects, since the bear was near a ranching area.

"Actually, I kind of believe they're down there," wrote naturalist Rick Bass, whose book *The Lost Grizzlies* documents the search in the San Juans. "There is a place in our hearts for them, and so it is possible to believe they still exist, if only because that space of longing exists." Faith, yearning, hope, and biology intersect repeatedly in the stories of these living ghosts, and the more arresting the animal, the stronger the grasp it has on us. That helps to explain the potency of golden toads and Colorado grizzlies—and brings us to the blackwater bayous and cypress swamps of the Old South, and to the oh-so-potent Log God, the woodpecker that will not die.

On a hot and muggy April morning, Steve Shively and I were hiking deep in the bottomland forests of eastern Louisiana, a landscape that is at least as much water as it is solid ground—a place of sloughs, sluggish rivers, oxbow lakes, bayous and swamps with towering cypress and tupelo hung with sheets of Spanish moss. For several years, this region had been withering under a drought, but a month or two before, the rain and floods had returned with a vengeance, and every mosquito egg that had sat quiescent through those long, dry years hatched at once. Depending on which old-timer you talked to, it was the worst mosquito season in thirty years, fifty years, or—and this was the most common sentiment—ever.

I'll admit the mosquitoes weren't as bad as the absolute worst I've experienced, in Alaska or northern Canada, but it's hard to convey just how bad they were without being melodramatic. They followed us like plumes of smoke, crowding the air around our heads and bodies, blackening our legs and arms. Despite the humidity and the heat, Shively—a thin, wiry man in his mid-forties with a full dark beard touched with gray—wore a heavy, long-sleeved denim work shirt with the logo of his employer, the Louisiana Department of Wildlife and Fisheries, embroidered on the breast pocket. His legs were protected by jeans, his hands by thick work gloves with the fingertips cut off, and he wore a red bandanna tied up so it covered his ears and neck below an orange cap; it looked ridiculous, but it wasn't long before I'd done the same, and we both wished we'd brought spares we could tie across our noses and mouths, too. Shively declined my offer of bug spray—"I'm trying to be pure. Besides, it just sweats right off," he said with resignation. I sprayed myself until I reeked, but he was right; it didn't do much good.

We both wore battered orange safety vests, because it was the tail end of Louisiana's spring turkey season and we didn't want to stumble onto a hunter who might assume the crashing in the brush was a gobbler—though frankly, I couldn't imagine anyone sitting motionless for hours with their back to a tree among the legions of mosquitoes. The bugs kept us to a brisk pace; Shively moved through the forest with a fast, purposeful stride, often consulting a battered compass whose old lanyard was threaded through the buttonhole of his shirt pocket.

We hiked and slogged and waded for hours through the forest, which at times reminded me of the seasonally flooded *várzea* of the Amazon, another place not fully land or water, and with (in my experience) considerably fewer biting insects. The bayous were a place John James Audubon knew well from his travels through Louisiana in 1820, which he recalled, with just a little poetic license, like this:

Would that I could describe the extent of those deep morasses, overshadowed by millions of gigantic dark cypresses, spreading their sturdy, moss-covered branches, as if to admonish intruding man to pause and reflect on the many difficulties which he must encounter, should he persist in venturing farther into their almost inaccessible recesses, extending for miles before him, where he should be interrupted by huge projecting branches, here and there the massy trunk of a fallen and decaying tree, and thousands of creeping and twining plants of numberless species! Would that I could represent to you the dangerous nature of the ground, its oozing, spongy, and miring disposition, although covered with a beautiful but treacherous carpeting, composed of the richest mosses, flags, and water-lilies, no sooner receiving the pressure of the foot than it yields and endangers the very life of the adventurer, whilst here and there, as he approaches an opening, that proves merely a lake of black muddy water, his ear is assailed by the dismal croaking of innumerable frogs, the hissing of serpents, or the bellowing of alligators! Would that I could give you an idea of the sultry pestiferous atmosphere that nearly suffocates the intruder during the meridian heat of our dogdays, in those gloomy and horrible swamps! But the attempt to picture these scenes would be vain. Nothing short of ocular demonstration can impress any adequate idea of them.

It was easy for me to stop, peering through the clouds of mosquitoes, and believe that little had changed in these forests since Audubon first saw them. There was still the "beautiful but treacherous carpeting" of wild irises, the choruses of amphibians, the sudden eruption of white, flashing wings as we scared flocks of feeding egrets from dimly lit pools. The woods were wide, the trees big. But the truth, as Steve Shively had been gently instructing me all day, lay just beneath the surface. The trees were big, yes, but only because plants grow fast down here. These were not the centuries-old giants that Audubon knew; the forest itself is a stripling, not much older than I. But perhaps the biggest difference between Audubon's day and my own was that we'd seen no ivorybills.

The ivory-billed woodpecker was nature's exclamation point, the personification of pizzazz—a full-throated yell of a bird with a scarlet crest, black-and-white wings like semaphore flags, and a walloping honker of a bill the color of old bone. It was big—as large as a duck or a

Ivory-billed woodpeckers, from the original painting by John James Audubon, who found the crow-sized birds to be common and conspicuous in much of the South.
(New-York Historical Society, accession no. 1863.17.066)

crow, with a 3-foot wingspan—and noisy, too, like someone blowing
into a megaphone with the mouthpiece of a clarinet, blasting out single
nasal notes that could be heard a half mile away. The ivorybill was a bird
with *impact*.

Many country folks called it the "kent," "kint," "caip," "kate," or some
other derivation of its raucous call. But more often, the names they used
for the ivorybill reflected the dazzle of seeing one of these huge birds
rowing through the light-splashed swamps on powerful wings. King of
the Woodpeckers, they called it. Log-cock. King Woodchuck. Giant
woodpecker. Log God. Like the smaller but similar pileated woodpecker, it was sometimes called the Lord God bird, or the By-God, because that's what a breathless greenhorn said when he first saw one: By
God, look at that bird.

The ivorybill lived in old growth, and it needed a lot of it, because it
occupied a peculiar ecological niche. Most woodpeckers chop away at
live or dead wood to expose the insects that live deep inside. But the
ivorybill focused its attention on a very specific resource—recently dead
trees still clad in bark, beneath which lived the thumb-sized larval grubs
of long-horned beetles. To find the bugs, the woodpecker would methodically peel away the tight bark, using its immense and powerful beak
as a prybar, eventually denuding the whole tree and leaving the bark
piled around its base in heaps. Of course, only a few trees are going to
be in this freshly-dead-but-not-too-rotten state at any given time, so a
pair of ivorybills needed a lot of room to roam if they were to find
enough to eat. One later study found that the territory of a single Lord
God bird might also support three dozen pileated woodpeckers, which
were much more flexible in their food habits.

Given what later befell the ivorybill, this high degree of specialization is usually portrayed as a maladaptive mistake—the classic case of a
species courting extinction by veering too far from the safe, secure middle ground of generalization. That overlooks the fact that the primal
South was a buffet table for a bird of the ivorybill's tastes, with tens of
millions of acres of ideal habitat. Consequently, it was one of the most
common and visible inhabitants of the great floodplain forests of the
lower Mississippi Basin, Gulf Coast, and southern Atlantic seaboard.
While floating down the Mississippi near the Missouri-Kentucky line,
just below its confluence with the Ohio, Audubon noted in his journal:

"*Ivory Billed Wood Peckers* are Now Plenty, Bears, Wolf &c but the Country extremely difficult of Access," while farther south he wrote of the woods being filled with "the constant Cry of the Ivory Billed Wood Peckers about us—scarcely any other."

Indians and whites prized the woodpecker for its bill and red head. "I have seen entire belts of Indian chiefs closely ornamented with the tufts and bills of this species," Audubon wrote. "Its rich scalp attached to the upper mandible forms an ornament for the war-dress of most of our Indians, or for the shot-pouch of our squatters and hunters." Since they were big, easy to find, and with a fairly low reproductive rate, it's unclear how well the ivorybill could withstand such pressure, but shooting was an annoyance compared with the real threat—the clearance of those old-growth forests.

It's hard for us, living in this age of at least tacit conservation, to imagine the scale of the nineteenth- and early-twentieth-century logging boom, in which the forest cover of virtually the entire eastern and southern United States was stripped to the eroded ground in a matter of five or six decades. No ecosystem was spared—not the white pine and hemlock forests of the North, the huge red spruces of the southern Appalachians, or the longleaf pines of the coastal plain. In the bottomlands of the South, the target was virgin bald cypress, sweetgum, water oak, and other species growing in the rich, flooded muck, trees that were in some cases a thousand years old.

Between the 1890s and 1920s, vast areas of the South were denuded of forest, and there was an almost precise correlation, scientists later found, between the arrival of the loggers and the local disappearance of the ivorybill. The Log God had its livelihood and home chopped out from under it, and in the space of a human lifetime it went from fairly widespread and common to a genuine rarity—which only served to put even more pressure on it, as skin collectors and curio hunters supplied growing numbers of private enthusiasts or museums with souvenirs. In just two years, 1892–93, a single collector named A. T. Wayne shot or bought from local hunters seventeen ivorybills from the Suwannee River in Florida—the last ones anyone ever saw in that region.

By the end of the nineteenth century, the woodpecker was widely assumed to be extinct, but in 1924, the species made the first of what would prove to be several unexpected reappearances. The discovery of a

pair in Florida was announced by Cornell University's distinguished ornithologist Arthur A. "Doc" Allen, who had been led to the nest by a local guide. Jubilation was short-lived, for the birds were summarily shot
by taxidermists who had—incredibly—a permit from the state to do
just that. Eight more years passed, the "extinct" label was dusted off
again, and once more the ivorybill confounded expectations, this time
when a freshly killed specimen was carried out of the trackless Tensas
River of eastern Louisiana. (This bird, too, was shot by someone with
official permission, but at least Louisiana had the sense to then suspend
all outstanding permits for woodpecker collecting.)

In the spring of 1935, Doc Allen and several colleagues, including a
young ornithology student named James T. Tanner, made a long trip
south from Cornell to Florida and then around the Gulf Coast to
Louisiana, looking for ivorybills. They found none in Florida despite
hard searching, but in a vast forest along the Tensas, owned by the Singer
Sewing Machine Company, they struck pay dirt—a pair of ivorybills
with a nest. Later they found a second pair, and in the years that followed, Tanner spent much of his time in the Singer Tract studying the
woodpeckers for his doctoral dissertation, which was published as an
Audubon research report and remains the only reliable, scientific account of the species' life history and behavior. For three years, 1937–39,
Tanner also covered more than 45,000 miles, crisscrossing the South to
look at every scrap of possible ivorybill habitat left, and his somber conclusion was that there were just twenty-two birds remaining—no more
than six in the Singer Tract and the rest in four areas of Florida. (For a
thorough and highly readable account of the ivorybill's history, including
Tanner's work, readers should turn to Christopher Cokinos's book,
Hope Is the Thing with Feathers.)

Despite the good news out of Louisiana, T. Gilbert Pearson, president of the National Association of Audubon Societies, all but wrote off
the ivorybill in 1936. "To-day it must be numbered among the species
we are accustomed to speak as being 'nearly extinct' . . . So far as the vision of the average man is concerned, the bird has already gone to join
the Dodo and the Great Auk." Pearson had seen the Louisiana birds not
long before, so he must have known firsthand what stunning creatures
they were. Yet in the spirit of the day, when conservationists tried to jus-
tify the preservation of even the most spectacular species on cold eco-

nomic grounds, he seemed to feel the King of the Woodpeckers came up a little short, and so he tried to pad its account: "The analysis of the food of the Ivory-billed Woodpecker indicates that this species, were it not for its small numbers, might be of considerable economic value. The insects which form the animal portion of its food are mostly of an injurious character . . . The vegetable portion of their food shows no indication that this Woodpecker is likely to take any products of agriculture."

Pearson's gloomy forecast for the ivorybill seemed accurate; the Singer management had sold the timber rights to the land holding the woodpeckers to the notorious Chicago Mill and Lumber Company, which began to clear-cut the 80,000-acre forest, a process already under way when Tanner and Allen arrived in 1935. By the early 1940s the situation was critical, and despite the overriding war effort, to which virtually everything else in America was held to be of secondary importance, four federal agencies, the Audubon Society, and the governors of four Southern states, including Louisiana, appealed to Chicago Mill to sell the timber rights to some of the remaining forest as an ivorybill sanctuary. The timber barons declined the proffered $200,000, however ("We are just money grubbers," Chicago Mill's chairman cheerfully informed the coalition), and the rest of the Singer Tract was chopped down.

The last time anyone saw an ivorybill on the Tensas was April 1944. The forest where the By-God had lived was busily being cleared, Cokinos notes, for no higher a purpose than to supply wooden tea crates to the British.

When we stopped moving, even for a moment, my ears filled with the hum of mosquitoes, and I had to breathe slowly and carefully to avoid sucking them into my nose and mouth. But this April morning was also full of birds, which gave us reason to stop and endure the insects—many of them migrant songbirds that had just flown across the Gulf of Mexico and were busily filling up on the cornucopia of bugs. There were wading birds of all sizes and shapes, from great blue herons with 6-foot wings to snowy and great egrets, tricolored herons, little blues, and nightherons. And there were plenty of woodpeckers—mostly red-bellied woodpeckers, a robin-sized species with a zebra-striped back and a crimson cap, which churred like angry gray squirrels; it seemed as though we were never out of earshot of a scolding red-bellied.

The Pearl River forms the southernmost border between Louisiana and Mississippi, north of Lake Pontchartrain and New Orleans. The Pearl River Wildlife Management Area, where we were, encompasses 35,000 acres of upland hardwood, marsh, and swamp forest—flat bayou country, which the highways cross on concrete pilings that carry traffic near the tops of the mossy cypresses. Yet despite its proximity to New Orleans and two bisecting interstates, this is still pretty wild land, where a person can become seriously disoriented in short order. And if you moved north or south, you could wander for a long while; Pearl River WMA is just one bead in a necklace of protected land along the state line, running from Boque Chitto National Wildlife Refuge in the north to Bayou Sauvage NWR on the shores of Pontchartrain, within the city limits of New Orleans. Even Steve, who knows the Pearl well, stopped often to check a compass bearing and his map before amending our course a few degrees and crashing back into the bamboo thickets.

The Pearl is about 200 miles from the Tensas and the old Singer Tract lands, but there's a good chance ivorybills also inhabited this area in the late nineteenth and early twentieth centuries. But by the time Jim Tanner got to the Pearl—a one-day stop on August 19, 1938, during a wide-ranging survey of potential ivorybill habitat in the South—it was a shadow of its original self, and he was dismissive of its potential: "I found these bottoms completely cut over, and know of no recent reports of Ivory-bills from there." Today, however, some wonder if Tanner was premature in his assessment.

It is a commonplace that if there is a Holy Grail of lost species, it is the ivorybill. I've always wondered why this one, of all creatures, elicits such a strong and nearly universal reaction. For birders, I can understand the magnetism: the ivorybill was so big, so brash, almost verging on the unreal, that anyone worth his or her binoculars would want to see one. The cachet of rarity was only icing on the cake. But why do so many regular folks—even those without the slightest interest in nature—know about the ivorybill and find its story so fascinating?

It may be the long dribble of provocative reports from the South, which periodically surfaced, often as not, on the front pages of newspapers across the country. Through the 1950s and 1960s, credible witnesses, including experienced birders and ornithologists, said they saw a "kaint" or two—along the Appalachicola River in Florida, for instance, or in the Big Thicket of East Texas, or the swamps of Louisiana. But with time, each of those last redoubts fell silent. In 1953, Roger Tory Peterson and the British naturalist James Fisher—in the midst of a fourteen-week, 30,000-mile trek across North America for a book they were writing—looked for ivorybills along the Chipola River of Florida; at least a few had been seen there in preceding years, and a small sanctuary had even been established. They found an old roost hole, but no bird. "We wondered, as we took a parting look at its last known haunt, whether the ivory-bill had finally joined the spectral company of the great auk, the Carolina paroquet, and the passenger pigeon," they wrote. Shortly thereafter, the sanctuary as such was eliminated.

December 1966: Ornithologist John V. Dennis reportedly sees a By-God along the Neches River in East Texas, while investigating claims that a few still inhabit the Big Thicket. A couple of years later, ornithologists searching in Florida find a snapped-off tree that exposed a nest hole, which contained the innermost secondary wing feather of an ivorybill—but there is no way to tell how old the nest, or the feather, might have been.

March 1971: A birder in the Santee Swamp of South Carolina plays a tape recording of an ivorybill (made during Doc Allen's 1935 expedition to the Singer Tract) and hears a response. No one sees a woodpecker, though many come to look, and skeptics wonder if the birder heard a loud frog, or even someone else with the same tape recording.

May 1971: Legendary ornithologist George Lowery, Jr., who as a young man saw the Singer birds, is shown photos of an ivorybill taken in Louisiana, which he considers authentic. The photos, however, are later widely rejected as a possible fraud.

Spring 1987: Mississippi State University professor Jerome Jackson plays the old Allen tape in a swamp in southern Mississippi, something he'd been doing across the South under a contract with the U.S. Fish and Wildlife Service, a last-ditch effort to see if the ivorybill might still survive. Until then they'd had no success, but this time Jackson and a graduate student were stunned to hear a reply—but again, they never saw the woodpecker, and their report, while intriguing, is not accepted as evidence of survival. By then, only the most Pollyannaish of optimists still held out any hope for ivorybills; many considered Jackson's search an effort in futility, his reported vocalization a simple misidentification. The ivorybill was dead and gone—but then came Cuba.

There were two subspecies of the ivory-billed woodpecker—*Campephilus principalis principalis* in the southeastern United States and *C.p. bairdii* in Cuba, which, while differing only slightly from their U.S. counterparts in the size of the bill, were unusual in that they inhabited highland pine forests as well as swampy lowlands. This bought them extra time, because while the bottomland forests were cut in the early twentieth century, significant tracts of mountain forest remained, and at least a few ivorybills, known locally as *carpintero real*, survived there through the 1950s. Proposals were even floated for a Cuban ivorybill refuge, but then Castro's revolution changed the political landscape and Cuba fell off the ornithological radar for most Americans. In fact, the ivory-billed woodpecker is often referred to as the only species driven to extinction by the Cold War.

Not everyone was convinced—it's that "absence of evidence" thing again. In 1985, Dr. Lester Short of the American Museum of Natural History checked many of the old sites in eastern Cuba and found what he believed was evidence of the woodpeckers in the form of freshly scaled trees—and the next year, a joint American-Cuban team found a couple of live ivorybills near Ojito de Agua. The news electrified the world's conservation community and made the front pages of newspapers around the world, but the cheering was premature; although Ojito de Agua was declared a sanctuary, it was far too small for even a single ivorybill territory, and it did nothing to stop logging on surrounding lands. Follow-up expeditions in 1987 and 1988 may have seen or heard distant birds—they couldn't be certain—but two extensive searches in the early 1990s found no evidence that the woodpeckers survived there. As had happened with Jim Tanner and the Tensas birds half a century before, the world had arrived just in time to witness the last ember go dark.

Famous as the ivorybill is, most people assume it is both the world's largest and rarest woodpecker, yet it is exceeded on one count and equaled on the other. The biggest of all was the closely related imperial woodpecker of northwestern Mexico, which measured a full 2 feet from bill to tail, compared to the ivorybill's 20-inch length. Both were members of the genus *Campephilus* (which means "caterpillar-lover," an odd choice for a group wedded to beetle grubs), and like the ivorybill, the imperial had the conical red crest in males, while the black topknot on females actually curled forward like a greased cowlick.

The imperial woodpecker lived in oak-pine forests on the high ridges and mesas of the Sierra Madre Occidental and the western edge of the central volcanic mountains; this was the same region inhabited by the extinct Mexican grizzly, and by Mexican wolves, which as far as anyone can tell now exist only in captivity. Unlike the swamp-loving ivorybill, the imperial was a creature of frosty highlands, usually above 7,000 feet, where it keyed in on old-growth stands of pine trees with lots of dead timber. Unlike many woodpeckers, the imperial seems to have been somewhat social, occurring in groups of five or ten. While uncontrolled shooting was a serious threat—its massive bill was a favored tool among Indians for removing kernels of corn from the cob, and its feathers and body parts were popular folk remedies—the biggest threat was again deforestation. By one estimate, 99.4 percent of the virgin forest there has been cut, much of it in the first half of the twentieth century.

That plundering of high-elevation forests sent the imperial wood-pecker reeling; it had disappeared from many areas by the 1920s, but it lingered in some regions through the 1960s or 1970s. In the mid-1970s, when the writer George Plimpton and birder Victor Emanuel traveled through the highlands of Chihuahua searching for it, they found loggers who said yes, they'd seen the big bird in years past, but the expedition found no convincing proof of its survival. They did find one man who re-called, with relish, how he'd shot a huge woodpecker fourteen years earlier and ate it for supper; it had been, he said, "*un gran pedazo de carne*," a great piece of meat. "Victor couldn't bring himself to ask how it had tasted," Plimpton wrote.

In the late 1990s, several biologists scoured the Sierra Madre Occi-dental looking for evidence of the imperial and talking to Indians and other locals. They concluded that seven sightings after 1965 were credi-ble, including two between 1991 and 1995—though in both cases, the witnesses saw only solitary females that appeared to be wandering no-madically. In April 1995, they found extensive workings, just a few months old, that they felt could have been made only by an extremely large woodpecker, but in nearly a month of fieldwork on that mesa, they never saw the bird itself, which must have moved from the area.

"In short, a few Imperial Woodpeckers may still exist, but neverthe-less extinction of the species seems inevitable. In all likelihood, all that will be left of the Imperial Woodpecker are some 120 skins in the mu-seum collections of the world," the team concluded.

If you're going to tell a skeptical world that you've seen the avian equiv-alent of a unicorn, it's probably best not to break the news on April Fool's Day.

David Kulivan, a twenty-one-year-old student at Louisiana State University, carried his shotgun into the Pearl River WMA before dawn on the morning of April 1, 1999, hoping to find the turkey gobbler he'd heard going to roost the night before. Instead, Kulivan says, at first light a pair of huge woodpeckers landed about 20 yards from where he sat motionless in camouflage. One was a male, with a bright red crest; it hopped around, making a call Kulivan thought sounded like "kent" or "cant," then they both flew to a tree even closer to him. By the time the birds disappeared into the forest, their calls still echoing through the trees, Kulivan was certain he'd just seen ivory-billed woodpeckers.

Kulivan, an experienced outdoorsman and a student in LSU's forestry and wildlife program, understood the gravity of what he'd seen, and the risks he would take in telling anyone; disbelief would be the least of the abuse he could expect. He debated saying anything at all, but in the end, when classes resumed a few days later, he took his natural history professor aside and dropped the bombshell.

Birders and biologists hear reports like this all the time, and they've learned to be skeptical; it's easy for a novice birdwatcher, seeing a pileated woodpecker, to jump to the wrong conclusion. A pileated, though not as big as an ivorybill, is still an impressive bird, more than 16 inches long, with a red crest and black-and-white pattern. The differences between the two species can be subtle, unless you know what you're looking for. A pileated has white patches on the primary feathers near the ends of the wings, which disappear when the bird perches; the entire rear half of an ivorybill's wings were white, both in flight and at rest. There was the bone-white beak on the larger bird (black in a pileated), and the ivorybill's habit of flying straight and smooth, without the undulating, swooping flight typical of other woodpeckers.

But the story Kulivan told was so persuasive, especially in light of his education and background, that the professor went to J. V. "Van" Remsen, curator of birds at LSU. Remsen and a panel of bird experts grilled the young man and found his assertion unyielding and his detailed description compelling; Remsen later said it was the most convincing ivorybill report he'd heard in thirty years. He and his colleagues in turn brought in the state wildlife agency, including Steve Shively, and plans were quickly formulated for field searches. Everything was kept strictly under wraps; because the ivorybill is such an iconic species, news that a few might survive in the Pearl would have brought a flood of birders, playing copies of Doc Allen's old tape and perhaps seriously disturbing any remaining woodpeckers.

For almost a year, the story remained largely secret. The state suspended a planned timber harvest near where Kulivan had been hunting, and searches were mounted on foot and with aircraft. While no one said they saw an ivorybill, some did say they heard a territorial marker known as a double tap, made, as Tanner noted, "by pounding with the bill on limbs or stubs, sometimes a single hard blow but more often a hard, double rap, *bam-bam*, the second note sounding like an immediate echo of the first." A double tap is a unique feature of *Campephilus* wood-peckers, and something that pileateds do rarely at best.

Conspiracies of silence rarely last, though, and news of the sighting spread in the Baton Rouge area. In January 2000, a newspaper in Jack-son, Mississippi, caught wind of the rumors and published the story, and all hell broke loose in birding circles. In an effort to harness the ensuing hubbub, Steve Shively and the state wildlife department organized the first of several mass hunts in the Pearl—a come-one, come-all blanket canvass of the management area. Participants were told to bring a com-pass and map, a GPS unit, lots of bug repellent, and a camera; they were warned to watch out for the abundant venomous snakes in the area, as well as crotchety old feral hogs, which can be dangerous. Please do not play tape recordings, they were admonished, which might screw things up for the woodpeckers and also mislead other searchers. When Shively and I met for our trek through the Pearl, the second group effort had just been conducted a few weeks earlier, in flooding rain that kept all but the most diehard at home. For Shively, the Pearl River was becoming a second home; he'd flown over it in a helicopter, waded its sloughs, and hiked its drier uplands many times, looking for ivorybills. But even though it was getting late in the season—too many leaves on the trees for easy birding, too many bugs and snakes for comfort—when I called he seemed eager for another excuse to get back in the bush.

Shively describes himself as "officially agnostic" on the subject of Lord God birds in the twenty-first century, trying to straddle the fence for as long as possible in order to keep himself open to evidence, pro or con. As for me, I came prepared to believe, but the Pearl made it hard. I had envisioned the Pearl River WMA as a deep and trackless wilderness, so I was struck by its paradoxical mix of accessibility and remoteness. While the place, by the nature of its wetlands, is tough to get around in, and liable to confuse a hiker who doesn't pay attention to his bearings, it is such a linear tract of land—stretched out along the river basin—that you're never really that far from the civilized edges, and dirt roads lace much of its higher ground. New Orleans is just 30 miles to the south, and Slidell, a city of 24,000, is only ten minutes away on I-59, which frames the western edge; I-10 cuts across its waist from east to west. After parking at a public shooting range we quickly hiked to where Kulivan had made his original sighting, and we could hear the slap-slap of semis going over expansion strips on the highway bridge. "And when that shooting range is going, it sounds like a war back here," Shively said.

We were threading our way through the woods when Shively suddenly dropped to one knee and began picking through dozens of small red fruits scattered on the ground. "You know mayhaws?" he asked, rubbing the dirt off one and eating it with evident relish. "It's a kind of hawthorn that they make a wonderful jelly from down here, but I like them raw, too." I could taste why; the fruits, which looked like tiny apples, were tart and juicy, the perfect snack for a hot, sweaty day. Shively looked up, figured out which of the thigh-thick trees growing by the slough was the mayhaw, and gave it a sharp kick with the flat of his foot. A shower of red pellets came bouncing down.

"I have a theory," he said as he sifted through the newly fallen fruit for the ripest ones, popping them in his mouth and spitting out the seeds. "I'm not going to find the ivorybill on a directed search like this. It's like in Faulkner's 'The Bear'—the boy doesn't see the bear until he finally leaves the gun at home. My theory is, I'm finally going to see the ivory-bill one day when I'm collecting mayhaws."

We walked on, eating mayhaws and admiring the lush woods, when Shively stopped short, peering down at his feet. A small cottonmouth was coiled near him, its body shiny and brown, banded with black, its chunky, sharply angled head pointing straight up. Shively spat a pale yellow seed and hit the snake's body, which quivered like an arrow that had just struck its mark.

"You'd better watch yourself, little guy, and make sure the wild pigs don't find you and eat you." The cottonmouth seemed unimpressed with the advice and held its ground, and was still standing at rigid attention when we walked away.

We saw lots of snakes that day, which for an amateur herpetologist like me was a nice consolation prize—a lovely Texas rat snake stretched out in a tangle of fallen branches, a long black racer that buzzed its tail like a rattlesnake, a ribbon snake, and two yellow-bellied water snakes. These last are big, heavy-bodied, and dark, much like cottonmouths, and while striding down a grassy strip of trail, Steve and I both stepped over a three-footer that lay between us, which bolted just as our stride crossed its back. I can't speak for Shively—he jumped, too—but it was, shall we say, an emotionally intense two seconds until I focused on the moving blur and realized it wasn't a pit viper.

We traveled through the forest at a brisk pace, stopping infrequently, because to do so brought down the mosquito legions, but from time to time we came across another mayhaw tree or a patch of ripe blueberries. The day was overcast but hot, and we swam in our own sweat, but the forest was beautiful, especially when we waded across the shallow sloughs, alive with tadpoles and wriggling fish, or edged along the much deeper bayous, where the brown-black water reflected the tendrils of Spanish moss that covered the tree branches. For several hours we pushed deeper and deeper into the swampy forest, through thick canebrakes—the native bamboo where Bachman's warbler once nested— and tangles of greenbrier, until at last we came into the sudden light of the river edge. The Pearl was turgid and muddy from the spring rains, moving strong and powerfully; the state of Mississippi was just over on the other bank, 60 or 70 yards away. After the slightly claustrophobic confines of the forest, it felt good to see the sun and feel a little moving air on our faces; the breeze even kept the mosquitoes to momentarily manageable levels, and I pulled the sweaty bandanna from my head for a few minutes, until we turned and headed back into the jungle.

We were working our way down the east edge of English Bayou, the very picture of a southern swamp, with cypress knees poking up like fingers from the still black water, and water tupelos with their swollen trunks, when several dark, purplish birds jumped into flight. They were little blue herons, and when we stopped to look, we realized we'd stumbled on a nesting colony of close to fifty pairs.

"You know," Shively said, in a deadpan voice, "the animal communicator said the ivorybills are somewhere close to herons."

There is something about any flamboyant lost species that whistles up the oddballs, and in this the ivorybill is no different. One of the groups searching for the woodpeckers was, while in the field, in cell-phone contact with a self-described psychic "animal communicator" in Florida who, in turn, claimed she was in touch with the spirits of the woodpeckers. (Without drawing conclusions, I will also say that this team is the only one claiming to have seen or heard an ivorybill during the state-organized hunts—a glimpse of one the first time and the sound of one calling the second.)

Shively, who is cordial but taciturn, didn't strike me as the sort of person to hold much truck with psychic phenomena, so I wasn't sure how to respond. "From what I've seen, you couldn't sling a dead armadillo down here without hitting a wading bird of some sort," I said noncommittally.

He went on as though he hadn't heard me. "The animal communicator also says the ivorybills like the color blue"—he patted his blue shirt and blue knapsack while giving me a significant smile—"but they don't like camouflage, because hunters give off 'negative energy.' Oh, and they don't like the smell of insect repellent."

"Which is all the more remarkable, since most birds have almost no sense of smell."

"Oh, you've got to learn to start thinking outside the lines," Shively said airily, flapping one hand dismissively before grinning hugely in his beard.

His open skepticism led me to ask him, bluntly, the central question: Did he think David Kulivan saw a pair of ivory-billed woodpeckers?

"In the two years since the report, there's been nothing really to corroborate it," Shively said. Some of the birders who have gone ivorybill hunting of late have reported widely on what they see as very suggestive evidence, like "scaled trees"—dead timber whose bark has been methodically flaked off, the typical hunting technique of an ivorybill searching for wood-boring beetle grubs. "The supposedly scaled trees I've seen had been dead for a long time, and the bark was starting to come loose," he said. "It was being pulled off, sure, but other woodpeckers will do that. Ivorybills pry it free when the tree hasn't been dead all that long, and the bark's still clinging on tight. I haven't seen anything like that."

Nor is the habitat what one would expect from the King of the Woodpeckers, famous for its affinity for big, old timber. As Tanner noted in 1938, virtually all of the Pearl was cut before World War II, and while the resulting second-growth is sizable, it can't compare with the giant tupelos and water oaks that once dominated the site, or the great, broken-top bald cypresses in the wetter places. Still, to someone used to the slow-growing forests of the northern United States, the Pearl looks as primal as when Audubon came through here. The trees' impressive girth has apparently fooled at least some of the recent ivorybill hunters, who have written about searching for the woodpeckers in forests they thought were seven or eight hundred years old. When I mentioned that, Shively slapped the rough bark of a tall, fat oak and laughed.

"That tree's not too much older than we are. It's a nice forest, but it's nothing special. There's nothing in this habitat that strikes me as being what ivorybills are supposed to need—but on the other hand, maybe they've become more adaptable. Some of the old writing said they were somewhat nomadic, moving around to find dead timber—though that one female that Tanner studied in the Tensas never moved, even when they cut everything out around her," Shively said.

Back and forth, pro and con, yes and no; even someone who's spent as much fruitless time in the field as Steve Shively can't shake himself free from the hope that the woodpecker is hiding somewhere, just beyond the next deep, gator-filled bayou.

"It sounds to me as though you really want to believe, even in the face of a lot of negative evidence that says maybe you shouldn't," I said.

"I've tried not to go one way or the other, unless I have some evidence—and of course, no one's ever going to come in with evidence that it's not there, proof of a negative. And sure, there's something exciting about the idea of stumbling onto an animal that's not supposed to be there—it's a *Valley of Gwangi* sort of thing, and the ivorybill fits that." But as we looked at a map of the Pearl River basin, I asked him if there were any refugia, during the years of frantic clear-cutting—any untouched places big enough for ivorybills to have hidden, from which they might later have emerged to the regrowing forests of the Pearl. He stared at the map for a long minute. "Well, there were some little pieces over here," he said, his finger tapping an area west of the river. "But not much, and that's all silviculture now, all tree farms." He fell quiet again. "No, there really wasn't a refuge."

"So that begs the question again—what did David Kulivan see?"

"Someone, a retired police officer, suggested we subject Kulivan to a lie detector test, but I'm not going to do that," Shively said. "It would be hard to believe he would lie, and hard to believe he just saw a pileated."

I mentioned something I'd read, that Kulivan's original report included details about ivorybill behavior that weren't widely known, but Shively corrected me. "The original report I saw, I'm not sure there was anything in there you couldn't get out of a field guide," he said. "Later, when Van Remsen interrogated him, he mentioned some other things, like the way the crest was cocked forward. But it wasn't until later, when I read the newspaper account, that it mentioned the double tap— that's the first I'd heard of that."

I don't know the answer, and neither does Steve Shively or anyone else. David Kulivan's garnered a lot of praise and withstood a lot of harsh criticism, but only the ivorybills of Pearl River—if any still survive—know the truth of the matter.

As Shively and I hiked back out of English Bayou, our sneakers squishing wetly in the mud and our tongues stained purple from ripe blueberries, I noticed weathered splashes of yellow and orange paint on many of the trees. The big timber sale, the one put on hold two years earlier when Kulivan made his report, was back on track. The powers that be had decided the ghost of a woodpecker was no reason to forgo cold, hard cash for logs.

There is a postscript to the story of the ivory-billed woodpecker. In the winter of 2002, the Carl Zeiss Sports Optics company, maker of high-priced binoculars, fielded a six-person team to conduct a systematic search of the Pearl River WMA by foot, boat, and off-road vehicle; the team included several prominent birders and biologists, including Martjan Lammertink, who conducted the unsuccessful searches for Cuban ivorybills and for the imperial woodpecker in Mexico. At the same time, remote listening devices were scattered around the Pearl by bioacoustic experts from Cornell University hoping to pick up the distinctive *kent* of an ivorybill. After more than a month in the field, the team reported hearing several double raps, though they saw only pileated woodpeckers in the areas from which the sounds came, and they found large roost holes and scaled trees they considered suggestive, if not definitive, evidence.

Attention was also rekindled in Cuba. Though overshadowed by the Pearl River sightings, reports had emerged around the same time that a few ivorybills might still survive in the mountains of southeastern Cuba. Secrecy was again the watchword; Americans from Audubon and the Cornell Lab of Ornithology were quietly helping the Cubans, but if the birds were actually there, everyone was playing their cards very close to the vest. All the world could do was wait, and keep its fingers crossed that the King of Woodpeckers had cheated death once again.

THREE

Chance and Calculation

As the long and (thus far, at least) fruitless ivorybill hunt in the Pearl River shows, finding a lost creature can be a grueling and by no means certain process. But the effort does pay off, and every year—sometimes every couple of months—someone announces the rediscovery of a ghost species.

There are two ways to reverse extinction—by chance or calculation, as an unmerited boon from Providence, or through concerted, focused effort. Many rediscoveries are the result of blind luck, and one could argue that simply stumbling through the boondocks is as good a strategy as any, but the fact is, those who do happen upon a missing organism by good fortune rarely have any idea of the significance of what they've found. As Louis Pasteur observed, chance favors the prepared mind.

It's hard to knock serendipity, though. When the first live coelacanth was unwittingly hauled up by a trawler from the depths of the Indian Ocean off South Africa, in 1938, it was hailed as a living fossil—until then, scientists had assumed the group of lobe-finned fish had become extinct about 75 or 80 million years ago. No more were seen until 1952, when it was learned that fishermen in the Comoros Islands north of Madagascar occasionally caught the behemoths—4 or 5 feet long, purplish and speckled with white. Over the years, more than two hundred coelacanths have been captured there, and another one hundred sightings made by divers, some of whom were able to film the huge fish in their natural habitat.

For half a century, it seemed clear that the waters of eastern Africa were the only home of the ancient fish. But in 1997, a California biologist named Mark Erdmann and his wife, Arnaz Mehta Erdmann, were honeymooning on Manado Tua, a small island near Sulawesi in Indonesia. They were wandering through a market when she pointed out an enormous, odd fish being trundled along on a handcart. Isn't that one of those fossil fish? she asked. Erdmann recognized it as a coelacanth, too, but he didn't realize that this one was more than 6,200 miles from where it should have been. The newlyweds took a few snapshots, though, and later they posted them on a Web site they created to celebrate their wedding—which is where two web-surfing Canadian coelacanth researchers found them in short order, calling Erdmann with the news that he and his wife had stumbled on a brand-new population of the world's most famous fish.

Not everyone was convinced; some thought the Indonesian find might be a hoax. So Erdmann returned to the islands in 1998, spending months talking to fishermen before another coelacanth—known locally as *raja laut*, king of the sea—was brought in alive. Erdmann and his wife were able to photograph it swimming behind a boat before it died (these deepwater fish never survive capture, probably because of the pressure change when hauled up), and genetic tests later indicated it was actually a new species, probably one that had been separated from the Comoros coelacanths for 2 million to 9 million years.

Rediscoveries often involve the accidental assistance of an unwitting third party—Indonesian fishermen with the coelacanth, or a hungry Andean weasel in another recent case, which solved a mystery dating back to the time of the Incas.

Archaeologists who excavated tombs of sixteenth-century Inca elite at Machu Picchu in Peru had long been puzzled by the presence of rat skulls among the human remains. These were not the bones of the small, skulking animals we think of when we hear the word, but were quite large—almost the size of small cats. The assumption was that the Incas had kept them either as pets or as food, but exactly what they looked like or what benefit they might have offered people was always a mystery, because as far as anyone knew, the "tomb rats" had become extinct along with the Inca empire.

But in 1997, Louise Emmons, a Smithsonian scientist working in the Vilcabamba, a dauntingly mountainous region northwest of Machu Picchu, got lucky. Emmons has as prepared a mind as Pasteur could have wished; her Ph.D. is in neurobiology and behavior, and for more than thirty years she has worked in some of the most dangerous and uncomfortable places in the world, studying jaguars in the Amazon, brush-tailed porcupines in Africa, tree shrews in Borneo, and bats in the Caribbean, among many other subjects. Emmons is widely recognized as the world's expert on tropical mammals, which is why she has for years participated in so-called rapid assessments in Latin America—the equivalent of a biological SWAT team of highly trained scientists who move into a remote and unexplored area and, in blitzkrieg fashion, quickly survey its biodiversity.

Emmons was in the Vilcabamba on one such expedition sponsored by Conservation International, part of a team that had been helicoptered to a cloud forest nearly 10,000 feet high, where they collected specimens in the cold, wet climate. One day she was hiking along a trail when she noticed a large dead animal lying on the ground—probably one of the prehensile-tailed porcupines that live in the Andes, she thought. But when she got closer, Emmons realized with a start that this was something she'd never seen before—a cat-sized creature with luxuriant gray fur, outsized whiskers, a long, bushy tail, and a white stripe running down its face. "Cuddly" is the distinctly unscientific way she later described it.

If that seems an odd word to use, bear in mind that there are more species of rodents—more than 1,800—than any other group of mammals, and a lot of them are rats. Many look pretty much as you'd expect—garbage-can gray, pointy nose, bare ears, and a naked tail. But there are gorgeous rats, breathtaking and lovely rats—and yes, even some that are cuddly. There is the maned rat of Africa, which reminds me of a shaggy, long-tailed bear, or the almost ethereal bushy-tailed cloud rat from the Philippines, which has a small, round face, plush black-and-white fur, and an extravagantly furred tail that is often longer than its body.

The rat—for Emmons recognized it immediately as some species of large tree rat—had just been killed, bitten through the base of the skull by a weasel that must have heard her coming and dropped its prey. It was almost 18 inches long, 8 inches of that its heavily furred tail, and weighed about 2 pounds. Because Emmons had literally written the book on Latin American mammals, she also quickly realized she'd stumbled onto something completely new—not just a new species, but an entirely new genus of rat. She later named it *Cuscomys ashaninka*, a double honorific for the nearby town of Cuzco and for the Ashaninka culture that inhabits the area.

It wasn't until she got back to the United States with the rat—now disassembled as a stuffed skin, a cleaned skull, and a pickled body—that Emmons uncovered the next twist in the story. She knew about the tomb rats that archaeologists had found when they dug up the burial grounds of Machu Picchu in 1916, and so she compared those bones with *Cuscomys*'s skull—and found that although they were different species, they belonged to the same genus. Suddenly the idea of being buried with a rat seemed a lot more logical, if the rats in question looked as sweet and cute as *Cuscomys*. Emmons plans to return to the Vilcabamba, hoping to learn more about the ecology of her newly discovered rodent—and confident that the original tomb rat, that mysterious species still known only from its dusty bones, is waiting to be found in the foggy, poorly explored mountains.

Tropical ecosystems as a whole, with their tremendous diversity of life, are also hotbeds for the rediscovery of lost species—there is simply more to misplace, and because the tropics remain relatively unexplored, the chance that a rare species will evade notice is that much higher. The tropical region with perhaps the highest rate of rediscovery is the island of Madagascar, off the east coast of Africa. Separated from the mainland for more than 100 million years, Madagascar evolved a unique fauna, particularly lemurs, an early branch of the primate tree that vanished elsewhere in the world but survived here.

The island's isolation was strong but not inviolate; the arrival of humans 2 million years ago started a cascade of extinctions that accelerated with European discovery and the French colonial era. About a dozen species of lemurs are extinct, including one the size of a small gorilla, and twenty-three of the thirty-two remaining lemurs are endangered. That tally isn't as depressing as it once was, though, because a number of lost lemurs have been rediscovered. They include the hairy-eared dwarf lemur and the greater bamboo lemur, the latter missing for eighty-five years before it was relocated in 1972. Also numbered among the newly quick is the aye-aye, which surely ranks as one of the most astoundingly strange beasts in the world. An aye-aye looks like a cross between a squirrel and Nosferatu the Vampire, with its long, furry tail, huge batlike ears, and skeletal hands with an extraordinarily thin, elongated middle finger it uses for fishing grubs out of dead wood. The animal's eerie pale eyes only compound the uncanny effect; little wonder the Malagasy consider it an evil omen. There were two species, both of which were considered extinct until the 1950s, when the smaller of the two was found alive in the wet forests of Madagascar, where it remains critically endangered.

I once asked a mammalogist who worked in Madagascar, and who was responsible for relocating several species of "extinct" lemurs, how he'd managed such a remarkable feat. "It's simple," he said. "Just go into the rain forest at night and look around. The French never bothered, because the French never went more than 20 miles beyond the nearest bottle of good wine."

He was kidding, of course; finding a lost species is rarely so easy. In 1993, researchers from the Peregrine Fund, a U.S.–based raptor conservation group, were conducting a survey in the Masoala Peninsula in northeast Madagascar when they spotted a large, long-tailed hawk. They thought it might be a Madagascar serpent-eagle, but that was unlikely; no one had seen one of the 2-foot-long raptors since 1930, and several intensive, well-organized searches for it had come up dry. But they decided to try again, returning to the area with equipment to trap and radio-track a hawk—only to find that farmers had already clear-cut the area for fields, the slash-and-burn agriculture known there as *tavy*.

The following year, however, Malagasy biologists trained by the Peregrine Fund were conducting a songbird survey in a completely different patch of forest within the peninsula. They'd strung the woods with mist nets, of a grade ordinarily too light and fragile for catching raptors, so it was double good fortune when the first serpent-eagle anyone had encountered in sixty years flew into the net and entangled itself without simply shredding the mesh and escaping. Capping the discovery, four years later Peregrine Fund scientists working in the area managed to find the first nest of the species ever seen. (Because of the Masoala Peninsula's biotic richness, the Madagascar government declared 840 square miles of it a national park in 1997.)

Sometimes it turns out that not only is an animal not extinct, it is actually fairly widespread but simply has been overlooked. The Madagascar red owl, a gorgeous species of barn-owl with brick-orange plumage, had been long considered extinct on the island, probably (so the thinking went) driven over the brink by competition from common barn-owls introduced from Africa. But one was found in 1993, the first confirmed record since 1934, and with more study scientists have begun to suspect that the owls are rather widely distributed, if still rare, in eastern Madagascar. Part of the reason for the oversight was that their call, though somewhat higher and sharper, had simply been mistaken for a barn-owl's for decades.

It's one thing to overlook a night-flying owl; quite another to miss a species because it was hiding behind the ice cream and a container of frozen peas. Everyone has a few odd, forgotten packages shoved in the back of the freezer, but experts thought the one Jim Anthony had tucked away for thirty-seven years might pave the way for the renaissance of a long-lost fish—and prove, in the bargain, how easily chance can become obsession.

Blue pike—not pike at all but a small relative of the walleye with huge, unearthly eyes and a pale bluish cast—were the mainstay of Lake Erie's commercial fishery from the 1850s until just after World War II, when they began to decline rapidly in the face of water pollution and overharvesting. By the mid-1970s, the species was feared extinct, although oddly colored walleyes that turned up from time to time kept alive the wishful notion that a few blue pike had survived. Others dismissed blue pike as not really a distinct species at all, just an oddly colored race of walleye.

The blue pike was only one of a variety of native fish lost in the Great Lakes, an extinction event to rival the near-loss of the Plains bison and Pacific salmon in both its ecological magnitude and its economic impact, and yet one that few Americans know anything about. Along with walleye, blue pike, and lake trout, a backbone of the Great Lakes commercial fishery was the whitefish, a diverse group of slim, silvery salmonids related to trout, including the ciscoes and lake herring. By one estimate there were forty species or distinct subspecies of whitefish in the Great Lakes, most found nowhere else.

The longjaw cisco, small and silvery with a deeply forked tail, was harvested for the smoked fish industry, while the 20-inch blackfin cisco, or "jumbo herring," was netted in immense quantities with the smaller deepwater cisco—up to 15 million tons from a single lake in 1885 alone. By 1900 the blackfin had been driven to the point of commercial extinction in many parts of the Great Lakes, and netters' attention had shifted to other species. The real blow, however, came not from too many gill nets but from a new enemy—the sea lamprey. This parasitic fish, native to the Eastern Seaboard but originally absent from the Great Lakes, wormed its way into the St. Lawrence River and thence through newly built canals to Lake Ontario by 1835, working its way progressively up the chain of lakes; anglers who used the larval lampreys as bait probably abetted its progress. Eel-like, the lamprey has a mouth straight out of a horror movie—a suction disk equipped with circular rows of sharp teeth, with which it battens onto a live fish and chews into the animal's guts.

The lamprey finished what the commercial netters had started; by the 1950s, the once-thriving lake-trout fishery had collapsed, and many of the whitefish had sunk into oblivion—deepwater ciscoes were extinct by 1955, the Lake Ontario kiyi by 1967, longjaw ciscoes by 1978. The blackfin cisco disappeared from its once-expansive range in the Great Lakes by 1969, but at least it has managed to escape extinction: a small population, classified by the government of Canada as threatened, survives in unknown numbers in Lake Nipigon, Ontario.

The glory days of Great Lakes fishing were becoming faded memories in the 1960s, when Jim Anthony was still a young man in the Lake Erie community of Conneaut, Ohio. The son of a commercial netter who'd worked on his father's boat, Anthony grew up with the stories of the lake's fishing wealth and helped his father catch and sell some of the last blue pike. So when he went fishing one day in 1962—with rod and line, not a gill net—and managed to catch a 15-inch fish, he stared open-mouthed at the critter flopping on his line and immediately realized it wasn't a run-of-the-mill walleye. So he plunked it into a bucket of water and started making hurried phone calls to state wildlife officials. Anyone want a live blue pike? he asked.

They didn't; finally, one office told him to just to take the fish back to the lake and let it go. But the stress had been too much for it, and the fish went belly up and died when he put it back. Anthony retrieved it, not quite sure what to do. Seemed a shame to throw it away—even if no one else appreciated its importance, he sure did—so he took it home and wrapped it up. Then it went into the freezer, where it remained for the next thirty-seven years, periodically rewrapped to keep it as fresh as possible. Anthony's wife, Mary Lynn, was under strict orders not to throw it away or allow it to thaw out when she was defrosting the freezer.

In the meantime, he became a lone-wolf advocate for blue pike, agitating for permission to set some nets, catch a few of the survivors he was convinced were still out there, and start a captive population. He cornered politicians, buttonholed agency staff. But once again, no one seemed interested, and since his father had died and Jim no longer had a commercial fishing license, he could do nothing.

Officials declared the blue pike formally extinct in 1983. By that time Jim Anthony, the onetime gill-netter, had long since become a barber. While he was cutting hair, he'd regale his customers with the story of the day he caught an extinct fish—and many of them, he admits, thought he was more than a little strange to have kept the evidence all these years. It's one thing to mount a trophy fish and hang it on your wall, but it's a might peculiar to keep a glassy-eyed fish stick next to the ice cube tray for four decades. Anthony was untroubled; though he was never sure what to do with the fish, he knew it was too valuable to discard. And he was right.

In 1998, someone stopped in the barbershop for a trim and gave Anthony a newspaper clipping he figured would interest him. Scientists were trying to determine whether or not the blue pike still existed, and so they were collecting specimens sent in by fishermen from the Great Lakes states and beyond. (There is a chance some blue pike eggs or fry may have been moved to other states before its extinction, since many large impoundments were stocked with walleye in the mid-twentieth century.) Anthony called up Dr. Carol Stepien, an ichthyologist at Case Western Reserve University in Cleveland who was taking part in the study, and offered her his frozen keepsake. Stepien was conducting genetic studies on fish that might be blue pike, though most, she said, lacked the trademark extremely large, close-set eyes, an adaptation to life in the gloomy depths. But Jim Anthony's fish, in surprisingly good condition despite its long deep-freeze, fit the profile of a blue pike pretty well. His might just provide the benchmark against which the maybe-pike could be measured.

Things were looking bright for a fish consigned to history for almost two decades. For a number of years, there had been provocative reports of small, bluish walleyes being caught in lakes in Canada that some fisheries biologists thought could be blue pike. In the spring of 1999, thanks to a flurry of media reports about Anthony's strange obsession and Stepien's research, interest in blue pike was running high. Because of the press coverage, an effort by the federal Lower Great Lakes Fisheries Resource Office to find and restore blue pike—a proposal that had been dead in the water for lack of money—got a kickstart when a Lake Erie fishing club ponied up $5,000 to match a grant from the National Fish and Wildlife Foundation. With Stepien's report on blue pike specimens coming out shortly, everyone was ready to jump on the bandwagon.

In May 1999, Stepien presented her findings at a meeting of the International Association of Great Lakes Research. The verdict: While Jim Anthony's fish had some genetic characteristics of a blue pike, it also had DNA from a typical walleye—in other words, it was a hybrid, probably the result of a female blue pike mating with a male walleye, perhaps because blue pike had become too scarce to find each other for mating. And while her tests on old samples of pure blue pike tissue seemed to settle the issue of whether it was a distinct species (it was, in her opinion), none of the recently caught fish they'd collected were true blue pike. "As far as I know today," she told the press, "the blue pike seems to be extinct. I'm not saying there may not be some somewhere. I just haven't seen them."

That hasn't stopped people from looking. Anglers regularly boat fish that look—more or less—like a blue pike, and the Native Fish Conservancy has posted a $500 reward for a certified pike or hybrid. Meanwhile, lab work continues in the hope of isolating genetic markers that would easily separate blue pike from walleyes, so that if anyone does find a surviving population of the fish, the real McCoys can be distinguished and a pure breeding population established.

While prolonged absence is often an indication of extinction, you can't always assume a species is gone just because it's been AWOL for a long time. This is especially true of seabirds, which spend most of their lives in the emptiest parts of the world's oceans. That's how the cahow in Bermuda was able to evade notice for three centuries, and it's why Dr. Dick Watling was so sure the Fiji petrel might still exist.

The petrel, a foot-long black bird with long, tapered wings, had been collected once, in 1855, and never seen again. Ordinarily, the passage of nearly 130 years without a sighting would be fairly clear evidence of extinction, especially given the ecological damage done to the Fiji Islands by introduced pests like pigs, cats, and rats. Petrels come ashore only briefly to breed, however, nesting belowground in burrows and coming or going only under cover of darkness—so even if they had escaped the ravages of alien mammals, they would require a great effort to find.

For a year and a half in the early 1980s, Watling and Ratu Filipe Lewanavanua visited the small Fijian island of Gau, which covers barely 56 square miles, searching for evidence of the petrel. But the hunt went poorly, and by April 1984 Watling was getting discouraged. Skirting dangerous reefs, they had cruised the eastern, or windward, side of Gau in a sailboat, speculating that adult petrels laden with food would use that easier approach when coming back to the island at dusk to feed their chicks; but they found nothing. They made repeated tramps up into the steep, rain forest–clad highlands, where they found signs that feral cats had been killing collared petrels, a more common species, but—for good or ill, depending on how you look at it—they found no evidence of dead Fiji petrels.

Nocturnal seabirds like petrels can be attracted by playing tape recordings of their calls, and by shining bright lights into the air. Of course, no one had a tape of a Fiji petrel, so Watling and Lewanavanua used the next best thing, recordings of collared petrels they'd made on Gau. They set up a spotlighting camp on a high, inland cliff that looked out spectacularly on Herald Bay, hauled up the heavy car batteries they needed for power, and set to work despite nearly constant rain and mist.

"April 30th, 1984, was the type of day I would ordinarily prefer to forget," Watling later wrote. "Certainly I could not persuade any of the villagers to stay overnight in camp. Wind-driven rain eddied back and forth across the ridge. The fire had succumbed—there would be no cooking tonight; everything in camp was drenched. I was tempted to slip into my tent—dry and warm. 'Another unsuccessful night,' I could simply have reported."

Instead, after dark he set up a small fluorescent work lamp and pow-ered up a handheld spotlight, which quickly attracted collared petrels drifting silently out of the wet darkness; these he grabbed and placed in cotton bags for later examination, their unhappy calls adding to the cho-rus coming from his tape recorder, which he had just turned on. Stand-ing back to check the sound output, Watling sensed something coming at his head out of the darkness and instinctively shied away as a bird clipped his ear and tumbled to the ground in a heap. It was the second Fiji petrel any scientist had seen. "A more undignified return to human awareness after 129 years of peaceful oblivion could not be imagined," he wrote. (Since then, five more petrels have been found on Gau.)

Getting smacked in the head is a helluva way to relocate a missing bird, but at least Dick Watling was looking for the Fiji petrel. If there is one story that epitomizes the role serendipity plays in the rediscovery of a lost species, it is that of the Australian night parrot.

About 9 inches long and looking very much like a dark, oversized budgie, the night parrot is one of the weirder members of Australia's de-cidedly eccentric avifauna. Discovered by Europeans in 1845 but not de-scribed for science for another fifteen years, it was rarely encountered by naturalists who penetrated the arid interior of the continent—in all, only twenty-three specimens were ever collected, several of them now lost. Early ornithologists did learn that the night parrot was entirely nocturnal, spending the day belowground in shallow burrows, where it also nested, coming out at night to forage for seeds (primarily from the native hummock grass known as spinifex, or porcupine grass, a keystone of many Australian deserts) and visiting widely scattered water holes. Night parrots were reluctant to fly, instead scurrying around on the ground like quail, but they were not flightless—in fact, it appears they were highly nomadic, ranging over most of central Australia in search of regions where heavy rains produced a local abundance of spinifex seeds.

Their nomadism, nocturnal timetable, and retiring habits conspired to make them among the least known of Oz's birds. Still, they seemed reasonably widespread through the 1870s and 1880s, though few collec-tors could be sure of encountering them except by accident. By the beginning of the twentieth century, however, night parrots had dis-appeared from their previous haunts, and in the years following World

War I, many Australian scientists sounded their death knell. The last specimen was shot in 1912; only a few years later, one author lamented: "There is little to record concerning this unique generic form save that it is now impossible to add much more, the absolute extinction of the species apparently being complete."

Not everyone gave up hope; the very qualities that made the night parrot hard to find would also tend to hide a small remnant population from discovery. In the 1970s, as Australian birders were conducting atlas surveys of the country's birdlife, they reported about twenty unconfirmed sightings, while a scientist from the South Australian Museum flushed four small night-flying parrots while conducting a search on camelback. Several ornithologists went so far as to suggest the night parrot was not only not extinct, it might not even be rare—just rarely observed. For support, they pointed to another deep-desert species, the Eyrean grasswren, a mousy little bird that had likewise not been recorded for almost eighty years but that proved—once birders learned where and how to look for it—to be abundant in the central deserts.

Theories are fine, but evidence was still lacking, and the night parrot came to exert a grip on the imaginations of Australians, similar to that of the maybe-extinct, maybe-not thylacine, or Tasmanian tiger—in fact, it's been referred to as "the thylacine of birds." In 1989, *Australian Geographic* publisher and flamboyant entrepreneur Dick Smith went so far as to offer a $25,000 reward for proof that this strange bird still existed.

Night parrots were a long way from Walter Boles's mind as he neared the end of a marathon, six-week specimen-collection trip across the top of Australia. A native of Kansas who had come to Australia in the 1970s to teach, Boles was accompanied by Wayne Longmore of the Queensland Museum and another Kansan, Max Thompson of Southwestern College. On October 17, 1990, they were in western Queensland, near the town of Boulia—deep in the desert heartland of northern Australia, a long way from anywhere.

"It was *stinking* hot," Boles remembered, sitting in the cluttered library of the Australian Museum's ornithology department in Sydney, where he is now curator of birds. The team was riding in two vehicles, and while most of them were fried from the 100-plus-degree heat— "None of us wanted to do anything but get somewhere else"—Thompson still wanted to try to collect an Australian pratincole, a small bird vaguely resembling a cross between a swallow and a sandpiper. When he spotted a flock off the road, he had the convoy pull over so he could stalk them across the stony desert, a bleak habitat known as a gibber plain.

"So we pull up, but we all said no way, it's too hot, we're not getting out of the cars." Thompson went off alone with his gun, and eventually came back with a pratincole and a plover he'd shot, both of which were starting to bleed. Boles, who'd walked back to see what Thompson had bagged, said he'd find a stick so Thompson could push some cotton wool down the birds' throats to plug up the bleeding.

"So I look down at my feet, to pick a stick off the side of the road, and I was practically standing on this dead parrot," Boles said.

The carcass was hardly in pristine condition. "It was flat, and it was just mummified; the ants had eaten most of the flesh," Boles recalled. The bird had probably been smashed on the grille of a truck—otherwise, Boles is sure that black kites, which are highly efficient scavenging hawks, would have gotten it first. A forensic pathologist later determined that the bird had probably been dead between three months and a year, preserved in the exceptionally dry desert air and carried for heaven only knows how far before it finally flaked off the truck grille—only to be spotted by one of the handful of people who would (first) pay attention to mummified roadkill and (second) recognize the feathered pancake. Like Louise Emmons with her cloud rat in Peru, the night parrot had been found by one of the few people who would realize what a prize he had—and most of the others were sitting a few meters away in their truck. Chance set the table, but a prepared mind spotted the feast.

"I picked up the stick and handed it to Max, and then I picked up the bird—we've got specimens of night parrots, so I knew immediately what it was. I stuck my head in the passenger side of the front vehicle, reached across, and said, 'There, Mr. Longmore, what do you think about *that*?' and handed it to him. Then I walked away, and he just sat there saying, 'Holy shit! Holy shit!'"

I assumed Boles must have been elated, too, but he said it didn't work that way. "Actually, I didn't feel anything for a while; it wasn't until later that the impact kind of settled in. Which I suppose justifies what one of my old girlfriends said, that I have the emotional range of a house brick," he said with a grin.

If Boles and his colleagues were taking the find with cool profession-alism, they were pretty much alone. They'd called the museum from Boulia to share the happy news, then vanished again—off to another re-mote outpost in Queensland for five more days of collecting.

"Suddenly everyone wanted to know where we were, and no one knew. What we didn't realize was, almost a year to the day before we found this thing, Dick Smith had offered his reward, good for two years, to anyone who could demonstrate the continued existence of the night parrot. And we didn't know anything about it."

With the reward—which eventually went to fund the Australian Mu-seum's night parrot research—stoking public interest, the parrot gener-ated a lot more attention than most rediscoveries of lost species. Once they got back to their respective institutions, Boles's and Longmore's phones rang off the hook for days. Queensland's minister for conserva-tion and the environment, accompanied by much of his staff, trooped en masse to the Queensland Museum (which claimed the specimen, al-though it lost out on a slice of the reward money), and later even an-nounced the news to the state parliament.

"It's in the official parliamentary record that we stopped to have a pee by the side of the road," Boles said. "Which is probably better than saying we stopped to shoot birds." (Nor was that the only time the real reason for the stop was fudged out of deference to public sensitivities, since not everyone understands the need to shoot wild birds for mu-seum collections. In an article the following year in *Australian Natural History*, Boles and his colleagues themselves said only that they stopped to "watch" some pratincoles, waiting until Thompson "obtain[ed] a suit-able look.")

There has been a concerted effort to locate living individuals since the night parrot resurfaced. Information packets were distributed widely across central Australia, detailing how to identify the species and whom to call if one should be seen. A flurry of reports followed, often from cattlemen driving their herds at night, as well as from kangaroo hunters, long-haul truckers, and bus drivers who flushed budgie-like parrots from the road after dark.

Follow-up expeditions were mounted to areas that produced credi-ble reports, with scientists trying a variety of techniques—mist-netting at water holes, using night-vision scopes and spotlights, searching for feathers or the remains of predator kills, making audio recordings—but all to no avail. Boles suspects that by the time a report comes in and an expedition is planned, the nomadic parrots have decamped and are a long way off. One hope was to catch a live night parrot and put a radio transmitter on it. "Even a few nights worth of data would have told us more than we have now," Boles said.

Even though no one has confirmed a living night parrot in close to a century—after all, the 1990 specimen could have been the last survivor—no one seriously believes the species is extinct. "It's the thylacine of the bird world, but unlike the thylacine, they *are* out there," Boles said. "I'd hate to think ours was the last one." While birders may allow wishful thinking to cloud their judgment, and thus taint their reports (Boles got a report from someone who said he'd seen a night parrot "at the same place he'd seen a thylacine"), the most credible accounts have come from nonbirders like cattle drovers who recognized the parrot as strange and distinctive but didn't attach a great deal of importance to the sighting until they saw the information packets later.

Even if the night parrot does survive, something happened in the last century to make it much rarer. It may be that the relatively large number of specimens collected in the 1870s and 1880s represented a fluke—an unusual concentration of birds due to the heavy rains and good seed production in those years. But experts suspect the degradation of spinifex grassland and the shrublands of the gibber plains by grazing, burning, and introduced plants has hurt the parrot, as it has a number of other birds and mammals dependent on these fragile ecosystems. Boles and others searching for the parrot have noticed, for instance, that the large, dense clumps of grass beneath which it would have burrowed and nested are now largely gone from many areas.

Introduced red foxes and feral cats may also have played a role, at least in some parts of the species' extensive range. In the 1890s, cats around Alice Springs killed many parrots, to such an extent that one establishment decorated its picture frames with the wings and tails of the "porcupine parrots" (as they were sometimes called) killed by the owner's felines. If true, this would be merely one example from many in Australia's history of mammals from abroad wreaking havoc on indigenous wildlife. (Boles's colleague John Blythe, of the Western Australia Department of Conservation and Land Management, notes that the same pressures have decimated mid-sized desert mammals, and suspects that only the night parrot's ability to fly has preserved it this long.)

When Boles finished telling me the story of the night parrot redis- covery, he asked if I'd like to see a few—not the pancaked specimen he found, which is in Queensland, but older specimens. I followed him through the back rooms and work areas, which as in most museums were musty, painted the same bland institutional colors as prisons, and cluttered almost beyond the point of allowing passage. We squeezed around a scientist patiently threading lengths of cord through dozens of specimen tags, and stopped in Boles's office, where he has a few re- minders of his Kansas youth—ratty old stuffed meadowlarks and a cou- ple of other American prairie birds that somehow wound up in the museum's collection.

"Let me take you into the vault," he said, fishing an old-fashioned key from his pocket and using it to unlock a heavy door in the next room. It was jammed with mounted specimens and bones, with a large cabinet against one wall filled with a hodgepodge of the rare and the vanished from around the world—a passenger pigeon and Eskimo curlews from North America, rare hybrid New Guinean birds of paradise. "We've even got the skeleton of a great auk in here somewhere," he said.

"This is a long way from Newfoundland," I said, surprised.

"Well, museums used to trade stuff between them. And don't forget, at one time, none of these were especially rare."

Boles opened a tray of very gray birds; I was reminded of Semper's warbler, though these were in a variety of sizes.

"Lord Howe Island thrush, extinct. Lord Howe Island starling, ex- tinct," he said, handling the specimen gently but with an almost careless sense of familiarity. "Lord Howe warbler, fantail, silvereye, all extinct." Lord Howe Island, a small jewel 500 miles from the Australian coast, re- tained most of its unique birdlife until a supply ship ran aground there in 1918 and black rats swam free of the wreckage. Today, nine of its fifteen endemic birds are extinct.

When Boles opened the drawer with the night parrots, I will confess my eye jumped first to the line of skins ranked down the middle—small birds, less than a foot long, but neon in their intensity, with fluorescent blue-greens, pinks, and reds. No wonder they named this species the paradise parrot. "That was possibly the first mainland Australian bird to go extinct," Boles said. Like the night parrot, it was also a victim of grassland burning and overgrazing, and while some still hold out slim hope for its survival, the fact that none have been seen since 1927 suggests it is well and truly gone.

The night parrots were less flashy, but no less attractive. Four of them were sequestered in a shallow cardboard box, each one—as promised—looking like a big dark-green budgie.

I've stood in just this position many times over the years, looking with mingled sadness and reverence at the last earthly remains of a species once vital and alive. Sometimes it feels like paying respect, which seems proper—but I also have to confess that at other times there is a peculiar sense of celebrity, like finally catching a glimpse of a famous person. How much more intense that feeling must be, I recall thinking, when the living creature materializes unexpectedly in your stunned and joyous hands.

Now that chance has played its part, the long, hard job of calculation and planning takes over. Despite more than a decade of failed searches and dry efforts, Walter Boles is convinced the night parrot is still out there; he and his colleagues just need better information about where it might be. And perhaps a more creative approach.

"You know what I'm thinking about doing? I might just set up shop at some of the all-night truck stops in the Outback and check the grilles of trucks when they stop for petrol. If we find a dead parrot, we ask the trucker where he's been, and that'll narrow it down in a hurry." He paused. "Unless the parrot's already been dead for nine months, like ours was." Only in the strange, twilight world of ghost birds would that plan make perfect sense.

Rediscovering a missing species can be a hard enough job, what with climate, distance, tropical disease, rugged geography, cutthroat bandits, and political instability conspiring against the searchers. One hurdle you wouldn't expect to encounter, though, is deliberate fraud—but for former Smithsonian ornithologist Pamela Rasmussen, the trail to one of India's legendary ghost birds was obscured by a messy tangle of lies, theft, and deceit dating back nearly a century.

Rasmussen—tall, blond, and strikingly attractive—is a specialist in the birds of southern Asia, with several newly discovered species of owls to her credit. In 1996, she was working on a new field guide to the birds of India when she came across an article about Colonel Richard Meinertzhagen that gave her pause. Meinertzhagen, who died in 1967 at the age of eighty-nine, was one of those extraordinarily colorful military characters that England occasionally produces—a spy during the Russian Revolution who claimed to have murdered more than a dozen Bolshevik agents, he was posted at various points to Africa and Asia, and eventually became chief of intelligence for British Field Marshal Allenby in the Middle East during World War I and a close friend of Lawrence of Arabia. A fanatical big-game hunter, he is memorialized, among other things, through the Latin name of the African giant hog, *Hylochoerus meinertzhageni*, whose skin he sent to the British Museum in 1902. (One Meinertzhagen biographer describes the hog as "sort of a nightmare composite of your ex-wife and a tax collector, though it is both rarer and has larger teeth than either.")

Meinertzhagen was, even from a young age, noted for his interest in ornithology and bird collecting, and he eventually donated more than 25,000 skin specimens to the Natural History Museum in London. Because of his extensive work on the Indian subcontinent, Meinertzhagen's bird collection and detailed records remain of great importance to ornithologists like Rasmussen.

But there apparently was a darker side to Meinertzhagen. The article Rasmussen read, written by British scientist Alan Knox, laid out a case of fraud against the colonel, demonstrating that a series of small Arctic finches known as redpolls from Meinertzhagen's collection had actually been stolen from other sources and their label data falsified. It was a serious charge: because museum specimens form the groundwork of many scientific studies, from distributional analysis to taxonomy, fraud in such a large, important collection as Meinertzhagen's would impact many researchers.

That included Rasmussen. She knew that more than a dozen species or subspecies of birds were included in the avifauna of India based on only single specimens in the Meinertzhagen collection, and if there was a chance that they were frauds that had been collected elsewhere, she might have to eliminate those birds from her field guide. On the other hand, Meinertzhagen was a tireless collector, and he might have found them just where he claimed he did, in which case the records were legitimate and should remain in the book. Rasmussen wasn't sure what to do.

By coincidence, the noted English ornithologist Nigel J. Collar was visiting the Smithsonian at the time, and when Rasmussen confided her problem to him, she was surprised to find that Collar had been a member of the committee appointed by the Natural History Museum to investigate Meinertzhagen's alleged redpoll frauds. Since she was planning to stop at the museum a few weeks later on a visit to London, he encouraged her to see the suspect Indian specimens for herself and to work with Robert Prys-Jones, head of the museum's Bird Group, who was examining the redpoll specimens on which Knox had based his allegations. But Collar told her that by simply looking at the skins, she'd probably learn nothing to settle the issue one way or the other.

At first, the fourteen specimens were indeed little help; as she'd been warned, Rasmussen couldn't really see anything that would tell her if the skins had been stolen from another collection and relabeled. These were not taxidermy mounts with glass eyes and lifelike postures but working scientific specimens—stiff as boards, stretched out, with folded wings and cotton showing at the eye sockets. The Natural History Museum has nearly a million such specimens, probably the largest such collection in the world, stored in vast cabinets with removable trays.

Though to some the practice seems anachronistic and even a touch barbaric in today's world—in fact, many birders are appalled at the notion of killing birds for scientific collections—skin specimens remain essential to many ornithological studies. I learned to prepare them as a kid working on starlings and pigeons in my bedroom, and honed my technique in college, but the process has changed relatively little since the days of Linnaeus or Audubon. I learned to begin by making a long incision down the belly of the bird, then easing the skin away from the muscle; this requires extreme care, because the skin is thin as tissue paper and tears easily. The leg bones are severed at the knee joint between the thigh and drumstick, and the humerus is cut midway to free the wings from the body. As the work progresses, the preparator uses white cornmeal to absorb any leaking blood or fluids that might otherwise stain the plumage. Eventually the skin is inverted like a sock from the bill, exposing the skull, which is trimmed and cleaned, with fresh cotton filling the empty braincase and eye orbits.

Now, using the body as a model, the collector takes a long, thin wooden dowel and builds a mannequin of cotton wound around the stick, approximating the size and shape of the original body; the skin is pulled over this and the incision sewn up. No attempt is made to make the bird appear alive—the eyes are filled with cotton and the bill points straight in line with the body; the legs are crossed and tied with a piece of thread. The final step is to fill out a label, which records the species and sex (determined by dissecting the body to check for ovaries or testes) and a variety of details about where and when it was collected. In the case of a new or unusual species, the amount of data that a conscientious collector includes on the label—in tiny, neat hand-writing—can be substantial, and usually refers to even more extensive field notes.

Most specimens are prepared along these basic lines, but Rasmussen knew that every preparator has his or her own approach to the process—little idiosyncrasies, shortcuts, and procedural quirks that should leave their unique mark on a specimen and that a careful eye might detect. This was especially true in the nineteenth and early twen-tieth centuries, when many of the collectors were self-taught and work-ing with whatever tools and materials they could find in remote, inhospitable regions. Such peculiarities had tipped off Alan Knox to the redpoll frauds.

"It's amazing, when you start looking at different people's speci-mens, how different their preparation styles are, and yet how consistent they tend to be, at least in a general time period and especially a certain expedition," Rasmussen told me on a sunny spring day when people were strolling the grassy Mall outside the Smithsonian's National Mu-seum of Natural History, where she kept an office. "People used differ-ent kinds of thread, and in particular different kinds of stitching, and different placements of the incision. Some preparators routinely skinned a bird under its wings, and some even skinned it on the back, but that's pretty rare."

Examining the fourteen British specimens, Rasmussen realized that every one showed a different preparation style, which was in itself suspi-cious; if Meinertzhagen had collected and prepared all the birds himself, as he'd claimed, the techniques should be roughly similar. When she went back to the storage cabinets and began to compare them to other specimens, she immediately began to connect those styles to collectors other than Meinertzhagen.

"It didn't take long, a few hours really, to start matching some of them up with the original series"—the word scientists use for a collection made during a particular expedition. "And it doesn't take an expert, either—I mean, in some cases it was just blindingly obvious." One example involved a magpie prepared in an unusual way, in a very flat style with an open incision, so that the stuffing was visible—a method often used by native collectors employed by Louis Mandelli, a tea planter in Darjeeling in the 1870s who was also a bird enthusiast. Rasmussen and Prys-Jones noticed that the magpie stuffing included strands of a moss-like substance—and when they checked other Mandelli skins in the collection, they found exactly the same material poking out of the hole. The Meinertzhagen specimen was obviously a fraud—it had been prepared for Mandelli, swiped, and relabeled at a later date by Meinertzhagen as if it had been his own.

It appears that Meinertzhagen used his reputation, and his free-ranging access to the museum, as a cover for his thefts, which Rasmussen and others believe must have occurred over many years. "He appears to have been taking specimens right along. We know of hundreds, but there must be thousands of frauds in this collection. That's quite a lot of work to take that many specimens—he wasn't accused of being lazy, because that's a lot of relabeling," she said.

Even at the time, there were suspicions about the colonel's behavior. Noted ornithologist Charles Vaurie wrote breathlessly to a friend: "I can say *upon my oath* that Meinertzhagen's collection contains skins *stolen* from the Leningrad Museum, the Paris Museum, and the American Museum of Natural History . . . He also removed labels, and replaced them by others to suit his ideas and theories." Rasmussen explained that in the early 1900s the collections manager at the museum informed the curator that he suspected Meinertzhagen was stealing skins. "The curator called Meinertzhagen in and asked him to open his briefcase, and there were nine specimens in it! And Meinertzhagen said, 'Oh, Dr. Bowdler Sharpe [the greatest curator of the Natural History Museum] always let my brother and me take specimens home when we needed to, to work on them there, and then we'd always bring them back.' "

"And he bought that story?" I asked.

She laughed. "I don't think so, no. But there was no way to tell it wasn't true, because Bowdler Sharpe was dead by that time. So Meinertzhagen was barred from the British Museum for a year; but someone eventually interceded and he got back in and eventually even got a passkey. Actually, back in the early days it was not all that easy to steal specimens. If you wanted to see greenfinches, you asked and they'd bring out boxes of greenfinches, and because they knew how many were in a box, it was difficult to steal large numbers of specimens without being caught. In fact, there are a number of reports filed by the in-charge saying, 'Sir, I regret to inform you that I have reason to believe Colonel Meinertzhagen has abstracted X number of greenfinches today.' But they never proved anything. In fact, they set up a sting operation, but Meinertzhagen was onto it."

One of the most important species in the Meinertzhagen collection was *Athene blewitti*, the Indian forest owlet. Discovered in 1872 by an amateur naturalist named F. R. Blewitt, it is similar to the little owl of Europe and the burrowing owl of North America—a chunky, round-headed owl about 10 inches long, broadly barred on the sides, with a heavy black rim to the round facial disk surrounding bright yellow eyes. Only seven specimens were collected, all from two areas of central India, separated by about 750 miles. It hadn't been seen in nearly a century, despite several well-organized expeditions looking for it; the handful of sight records and photographs attributed to it in the 1950s and 1960s were later dismissed as misidentifications of the very similar spotted owlet, which is common across India and Southeast Asia. In the 1970s, experts combed three regions where, based on old specimen records, the owl once lived, but turned up nothing. The depressing conclusion was that the forest owlet had slipped into extinction.

The last specimen on record was a bird Colonel Meinertzhagen said he collected in October 1914, but it was on Rasmussen's list of suspicious specimens, and after the frauds came to light, she was betting the owlet skin had been stolen from someone else's collection, too. But while the flattened magpie and a few other skins were relatively easy to link with their original collectors, the forest owlet was a much tougher nut to crack. The skin had obviously been restuffed—she and Collar could see where it had been opened and stitched over the original sutures—and then washed in solvent to degrease it. Proving where it

came from was going to be difficult, though, since there were no obvious external clues, as with the magpie, to link it to another collector.
But there was circumstantial evidence—a forest owlet skin known to
have been shot in 1884 by an amateur ornithologist named James Davidson was missing from that series.

"I knew that the Meinertzhagen specimen was remade, and I knew
there was a missing Davidson specimen, but I didn't know how I was going to link the two," Rasmussen recalled. One possibility might be to
open up the skin and look inside for clues, but everyone was leery of
that—the owlet was one of just seven specimens in existence, of a
species long considered extinct, making it extraordinarily valuable from
a scientific perspective.

Nevertheless, Rasmussen received permission from the Natural History Museum to bring the skin back to the Smithsonian, where specialists have perfected techniques for remaking old specimens without
unduly damaging them. They also borrowed the skin of another species
of small owl, stuffed by Davidson just two days after he collected his
missing forest owlet. Rasmussen was betting that a close examination
would reveal matches in preparation techniques between the two.

She was right. The researchers quickly found a few unique markers
in Davidson's work, most notably a quirky way he had of skinning out
the upper wing and stuffing the cavity around the radius and ulna with
cotton, something few other collectors bothered to do. The forest owlet
showed the same preparation—and when the scientists pulled out the
new stuffing that Meinertzhagen had packed into the cavity, they found a
small wad of greasy, yellowish cotton, left over from the original preparation and untouched by the degreasing solvents. Rasmussen sent a sample of that cotton, plus some from the known Davidson specimen, to the
FBI crime lab, which confirmed that they were similar. The damning
physical evidence, coupled with a lack of any mention in Meinertzhagen's own diary from 1914 of what should have been a momentous discovery, showed he had been lying about the owl, too.

At this point Rasmussen was still mostly concerned with determining which Meinertzhagen specimens, if any, should be included in her
Indian bird field guide. But she also realized that if the colonel had been
lying about where he collected the forest owlet, then everyone who had
been searching for the species using his labels as a guide might well have

been looking in the wrong place. Perhaps, with a little more detective work, she could determine where the owl really once lived—and just might still survive.

The Indian subcontinent is (or at least was) home to a number of storied lost species. One is the Himalayan quail, a dark greenish bird with a blood-red bill and a white eyebrow, originally collected in Uttar Pradesh in the 1860s and 1870s before it vanished—just why, no one can say. Several concerted searches have failed to turn up any evidence of its survival, but there have been unconfirmed reports of sightings from time to time, and the World Wildlife Fund of India recently called for additional efforts to relocate it.

Considerably more attention has been paid to the case of the pink-headed duck, perhaps because of its improbable but accurate name—this large duck had a chocolate-brown body, while its neck and weirdly triangular head were bright pink. Apparently never common, it inhabited quiet waters in the jungles of northeastern India and neighboring Burma. The last wild individual was seen in 1939, and although a few ducks were kept in captivity, they never bred well; the last one died in France in 1944, having made it most of the way through World War II.

Once again, unsubstantiated reports over the years have kept alive the hope that the pink-headed duck may still be extant, although experts attribute most of them to confusion with another, vaguely similar duck, the red-crested pochard. That hasn't stopped a number of people from combing the Indian hinterlands for the legendary bird, however, including the American writer Rory Nugent, who had more success encountering Gurkha separatists, pirates, and occult curses than in finding the missing duck.

One Indian ghost bird did return from the dead—a peculiar shorebird known as Jerdon's courser, which prefers rocky, open patches of scrub amid thicker jungle. As with many lost species, it appears to have been rare to start with; originally collected in 1848, it wasn't seen again for a quarter-century, then vanished once more until 1900, after which it disappeared completely. Two major surveys failed to turn it up, and few people had any doubt of its extinction—until 1986, when a year-long search by the Bombay Natural History Society relocated it in

Andhra Pradesh. The discovery came just in time: the site where the bird lived was about to be developed for an irrigation project but instead was turned into a wildlife sanctuary.

Richard Meinertzhagen claimed to have shot his forest owlet in 1914 in Gujarat, not far from the Arabian Sea. Because his was the last record anyone knew about, people had focused their efforts to find the owl there—which meant that using Meinertzhagen's label data as a clue, they had been looking for the forest owlet in a part of India where the species may never, in fact, have been found.

With the fraudulent specimen correctly identified, Rasmussen pulled out her maps and started looking up the collection locations of the seven known specimens—which in itself caused some head-scratching. "Once we'd worked out that these really were the sites, it still wasn't easy to

track them down, because the names have changed, the spellings have changed. But it turned out that none of those sites could have been above 500 meters in elevation." This was significant, because until then, most of the accounts of the forest owlet indicated that it lived in hills or mountains—and thus the previous, unsuccessful expeditions had focused on highlands. "When we realized that people had been going to hills to look for the owl, it was pretty clear that they hadn't been looking where the specimens had come from. Not too far away, but in order to declare something extinct, you have to look in the right places." Pam Rasmussen decided she'd look in the right places.

It's one thing to make that spur-of-the-moment decision to go after a missing animal, when the adrenaline and excitement are running at flood and anything seems possible. But reality eventually seeps back in, as it did for Rasmussen as the expedition approached.

"I never did expect to find it—before we set out, I asked a couple of my colleagues what they thought my chances were, and one of them gave me one in a thousand odds. I had a higher chance of being killed in a car wreck than of finding this bird, and the closer it got to the time to go, the more I felt it was silly to even try."

In November 1997, Rasmussen and three colleagues—Ben King of the American Museum of Natural History; David F. Abbot, a Virginia birder and artist; and their driver and translator, Ranjan Kumar Pradhan—set out on a 750-mile trek across central India to look for the owlet. They started in the eastern states of Madhya Pradesh and Orissa, exploring remnant forests close to where the original specimen had been taken. They were hamstrung by a lack of basic knowledge about their quarry, however; no one, for example, had ever recorded what the call of the forest owlet sounded like, which would be a formidable obstacle. They tried wandering the forest at night, squeaking or pishing to attract birds, and they found a variety of owls—but never the forest owlet. Fortunately, Davidson, who had collected more of the species than anyone else, had noted in the 1880s that the bird often perched in the tops of high, bare trees during the day, for unlike many owls, it and its close relatives are at least partially diurnal. That at least gave the team something to go on, and they began to concentrate their energy on the hours around dawn and dusk.

As the days dragged on without any success, the team's spirits began to flag. "We endured days of absolute tedium and boredom—those are not exciting birding places," Rasmussen said. Some of the members were lobbying to pack in the owl hunt and enjoy the remaining days, maybe take a side trip to a couple of waterfowl-rich lakes. But the thought of coming back empty-handed led them to push on to western India, to Maharashtra, where Davidson had taken his series of owlets. With a couple of days of field time left, they spooked through the Akrani Hills near Shahada, where the lowlands were completely stripped of forest and only a few patches of scrubby, degraded woodland remained in the lower hills.

"I had pretty much given up on it, but our hopes were a little bit raised when we saw the forest. In fact, we'd been up since 4:00 that morning, videotaping, and we'd seen quite a lot of things—we'd seen really nice views of mottled wood-owl, and we'd seen common quail on the road and videotaped that as a reference for our field guide," Rasmussen recalled. "It was getting late—it was nearly 8:30 in the morning—and it was getting hot. I was a little way behind Ben and David on the road, opening my water bottle, when Ben said, 'Look at that owlet.' He said it so quietly, but as soon as I saw what he was looking at, I dropped my water bottle. There had been lots of owlets around—there were jungle owlets all over the place, they're noisy and common. But I could see that it wasn't one of those."

The trio were silent for a moment, until Rasmussen whispered that she didn't see any spots on the top of its head, the field mark of the common spotted owlet. There were other differences as well. "It was chunky—it was not the thin, delicate shape of a spotted owlet. It had this sort of grayer tone, and was basically unspotted. It had big white feet, its claws were huge, and the legs and the lower underparts were fluffy and white. The spotted owlet isn't nearly as fluffy, and there's no part that you would call white.

"Knowing there had been no records for 113 years, and then to suddenly see this bird—I was in a panic, because I desperately wanted to document it. First, I didn't want to have to trust my own opinion; I wanted to be able to prove it to myself beyond any doubt, and to anyone else. I'm a big skeptic of sight records, not just other people's, but mine as well, and in this case, there'd been so much confusion about the bird. It so often happens when you're birding that you glimpse something and then you never see it again, and you never satisfy yourself as to what it was. So I was in a panic, because if I started videotaping right away I probably wouldn't get a decent look with my binoculars. As it turns out, the bird was going to just sit there—it was totally unconcerned, just totally oblivious to all this. Like, 'Who are you people?' "

The owl proved to be surprisingly tame, unruffled by the three birders or by the constant foot and livestock traffic along the road; although its habitat had been reduced to small fragments and it had been forced out of the plains where it had once lived, it had evidently adapted to some degree to its reduced circumstances. Before the team left two days later, they even found a second owlet.

When Rasmussen and the others returned to the United States and announced their find the following month, the media attention was remarkable and, for the scientists, a bit bewildering in its intensity. *The New York Times,* the *Times* of London, and other major newspapers and wire services ran prominent articles; it was featured on the evening news, in magazines, and on the Internet. But once the hullabaloo died away, everyone realized there was still a great deal to learn about the owlet—about its diet, its habitat, its range. Seven months after the rediscovery, Pam Rasmussen was back in India, organizing a team from the Bombay Natural History Society to study the owl. They found eight in a 30-mile-wide area, but Rasmussen was also shocked to discover that in the short time since she'd left, farmers had substantially reduced the small islands of hill forest supporting the bird.

All of which highlights a problem, frequently overlooked in the elation at the rediscovery of a missing species: the question of what comes next, after the champagne toasts have been drunk and the backs have all been patted. Except in the oddest of circumstances, the resurrected creature is usually hanging on by its nails, its long-term survival still very much an open question. Dreams become problematic reality—and often it turns out that ducking the bullet was the easy part.

FOUR

The Noble Living

❧

. . . There is
One great society alone on earth:
The noble Living and the noble Dead.
—William Wordsworth, *The Prelude*

In the spring of 1843, John James Audubon—aging, frail, and largely toothless—made one last expedition of discovery, up the Missouri River to Fort Union, on what is now the border of North Dakota and Montana. Frequently in his journals of the trip, he refers to "Prairie Dogs, or, as I call them, Prairie Marmots." It was hard to avoid noticing them—Lewis and Clark spoke of the "infinite numbers" of these roly-poly rodents, which lived in vast towns whose dimensions beggar belief. A century after Lewis and Clark, for example, the biologist C. Hart Merriam carefully tabulated "prairie marmots" at a colony in Texas that covered at least 25,000 square miles—an area the size of southern New England—and estimated their number at more than 400 million.

On his Missouri trek, Audubon and his companions scoured the Plains daily for new species of mammals, for the old man was working on his last great project, *The Viviparous Quadrupeds of North America*, a three-volume opus co-written with his friend the Reverend John Bachman and illustrated with help from Audubon's two sons, John and Victor. Yet, for all their hunting, they managed to overlook one unusual resident of the huge prairie dog towns—a good-sized weasel with dark legs and a robber's mask. The animal was known to fur trappers, who occasionally caught it in their sets, but not to science—until 1849, long after Audubon had returned home to New York, when a mountain man from Wyoming sent him the skin of one, stuffed with sagebrush.

The aging artist died in 1851, the same year that the volume of *Quadrupeds* was published containing a painting and description of the creature he and his co-author had dubbed *Mustela nigripes*, the black-footed ferret. "It is with great pleasure that we introduce this handsome new species," Audubon and Bachman wrote. Going by guesswork and their experience with other weasels, they surmised the ferret "feeds on birds, small reptiles . . . eggs . . . hares," and other mid-sized vertebrates, and the painting of the ferret, by John Woodhouse Audubon, shows it peering down a grassy bank into the egg-filled nest of a songbird. But the naturalists admitted they knew little about the ferret's habits.

Nor were they to learn more; no other ferret surfaced for the next

A black-footed ferret investigates a bird's nest in the original John Woodhouse Audubon painting from *The Viviparous Quadrupeds of North America*, the first time this enigmatic species was described for science. Biologists later realized that the ferrets eat almost nothing but prairie dogs, a specialization that led to their near-extinction on several occasions. (New-York Historical Society, negative no. 75037)

quarter-century, leading some (including Spencer Fullerton Baird, the assistant secretary of the Smithsonian Institution) to publicly question the veracity of the original report. This is perhaps understandable, since in those days scientific fraud was not unheard of, and Audubon, though generally honest, had a reputation for shooting from the hip that alienated more scientifically precise folk like Baird. Perhaps this erstwhile "ferret" was such a hoax, they wondered, or at best a misidentification.

It wasn't, but it is appropriate that the black-footed ferret entered scientific notice amid mystery and controversy, because the century and a half since its formal discovery has been a continuing series of puzzles, miscalculations, premature relief, and equally premature despair. Overlooked for so long, it was nearly exterminated before anyone noticed— and then when it actually was declared extinct, not once but several times, it confounded the experts by reappearing each time. Even today, with all the razzle-dazzle of high-tech conservation science on its side, the ferret's future is anything but secure.

Black-footed ferrets are phantoms: secretive, highly nocturnal, almost entirely subterranean. What Audubon and Bachman didn't realize, and what it took biologists more than a generation to learn, is that a prairie dog town is a ferret's entire universe: shelter, larder, birthing chamber, and tomb, all in one. No other North American mammal is so specialized in its diet and lifestyle, so utterly dependent upon a single other species for its very existence. Extreme specialization is always a gamble; when times are good, a specialist may thrive, but changing conditions may leave it unable to adapt, and ultimately unable to survive.

Prior to white settlement, times were certainly good for ferrets. The five species of prairie dogs on which they preyed, most notably the black-tailed, were found from Saskatchewan and Alberta south to northern Mexico and west to Arizona, Utah, and Montana. Ernest Thompson Seton, the early-twentieth-century naturalist, did a few back-of-the-envelope calculations and declared that the presettlement prairie dog population may have totaled 5 billion animals, a guesstimate that modern scientists find plausible, perhaps even a bit conservative. To put that in perspective, it is a figure equal to all the wild birds, of all species, living today in North America, and was perhaps one hundred times the presettlement population of bison, that usual standard by which we judge unimaginable abundance.

That's a lot of ferret food, and the long, lanky weasels occupied an expansive range that almost perfectly mirrored that of three prairie dog species—the black-tailed across much of the Great Plains, white-tails in the shortgrass foothills of the northern Rockies, and Gunnison's prairie dog in the Southwest. And in contrast to the highly gregarious dogs (which despite their name are most closely related to ground squirrels), black-footed ferrets, like all weasels, are somewhat surly, asocial beasts, spreading themselves thinly over the land. Ferrets like elbow room. Even so, biologists working from historical records of the acreage covered by dog towns in the Old West and the known population density of wild ferret populations, think there may have been as many as 5.6 million blackfoots in the days before settlement—roughly one for every thousand prairie dogs.

Through the nineteenth and early twentieth centuries, black-footed ferrets were curiosities, collected for museums or taken (usually by accident) by trappers, since their pelts had little commercial value. But for the most part, no one paid the slightest attention to them—while paying a great deal of attention, little of it admiring and most of it punitive, to the prairie dog. Ranchers, looking at miles and miles of pockmarked rangeland given over to prairie dog towns, pronounced them a grass-eating, cow-competing, hole-digging, horse-laming pest, and the government obliged by declaring wholesale war on prairie dogs.

Strychnine was the weapon of choice, and there are plenty of historical photos that testify to its lethal efficiency—huge pyramids of bloated prairie dogs, representing the relative handful that died outside their burrows; in one especially macabre snapshot from 1921, taken from a high vantage point, "U.S. Biological Survey" (the precursor of the U.S. Fish and Wildlife Service) is spelled out in neatly arranged piles of the dead animals. That strychnine is a secondary poison, killing the predators and scavengers that fed on the dead and dying rodents, was only an added benefit, since the government was also shoveling money into various other "varmint" eradication campaigns.

The feds stinted on neither effort nor money, and to say it worked is an understatement. In the short period from 1916 to 1920, for instance, prairie dogs were poisoned on 47 million acres of land stretching across six states, from the Dakotas to New Mexico. As late as 1908, a prairie dog town covering 1,000 square miles and containing 6.4 million ani-

mals occupied New Mexico's Animas Valley; two decades later, it was
down to just 50 acres. Between 1920 and 1960, federal, state, and private poisoning efforts in North Dakota reduced prairie dog colonies in
that state to about 20,000 acres, just 1 percent of their original area; by
1978, that figure was down to just over 9,000 acres. South Dakota,
which in the 1920s had 1.2 million acres of dog towns, now has less than
a quarter of that—but that slim total represents a third of the continent's surviving prairie dogs.

Add to that more than a million acres of grassland converted to
crops, plus the fragmentation of habitat from development and roads,
and it's no wonder that prairie dogs have been eliminated from an estimated 98 percent of their original range in the United States. Even the
black-tailed prairie dog has been so reduced in numbers and extent that
the National Wildlife Federation and other organizations petitioned the
U.S. Fish and Wildlife Service in 1998 for its protection under the federal Endangered Species Act; the agency agreed that the dogs merited
"threatened" status, but declined to offer them full protection on the
grounds that other species in the region were in even deeper trouble and
more deserving of limited resources. While the petition prompted the
U.S. Forest Service to suspend poisoning programs on all twenty national grasslands, it left other branches of the U.S. Department of
Agriculture unmoved, including the USDA's Wildlife Services (formerly
known as Animal Damage Control) division, which still facilitates poisoning campaigns.

Today, the largest and healthiest towns are generally on federal land
and Indian reservations, though even some national parks, like Badlands
in South Dakota, poison their colonies to avoid lawsuits from neighboring ranchers. Theodore Roosevelt National Park, along the Little Missouri River in western North Dakota, preserves a slice of the landscape
Audubon explored, complete with his "prairie marmots." On a windy,
overcast spring morning a few years ago, I worked my way down one of
the park's long, twisting canyons cluttered with junipers, spooking mule
deer, finding the pugmarks of bobcat in the dried mud, and keeping a
cautious eye out for the bison whose deep hoofprints made the trail uneven and difficult to walk. The canyon walls were corrugated layers of
buff, gray, and black, the legacy of ancient volcanic ashfalls, compacted
to rock and deeply eroded with time. A Cooper's hawk, so dark blue it

looked black, bolted out of the undergrowth, and I found the remains of its meal—a sharp-tailed grouse, plucked feathers surrounding it like a halo, and the breastbone, picked utterly clean, still wet and faintly pink.

The canyon opened up onto a wide plain, rimmed on one side by a high wall and falling away in the other direction to the distant river, fringed with a band of freshly green cottonwoods, where a line of bison moved with ponderous dignity. The wind carried the sound of high-pitched, staccato yips to me, and I realized that the land ahead was dotted with low, conical mounds, among which dozens of small bodies were darting. My approach caused an uproar in the town, a gossipy chatter of alarm barks, though once I settled in at the edge of a small draw, only my head and arms visible among the sagebrush and grass, the prairie dogs paid me little further heed.

The park's prairie dog colonies, covering only a few hundred acres, are by historical standards insignificantly small, but it was enough to give me a sense of life in a black-tailed prairie dog town. As their suspicion ebbed, the rodents popped up, little pear-shaped sentinels that are the very definition of "potbellied"; holding grass in their paws as they fed, they looked for all the world like fat men with their heads bobbing in prayer. Occasionally, one would stand completely erect, throw back its head, and give a loud, two-note whistle, which scientists believe may signal a territorial warning or give the all-clear to other dogs. If the latter, then they were choosing to ignore not only me but also a pair of golden eagles perched in a shaft of morning sun on the rimrock above the town.

The constant bustle of movement was impressive, but the real artistry of a prairie dog town is hidden out of sight. Each burrow complex, which may reach 15 feet underground and extend for 10 or 20 yards, has side chambers that serve as nurseries, hidey-holes, and latrines; the multiple entrances, set in low mounds, act as chimneys, drawing the constant grassland wind belowground to freshen the air. Prairie dogs are talented architects, but they are remarkable from a behavioral perspective, too. Biologist John Hoogland, who has studied them for more than twenty-five years, has found that they are a bundle of contradictions—females will kill and eat the litters of their close relatives early in the breeding season (in some colonies, half the babies die this way), but later in the summer, for reasons that remain unclear, will share their precious milk with pups that are not their own.

Prairie dogs are what ecologists refer to as a keystone species—one that plays such a central role in the functioning of an ecosystem that its removal may send the whole edifice crashing down. Prairie dog holes provide nest sites for burrowing owls and threatened swift foxes, shelter for foot-long tiger salamanders and prairie rattlesnakes (which do not, popular wisdom aside, live in perfect harmony with their hosts—the snakes will cheerfully eat dog pups if they can). The mountain plover, a bird in such dire straits that it is listed as threatened under the Endangered Species Act, prefers to nest on the bare earth of towns, while a constellation of raptors—ferruginous hawks, golden eagles, prairie falcons, red-tailed hawks—patrol the skies overhead, watching for an opportunity to snatch a meal.

A town may attract nearly 170 other species of animals, and studies have shown that the area around a colony has three times the density of wildlife as a prairie without one. And while prairie dogs certainly eat a lot of grass, denuding the ground at the center of an old colony, they also fertilize and aerate the soil, so that bison actively seek out the more nutritious graze around the edges of a town, or in newly settled spots. The fact that bison grazing in dog towns gain weight faster than those feeding in the absence of prairie dogs has led some biologists to dispute the long-held belief, which drives poisoning campaigns, that the chubby ground squirrels compete with ungulates for food.

In the past few decades, we've learned a fair bit about prairie dogs, but ferrets—which are more closely tied to them than any other species beneath their umbrella—remain a slender, sand-colored mystery. The only way to see them, under normal circumstances, is to probe a dog town at night with a powerful spotlight, hoping to get a glimpse of their brilliant emerald eyeshine in the beam. They're easy to overlook, and so for a very long time no one had a clue about how the ferrets were faring as poisoning programs mopped up one dog town after another—though Ernest Thompson Seton, alarmed by the mass poisoning of prairie dogs, predicted trouble for the ferrets as early as the 1920s.

Assumptions are dangerous things in wildlife management. In the 1950s, even though few ferrets were being seen, most Western game agencies assumed they were still found across most of their historic range, albeit in low numbers and widely scattered. What no one realized is that the ferret population had become badly fragmented—broken into small islands of prairie dogs and their attendant weasels, instead of forming a contiguous blanket across the Plains. Isolated from each other, each pocket of ferrets faced a much greater risk of local extinction, with no hope of subsequent recolonization. And now both species had a new danger to contend with: sylvatic plague, the same bacterium that causes bubonic plague in humans, which is transmitted by infected fleas. Probably introduced to North America from Asia by humans, it spread quickly through small mammals in the West in the early twentieth century, appearing in prairie dogs in 1946.

Because the disease is exotic, the rodents have no natural defense against it, and mortality may be almost universal, causing the swift and catastrophic collapse of a prairie dog town. While plague also infects ferrets, the loss of their prey is an even bigger problem, and plague outbreaks destroyed entire ferret populations one after another. By the 1960s, blackfoots had disappeared from all but ten of the 130 counties and provinces where they had been found just eighty years before, and even in those ten counties, ferret sightings were rarities. Just a few years later, government scientists were debating whether to officially declare the animals extinct.

In the late summer of 1964, the black-footed ferret made its first reappearance. A small population was discovered on a farm in Mellette County, in southwestern South Dakota—a state with lots of prairie dogs, but also with one of the most aggressive eradication campaigns in the country. This time the weasels got plenty of attention. Federal and state researchers conducted intensive surveys that showed ferrets were scattered at low levels across an eight-county area that corresponded with the highest concentration of black-tailed prairie dogs in the state.

Over the next decade, biologists filled in many of the blanks in their understanding of ferret ecology and life history by trapping, marking, and watching the wild animals. They found that while prairie dogs usually composed 90 percent of the predator's diet, the ferrets were also opportunistic, taking rabbits, voles, mice, gophers, ground squirrels, birds, and even insects when the chance presented itself. They were not wanton killers; a single prairie dog, which outweighs an adult ferret two to one, would provide food for four or five days. Ferrets were solitary, except during the late-winter breeding season, when males and females would briefly share burrows. After a 45-day gestation period, the females would give birth to a litter of as many as five kits, but juvenile mortality was high, with up to 80 percent of the youngsters disappearing before they reached adulthood—victims, usually, of a host of larger predators, from great horned owls to coyotes and badgers.

It was also clear they were, as a species, in deep trouble. Despite many searches, no other colonies had been found, and black-footed ferrets were thus among the first species to receive protection under a sequence of federal legislation, starting in 1966 with the Endangered Species Preservation Act and culminating with the current Endangered Species Act (ESA) of 1973, which recognizes several levels of risk. An "endangered" species is one that is in danger of extinction throughout all or a significant portion of its range, while those listed as "threatened" are likely to become endangered in the foreseeable future.

The ESA is the junkyard dog of American wildlife laws, the only one with enough teeth to make a difference. That's why it has been so widely used by conservation groups, often as a blunt instrument to force broader management changes at a landscape level (witness the spotted owl imbroglio) and why it's been so hotly vilified by its opponents. Administered by the U.S. Fish and Wildlife Service (USFWS), it is supposed to provide not only a legal shield against direct persecution but the designation of so-called critical habitat that receives more stringent protection and a recovery plan to guide restoration efforts. But because funding for endangered species work is chronically short (often choked off by politicians who oppose the ESA), habitat designation and recovery plans are often delayed for years, if not indefinitely.

And just because a lost species might be found in the United States does not mean it would automatically receive ESA protection, however rare it might be. Some ghost animals, like Eastern cougars and ivory-billed woodpeckers, were added to the federal endangered list when the law was created and remain on the list today; thus any surviving population would be immediately covered. But let's say instead that someone does miraculously find a blue pike swimming around in the Great Lakes. The pike was listed as federally endangered in 1967, but it was "delisted" in 1983 because it is considered extinct. If rediscovered, it would have to undergo the long, bureaucratic, and politicized process of being placed on the list again—a process that is often driven more by outside lawsuits than by need or science, and that can drag on for decades because of a lack of funding and manpower within USFWS. Almost three dozen species have become extinct while waiting for ESA listing—the conservation equivalent of letting an emergency room patient die in the corridor while waiting for a bed.

Even having the new endangered species law for backup was of marginal help to the ferrets, since differing divisions within the federal government were both aiding and exterminating the animals—USFWS was working to preserve them in the wild in South Dakota, even while the Animal Damage Control unit was spearheading prairie dog poisoning campaigns in the same region. Not surprisingly, things weren't going well in Mellette County. Over the course of a decade, biologists documented only eleven litters in the colony, and found that the ferrets weren't expanding into suitable adjacent habitat; adding to the problems, there was growing friction between landowners and wildlife biologists that could jeopardize the study. Amid rising concern, six wild ferrets were captured in 1971 from areas slated for prairie dog poisoning and shipped from South Dakota to the Patuxent Wildlife Research Center in Laurel, Maryland, a USFWS facility with experience in captive breeding. In fact, for the three years prior to this, Patuxent staff had been experimenting with Siberian ferrets, the blackfoot's closest relative, using the more common animals as surrogates to test a variety of handling and propagation techniques.

The idea was to establish a second population as a safeguard against a calamity in South Dakota, like an outbreak of plague or canine distemper, a common disease that is fatal to ferrets. Hoping to protect the newly arrived ferrets from infection, biologists at Patuxent inoculated them with a modified live-virus distemper vaccine. Such a vaccine is safe for most animals, including Siberian ferrets, 150 of which had already been vaccinated. What the Patuxent researchers didn't know—what nobody knew—is that the live-virus vaccine was deadly to blackfoots. Whether because they simply had a different immunological system than their Asian relatives, or because inbreeding had weakened their systems, four of the six ferrets, all females, died from the very disease the biologists were trying to prevent, leaving Patuxent with just two males.

It was a crushing blow, but the Patuxent team, led by USFWS biologist Conrad Hillman and Patuxent veterinarian Jim Carpenter, pushed ahead. Another ferret was shipped to Maryland in 1972, and two more the following year—and now with a terrible sense of urgency, because the Mellette ferrets were vanishing, with the last survivors disappearing in 1974. One of the surviving females would have nothing to do with the remaining males; however, the other female was more compliant and gave birth in 1976 and again in 1977—but in both cases the young either were stillborn or died quickly. Nor did the adults thrive; black-footed ferrets are prey to a variety of diseases, including pneumonia, and the humid climate in eastern Maryland obviously didn't suit them. The ferrets battled a succession of illnesses that whittled away at the meager captive stock, until the last of the wild-caught animals died at Patuxent of cancer in 1979, leaving the researchers like Hillman and Carpenter who worked with them feeling emotionally battered.

With the Mellette population gone, too, Hillman hunted across the Plains, looking for a miracle in the form of an unknown ferret colony—but with no success. He and other searchers found bones, but no live ferrets, and a year after the last Patuxent female died, USFWS slashed the ferret recovery budget, prompting Hillman, a fourteen-year veteran of ferret work, to quit the agency in disgust. He was sure ferrets still existed out there somewhere, but this time, many experts agreed, Audubon's "handsome species" was well and truly gone.

Hillman wasn't the only one to keep faith with the ferrets. A private biologist named Tim Clark, who ran a company called BIOTA, based out of Jackson Hole, Wyoming, got enough grant money from private conservation groups to keep poking around the Great Plains, checking prairie dog colonies with the fading hope of finding ferret sign—green eyes glowing in a spotlight, long, twisted skeins of gray scat, troughlike trails in the snow, or the distinctive trench that a ferret digs at a tunnel mouth. Best of all would be a plugged hole—a mound hurriedly packed shut by prairie dogs to seal a ferret inside, with a smaller hole where the weasel clawed its way out. But as Clark checked eleven states over the course of a decade, even offering a small reward for information, he never found any proof of ferrets. Pretty soon, he was one of the few people with any serious hope that ferrets survived, and it's hard to say how serious even Tim Clark's conviction was toward the end.

All that changed in September 1981, at a ranch near Meeteetse, in northwestern Wyoming along the headwaters of the Greybull River. It is classic shortgrass prairie country, out there in the Bighorn Basin: wide and high, frigid in winter and blistering in summer, windy almost all the time, with sere and sparse grasslands that lap the Absaroka range to the west. White-tailed prairie dogs are still fairly plentiful out here, in part because some of the ranchers take a more forgiving attitude toward them than cattlemen in other parts of the West, and in part because white-tails live in more diffuse colonies than some of their relatives, keeping a lower, less antagonistic profile.

One night Lucille and John Hogg, who have lots of prairie dogs on their ranch, heard their blue-heeler dog, Shep, mixing it up with some animal outside the house; the ruckus was loud enough to wake them. When John checked the next morning, he found the carcass of a creature he didn't recognize lying limp near Shep's food dish. He was going

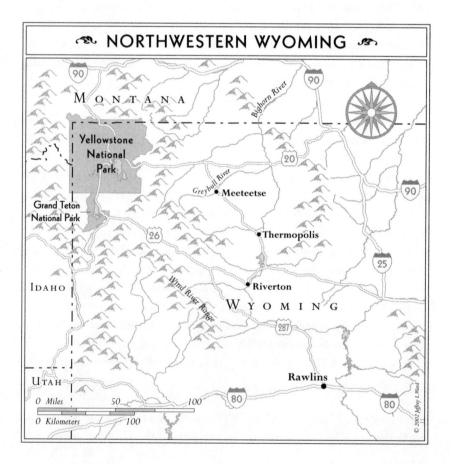

to toss it out, but it was so pretty—long and slim, yellow-brown and black—that Lucille suggested he take the animal to a local taxidermist. The shocked taxidermist knew exactly what the Hoggs had found, and the breathtaking news soon spread among conservationists.

And so a mixed-breed ranch dog defending his chow accomplished what biologists had failed to do for nearly a decade. Soon there were biologists swarming over the ranches around Meeteetse—Clark and his colleagues from BIOTA, the U.S. Fish and Wildlife Service, and the Wyoming Game and Fish Department, which was eventually given the lead role in the study and recovery of the recently mourned, but now very much alive, black-footed ferret. Intensive surveys followed, and by the next summer, the scientists estimated (based on an incomplete survey) that there were sixty-one ferrets in the area, twenty-one of them adults. By the following year, the population was thought to be eighty-eight, and by 1984 it had risen to 129, forty-three of them adults.

By 1983, when it was clear that the ferrets were doing well in Meeteetse, there was a lot of pressure on Wyoming Game and Fish to bring some of the animals into captivity, to establish a reserve population in case of problems in the wild. Of course, no one really knew much about keeping blackfoots in captivity, and the previous experience with the South Dakota animals kept at Patuxent didn't bode well. So the state, which had a firm policy anyway about keeping the ferrets in the wild—and in Wyoming—refused. When Game and Fish finally agreed to captive breeding, it was on the condition that the ferrets be housed in Wyoming, under state control, even though suitable facilities were not yet available, and despite offers from a number of institutions with exemplary track records in breeding endangered species, including the National Zoo's Conservation and Research Center in Virginia. Meanwhile, relations between the various government agencies, Clark's consulting firm, nonprofit organizations, and everyone else concerned with ferret recovery, which had been strained for years, were getting progressively worse.

There was a lot of bickering and politicking over the issue of plague control, among other things, since worries about an outbreak were always in the back of biologists' minds. Some time after the ferrets were discovered, fleas from the prairie dog burrows were tested and found to be carrying plague. The federal Centers for Disease Control and Clark's company pushed for applications of the pesticide DDT in the dog burrows, while others renewed their call for captive breeding, some even suggesting that all the ferrets be trapped out of the wild. Wyoming Fish and Game once more nixed the removal of ferrets from the wild, but in 1985, under great pressure, they did finally agree to treat something like 100,000 prairie dog burrows on 6,700 acres with the insecticide Sevin, in order to control sylvatic plague.

Whether or not the spraying program was necessary remains a subject of contention; it later became apparent that the plague outbreak had already pretty much run its course by the time the spraying started, and just a month after it ended, the number of fleas was back to pretreatment levels. But soon no one was thinking about plague, because that's when things started to go sour for *Mustela nigripes* all over again.

Shep, the Hogg's ranch dog, had treated that first ferret near his food dish just like any other interloping critter, but he was the last to do so. Snatched back from presumed extinction, the ferret was universally regarded as the most endangered mammal in North America, and handled with kid gloves—or, to be more accurate, with cloth face masks and latex surgical gloves. Scientists knew that black-footed ferrets were susceptible to a wide range of diseases besides plague—human influenza was a killer, and so was canine distemper, to the extent that team members couldn't work with ferrets if they'd been near a dog within the preceding two days. Ferrets also contract coccidia, which is common in cats and dogs, and cryptosporidia, a widespread protozoan found in contaminated water supplies.

During the summer of 1985, the folks doing nightly spotlight censuses realized something was amiss: an area that had been densely populated by ferrets the previous year was suddenly empty of them. Biologists surveyed more of the ferret range and found the same disturbing trend—local populations had vanished or declined drastically. By late summer, biologists could account for only 58 ferrets, down from the record high of 128 animals the year before. Those they saw didn't act normal; they seemed sluggish, lying around the mouths of their burrows, not at all their usual, hyperactive selves. And the bad news kept coming. When state biologists fanned out to trap and mark the remaining ferrets that September, they caught just 10, suggesting an overall population of barely 30 remaining on the Plains. By October, that estimate was down to 16. The ferrets of Meeteetse were in the middle of an appalling crash, declining by 50 percent every thirty days.

Throughout that summer and into the fall, Wyoming Game and Fish continued to insist there was no real need for alarm, disputing the field team's assertion that the population was falling fast, refusing requests to allow blood samples to test for unknown diseases, and insisting that no ferrets be brought into captivity until after the annual population survey in September, as had been agreed to before anyone knew about the crash.

At last, the mark-and-recapture surveys were finished, and six ferrets were taken out of the wild and sent to a new state captive breeding facility at the Sybille Wildlife Research and Conservation Education Center near Wheatland, Wyoming, where they were kept in a communal enclosure. One of the newly caught ferrets started sneezing, but was placed in the group cage anyway, as was a seventh ferret caught a few days later; soon, four of the animals were infected, and though some of the animals lingered for weeks, all eventually died. The culprit, pathologists quickly determined, was canine distemper, which because of its incubation period could have been contracted only in the wild. Worse, distemper is a disease with a 100 percent mortality rate in ferrets. (For a detailed account of the Meeteetse epidemic, I recommend *Prairie Night: Black-footed Ferrets and the Recovery of Endangered Species*, by ferret biologists Brian Miller, Richard Reading, and Steve Forrest.)

This discovery, with terrible implications for the survival of the Meeteetse population, set off another round of acrimony and finger-pointing. While the disease might have arrived on the Greybull in any number of ways—it was later found to be present among coyotes in the area—it's also possible that the dozens of volunteers who had been busily visiting tens of thousands of burrows that summer to dust for fleas had inadvertently carried the virus with them. By trying to thwart one disease, critics said, wildlife managers may have introduced an even worse one. However it got there, distemper was eviscerating the Meeteetse population.

With the captive ferrets dead and the wild population in free fall, the ferret recovery team decided to trap whatever surviving animals they could in a last-ditch attempt to start a breeding program. In September 1986, biologists trapped wherever there was any sign of ferrets in the Greybull country, catching seventeen animals—six males and eleven females. The following February they caught the final holdout, another male.

In the years that followed the Meeteetse disaster, there was recrimination aplenty, much of it directed at Wyoming Game and Fish, which had steadfastly refused to bring ferrets into captivity when there were lots of them. Had the state done so, critics said, they could have carefully selected a good mix of sex and bloodlines to ensure the best genetic diversity. Instead, they had to scramble to get whatever tag ends were left following the epidemic, and the results reflected that; genetic analysis later showed that only four founding bloodlines were represented among the captive population of eighteen animals. The ferret gene pool had clearly suffered an irreparable blow, and even if these ferrets could be persuaded to breed, the species would be hampered by the effects of severe inbreeding.

Game and Fish also took flak for keeping all six of the first captives in the same enclosure and adding a visibly ill ferret to the bunch—what seems a glaringly obvious breach of the old, commonsense, eggs-in-one-basket rule. In truth, everyone involved with ferret recovery in those days was making it up as they went along; no one had ever worked much with captive ferrets, and the blackfoots are exquisitely sensitive to all sorts of stresses and pathogens, to a degree not seen in Eurasian and Siberian ferrets, their closest relatives.

And what of the Hoggs, whose dog found that first ferret in 1981? They later told a reporter that if they had it to do over again, they'd have chucked the dead animal over a fence and kept their mouths shut.

In 1986, writer Peter Matthiessen published a revised edition of his classic book *Wildlife in America*. In it, he recounted searching in vain with biologists the previous summer, at the height of the distemper epidemic, for ferrets that seemed headed for extinction once again.

> This very evening, one of the last ones will sit upright in its burrow, eyes glinting a strange green in the prairie starlight. At

night, the stark landscape appears eternal, but it is cattle-pocked and fenced, and the buffalo and wolves are long since gone.

The ferret is millions of years old. When this elegant slip of life returns to the earth for the last time, and a few grains of sand roll down behind it, the secrets of the long journey that brought it from Siberia to North America many thousands of years ago will disappear. There is starlight on the pale earth at the hole, but the hole has been taken over by spiders, and the land is empty.

At some point you have to ask the question: How joyful, really, is the resurrection of a species, if the modern world cannot find a single safe haven for it, and if it seems doomed to slip into limbo once more anyway? It's an issue conservationists have had to struggle with repeatedly over the years with lost species, which sometimes reappear, blinking like Rip Van Winkle, in a landscape no longer able to support them, or incapable of recapturing the skills needed to live in the wild.

We've all seen a Barbary lion—at least, a three- or four-second glimpse of one. The old MGM Studios lion, the one with the magnificent mane that roared in black-and-white at the beginning of classic movies, is thought to have been a Barbary—a large subspecies of the African lion, *Panthera leo leo*, that once lived from Morocco to Egypt. This was the lion that fought gladiators and ate Christians in the coliseums of the Roman Empire, that Crusaders hunted and whose image they wore in heraldry on their shields. Barbaries were among the most striking of all the world's twelve or thirteen races of lion—exceptionally large, with males reaching 500 pounds and 10 feet in length, bearing a heavy, dark mane that stretched all the way along the belly to the groin. A typical savanna lion from the rest of Africa weighs about 350 pounds and has a sparser, tan-colored mane; some populations lack the mane almost entirely.

But as human populations rose and guns spread through the region, Barbary lions (also known as Nubian or Atlas lions) became rarer and rarer. They were gone from Libya by the eighteenth century, and the last Tunisian specimen was killed in 1891. Finally they were forced back up into the Atlas Mountains of Morocco, where the last was shot in the 1920s. For nearly eighty years, everyone assumed that *P.l. leo* was extinct; unlike many big cats that have vanished, there wasn't even a sniff of a rumor from the wild to keep hope alive. Nor was the Barbary the only lion subspecies to suffer this fate. The Cape lion of South Africa, *P.l. melanochaitus*, was shot out of existence in the nineteenth century; like the Barbary, it was adapted to a higher, colder climate than the typical lion, and so was larger and more heavily furred.

Sometimes a lost species reappears, like a vision, in a wilderness setting; sometimes it winds up dead next to a ranch dog's dish, like the ferret. The lion of the Romans made such a less-than-regal entrance. In 1996, the owner of the itinerant Akef Egyptian Circus—a motley collection of performers, big cats, livestock, and pythons—abandoned his bankrupt enterprise in Mozambique, one step ahead of authorities who believed his main occupation was trafficking in chimps and other endangered species. Among his sick and malnourished charges were three lions, which eventually found their way to the Hoedspruit Research and Breeding Centre for Endangered Species in South Africa, which specializes in working with large carnivores like wild dogs and cheetahs.

It wasn't until the cats were at Hoedspruit, though, that staffers realized that one male, named Giepie, was a lot bigger, shaggier, and darker than most African lions—he was, in fact, a dead ringer for the supposedly extinct Barbary lion. As word of the find spread, zookeepers around the world began to reexamine their own lions, some of which had Barbary-like manes, leading to the suspicion that they could be descendants of Barbary lions captured decades ago. The Rabat Zoo in Morocco has two dozen, descended from a royal collection, while a zoo in Addis Ababa, Ethiopia, has eleven lions that were once the living symbols of Emperor Haile Selassie, until a coup toppled "the Lion of Judah" from power in 1974. A South African scientist named Hym Ebedes believes the Ethiopian cats may also be Barbaries, while another South African, zookeeper John Spence, recently announced that two cubs at a zoo in Siberia were in fact long-lost Cape lions.

Or not. No one knows where the circus lions came from, and zoo lions from many sources have no doubt interbred for generations, blurring any regional distinctions their ancestors may once have had. The dark-maned captives of today may be nothing more than an accident, a genetic hiccup. To find out, Oxford University scientists have begun to examine DNA from old skeletal specimens of undisputed Barbary lions, comparing it to the genes of sub-Saharan races of lion in the hope of finding unique genetic markers that would distinguish the northern sub-species—and, perhaps, put a firm identity on the Barbary-like captives, and then pinpoint which have the purest bloodlines to preserve through captive breeding.

But should the lions prove to be the real McCoy, a stickier problem arises—what to do with them. Morocco has designated 98,000 acres in the Atlas Mountains as a release site, hoping the cats could become a tourist attraction, while others have advocated placing the Barbaries instead in South Africa's highlands, as a near-replacement for the extinct Cape lion (assuming, that is, that the cubs from Siberia do not prove to be a reincarnation of that animal). But talk of reintroduction skirts the far greater problem of behavior: after generations in captivity, the lions in question have lost any sense of how to survive in the wild—those from the circus in Mozambique, which had spent their entire lives in cages, were terrified of moving leaves and running water when first released into open enclosures. Large social predators like lions depend on teaching—a cultural transfer of information between the generations—to turn an inexperienced youngster into an efficient hunter. Happy thoughts of *Born Free* aside, this is a nearly impossible process for humans to duplicate.

Sometimes, snatching a vanishing species from the maw of extinction is the easy part. It's a lesson that those working with black-footed ferrets also learned.

Following the distemper epidemic in Meeteetse in 1986, people kept hoping that another colony of wild black-footed ferrets would turn up to supplement both the numbers and the genetics of the captives. One conservation group offered a $10,000 reward for news of ferrets, but it went begging. There were rumors, though—mostly the friend-of-a-friend sort about someone who had ferrets on his ranch but didn't want those damned biologists messing them up. And there may have been something to these rumors; the West is big, and antigovernment suspicion runs deep. But in the more than fifteen years since the Meeteetse epidemic, no one has offered proof of any other wild population of black-footed ferrets, and almost everyone now thinks they were truly gone in the wild after the last male was trapped in 1987.

That put the survival of the species on the slim backs of the eighteen animals caught in the wake of the epidemic and held at the new state breeding facility at Sybille. The first year, 1986, none of the captives bred; it looked like Patuxent in 1976 all over again, and a lot of ordinarily optimistic people were writing the species' epitaph. But in 1987, much later in the season than anyone had dared hope, two of the females gave birth, producing seven kits—and unlike the situation at Patuxent a decade before, the babies survived. The next year, twelve females raised thirty-four kits. Managers were learning how to handle blackfoots, how to avoid stress, how to manipulate pairs. For instance, they were using a technique developed at Patuxent years earlier called vaginal cytology, in which the tissues of the female's reproductive tract are monitored to assess breeding condition—fine-tuning the timing and greatly increasing the chances of a successful mating when she is placed with a male.

Even before the first captive births, the recovery team had turned to the Smithsonian's Conservation and Research Center, an adjunct of the National Zoo located in Front Royal, Virginia. CRC has a remarkably successful history with animals like big cats that are tricky to breed in captivity, and the recovery team members hoped they might be able to develop "assisted reproduction" techniques for ferrets, like artificial insemination (AI), should all else fail. Even after some of the captives started breeding on their own, CRC still became the first of six facilities, besides Sybille, to serve as ferret breeding sites; there would be no more holding all the eggs in one basket.

Long before it became the zoo's research center, CRC was a federal remount station, supplying cavalry horses and mules for the Army; in 1975, the zoo acquired the 3,200-acre facility as a captive-breeding site, and today dozens of species of critically endangered birds and mammals live in this pastoral setting in the foothills of the Blue Ridge Mountains—among them scimitar-horned oryx from northern Africa, Eld's deer from Burma, red pandas from Asia, and several species of Pacific island birds like Guam rails and Micronesian kingfishers.

By the time CRC received its first ferrets in 1988, everyone had calmed down a bit, reassured by the two litters the previous year, and decided the Smithsonian staffers should focus on natural reproduction instead of artificial means. And so they did through the mid-1990s, until a grad student, examining breeding records, realized that up to half the males weren't breeding each year—an obvious threat to some crucial bloodlines in this small, highly inbred species. (Every ferret since 1986 has been logged in a species survival plan, or SSP, stud book, which records its lineage and matings, so that bloodlines can be tracked. Ferrets are ranked by their degree of relatedness to other ferrets—those with the fewest relatives are ranked highest, and are considered the most important for the breeding program.)

So Dr. JoGayle Howard and her colleagues at CRC set to work, experimenting first with domestic European and Siberian ferrets, the blackfoot's closest relatives. Howard is the zoo's chief theriogenologist—a fancy way of saying a veterinary reproductive specialist—who specializes in highly endangered wildlife like cheetahs and clouded leopards. While many of the old, wood-frame administrative buildings at CRC still have a distinctly military simplicity about them, the veterinary hospital where Howard and the center's vets work is stark and modern, with surgical rooms large enough for their biggest charges. On my first visit to CRC, as I followed Howard into the room where she'd be working on ferrets, I spotted workers wheeling a drugged deer on a large, low dolly into an adjacent suite.

Our patients, by contrast, fit into three plastic cat carriers. In each was a small, narrow wire cage barely 6 inches wide and a foot and a half long, holding a ferret. One of the lab's technicians, a petite, dark-haired woman named Lisa Ware, removed one of the holding cages and placed it on the table, and I got my first view of a live black-footed ferret— Benjamin, SSP #1501. He was a five-year-old male nearing the end of his reproductive life, and thus it was especially important to get his genes into the mix.

I was struck first by his color, a lovely faded buff sprinkled with chocolate, darkening imperceptibly to black on the legs, as though he'd waded through soot. Bright eyes sparkled out of the robber's mask, and his ears were short and rounded, nicked along the edges. Then Ware opened one end of the cage and pushed in a heavily gloved hand, and the ferret exploded with angry chirps and a ferocious attack. I marveled at how fluidly it moved within the cramped confines of the tiny cage, flowing back on itself as though it had no spinal column, no bones at all, almost squeezing through the gap between the wire and her fist. It pressed the attack again and again; if these animals were the size of golden retrievers, no one would ever dare leave their house.

Pinned at one end of the wire tube, the ferret could do little more than squeak as Howard lifted a pinch of skin and gave it a quick injection of Ketamine; within moments, the ferret was immobile. Ware slid him out onto a cloth-covered heating pad on the surgical table and put drops in his eyes as Dr. Mitch Bush, the head vet at CRC, eased the animal's muzzle into an oxygen cone.

Ever since their near-brush with extinction, black-footed ferrets have become minor celebrities, and Benjamin had an entourage watching his progress, including two other magazine writers and a videographer who had rigged multiple cameras, tripods, and bright lights. We all wore surgical masks to prevent the transmission of flu and other diseases, and those who handled the ferrets were also gowned and gloved.

To collect the sperm, Howard inserted a rectal probe into the drugged ferret, using low-voltage electrical charges to stimulate its testes. Howard was doing noble work, obviously, but it was hard not to feel a little sheepish being part of a media contingent raptly watching a woman work a rectal probe with one gloved hand and hold a small, furiously red ferret penis with the other.

Howard lifted the tiny droplets of semen in a pipette—"There's not much, but it's very concentrated," she said—and transferred the semen to vials of nutrient media, from which graduate student Rachel Moreland quickly took a sample to place under a microscope. Everything—the pipette tips, the plastic tubes of liquid nutrient into which the semen was placed, the microscope slides—was warmed to about 100 degrees, just below a ferret's body temperature, so the sperm wouldn't be cold-shocked.

But the video monitor hooked to the microscope showed bad news—no sperm at all. Judging from the small size of his testicles, Benjamin wasn't in breeding condition yet; for reasons that are still a mystery, the male ferrets at CRC often lag weeks or months behind the females in their breeding cycle, making both natural and assisted reproduction problematic. After a few more tries it was clear that Benjamin was a bust. He was handed to Moreland to hold as he came out of anesthesia, and another carrier cage was brought into the room.

"Bachelor number two is Reid, better known as number 1637," Howard announced in a game-show voice. From the beginning, it was clear that Reid was in breeding condition, and the first batch of semen to go under the microscope was full of sperm—though many of them were deformed, with bent or folded tails, unable to move. This is typical of black-footed ferrets—typical, indeed, of most badly inbred species, one reason why conservation biologists try so hard to preserve a lot of genetic diversity in endangered species populations. Just in case Reid was a flop, too, Howard had an insulated container sitting in a corner, cooled with liquid nitrogen and containing tiny yellowish pellets of frozen ferret semen. But there appeared to be enough active, normal sperm in Reid's subsequent samples that Howard gave the go-ahead for the next step: inseminating a female.

Her name was Bonnie, and she was roughly half the size of the larger males, a delicate creature the color of old bone and charcoal. The drugs quickly rendered her inert, slouched against the wire in mid-bite, until she was poured out into Ware's hands for surgical preparation. The ferret was so small, swallowed up by the big room, the equipment, and the crowd of bustling, tense humans, that it was hard not to wonder whether it was worth the effort. This is unfair, of course, and on more than an ecological level; I suspect the thought wouldn't even have occurred to me if Howard and the rest were working on some big, impressive ungulate or a large cat—something with a commanding physical presence even in a drug-induced torpor. Ferrets are beautiful, but their presence, their impact, is mostly force of personality—that ferocious bravery I saw when Ware stuck her gloved hand in the squeeze cage and the ferret turned on her without hesitation, conveying the sense not of fear, but of outrage.

But now, in this clinical context, the ferret suddenly seemed inconsequential, unsubstantial, as though it had evaporated when the anesthesia took effect and left only its memory behind on the operating table. I found it almost impossible to imagine that limp form, not much larger than a tube sock, moving through the darkness of a High Plains midnight, sliding down burrows like quicksilver, the dark angel of the prairie dog town.

Around me, the vets and scientists moved with practiced assurance, though their confidence was the result of a long process of trial and error. When Howard started AI research on ferrets, using European and Siberian surrogates, she knew that a nonsurgical technique of the sort used on dogs and cows—simply squirting the semen in the vagina—wouldn't work. Ferrets require copulation to induce ovulation; it's no surprise that poking an anesthetized ferret with a pipette wouldn't get her in the mood. So they give each female ferret a shot of a hormone, which causes her to release her eggs twenty-four hours later. But even with the ferrets ovulating on time, the researchers discovered that just placing the semen in the vagina still wasn't working. A ferret's uterus, it turns out, has a peristalsis motion, like that of a swallowing throat, that moves the sperm up to the waiting eggs. Under anesthesia, that movement stops.

"So we thought, Okay, we'll put the sperm right where it needs to be," Howard said. "We stole the laparoscope from human reproductive technology, and now we use it for all sorts of surgical procedures." A thin metal tube with a light and camera that functions like a telescope, the laparoscope allows Howard to peer inside a ferret's body, locate the uterus, and guide the sperm to precisely the right spot.

Bonnie was ready; her abdomen had been shaved and scrubbed with bright yellow disinfectant, and all but a few square inches was hidden beneath billowing blue surgical drapes. Howard made a tiny incision and used a small hand pump to slightly inflate the abdomen, just like pumping up a tire; then she eased the metal stem of the laparoscope into the hole, pushing it home with an audible "pop!"

An assistant connected the lap unit to a camera and video monitor, and suddenly we had a Technicolor view of Bonnie's innards—the greenish globe of the bladder, netted with capillaries; the soft folds of the intestines; and the twin horns of the pink, forked uterus, into which Howard carefully inserted the thin catheter, which looked as big as a crowbar on the monitor. Moreland uncapped the end, shot in an almost invisible amount of semen from a syringe, followed by a tiny squirt of air. Moments later, the procedure was repeated on the other uterine horn. Then the scope was withdrawn, and with a few sutures Howard closed the incisions. Shortly thereafter, Bonnie was moving groggily in her carrying cage, her head wobbling. That's it; it seemed a little anticlimactic, but if all went well, in about forty-two days Bonnie would crawl into her nest box and produce a litter of wriggling, black-masked babies, helping to move the species just that much further from oblivion.

When I visited CRC, in the spring of 2000, things were looking pretty good for black-footed ferrets—far better than anyone would have predicted just ten or twelve years earlier. By 1991, the captive population had risen far enough to allow biologists to reintroduce the species to the wild in the Shirley Basin of southeastern Wyoming, where the following year wild kits were produced for the first time. Since then, ferrets have been released at sites in Wyoming, South Dakota, Montana, Utah, Colorado, and Arizona. At the time of my visit, the total population numbered more than 500, with 220 in the wild, 170 of them in South Dakota alone—a number significantly higher than Meeteetse at its pre-epidemic peak. The previous summer, almost 450 kits had been produced in captivity, about half of which were released into the wild, where predators, starvation, and disease would inevitably pare back their numbers.

"It gets better and better every year, as we get better at it," JoGayle Howard had told me, after finishing up with Bonnie. "Last year for the first time they actually held off breeding some females because we had so many." Yet the optimism was somewhat premature; that summer was an inexplicably bad year for the CRC ferret program, with a large number of babies dying shortly after birth. Nor did Bonnie fulfill her promise. Six weeks after her insemination, she was placed under twenty-four watch, with volunteers monitoring her nest box on a grainy black-and-white video screen through the night, but she never gave birth. Nor was it an especially good year at other ferret-breeding facilities around the country—not a symptom of pervasive problems, ferret experts said, just one of those bumps in the road that crop up every so often with any captive-breeding program.

Even when things are humming along in captive facilities, the problems that doomed wild ferrets the first time remain. The black-footed ferret recovery plan—the official document, drafted in 1988 under U.S. Fish and Wildlife Service auspices to guide the recovery process—set an ambitious goal of 1,500 wild ferrets in at least ten populations by 2010. "Black-footed ferret populations must be large enough to accommodate variations in their demography and environment that tend to draw them toward extinction in the short term, as well as large enough to preserve existing heterozygosity"—a ten-dollar word for genetic diversity—"and provide the potential for species evolution," the recovery plan states. That means that ferrets must be abundant enough, and widespread enough, to absorb temporary, local crashes from plague and distemper outbreaks.

But while the plan calls for reintroductions on prairie dog colonies of at least 10,000 acres, managers have sometimes had to settle for tracts only half that large—there simply aren't that many big dog towns remaining, thanks to continuing eradication campaigns and growing human development. Nor has the disease threat eased; blackfoots are no longer being released in Wyoming, for instance, because of recent epidemics that walloped prairie dogs and ferrets there. Only South Dakota is free of plague, a situation that may have more to do with luck than anything else—and making that state's leadership role in ferret reintroduction a tenuous one.

Vaccine research on sylvatic plague is under way, but Howard compared its complexity to that of creating an AIDS vaccine. Success, in her opinion, is at least ten years down the line—not only must the vaccine itself be developed, but an effective remote delivery system has to be worked out for use on wild ferrets. Conservationists also need a killed-virus vaccine for canine distemper in ferrets, since the commercially available vaccine is the live-virus form that wiped out the first batch of captive animals at Patuxent in the 1970s.

At the time of this writing, ferret biologists exploring reintroduction sites were looking beyond the U.S. border for the first time, to Chihuahua in northern Mexico, home of the largest remaining black-tailed prairie dog colony in North America, which experts believe holds great promise for establishing a significant ferret population.* But certifying a release site takes time—prairie dog burrows throughout the colony must be swabbed for fleas and the insects tested for plague; if that hurdle is cleared, then coyotes and other predators are trapped and tested for canine distemper.

None of this comes cheap; by Howard's estimation—factoring in the cost of six breeding facilities, staff, transportation, and on-site costs for releases—each captive-bred ferret costs in the neighborhood of $10,000 to produce. For that reason, it makes a lot of sense to be sure that the ferrets being released have the skills they need to survive—and that, in turn, is hard to do when you must rear the animals in isolation conditions to prevent disease.

---

*As this book went into production, the first eleven black-footed ferrets from CRC were released in Chihuahua, about 140 miles south of El Paso, Texas.

While most of the breeding facilities raise their ferrets in what amount to lab settings, CRC quickly took a different approach. Inside an L-shaped building that once housed Australian tree kangaroos, CRC collections manager Linwood Williamson opened a door—one with a large sign warning that this was a quarantine area and that gowns and masks were required beyond that point—and gave me a peek inside. Several of the ferret keepers, suitably robed, moved down a long, sunlit central corridor. To either side were ranks of dirt-floored enclosures, wire-mesh-fronted and containing wooden nest boxes with black plastic pipes poking out as erstwhile tunnels. Cages the size of the average bathroom were connected by small, locked doorways to others only half that big.

"The large enclosures are for the females, and the smaller pens are for the males," said Williamson, a big, bearded Virginian with a rich drawl and a pinch of snuff in one cheek. "That way, when it's breeding season, all we have to do is open the door and let them get together, without the stress of trapping and moving the ferrets." Each cage was also connected by a door to large outdoor pens, each the size of a big dog run, still closed off to the ferrets on this spring day.

The outdoor runs are the key to CRC's ferret-rearing philosophy. Each one has a concrete floor buried three feet in the ground and a chest-high mound of dirt covered with scraggly clumps of grass and weeds, pockmarked with burrows. That's where Edith and Archie come into the picture—a pair of black-tailed prairie dogs that, along with several other pairs like Franklin and Eleanor, are key to preparing the ferrets for life in the wild. "Basically, we use these guys as diggers, and we move them from cage to cage," Williamson said. By the time the rodents have finished remodeling a dirt mound and are moved to their next assignment, the ferrets have a real prairie dog burrow to occupy, complete with authentic smells—a foretaste of life on the plains.

After the ferret families are moved outdoors, their daily diet of ground-up prairie dog (not the digging crew, I was assured) is supplemented with live prey—hamsters at first, but eventually the ferrets graduate to live prairie dogs, brought in from the Plains and held in quarantine for several weeks to ensure they aren't carrying sylvatic plague. Black-footed ferrets seem to know instinctively to use a neck bite, gripping the prairie dog's throat with their unusually long canine teeth and suffocating it, but proficiency comes only with practice, and learning to safely tackle the 4-pound rodents, which may weigh twice as much as the ferrets, is the final step in this long preconditioning program.

"So they're used to hunting, and going underground to take cover. The only thing we can't do is teach predator avoidance, because it would be too dangerous. But we limit their contact with people, and if someone walks down here—zip, they're underground," Williamson said. Some years ago, in an attempt to instill fear of predators, scientists at CRC did experiment with a stuffed badger skin mounted on a radio-controlled car (and dubbed, inevitably, "Robo-Badger"), but the results were inconclusive.

"Most facilities don't have the kind of space we have—their ferrets are kept in small enclosures on raised platforms, with a nest box in the middle and black pipes connecting them—there's no dirt, no natural burrows," Williamson said. JoGayle Howard agreed that the process makes a big difference. "Preconditioned animals have three to ten times the survival rate of those that have never seen a burrow or a hole in the ground," she said. "Our ferrets are big, they're bulky, they run around and dig—they're just good-looking ferrets. I think by keeping them outside, on dirt, in big enclosures, we've avoided a lot of the management problems other breeding facilities have had."

Later that summer, on a muggy July day, I was back at CRC for a visit. A few days before, the biologists had given up hope on Bonnie's birth, but they showed me a video monitor labeled CHELSEA, on which we watched a mother ferret and a single kit born a couple of weeks earlier; at first the two were asleep, curled head-to-tail like a furry yin/yang symbol, but soon the baby began to nurse on its sleeping mother, kneading her belly with its tiny black paws.

Chelsea's kit was cause for optimism in a year that had been rough on the ferret team. A third of the kits born that summer had died, including four out of a litter of five born to a small female going through her first reproductive season, Williamson told me. The kits were near weaning, a stage when keepers begin providing supplementary food to the family. But unknown to the staff, the young female's milk had dried up prematurely, and the hungry babies quickly weakened and died.

Learning from the tragedy, Linwood's staff changed their routine. Females with litters will receive extra food earlier than was once thought necessary, and the CRC keepers may remove the young kits from the nest box to weigh them—a tradeoff of unclear advantage, since the information about the health of the babies comes at the price of increased disturbance. But such is the lot of those who work with endangered species; the process is an endless series of trials and inevitable errors, a constant refinement of technique and theory as scientists try to figure out what makes these rare and often delicate creatures tick. It is art as much as science, so complex that it has been compared to trying to build an airplane without instructions.

With Linwood's permission, I settled myself into the tall grass behind the ferret building, where I had a good view of one of the outdoor runs. While it hadn't been a banner year for the ferrets, there were still nearly two dozen kits growing here, and I was anxious to get a glimpse of some of the older ones, which had been moved outside. Because of those perennial disease concerns, however, I was looking through a chain-link fence, across a wide gravel pathway, and through another wire mesh screen.

For almost twenty minutes, nothing moved except a cloud of biting gnats around my head. Then, just as I began to shift position to ease a cramping muscle, a ferret popped from a hole like a Jack-in-the-box—slim, its back curved, eyes gleaming from its dark mask. A second animal, a carbon copy of the first, periscoped up for a look, and I froze, holding my breath; but within seconds they collapsed in a rough-and-tumble wrestling match, chasing each other with that humping, caterpillarish run that all weasels share, like a Slinky covered in fur, and disappeared from view.

A few minutes later, the ferrets edged back into the sun, then bounced through the open doorway to their inside cage, where the keepers had placed a tray of chopped-up prairie dog meat. One of the ferrets grabbed a chunk, glanced quickly over its shoulder, then bolted down a burrow to eat—no slow, leisurely, dangerous meal in the open for them. Captive-bred or not, these animals obviously retained a wild ferret's mistrust of the open air, where death comes on fast, silent wings.

It is likely that the ferret will always need some degree of intensive management, probably including captive breeding and trap-and-transfer of wild-bred animals. Unless there is a sea change in attitudes on the ranches of the West toward prairie dogs, and an uncharacteristic willing-ness to share the land with Audubon's prairie marmots, the ferret's range will remain dangerously fragmented, subject to local extinctions from disease and chance. Summing up the carnage from plague, eradica-tion programs, and habitat loss to development, one USFWS biologist told *The New York Times* he didn't expect the ferret would ever recover enough to be downlisted from endangered to threatened. Nor is the track record for reintroductions as a whole encouraging; the National Zoo, CRC's parent institution, found that of 145 such projects involving 115 different species, only 16 resulted in self-sustaining populations—and only half of those were endangered species.

But faith is sometimes all you have left to work with, and the ferrets, by their very existence, prove that you should never count an organism completely out. By autumn, the kits I was watching scramble in the dust would be loaded, along with their mother and several other families, into specially outfitted pet kennels at CRC and shipped West. A few weeks earlier the U.S. Fish and Wildlife Service had assigned them to a new ferret reintroduction site on Sioux land along the Cheyenne River in South Dakota. Some would be fitted with tiny radio collars, but most would simply slip out of their cages and into the anonymous night, smelling for the first time the rich odor of sagebrush, hearing the coo of burrowing owls, then gliding down a prairie dog hole to begin the predatory life that nature intended for their species. They would be part of a wild place—which would have become just a little bit wilder in the process.

FIVE

The ABC's of Ghost Cats

I've lived my whole life in the central Appalachian Mountains, rich country for a naturalist—full of deer, black bear, bobcats and coyotes, otters and fishers, wild turkeys, and even growing numbers of elk. But for all their diversity, the mountains are incomplete; the wolves and lynx that once roamed here are gone, as are the bison that once moved through the fire-scarred meadows and shadowed forests of the western plateaus, and the flocks of passenger pigeons that once darkened the skies.

But the loss I have always felt most keenly, the one that seems so hard to accept when I stand on a high escarpment and look out on a universe of rolling green ridges, is the mountain lion. Once, all of the Appalachians—all of this continent—belonged to the big cat known, depending on the region, as the cougar, puma, mountain lion, panther, painter, or catamount. They were wiped out here nearly a century ago, but they were once common in the old-growth forests of oak, pine, and hemlock that covered my part of Pennsylvania. Up near State College, one man alone turned in more than six hundred cougar scalps for the bounty over a fifteen-year period in the 1860s. Today, thanks to that kind of destructive diligence, the only mountain lion remaining there is Penn State's famous Nittany Lion, a stuffed, somewhat moth-eaten specimen left over from those frontier days.

Officially, the Eastern cougar, the subspecies *Puma concolor cougar*, which was once found from the Maritimes to the Carolinas and west to the edge of the prairie, is extinct. (The handful of Florida panthers sur-

viving in and around the Everglades belong to a separate race, *P.c. coryi.*)
But people keep claiming they see lions or their tracks up and down the
Appalachians, in the woodlots of the Midwest, the hills of the Ozarks,
and the forests of New England and southeastern Canada.

Some of these people are mistaken, or deluded, or easily gulled by
wishful thinking; they see a lanky brown dog cross the road at night and
jump to the wrong conclusion. But while many reports are in error, not
all of them are. Enough witnesses are sober, sensible people with a solid
background in wildlife—hunters, biologists, photographers—that their
claims cannot be easily dismissed. Nor can one ignore the physical evidence; every so often a cougar turns up dead in the East, or someone
gets a good photograph, or finds droppings from which hairs and DNA
samples can be isolated. A few years ago the Philadelphia area was in a
ruckus, following eyewitness accounts of a cougar stalking suburban
backyards and killing deer on the edges of golf courses. That one had a
collar—somebody's exotic pet, escaped or released and by some miracle avoiding death on the urban highways. Maybe that's how the other
Eastern cougar reports start, too—like the small female puma shot in
northwestern Pennsylvania in 1967, which on close examination proved
to be of Latin American stock.

The Eastern cougar is the lost species with the greatest resonance for
me; ever since I was a child, I've tried to wish wild mountain lions back
into these rugged old hills, because a big cat changes the landscape in
dramatic ways. I remember finding fresh lion tracks in a remote canyon
of the Chisos Mountains of West Texas, or the night when, returning
from a solo walk in the jungle of Belize, I found jaguar pugmarks neatly
superimposed on my own bootprints; it seems the huge spotted cat had
been following me, which explained the prickling I'd felt on the back of
my neck. From that moment on, the forest almost shimmered to my
eyes, with an edge of danger and excitement that magnified the wilderness. I want that kind of luster restored to the bruised mountains of my
home—and there is no longer any doubt that at least a few cougars are,
indeed, living in the wild in the East. In the 1990s, DNA evidence from
droppings confirmed their presence in Vermont and western Massachusetts, among other locations, and an apparently healthy male cougar,
showing no signs of captivity, was killed by a train in southern Illinois in
the summer of 2000, having perhaps wandered up out of the Ozarks.

But still unresolved is the question of whether, and how many, cougars live in the bulk of the East, especially in the central and southern Appalachians.* If you go by the number of sightings reported each year, the Eastern United States must be awash in large tawny felines—the Eastern Puma Research Network, a husband-and-wife operation based in Maryland that tracks such reports, recorded more than 2,200 sightings in just a ten-year period, which has led them and others to conclude that cougars are firmly established in the region, their presence hushed up by nervous governments, the evidence spirited away. (A biologist friend of mine jokes that all the dead Eastern cougars whisked off over the years are stored at the legendary Area 51 in Nevada, "right next to the hangar with the crashed UFOs and alien bodies, and down the hall from where they keep the JFK conspiracy stuff.")

Most of the game wardens and agency biologists I know take a highly

---

*Some biologists have taken a serious look at the question of Eastern cougars, but their findings are inconclusive and are sometimes at odds with each other. The first to do so was Bruce S. Wright, a Canadian student of pioneering conservationist Aldo Leopold, who became intrigued with reports of Eastern mountain lions when he was a young man in the late 1930s in New Brunswick. Wright spent the next forty years following up on sightings, publishing two books on the subject, and providing professional credibility to the notion of cougars in the East, which he believed were present in eastern Canada and represented surviving original stock.

In the late 1970s, U.S. Fish and Wildlife Service biologist Robert L. Downing undertook an investigation of cat reports in the southern Appalachians from Virginia to northern Georgia, particularly along the scenic Blue Ridge Parkway. Downing, who was also the principal author of the USFWS's Eastern cougar recovery plan, spent the better part of five winters looking for tracks along the road, often in what he admits were less-than-ideal tracking conditions, without finding any cougar sign he considered indisputable.

"In view of the poor tracking conditions, the best evidence of cougars was the high volume of sighting reports," Downing wrote some years later, after his retirement from the agency. "Investigators elsewhere do not regard sighting reports highly, and I have little doubt that 90 to 95 percent of the reporters were mistaken. Nevertheless, it remains difficult to believe that all were mistaken, as many reporters were highly qualified and had ample opportunity to observe the animals closely." As optimistic as Downing may be about the chance for cougars in eastern Canada, northern New England, and a few other parts of the East, he also notes that the "low but consistent rate of roadkills in Florida and the West suggests to me that automobile traffic is a search tool of sorts, and that vast areas of the East have, with high probability, already been 'proven' cougar-free based on high traffic volume and the lack of documented roadkills."

cynical view of the cougar reports; they've heard too many tall tales, chased too many will-o'-the-wisps in their younger and more enthusiastic days, to pay much heed to eyewitness accounts unsupported by physical evidence. "I call them UFOs, unidentified feline objects," says another biologist of my acquaintance. "They're our greatest success—I get more reports of them than I do of bald eagles. They didn't cost us a thing to reintroduce, they don't get killed on the highway, so we never have to pick them up, and they never eat deer or little kids."

But as the Illinois cat shows, there are at least a few cougars in the Eastern woods. The unanswered question is where these cats have come from. Are they lucky pets that survived abandonment, and if so, are there enough of them to find one another, breed, and produce a self-sustaining population? Or are they, as many people insist, the relict holdovers of the true Eastern cougar, *P.c. cougar*, which may have clung to existence in the deep woods of New Brunswick and Ontario, or the hills of the mid-South, later to recolonize the Appalachians and the forests around the Great Lakes? The question is more than academic; the Eastern cougar was added to the federal list of endangered species in 1967 and remains there, and thus any population shown to be of the original wild stock would enjoy full protection under the nation's strongest environmental law. On the other hand, escaped cats of Western or Latin American origin would have no standing under the ESA at all but would be subject to the vagaries of local protection, if any.

How reliable are those eyewitness sightings? One measure of their veracity may be the large number—between a quarter and a third—that involve black panthers. This is more troubling than it may at first appear. While black leopards and jaguars are fairly common, I know of only two documented cases of black cougars, nor is melanism at all common among North America's other wild cats, with fewer than a dozen black bobcats recorded, almost all in Florida. (This has not stopped some of the amateur cat-hunters from claiming the black panther is a distinct but heretofore undescribed species of large cat.)

Interestingly, black panther reports tend to come most frequently from those areas where documented populations of wild cougars don't exist; there are few reports of black cats from places like West Texas or Utah or Montana where there are healthy numbers of mountain lions. This leads skeptics to believe that black panther reports, and by extension most Eastern cougar sightings, come from people who didn't see what they thought they saw.

At times, it can be hard to believe one's own eyes. Not long ago I was talking to a friend and colleague who is both one of the most experienced field naturalists I know and the author of a book about the endangered Florida panther. We were discussing a trip he'd made recently to a stand of virgin hemlock in central Pennsylvania that we both know.

"I was retracing my route, working back out past the hickory overlook, when I saw a black panther," Chuck said in a matter-of-fact tone that stopped me dead.

"There was this large black—coal black—animal in the middle of the road," he continued, "two, maybe two and a half feet tall, with a long, sinuous tail that curled up at the end. Really sleek, with a close coat. The head was low, but then it lifted its head, very feline and catlike, and took two long bounds down off the side.

"I ran up and looked down the hollow, where there had been an old clear-cut years ago, and way, way down I saw a little shard of black. I got the binoculars on it and had to wait a while before it moved—and when it moved it was as cautious and catlike as you can imagine."

By now I was holding my breath.

"But finally, it moved where I could see it. And, of course, it was a Labrador," Chuck said. The dog was thin but appeared healthy, and moved with a feral caution that convinced him it was running wild, not someone's pet.

"You know, when I first saw it, I thought, Oh, it's a black panther, but then I said, Wait a minute, it can't be. But if I hadn't looked, if I was perhaps a little more credulous . . ." He let the thought trail away.

Chuck had wanted to believe, just for a moment, even knowing it was wishful thinking. As with many lost species, the Eastern cougar— brown or black—is less a concrete, biological organism than it is a talisman, a totem of wilderness to which people can pin a lot of their dreams, like my wish for wilder Appalachian Mountains. Even after long talks with those who study human psychology, I cannot explain what it is about big cats, especially, that strikes such a deep chord in us, but the connection is there—in our mythology, in our folklore, in our fears. Of all the lost species that may still haunt the globe, few have the evocative power of these ghost cats. More than almost any other extinct animal, people want to believe—maybe *need* to believe—that big cats still linger on the wild margins of their urbanized world.

I recall a story told to me by John Seidensticker, the curator of mammals at the National Zoo and one of the world's experts on tigers. Dr. Seidensticker holds the unenviable distinction of certifying the extinction of an animal he once studied—the Javan tiger, one of the world's eight races of *Panthera tigris*. Although perhaps three Javan tigers still existed in Meru-Betiri National Park when Seidensticker and his Indonesian colleagues worked there in 1979, since that year there has been no evidence of surviving tigers anywhere on the island.

Yet, as Seidensticker explained, even today many Javanese still believe that tigers live in their forests—people have told him about encountering the striped cats beside streams, or near temples, even though there is no chance that the species still clings to existence on that small island. He does not see this as a willful attempt to deceive him; the deception, if that is the right word, goes much deeper. "Animals as metaphysically important as tigers live on in our minds after they are gone," he once wrote; it takes more than the biological process of extinction to purge an animal as central to a society's life and belief as the Javan tiger.

And so the Javanese still see tigers where there are none, because they need to see them. That may be why so many Americans believe they see cougars (or black panthers), even in the most unlikely settings. Nor is the urge to populate the landscape with charismatic predators restricted to those places where they existed in the recent past. That's why, for a time, we will turn away from the hunt for vanished animals and look instead for those with no right to be where many people say they now are. There were, I was about to discover, even less probable places to find ghost cats than the Appalachians.

Morning sun shone on the small medieval market town of Tewkesbury, in the heart of central England. Although it was still early, the main streets were already filling with shoppers, ducking into half-timbered Tudor buildings in the shadow of the huge twelfth-century abbey church. On the River Avon, which flows through town beneath arched bridges, elderly strollers fed the ducks among brightly painted canal

boats. It was, in short, the perfect day to head out into the British countryside in search of black panthers.

Let me say that again, slowly: We were looking for wild leopards. In
Great Britain.

And not up in Wales or Scotland, either, where there is still some
marginally wild land, but smack in the middle of Gloucestershire and
Worcestershire, in the manicured, hedgerow-bounded farmland of
Shakespeare country, where village church towers are the highest thing
on the horizon—and where red foxes and badgers are supposed to be
the pinnacle of the local food chain.

Tell that to John Keel and his son Richard, whose family farm lies
east of Worcester, near the little village of Himbleton. A few years ago,
they lost thirty-eight sheep from their pastures; their neighbor lost
thirty. Dead or missing livestock is nothing unusual, even in England;
free-running dogs often kill sheep, and thieves sometimes steal them.
But this, the Keels said, was different.

"If a dog kills a sheep, there's wool all over the place," John Keel said,
standing in the shade of an equipment barn on a quiet morning in August, as Richard wiped tractor grease from his hands and nodded assent.
"In this case, there was just one spot of wool left. And if someone's stealing sheep, you know when that's happening."

The Keels felt certain this was something else, if only because their
hounds and border collie were restless, and the old mare and the other
stock were on edge. Besides, there were all the stories they'd heard
from others around the village—stories of huge black cats bounding
through the beams of headlights, or scaring the bejesus out of people
walking their dogs along the network of public footpaths that lace the
countryside. The newspapers were full of reports of black panthers (as
melanistic leopards are known) and pumas, not only locally but from
around the United Kingdom—the so-called Beast of Bodmin Moor in
Cornwall, the Beast of Exmoor in Devon and Somerset, and the Powys
Puma in Wales. Because Great Britain never had any native large cats, all
are thought to be the descendants of exotic pets, released to the wild
more than twenty-five years ago, when laws restricting their ownership
were passed.

For the Keels, the matter came to a head one morning a couple of
years ago when they had to deal with a sick ewe and her two lambs. The

ewe had come down with mastitis, so John and Richard separated the three from the flock and put them in an empty pasture. When they returned to check on them later in the day, one of the 50-pound lambs had been killed, its neck torn horribly and deep slash marks on its side.

They picked up the phone and rang Quentin Rose. A former zookeeper specializing in big cats, Rose now lists his occupation as "professional dangerous animal trapper and consultant," and makes his living recapturing escaped zoo animals and the like. But he has also been following reports of large wild cats in England for seventeen years, and it's now rare for several days to go by without a call like John Keel's.

"I've done hundreds of postmortems on livestock, and the vast majority are animals that have died a natural death and been scavenged by foxes and badgers," Rose said, as we stood with the Keels. "Often the front leg is completely gone, and farmers refuse to believe that a fox could remove a leg like that. The next most common category are dog kills, and I always assume it's a dog, unless I can prove otherwise. But I have confirmed six big-cat kills," Rose said. The sheep on the Keel farm, he was sure, was the work of a leopard.

As I stood in the Keels' farmyard listening to Rose recall those events, a European robin sat on a wooden fence rail behind us and poured out a cascade of clear, tinkling notes, its orange breast catching a shaft of low morning light. It was such an incongruous moment for me, trying to mesh the tranquillity of an English summer at its richest and most luxuriant with the blood and violence—the wilderness edge—that a large predator brings to any landscape.

Of course, many people would find the idea of a big cat prowling the Worcestershire farmland, snatching sheep and terrorizing elderly walkers, not only incongruous but perfectly laughable. But despite the publicity and the often silly nicknames like the Fen Tiger and the Norfolk Gnasher given by the press, many in the United Kingdom—including police officials, members of Parliament, and the military—treat exotic big cats as an accepted, and increasingly worrisome, fact of life.

Each year sees a growing number of eyewitness sightings and livestock kills, ranging from vague reports of catlike animals darting across country roads at night to large tracks found near dead calves or sheep. Nor do they come mostly from the United Kingdom's more remote sections; in one recent year there were more than three hundred big-cat

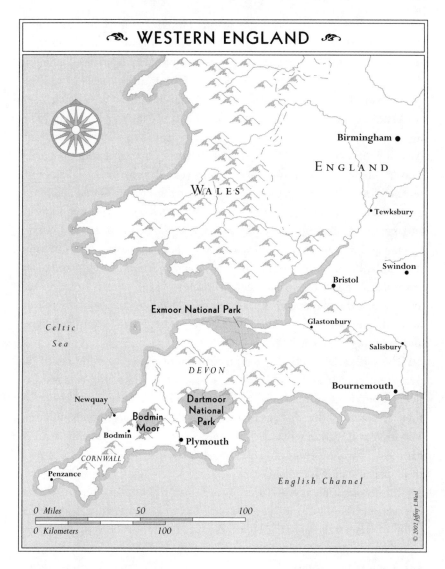

WESTERN ENGLAND

Birmingham

ENGLAND

WALES

Tewksbury

Swindon

Bristol

Exmoor National Park

Glastonbury

Celtic
Sea

Salisbury

DEVON

Bournemouth

Newquay

Dartmoor
National
Park

Bodmin
Moor

Bodmin

Plymouth

CORNWALL

Penzance

English Channel

0 Miles   50   100

0 Kilometers   100

© 2002 Jeffrey L. Ward

reports from about thirty English counties, most from the moorland and
farms of central and western England, but some coming from the sub-
urbs of London, along with many in Wales and a few in Scotland.

Most remarkable of all was the claim, made by an eleven-year-old
boy in eastern Wales, that a black leopard he surprised in a hayfield had
slashed his face with its paw, and bit him on the head before fleeing. For
a week, until a fuel crisis nudged it off the front page, British newspa-

pers were full of photographs of Joshua Hopkins, four long lacerations across the left side of his face; it is a measure of how seriously authorities took the incident that helicopters equipped with infrared imaging devices scoured the landscape, while leopard-hunting experts from Zimbabwe were brought in to assist with the search—all without luck.

With me on the Keel farm was Dr. David S. Maehr, a lean man in his mid-forties with a blunt face and close-cropped salt-and-pepper hair. Now a professor at the University of Kentucky and an expert on black bears, Maehr is best known for his nine-year stint as the head biologist on the Florida panther project, working for the Florida Game and Fresh Water Fish Commission. He and his colleagues slogged through swamps and sawgrass, chasing the endangered cougars with packs of hounds, treeing and darting them, following their tracks and sign, and examining their kills. I'd brought him to England as an objective expert—to talk to witnesses like the Keels and the cat-hunters like Quentin Rose, to examine the evidence and make a professional judgment about the likelihood that exotic and potentially dangerous large cats really are living and breeding in Great Britain.

This isn't a uniquely English phenomenon, either. In addition to the persistent cougar reports in the Eastern United States, big cats are frequently reported in Australia, where felines never occurred in the wild; they are supposedly the result of released or escaped pets, including World War II military mascots brought over from the States by American GIs. But none can compare, for sheer improbability, to the notion of leopards stalking England.

Yet my skepticism was shaken twice, first when John Seidensticker at the National Zoo put me in touch with Douglas Richardson, former curator of mammals at the London Zoo and now director of the Rome Zoo. "Unlike some others, I hesitate to suggest that there is anything like a thriving population of these animals in the U.K., but I am in no doubt that there are, or there have been, big cats at liberty," Richardson said. "Hard, indirect evidence has come in the form of injuries and kills to domestic livestock that showed all the signs of a classic big-cat attack."

Richardson, in turn, suggested I contact Quentin Rose, whom he knew from their years together in zoo work, and who was, he said, methodical and quick to rule out questionable evidence. Rose, as it developed, was kind enough to devote a substantial amount of his time to showing us around central England, introducing us to the landscape and the witnesses. And in the process he shook my skepticism again—because Quentin Rose was, very obviously, not a kook.

When Rose—a slim, athletic man in his mid-forties with a square forehead framed by thinning hair—arrived that day at the Keel farm, he brought with him some of the tools of his trade: latex gloves, a skinning knife, a tape measure, and a video camera. We had already seen the tape of his postmortem of the dead sheep, which had a great, bloody bite to the neck; we could see Rose's gloved fingers probing what he believed were the holes made by a cat's canine teeth, 3½ inches apart. Then he skinned the lamb, revealing a tremendous amount of bruising at the throat and ribs (an indication that the injuries were inflicted while the animal was still alive, and not by scavengers) and deep lacerations farther back on the abdomen, spaced about right to be feline claw marks. The rib cage was crushed on one side, the result, he believed, of a smashing blow from a leopard's paw.

"I reckon that if a man took a sledgehammer to a sheep, he couldn't do that much damage," he said as the tape ended. "Well, that's about it, though when I was done with the postmortem, I brought one of the legs home with me," Rose said.

"To study it further?" Maehr asked.

"No," said Rose, surprised at the question. "To eat it."

No sooner had Rose driven the 15 miles home to Tewkesbury, mutton in hand, than the Keels called again, frantic with worry. Whatever the predator was, it had returned, killing the second lamb in that pasture. Speeding back in the gathering darkness, Rose crept his way into a woodlot bordering the field, where he heard something crashing in the underbrush.

"Then I heard the cough of a leopard—a sound I've heard hundreds or thousands of times in zoos. It cut through the woods like a knife," he said. "I was unarmed, it was getting dark, and it was warning me off." And so he did what seemed the prudent thing—he backed away, conceding the field to the unseen predator.

Based on the number and distribution of reports like the Keels', Rose estimates there are about one hundred large cats living in the

United Kingdom, a population that he contends is growing with each passing year as they breed and spread into new areas. "I've documented thirty-two areas of regular, reliable sightings for puma and twenty-nine for leopards," he told Maehr and me the day we arrived, opening a series of large topographic maps covering central England. On these he had meticulously mapped a decade's worth of cat sightings and livestock kills that he considers legitimate, marked with small adhesive colored dots inked with the date in tiny handwriting.

"Black dots are leopards, orange are pumas, and these pale blue"— Rose's finger tapped several tight clusters north of London—"are caracal lynx." Now he drew large circles with his fingers, encompassing groupings of markers. "This is the Fen Tiger here, and this is the Surrey Puma—I simply ran out of room for dots for it—and this"—indicating a spattering south of London—"was a leopard." The dots were not scattered randomly around the country but were grouped in places where the maps showed loose networks of small woodlots, snaking across the farmland. For instance, east of the city of Worcester, where the Keel farm lies, was a swath of black leopard reports perhaps 15 miles long and only a few miles wide, all centered along a series of forest fragments.

By plotting eyewitness accounts, Rose believes he can track the movements of individual animals and even (based on sightings of cubs) their reproduction. And that has him particularly worried, for unlike some folks who are thrilled at the thought of large predators in the United Kingdom, Rose sees little but trouble ahead.

"They're breeding, there's no doubt about that, so I have four main concerns. One is their effect on indigenous wildlife, the second is the effect on livestock. The third is the welfare of the cats themselves, from farmers and vigilante groups. But the fourth is the threat to human life from a wounded animal, particularly a wounded leopard."

It is this last point that has brought Rose the most attention; he has been widely quoted in the British press in recent years, suggesting that big-cat populations in Britain are poised for explosive growth, and raising the specter of man-eating leopards. To Rose, the incident in Wales, in which the boy claimed to have been slashed across the face, was an all but inevitable near-miss.

Unlike North America or mainland Eurasia (where Caspian tigers and leopards once ranged to Turkey), Great Britain had no native large cats after the extinction of the cave lions of the last ice age. There are ambiguous travelers' tales of catlike animals in Britain dating to at least the sixteenth century, but the big-cat phenomenon didn't really establish itself in the public's mind until the 1970s and 1980s, with the fabled Beast of Exmoor. Here, in the high and empty moorland on the north coast of Devon and Somerset, farmers claimed losses of sheep to an animal usually described as a large black or tawny cat; one London newspaper offered a thousand-pound reward for it, and Royal Marine commandos were even called out in the mid-1980s to comb the farms and pastures. They had no more success than a local cat-hunter who built large cage traps, baited them with tripe—and caught a pig.

The British media has had a field day with the subject, and seems especially fond of the sinister word "beast"—the Beast of Gloucester, the Beast of Bala, and my current favorite, the Black Beast of Inkberrow, which has such a Gothic ring to it that I will be terribly disappointed if it proves to be merely a panther. It wouldn't be the first anticlimax. The Beast of Bala, blamed for the death of lambs on a farm in Wales, was eventually shot by a farmer—who discovered it was a harmless lemur, escaped from a local zoo.

While the general public seems to view the periodic waves of big-cat reports with a mix of casual acceptance or skepticism, there is a core of fervent believers, to whom the felines are known as ABC's—"alien big cats." That's "alien" as in exotic, not extraterrestrial, though there is a small subset of aficionados who do believe there is a connection between ABC sightings and UFOs, crop circles and (I kid you not) El Chupacabra, the legendary vampiric "goatsucker" monster in the Caribbean.

Nor is that the only imaginative theory that tries to account for the presence of huge cats in the clotted-cream countryside of western England; some people insist they're saber-toothed holdovers of the ice ages, or a modern hybrid between escaped jungle cats and domestic tabbies, or some wholly undescribed species of feline that managed to escape the notice of both ruthless gamekeepers and generations of zealous English naturalists. Others, taking a page from the region's long Celtic and Saxon history of spooks and ghost animal stories, insist the cats are direct manifestations of the supernatural, along the lines of the spectral black dogs with glowing eyes that have been whispered about for centuries in much of Britain. It may not be very good science, but it makes for great tabloid copy.

The most common and logical explanation, however, is the Dangerous Wild Animals Act of 1976. Until that time, there were no national laws in Britain controlling the ownership of exotic pets like cougars or African lions, which were for a time coveted by rock stars and blue-collar workers alike. It wasn't unusual to see some supermodel striding down the sidewalk in a swank London neighborhood with a cheetah on a leash, the cat as slim and elegant as its vapid owner, or to find a slapdash cage in the back garden of a working-class neighborhood with a jungle cat or mountain lion cub inside.

That changed when, in the early 1970s, a child was mauled by a captive cat and Parliament passed the wild animal bill in response. Owners were given three choices: qualify for a costly permit, donate the animals to zoos (which were subsequently swamped with calls and unable to accept even a fraction of the offered pets), or have them put down. Of course, people had a fourth alternative—dump their pets in some lonely spot. Speculation has long been rampant about such extra-legal releases, and in recent years, as the number of cat sightings has grown, a few former owners have come forward to 'fess up.

One of them, Leslie "One-Eyed Nick" Maiden, a colorful sixty-three-year-old former lion tamer who lives near Birmingham, admitted that he had released a black leopard and a cougar in the Pennines of north England's Peak District in the late 1970s; he said he'd been given the animals by people who couldn't comply with the new law. "I've always been an animal lover. But people came to me with the animals, saying they would have to put them down. I had no option," he told the Birmingham *Post*. "At first I was a bit worried about how they would get on, because they were so tame, but I went up to the moors a few weeks later [and] I saw the bones of sheep and pheasants, so I think they adapted pretty well." Interestingly, Maiden broke no laws. Until the loophole was closed recently, there was no legal recourse to stop someone from liberating big cats—or elephants, for that matter.

If the cats did adapt to the English countryside, they wouldn't be the first; Great Britain is overflowing with exotic wildlife brought there over the centuries, from American mink, Canada geese, and gray squirrels to Chinese pheasants and fallow deer introduced by the Romans. Muntjacs—pig-sized Asian deer with sharp tusks jutting down from their up-per jaws—are now almost ubiquitous across southern England, as are the small Asian elk known as sika. There are even feral populations of the red-necked wallaby, a mid-sized kangaroo that established itself as a re-sult of escapes. On top of that, a menagerie's worth of small, exotic fe-lines have turned up around Britain—an Asian jungle cat weighing 15 or 20 pounds that was found dead in Shropshire in 1989; several leopard cats, a small spotted Asian species, shot or found dead in the late 1980s and early 1990s; an ocelot shot in Lancashire after it attacked a hunting dog in 1981; an African caracal—a beautiful red-brown animal with long tufted ears—shot while stalking sheep.

But none of these are large cats. For all the hundreds of reports in the United Kingdom each year, there is just one documented specimen to show for all the fuss. In 1980, a farmer named Ted Noble in the cen-tral Scottish Highlands set a cage trap on his property and baited it with a sheep's head, hoping to catch the animal that had been killing his live-stock. He caught a female cougar—an animal originally described in the local press as snarling and savage, but which, when transferred to the nearby Highland Wildlife Park, was declared to be quite tame, rather elderly, and decidedly overweight, probably having been released shortly before it wandered into Mr. Noble's trap. The cat was named Felicity, and remained at the zoo (where she enjoyed having her belly scratched) until her death in 1985, after which she was stuffed and placed in an In-verness museum.

But if there are few warm bodies to show for it, the eyewitness re-ports continue apace, at a rate of several hundred a year from all across Britain. Here's a recent sampling:

- November 1998. A man dropping his children off at school re-ports seeing an African lion with a bloody mane near Dartmoor in southwest England, and a pawprint found by police is identi-fied as a lion's by personnel from the Dartmoor Wildlife Park. Four days later and 12 miles away, "huge tooth marks" are found on a tin of cat food that had been pulled from the garbage at an isolated farmhouse, and a partial track is discov-ered in the yard; staff from another zoo identify the tracks as possibly from a mountain lion. Two teams of dog handlers, accompanied by armed police squads, comb the countryside without success, but police soon have a bigger worry on their hands—shotgun-toting vigilantes trying to find the animal on their own.

- August 1999. Six lambs are killed near Carmarthen in western Wales, and locals insist they have seen a puma, as the Brits usually call mountain lions. "It would have taken at least two, maybe three, pumas to make this mess," farmer's wife Yvonne Edwards told the press. "I'm too scared to let my sons play in the fields now because we don't know what's out there."
- September 1999. A large black cat is reported by a woman in Dorset, who also says she found the carcass of a "savaged" deer. (The unfortunate livestock and deer in these reports are never merely killed or eaten, but almost always "savaged.")
- November 1999. Royal Auxiliary Air Force volunteers in Cornwall, some newly returned from service in Kosovo, spend a weekend lying in freshly dug foxholes and using night-vision scopes and motion detectors in an attempt to find the Beast of Bodmin Moor. Known formally as Operation Last Look, the maneuver is immediately dubbed "Operation Pussycat" by the press; the soldiers report seeing nothing more threatening than ponies.

We met Rose early one morning for a tour of local panther hot spots and a chance to meet some of his witnesses. Following the directions to his cottage with some bewilderment down the main street of town, we found a small, vaguely trapezoidal door wedged between a hairdresser's and the St. George pub. Inside was a long corridor, with beams low enough to threaten our heads, opening onto a tiny brick courtyard full of flowers. The cottage sat a few feet from the grassy edge of the River Avon, on which floated restored canal barges and pleasure boats, with no trace of the bustling commercial zone a few yards behind us. It was like going down Alice's rabbit hole.

As Rose gathered up his equipment in the small kitchen, I bumped into a box of well-worn foot snares with rusty trigger pans—the same sort Maehr uses to catch black bears in Florida, as it turned out, but that

Rose uses to catch escaped exotics like tigers, a European lynx that had been killing sheep, and an orangutan that reacted badly to its medication and smashed its way out of its enclosure twice in the same night.

"Is there enough of that work to keep you busy?" Maehr asked.

"I could work every day if I wanted to," Rose said. The trouble is, although the police often call him out in such cases, they don't always reimburse him for his trouble. Indeed, much of his time is devoted to pursuits like the cat-tracking, for which he receives no income, or his long effort to develop a humane foot snare, prompted by his travels in northern Canada with Native trappers whose economy was devastated by anti-fur campaigns in the United Kingdom and the United States.

Because he might get an escaped-animal call while we were out, Rose loaded his small Toyota with a jumble of equipment, including a tackle box of darts and immobilizing drugs, and a metal noose-pole. Then off we sped, down narrow country lanes wedged between towering blackthorn hedges, so close that his sideview mirror often slapped the leaves. In the singularly named village of Upton Snodsbury, Rose introduced us to a lovely woman named Liz Cash, who'd had what he considers a reliable sighting of a leopard.

Mrs. Cash had been walking her two English setters through pastureland near a small wood in early September five years ago. "It was quite early in the morning, and I was walking up a hill on the side of the hedgerow, and I just happened to turn around, like you do to take the view of the countryside," she recalled. "My dogs were way out ahead of me, and I suddenly saw this black cat inching along the hedgerow, a hundred yards away. I knew people had been talking about the sightings in this area, but I just couldn't believe what I was seeing—for I knew very well that it wasn't a domestic cat. It was big, the size of my English setters, but what really struck me, I remember, was that really long tail.

"I stopped, and it stopped, and I was quite frightened—because I'm down there on my own, and what worried me was that my dogs would see it and go after it. But luckily they didn't," Mrs. Cash said as we sat in her sun-drenched kitchen. "I decided to go back the way I came, and it just turned round and slunk off the way it came."

Mrs. Cash told the story simply, without theatrics, and with absolute conviction. The one constant about these sightings, as we soon learned, is the witnesses' unshakable belief in what they've seen, a sincerity that shines through, however unlikely the tale may sound at first blush. We met the Bowden brothers, Les and Brian, who farm about 1,000 acres not far from where Mrs. Cash had her sighting; they've seen what they believe are black leopards a number of times. "I can always tell when it's been about," Brian shouted over the roar of machinery from their milking barn. "I've milked cows all my life, and some mornings they are so crazed that they just can't be milked. Sometimes they'll take out 50 yards of fence, just go through it in a stampede."

Rose approaches the big-cat question a good deal more objectively than do most of the amateurs chasing panthers, who often seem more determined to maintain the English tradition for eccentricity than to get at the truth. And many of the stories he passed along had a ring of authenticity, like the one about two poachers walking at dusk through a hilly pasture dotted with huge old linden trees, in one of which they surprised a leopard draped over a branch—typical leopard behavior in Africa or Asia. They were so shaken by the experience that they went to the landowner, confessed their trespassing, and told what they'd seen.

Rose took us to the field; flocks of wood pigeons flapped explosively from the trees as we walked among them, and Eurasian goldfinches, with yellow wing patches and bright red faces, twittered out of stands of dying thistle. Maehr looked around at the rolling grazing land, with long ribbons of woods running through the valleys. "This actually looks pretty good for leopards—better than for mountain lions, anyway," he said. "I mean, leopards are an open-country species, and this mix of fields and small woodlots is a lot like the savanna and riparian corridors they use in Africa."

Yet, for every couple of plausible stories we heard, Rose would tell us another that had Maehr and me shooting each other sidelong glances. There was, for example, the elderly woman walking along a public footpath who found a black leopard sleeping in the tall grass and prodded it awake with her cane. (Rose admits he got that one secondhand, however.) A whiff of special pleading came with a lot of the accounts, not only from Rose, but from other British cat-trackers trying to explain why English cats don't always act like big cats in other parts of the world. For instance, mountain lions invariably bury the uneaten remains of their prey beneath a huge scraped pile of dirt, leaves, and sticks; to my knowledge, no one in England has confirmed such a buried kill, even though a lot of dead livestock has been blamed on pumas. Why the discrepancy? Well, we were told, the cats are scared off by walkers or dogs or farmers before they have a chance to bury it.

The list of such inconsistencies grew as we traveled, until the arguments began to sink beneath their accumulated weight. Why do so few people claim to find big-cat scat? Because British leopards and pumas always bury their feces, a behavior that is much less rigid in, say, the Western United States, where it's not unusual to find exposed mountain lion droppings, which may function as territorial scent-marking posts. If there are so many large cats in the country, why has Rose, by his own admission, found only three tracks he considers authentic? Because the animals avoid stepping in mud, he says. Why, in this land of wool and mutton, hasn't he been able to attribute more than six livestock kills to cats? Because, we were told, leopards prefer wild game like deer, hares, and other wildlife to sheep, and drag away the lambs that they do kill. (Rose also said that in his experience, leopards in zoos don't like the texture of wool in their mouths.)

And finally why, in a countryside of twisting roads, congested motorways, and fast drivers, hasn't one of those hundred-odd leopards and pumas died after being struck by an automobile? In southwest Florida, cars would kill several of Dave Maehr's panthers every year out of a population of barely seventy animals, with far fewer roads in an immensity of soggy wilderness.

"We've had roadkills in Florida on some of the most desolate, untraveled country roads in the state," Maehr said. "In Florida, some panthers demonstrate an aptitude for figuring out traffic, but there are always those animals who don't—first time they set foot on a road, they get run over. They don't learn from another cat telling them, they have to learn from experience. You're always going to have a naïve, or very stupid, or neurologically challenged cat that's going to get run over. After twenty-five years of this stuff in the U.K.—especially if there's reproduction going on—there'd have to have been roadkills."

I'd met Dave Maehr long before I asked him to accompany me to England. He has a reputation for speaking bluntly and candidly, even at the expense of injured feelings, and I was a little worried about how he'd respond to Quentin Rose and the others we had arranged to meet. I was pleasantly surprised, then, at how carefully neutral Maehr was—

not just diplomatic, but consciously objective. Rose was obviously disappointed that evidence which to him was conclusive struck Maehr as much weaker, but over the course of our time together we struck up a friendly working relationship based, so far as I could tell, on mutual respect.

In fact, the only time in the whole trip that Maehr's impatience came close to overcoming his diplomacy was during a meeting we had with a zealous amateur cat-hunter in Cornwall, a man named Mike Thomas who runs a small zoo in a resort town on the coast. He'd come to my attention because he'd been widely quoted in local press accounts about the Beast of Bodmin Moor, described as a cat expert in part because he keeps several cougars on display at the zoo. Even before we left for the United Kingdom, Maehr and I debated whether to talk to Thomas, because many of his comments to the media about the Beast struck us as pretty absurd and Rose had suggested we save our time. Maehr wanted nothing to do with him, but I finally decided it was worth taking note of the fringe.

Thomas was hospitality itself, rummaging in his cluttered closet to haul down box after box of plaster track casts and stacks of photograph enlargements. Maehr had come along reluctantly, and sat tensely, arms and legs crossed, the muscles in his jaw working, his whole body language radiating discomfort even as his voice remained even and professional.

"Now then, this was found at the site of a sheep kill in Devon," Thomas said enthusiastically, opening a sheet of bubble wrap and handing Maehr a chunk of plaster with an enormous footprint, perhaps 5 inches across, on it. Maehr turned it over in his hands a few times, looking silently at it for a minute.

"Well, you see, that's a dog," Maehr finally said, handing it back.

"No, no," Thomas protested, "it's much too large for that. Even an Alsatian's print would be a quarter that size."

"But so would a cougar's. A mountain lion track isn't nearly that big." He pointed out the lack of several characteristics of big-cat prints—the so-called lead toe, which pokes out ahead of the other digits, or the way the whole footprint should be skewed asymmetrically to one side, or the rear edge of the footpad, which wasn't scalloped into three lobes like a cougar track would be. And this cast showed several clear claw marks, which are rare on cat prints.

"Yes, well." Thomas stopped, then reached back into the box, where we heard the rustle of more bubble wrap. "Right. Well, that isn't conclusive, is it? But take a look at this—this was one of the tracks found at a savaged sheep in Cornwall, and I think you'll agree that this is definitely a puma."

Maehr looked at the cast; even I could see the claw marks from where I was sitting. "Um, that's a dog, too."

And so it went for the better part of an hour. Thomas rummaged in his boxes, pulling out more casts, gruesome photo enlargements of half-eaten sheep, blurry pictures of unidentifiable dark smudges, and (in one case) a very sharp photo of what to us was clearly a small, potbellied black dog, sitting on its haunches by a farm water tank, which we were told was a panther. The tracks were of dogs, or so ambiguous Maehr couldn't tell what species, if any, had made them. None of the photos, in Dave's estimation, showed the typical signs of a cat attack—crushing bite wounds to the head and a neatly disemboweled carcass with the gut pile dragged off and buried separately. Yet each piece of evidence was presented with an air of triumph—as though *this* was the clincher. And each time, with patient tact, Maehr would demur and hand it back.

Thomas also regaled us with his pet theory that the black Beast of Bodmin Moor was a hybrid between escaped pumas and native Scottish wildcats, a tabby-sized feline that's been widely assumed to be extinct in southern Britain for years. Maehr looked as though he was going to pop a vessel, so we made our goodbyes and I hurried him out the door. We were barely out of the man's office when Maehr exploded.

"What absolute *bullshit*! What a load of crap!" he railed, pulling on a denim jacket with sharp, angry movements. "How anyone who pretends to know *anything* about these animals, or even simple taxonomy, can think that cougars are hybridizing with wildcats is beyond me!" Passersby turned to stare, and mothers pushing babies in prams hurried away in alarm.

You can look at a lot of the evidence for yourself—cat enthusiasts have embraced the Internet in a big way, and many Web sites show photos of alleged panthers, tracks or plaster casts of pawprints. Their attention to spelling and grammar might be a bit more rigorous, but their earnestness is endearing; one of them cautions people to be careful should they encounter a puma, as the species has caused "serious fatalities" in the United States. Many sites feature stills from videotapes purporting to show big cats, almost invariably black; the majority of images are so enlarged and fuzzy that they could be almost anything, but the few that show the animals in relation to their surroundings—trees, hedgerows, and in one case an industrial brickyard—looked to my increasingly skeptical eyes to be big house cats, with none of the lanky proportions you see in cougars or leopards.

And then there are the tracks. Much is made of their size and roundness, but even if you overlook such subtle characteristics as a cat print's asymmetrical shape, or the scalloped rear edge of the footpad, it's hard to account for claw marks—dog tracks usually have them, cat prints rarely do. Yet most of the tracks offered as leopard or puma evidence show unmistakable claw impressions. Tracking and woodscraft seem, alas, to be dying arts in Britain.

There has been at least one official government investigation into the big-cat question. In 1995, under pressure from politicians and farmers, the Ministry of Agriculture, Fisheries and Food sent biologists Simon Baker and C. J. Wilson to Cornwall to investigate the Beast of Bodmin Moor, blamed for waves of stock killing. Baker and Wilson spent six months plotting sightings, talking to witnesses, examining photos and track casts, and looking at a half-dozen dead sheep and calves supposedly killed by cats.

They analyzed a series of still photos and videotape that the photographers claimed showed the Beast—some of which, at first blush, are rather convincing. In one, a sleek black feline leaps over a tumbledown stone wall, in relation to which the cat looks very large; but when Baker and Wilson visited the site, they found the wall was unusually low and that the animal crossing it could have been no taller than 12 inches at the shoulder. Likewise with a famous piece of 1993 footage from Bodmin Moor, much ballyhooed at the time, which purports to show a black panther crossing a pasture and disappearing beneath a tree. Baker and Wilson relocated the spot and found that the "tree" was a shrub, and when they photographed a black house cat in the same position, it and the supposed Beast appeared identical.

Baker and Wilson concluded that none of the evidence they'd seen supported the notion of big cats in Cornwall—a finding that sparked much local outrage. Then, less than a week after the report was made public, several teenagers playing on Bodmin Moor found the skull of a huge cat bobbing in a creek near a popular waterfall. Here, the believers said, was proof that the skeptics couldn't ignore. The skull was taken to the Natural History Museum in London, which confirmed it was that of a young male leopard—but also noted that the bone was covered with fine cut marks, consistent with someone having skinned it with a knife, and that the back had been sawn away, a practice typical when preparing a leopardskin rug. A museum mammalogist found the clincher inside the skull itself—the egg case of a species of tropical cockroach, a bug unlikely to be found in chilly, damp England. "The conclusion is that this particular leopard skull came to Cornwall only by human agency," the museum's report notes dryly.

The town of Bodmin has an ambivalent relationship with the monster of the neighboring moor. Although growing numbers of people now visit the region specifically to look for the cats (along with visiting the Daphne du Maurier museum at Jamaica Inn, and Dozmary Pool, where King Arthur's sword Excalibur is said to lie), the employees of the tourist information center in the Shire Hall are instructed not to give opinions pro or con on the Beast's existence, instead directing visitors to a bland, intentionally noncommittal display on the subject in the upstairs interpretive gallery. ("As to the identity of this mysterious 'beast,' it is open to conjecture . . . No doubt it will continue to provoke widespread discussion around many a Bodmin table until some positive proof of its existence is found.")

A huge papier-mâché effigy of the Beast leads the annual street procession during the town's Heritage Day each summer, but we found none of the expected trappings of a certified tourist attraction. "You mean no one around here has thought to make a damned T-shirt with the Beast of Bodmin Moor on it?" Maehr said in bewilderment one day, after we'd spent several hours walking and driving to every tourist dive and knickknack shop we could find, looking for souvenirs he could take home to his kids.

Before going to England, I spoke at some length with Simon Baker about his investigation. "Nothing we looked at stood up," he said. "That doesn't prove a negative, of course. That's not to say there can't be a cat out there—they're held in zoos, a few people may have them illegally— but I find it hard to believe that we have a breeding population. The sightings are almost always of either pumas or melanistic leopards. If the reports were correct, we would have to have some sightings of spotted leopards, since spotted leopards are much more common in captivity. But we never do."

If there really aren't scads of wild cats roaming Britain, why the constant claims, why the rampant public interest that grows every year?

"The more I think about this, the more I'm convinced this story isn't about cats at all. It isn't even about wildlife," Dave Maehr said one day, as we were driving to another interview. "It's about people."

The South West Coast Path, a British national foot trail, hugs the edge of Exmoor National Park—not a park in the North American sense of publicly owned wilderness, but an especially scenic 267-square-mile chunk of north Devon and Somerset, home to 11,000 people in villages and farms, and a lot of sheep, feral ponies, and red deer. Exmoor also holds a special place in the history of British big-cat sightings, as home to the Beast of Exmoor, which has been reported off and on since the 1970s— though the description is rather fluid. Sometimes it is described as a black cat more than 8 feet long, at other times ginger-colored and the size of a spaniel. One local naturalist, who said he spotted the beast while he was birding, described it as "black and rather otter-like," while others said it resembled a dog. (No kidding, snicker the skeptics.)

Maehr and I followed the Coast Path past Countisbury Church, its gray tower furred with moss, with large slate headstones leaning in the small churchyard beneath wind-twisted yews. Aside from this tiny grove of trees, though, the landscape was bare—grass and purple heather surrounding islands of yellow gorse, with cliffs dropping away from us a thousand feet to the sea; from where we stood, it was hard to tell the wind-torn whitecaps from the gulls and fulmars that sailed over them.

When the trail left the lee of the hill above us, a wind of 45 miles an hour walloped us hard, making walking treacherous on the scree-covered slopes. Maehr moved on ahead, out of sight around a bend, as I hung back to take some pictures, and in an incautious moment I missed my footing on the loose rock. My feet flew out from under me in a clatter of loose stones, and I frantically spread-eagled my arms and legs, the heavy tripod dragging, before clawing myself to a precarious halt. There was no cliff edge, just a steep, unimpeded drop to the ocean and a carpet of egg-sized rocks to speed the unwary along; if I slipped again, I

would accelerate nicely and shoot off into empty space, no doubt surprising the much more aerobatic fulmars far below.

Moving more carefully, I rejoined Maehr, and we hiked on for several hours, both of us struck by the land's resemblance to the Big Sur
country of northern California—a place, he noted with irony, full of
mountain lions and lion sign. Here, though, there was nothing but the
omnipresent spoor of sheep: tracks, dung, and tangled clots of shed
wool quivering in the wind.

"Goddamn sheep are everywhere," Maehr grumped. Wherever the
path held water, the mud was pocked with hoofprints. "So where are all
the cat tracks, if there're so many mountain lions and leopards around?"

"But would a cougar even use a trail like this?" I asked, wondering if
perhaps a cat would prefer to stick to the thick bracken fern in the hollows, or the dense heather.

"You kidding? Mountain lions *love* trails—if this were Monterey,
there'd be old fossilized lion crap and fresh lion crap everywhere along
this path. And I don't know about leopards not liking the taste of wool,
but cougars don't mind it a bit. They'd eat these sheep in a second."

"Ah, but these are the Ghost Cats," I reminded him. "They eat not,
neither do they shit."

"And they don't leave tracks—they must walk 2 feet above the
ground," he said, shaking his head.

Despite the sincerity and intelligence of some believers like Quentin
Rose, and a genuine desire (at least on my part) to believe that there
were reproducing populations of cougars and leopards in the United
Kingdom, we came away unconvinced. I am prepared to acknowledge
the chance that one or two big cats may, even today, eke out a solitary
existence in Britain, having been recently dumped in the wild like Felicity the Scottish cougar. But Maehr pointed out to me that any cats released in the 1970s, in the wake of the Dangerous Wild Animals Act,
would now be long dead—and the chance that those few had found each
other, mated, and built a population large enough to carry on for thirty
years, while not leaving any physical sign of their presence, was impossibly small.

A cynic would chalk up the persistence of the ABC phenomenon to
gullibility, mass hysteria, or attention-seekers, and these may indeed
contribute. On one or two occasions, people may even have seen actual
big cats; perhaps those released in the 1970s provided the factual kernel

around which the feverish big-cat sensation has grown up, a snowball effect that has ballooned with time and overheated press reports.

But the fact is, human beings are pretty lousy observers, and psychological research shows that eyewitness testimony is often riddled with
errors and outright (if unintentional) fabrication, subject to the vagaries
of interpretation based on preconceptions and biases. The fact that there
are so many black panther reports may also reflect a common optical il-
lusion—black objects look bigger at a distance, especially if, as on a
moorland, there are few landscape features like trees against which to
judge size. If people who have been reading about panthers in the neighborhood catch a glimpse of an animal scuttling across the road late at
night, their brains may take the ambiguous shape of a muntjac or the
neighborhood dog and stuff it into the mental box labeled "big cat." And
if they see a large black tomcat slinking across a pasture or moor, they
may also jump to the wrong conclusion.*

Simon Baker, the biologist who investigated Bodmin Moor, thinks
that's what often happens with big-cat sightings in the United Kingdom.
"That's not to say that people aren't genuine in their reports, and it's
wishful thinking," he said. "They just don't give much thought to it.
They've heard the reports, they see something, their mind processes it,
and they say, Yes, that must be what it was. They don't realize that the
eye isn't a camera; it's open to interpretation."

But I think all these explanations are only partially correct and overlook a larger, deeper truth—that there is a powerful force at work here,
capable of conjuring exotic cats from a landscape that on the surface appears wholly unable to support them.

It was late evening, some days after we'd parted company with
Quentin Rose, and the wind was howling again as Maehr and I climbed
the sides of Rough Tor, a high, rock-capped hill near the center of Bodmin Moor. With the exception of a few pine plantations, the land was almost completely treeless. To our east rose Brown Willy, at 1,400 feet the
highest point in Cornwall, and around us were scattered the remains of

---

*One well-known example of this phenomenon occurred in 1978 in the Netherlands,
when a small red panda escaped from a zoo. After the escape was reported widely in
the press, more than a hundred people from across the country called authorities to
report seeing the animal—which had, it turned out, been hit by a train within a few
hundred yards of the zoo.

thousands of years of human settlement—Neolithic stone circles, long-house foundations making oblong dimples in the sod, medieval field walls. The omnipresent sheep and a few ponies shared pastureland that rolled to the horizon, with ravens and common buzzards riding the up-drafts.

This is as wild as the land gets in Cornwall, but still it was crawling with people—hikers, picnickers, sweethearts walking hand in hand, families with small children. Rose told us he believes the cats are comfortable living close to humans, lying up for the day in hay barns, small woodlands, or trees; but here, as in Exmoor and Gloucestershire and everywhere else we visited, it seemed to us that there was no decent place for a cat to hide—no core of wilderness into which it could withdraw, no refuge beyond the endless press of humanity.

The very domestication that pervades Britain, rendering it such an impossible place for big cats, may also make the notion of exotic predators so compelling, so seductive, to the British themselves. We want the world to be more mysterious than it looks in the plain light of day, a more exciting place than we know it to be. We want there to be hidden valleys and unclimbed crags, forests where the shadows linger, rivers whose sources remain unknown. We want to blur the sharp edges of certainty. The general public acceptance of the idea of British big cats, which at first I took to be another example of overly credulous modern society, I later saw in a different light—an unarticulated longing for a less denuded, less denatured environment.

The greatest expression of wilderness is not stirring mountains and empty spaces but big, powerful predators—brown bears in Kamchatka, leopards in the Okavango, tigers in the Sundarbans—the potentially dangerous creatures that still sit a notch or two above us on the food chain, imposing upon us a humbler self-image. The presence of a large carnivore can redeem a diminished landscape and restore some of its luster, like the jaguars that have filtered back into southern Arizona in recent years, or the wolves that again balance the ancient bear-lion-canine triumvirate of the northern Rockies.

But Britain has been shorn of its big predators for centuries. The last lynx died out before the Romans, the last brown bears in the tenth century, and the last wolf was run down in the Scottish Highlands in the 1740s. It is hard to see a red fox or a badger as the heirs to wilderness;

they are beautiful, but they cannot fill the empty space in the land or in a human heart. So sometimes, if the countryside does not supply them, people build these spectral beasts for themselves, from twilight, mist, and unspoken, unacknowledged yearning. In the Appalachians, the ghost cat is the Eastern cougar, its legend built on the possibility, however slim, of truly wild relicts. In Britain, which never had big cats of its own—where the land is tamer and the psychological need perhaps greater—the great black cats have been pulled from even thinner air.

Dave Maehr thinks the compulsion to look for predators, even where they have no logical place, is a deeply buried one. "After all, 99 percent of the human species' existence took place in competition with things that would rather eat us than run away from us," he said, looking out over Bodmin Moor, as the lowering sun set everything into sharp relief. For most of our history, we marked these growing shadows of evening with trepidation, always watching beyond the fire for the long, supple silhouette and the glint of green eyeshine that might mean death. The danger is gone, but the reflex remains, and we still imbue the lonely, empty places in our personal landscape with monsters—or with Beasts. The ghost cats of Britain, slipping through churchyards and oak woods, across the moors and between the hedgerows, fill such a craving admirably.

This notion of black panthers as a surrogate for Britain's lost wild soul would also explain something that had troubled Maehr from the beginning—why even the best of the cat-hunters, like Rose, never seem to take the logical, final steps to get solid, defensible proof.

"There seems to be this jump from possibility to reality, without that middle ground of science in between. People ought to be doing things on a systematic level, in the field—walking transects, doing track counts, adding some credibility to it. Of course, they don't want to hear that sort of thing. They want to leave the possibility open," Maehr said quietly. "And I understand that. They don't want to finish the book. But it may well be that the book was finished when the last wolf was exterminated from the U.K." And with that he lapsed into silence, staring into a twilight that both of us knew in our bones sheltered no flesh-and-blood cats, only an overly civilized country's longing for something older, wilder—and perhaps irrevocably out of its reach.

SIX

Cruising the Crypto-fringe

When I was starting junior high in the early 1970s, I picked up a morning ritual from my mother. I'd eat breakfast while watching the early newscast on the *Today* show before running out the door to catch the bus to school. This led to my becoming a lifelong news junkie, but at the time I had a different, very particular reason for listening to Frank Blair read the headlines in his stentorian voice. My mother and I had an agreement—if the good people at *Today* announced the capture of the Loch Ness monster, I got to stay home from school and watch the unfolding drama.

This may seem like a pretty screwy arrangement for a thirteen-year-old to make with his parents, but I was deadly earnest. I'd first read about Nessie a couple of years before and was instantly hooked; as with a lot of kids, the idea of a huge, prehistoric reptile fed right into my childhood obsession with dinosaurs, and Nessie in turn opened up a netherworld of outlandish animals. I trawled the local libraries for books on Sasquatch, boned up on the famous Gloucester sea serpent, and scared myself silly late at night reading about UFOs and then scanning the skies for mysterious lights. All this extracurricular study caused my long-suffering parents to roll their eyes, but it only confirmed my adolescent hunch that the world was a big, exciting, largely unknown place.

The news bulletin never came, of course, but my interest in weird and unknown beasts did not flag. I later learned this discipline even has a name—cryptozoology, from the Greek roots meaning "the study of hid-

den animals," and that it is the province of zealous amateurs and professional scientists, though the term "cryptozoologist" is loosely applied to
both, regardless of academic training.

Separating the real from the imaginary here becomes problematic,
especially when often all there is to go on are rumors, hearsay, the accounts of hyperventilating witnesses, blurry photographs, and physical
evidence—hair, feces, even whole bodies—that has a suspicious habit of
disappearing before anyone can run a rigorous analysis on it. Skeptics
tend to dismiss cryptids, as the animals are commonly known, as the expression of universal archetypes—the bogeyman, the hairy ogre hiding
beyond the firelight, the hostile power of nature personified in sea serpents or dragons. The same tendencies that manufacture black panthers
in England might explain a lot of the accounts that fill the *Journal of Cryptozoology* and other publications.

Nature has a nearly infinite ability to confound our expectations,
however, and hidden among the certifiably wacky, there are some tales
with the ring of truth. The realm of lost species is a continuum, after all,
which explains why a Scottish lake monster may deserve the same attention as the Indian forest owlet. At one end are animals like Semper's
warbler, supposedly extinct species that logic suggests might still exist in
some poorly explored wilderness. Further along the line you encounter
animals like the imperial woodpecker or Tasmanian tiger, which were
once common but are now almost certainly gone, yet whose extinction
no one can prove with any certainty. Well into the shadows you come
across what I think of as the maybe-fauna, those rumored species whose
existence seems plausible but is as yet undocumented—animals like the
mysterious Bili ape of the Congo, or the snake-eating cow of Cambodia
called the *khiting vor*, or the giant black bear of Kamchatka in Siberia,
which was reported in the 1920s by Russian hunters.

Out toward left field, though, things begin to get seriously weird;
you bump into those big cats in Cornwall, for instance, species that appear to live more in the minds of believers than in flesh and bone. And if
you creep beyond even the Beast of Bodmin Moor, you enter the shadowed fringe where science, faith, and whimsy merge. Look around; this
is the home of sea serpents and lake monsters, of condors the size of
747s, giant turtles in Vietnamese lakes, ice age ground sloths in the
Amazon, dinosaurs in the Congo, and a veritable United Nations of

huge, hairy "wild men" almost everywhere, from Skunk Apes in the Everglades to yeti in the Himalayas and a "monkey-man" terrorizing New Delhi in the summer of 2001 to such an extent that frightened apartment dwellers leaped to their deaths when they heard that the beast was nearby. And even *that* is just the first incline on a bizarre and slippery slope, one that eventually leads to UFOs, Mothman, and the Caribbean vampire known as El Chupacabra.

This is the world of cryptozoology, and while it is the haunt of many a flaming lunatic, certain that the Jersey Devil or a saber-toothed tiger lives in the woods just across the street, it is also the specialty of a lot of very level-headed, well-respected scientists who are convinced the world is a damned sight less catalogued than the rest of us would credit. Naysayers—noting, for example, that eyewitnesses in New Delhi described the monkey-man as wearing dark glasses, an unlikely accessory for an animal—are inclined to dismiss the entire cryptozoo. But this is a mistake. Cryptozoology fails on many of the specifics, but as recent discoveries of unknown animals in the deep oceans and Asian jungles show, Earth still has a lot of surprises. In a sense, cryptozoology is just the search for mundane lost species painted on a larger and much more colorful canvas, and it's worth taking a detour through improbability and the occasional outright hoax for the light they shed on the nature of desire and the power that mystery holds on our imaginations.

So perhaps the place to start is with Nessie, without question the world's most famous unknown animal—one that perhaps suffers from overexposure, given the rich variety of lesser-known cryptids said to inhabit the globe, but also the monster that is at once among the least biologically probable and the most thoroughly investigated. The background is familiar: Loch Ness is a slender lake, lying in the deep geologic fault line known as the Great Glen, which cuts southwest to northeast across central Scotland—a narrow body of water some 24 miles long and a mile wide, about 700 feet deep in places, connected to the sea by the 6-mile length of the River Ness. Its cold water, drained from the surrounding mountains, is stained with peat and extremely turbid, with visibility of just a few feet—an appropriately sepulchral home for an unknown animal. The earliest mention dates to A.D. 565, when St. Columba used the sign of the cross to drive away "a certain water monster" in the Ness that was attacking one of his followers—thus raising Columba's stock considerably with King Brude and his Picts, the object of the saint's mission. The monster then disappears from the historical record for nearly 1,400 years, resurfacing (pardon the pun) in the nineteenth century in the form of kelpies, or water-horses, a malicious aquatic form of Scottish sprite able to take the form of a horse, which when mounted leaps into the water and devours the rider.

Kelpies are a dime a dozen in Scottish folklore, but things got interesting at Loch Ness around World War I, when locals began reporting weird beasts in the water. In 1916, the head gamekeeper of a large estate claimed that an enormous animal surfaced near his boat while he was fishing, and in 1932, a woman said she witnessed a crocodile-like something or other with tusks and a long snout in the River Ness. Newspaper reports spoke of strange fish. But the watershed year for Loch Ness was 1933, when construction crews were blasting a new roadbed along the northern shore of the lake; many have since speculated that the explosions stirred up the monsters. In March of that year, a hotel manager named Aldie Mackay was driving along the loch when she saw what she described as an animal similar to a whale; the story leaked to the Inverness newspaper, and the modern hubbub began. In July of that same year, a couple driving by the loch in midafternoon said they saw a huge beast clumping across the road several hundred yards away; unlike Mrs. Mackay's sighting, this time the witnesses insisted the creature possessed a long, sinuous neck. (The couple had reportedly watched the stop-action dinosaurs in *King Kong* not long before and said the monster they saw looked like one of the beasts from the movie.) The story was picked up by the international press, and all hell broke loose in the Great Glen.

Reporters descended on Inverness and the smaller hamlets around the loch, and a circus even offered a reward of £20,000 for the capture of a live monster. When the local water bailiff said he'd seen something with a long neck like a plesiosaur in October, the news went around the world (though no one paid attention when, some weeks later, the same fellow had a second sighting and realized he'd been fooled by cormorants distorted by heat waves coming off the lake). In January 1934, the *Daily Mail* of London sent actor and noted big-game hunter Marmaduke Wetherell to the loch to get to the bottom of the mystery.

Wetherell quickly found what he described as the monster's footprints along the lakeshore, from which he made plaster casts that were sent to the British Museum (now the Natural History Museum) for analysis. The verdict: A hoaxer—no one knows if it was Wetherell or someone duping him—had used a wastebasket made from a stuffed hippo's foot to make the impressions.

For most of the twentieth century, the best evidence for the presence of an unknown animal in Loch Ness was the famous "surgeon's photo," taken on April 19, 1934, by London physician R. Kenneth Wilson. This is *the* quintessential Nessie picture, the one everyone on the planet (with the possible but not certain exception of stone age Indians in Brazil) has seen—a curving saurian neck, a little head and wide back silhouetted against the black-and-white waves. Wilson said he'd driven up to the loch from London to visit a friend and to photograph birds, and he snapped the photo when he noticed a disturbance on the surface of the water. Wilson's position in society gave him instant credibility, and his photo became one of the key pieces of evidence for the monster's existence. But more than that, it solidified the universal image of Nessie as a plesiosaur—no more roaming the beaches on stumpy legs, she was assumed to be a form of flippered, Mesozoic marine reptile that had become landlocked in Scotland, feeding on salmon and ducking the cameras.

Matters died down considerably after the mayhem of the early thirties; by the 1940s the world had other things to worry about, notably Hitler. The 1950s saw an increase in interest, though, along with a number of sensational sightings, including a four-minute piece of motion-picture footage by an amateur monster-hunter named Tim Dinsdale, which showed a dark object moving across the loch and then turning parallel to shore. The British Joint Air Reconnaissance Intelligence Centre examined the film and concluded the object was "probably animate," but later investigators—most of whom held Dinsdale, who spent the rest of his life searching for Nessie, in high personal regard—felt his film showed nothing more than a distant motorboat.

Still, thanks in part to the Dinsdale film, the 1960s and 1970s were heady days for those with a passion for mysterious monsters all over the world, and for the first time, serious scientists began to get involved in the search for answers. In Scotland, one of those convinced by the sheer mass of eyewitness reports and photos from the loch was Sir Peter Scott, one of England's most prestigious naturalists. The son of revered Antarctic explorer Robert Falcon Scott, Sir Peter was one of the founders of the World Wildlife Fund, and an accomplished bird artist as well as a scientist. Scott had long been fascinated by Nessie; in 1962, he was among a small group that established the Loch Ness Phenomenon Investigation Bureau, which took the first rigorous steps toward examining the reports. The bureau's scientific director was a maverick Ph.D. from Chicago, Roy Mackal, who had made his professional reputation as a biochemist and engineer but went on to devote much of his life to cryptozoology. The LNI, as the bureau was commonly known, set up telephoto movie cameras to provide nearly constant surveillance of the lake, in the hope of bettering the kind of fuzzy, blurred photos taken over the years by amateurs; they got a war-surplus searchlight to watch the loch after dark and even set off explosions along the shore to simulate the road-blasting of the 1930s, which was thought to have sparked the first rash of modern sightings.

Meanwhile, the interest in Loch Ness brought to light stories about a lot of other lake and sea monsters around the world—"Ogopogo" in Lake Okanagan, British Columbia (with similar beasts in many neighboring lakes); "Champ" in Lake Champlain in New England; "Bessie" in Lake Erie; "Caddy" in Cadboro Bay off Vancouver Island. There were said to be unexplained animals in lakes and rivers all over North America and beyond—Bear Lake on the Utah/Idaho line, Flathead Lake in Montana, the White River in Arkansas, Alkali Lake in Nebraska, some three hundred bodies of water in all around the world. Monster-hunters with a knack for biogeography noticed that almost all the reports came from deep glacial lakes within a narrow latitudinal band around the Northern Hemisphere, many of which do not freeze, which struck them as an indication that they were dealing with a true biological phenomenon. Chambers of commerce with a knack for marketing noticed a business opportunity, and many community festivals were established to celebrate whatever beastie—invariably given a cute nickname like Slimy Slim or Tahoe Tessie—inhabited the local waterhole. Most are cut from the sea-serpent mold, but not all. Since the 1950s, Churubusco, Indiana, has celebrated Turtle Days every June, commemorating the Beast of 'Busco, said to be a giant turtle in nearby Fulk Lake.

Cryptozoologists tend to dismiss the Beast of 'Busco as nothing more than an unusually big alligator snapper, but figuring out what the other monsters really are has proven a good deal harder. Thanks to Nessie, the average person conjures an image of a plesiosaur, but scientists like Roy Mackal who have investigated the sightings have proposed some fascinating alternatives. In his 1980 book *Searching for Hidden Animals*, Mackal lays out the case for some sea serpent and lake monsters in the Pacific Northwest to be zeuglodons, a form of early whale typified by *Basilosaurus*. Zeuglodons are known from Eocene fossils dating back about 40 million years, and had a long, sinuous body and a narrow head. What's more, he notes, the many lakes and rivers in Washington and British Columbia in which monsters have been reported are connected to the Columbia River drainage, making it possible that migratory proto-whales could have ascended the river and become isolated in the lakes.

Mackal also hypothesized that Champ, the monster of Lake Champlain, was a zeuglodon; in this case, a river ascent would not have been necessary, for the lake was, until a few thousand years ago, an arm of the Atlantic, and a whale fossil has been found along its shores—though the remains not of a snakelike proto-whale but of a modern beluga. Whatever Champ is, it is usually described as 25 or 30 feet long, with a humped back and a long, curving neck. The first recorded sighting was by no less a person than Samuel de Champlain in 1609, but the most famous came in July 1977, when Sandra Mansi and her fiancé said Champ surfaced 50 yards from where they were watching Mansi's two children playing in the water near St. Albans, Vermont. The single snapshot Mansi took shows a dark body with a long, curved neck turned to one side, water glistening from it, as the monster moves away from her toward the far lakeshore. It is by far the best evidence for Champ, though not everyone accepts the picture at face value, in part because Mansi waited three years before coming forward with the print and had lost the original negative.

But unlike Loch Ness and Lake Okanagan, Champlain freezes solid in the winter, which makes the survival of air-breathing vertebrates, be they reptilian or cetacean, a bit of a puzzle. Champ proponents have suggested that the beasts may hibernate, or perhaps create breathing holes, though none of the ice fishermen who throng the lake report finding anything of the sort. A popular theory is that Champ spends the winter in hypothetical underwater caves that are somehow connected to the surface through equally hypothetical tunnels, thus providing it with an air supply.

Unfortunately, stretching for an explanation is nothing new in cryptozoology. F. W. Holiday, a writer much taken with paranormal topics, devoted an entire book to the hypothesis that Nessie was an enormous slug; as evidence, Holiday pointed to similarities between sightings and photographs of the loch creature and *Tullimonstrum gregarium*, a fossil invertebrate, possibly a mollusk, with a bulbous body, a long, necklike proboscis, a triangular tail, and two odd appendages about where flippers would be on a vertebrate. Never mind that *Tullimonstrum* was roughly 300 million years old and the largest specimen recovered from Illinois strip mines was barely a foot long.

The ability to strain at gnats while swallowing camels surfaces even among some of the field's scientific leaders. Take the case of the White River monster, news of which first broke in the summer of 1937 near Newport, Arkansas. Witnesses said they saw something inexplicable in a deep channel of the river; some described it as a large fish, but others said it was as much as 12 feet long and 5 feet wide, and still others claimed it was the size of a boxcar. Many witnesses agreed that its skin appeared to be peeling or sloughing off, and some thought they saw a horn in the middle of the head. Sightings continued for years, and in 1973 the state senate even passed a resolution granting the beast legal protection.

The fact that some witnesses thought the "monster" was simply a large sturgeon or catfish might give one clue to its identity, but to some cryptozoologists, there are better candidates. "The White River case is a clear-cut instance of a known aquatic animal observed outside of its normal habitat or range and therefore unidentified by the observers unfamiliar with the type," wrote Roy Mackal. "The animal in question clearly was a large male elephant seal, either *Mirounga leonina* (southern species) or *Mirounga angustirostris* (northern species)." Mackal has a point; elephant seals are big (up to 20 feet long and weighing 4 tons), males have an inflatable snout that might be mistaken for a horn, and when molting their short, dense fur, they have a patchy, peeling appearance.

But there are only two populations of elephant seals in the world, and both are a long way from Arkansas. The northern elephant seal is found along the California and Baja coasts, and so can be easily discounted, unless one hitched a ride across the Rockies; the southern species breeds on sub-Antarctic islands and the Valdez Peninsula of Argentina, so is, at least, in the right ocean. It is at least marginally conceivable that one might have bolted 8,000 miles north, crossed the Caribbean and the Gulf of Mexico, ascended the Mississippi River, dodged barge traffic, and eventually swum up the White River, where it somehow found the hundreds of pounds of food it would need to eat per day—that's a lot of bluegills and bullheads, since the squid these animals normally prey upon are a little thin in those parts. It also must have forgone the elephant seal's normal habit of hauling out on a beach from time to time—and it supposes that this huge, blubber-encased animal, insulated for diving into the frigid depths of Antarctic waters, wouldn't immediately keel over from heat stroke when exposed to an Arkansas summer day.

(Mackal also ascribes the Alkali Lake, Nebraska, monster—reported in the 1920s—to an errant elephant seal that ascended the Mississippi and Missouri Rivers, even though the lake in question is nearly 200 miles from the Missouri. While it is true the seals do sometimes make much shorter overland crossings, it's hard to believe folks could have missed a 20-foot, 8,000-pound fleshy slug creeping along on its belly through the high sandhills and arid, prickly pear–studded pastures of northwestern Nebraska.)

In the early years of monster-chasing, after Nessie became a global celebrity, a number of elaborate cage traps were built at Loch Ness to catch her. But with the 1970s, crypto-hunters shifted to much more sophisticated equipment, especially a new generation of optics. Starting in 1970, a Boston attorney and physicist, Dr. Robert Rines, and his Academy of Applied Science undertook annual expeditions to the loch, armed with automatic submersible cameras and strobe flashes that had been designed by Dr. Harold Edgerton of MIT, the pioneer of high-speed flash photography. They documented an abundance of salmon and large eels in the lake, as well as something considerably less banal. At

1:50 a.m. on August 8, 1972, a camera set at a depth of 45 feet captured two riveting images, showing a large rounded body with a diamond-shaped flipper. The grainy images were later computer-enhanced by NASA's Jet Propulsion Laboratory, and by combining the photographic evidence with simultaneous sonar data from that night that showed a moving object, Rines and his colleagues estimated the flipper was about 6 feet long and the entire organism up to 66 feet in length.

Though skeptics said the pictures showed an anchor fluke or some other man-made object, and questioned whether the NASA enhancement had altered them too much, the Rines photos were a sensation. They were followed in 1975 by two more (among just six photos out of two thousand that had any discernible image) that purportedly showed the animal's body—one taken at a depth of 35 feet, at 4:30 a.m., which may show a large, plesiosaurish creature with a long, thin neck, squat body, and two appendages about where you'd expect front flippers to be; the other, nicknamed the "gargoyle photo," was thought to be a close-up of the head of the monster. Skeptics suggested that with its oddly bumpy appearance it looked a lot more like a tree stump, and on this, they carried the day—a follow-up expedition in 1987, using sonar and underwater television in the same area where Rines's camera had been moored, brought back sharp images of a tree stump that was, despite twelve years of decomposition, a dead ringer for the alleged monster head.

After the photos were released, Peter Scott and Rines even went so far as to publish a brief article in the prestigious British journal *Nature*, "Naming the Loch Ness Monster." Noting that the recently passed Conservation of Wild Creatures and Wild Plants Act required that any animal receiving legal protection have a common and scientific name, the pair said it was better to be safe than sorry, "even though the creature's relationship with known species, and even the taxonomic class to which it belongs, remain in doubt." The name they proposed was Nessie or Loch Ness monster, *Nessiteras rhombopteryx.* "The generic name *Nessiteras*, a neuter noun, is a composite word combining the name of the Loch with the Greek word *teras*, genitive *teratos*, which was used by Homer and onward to mean a marvel or a wonder, and in a concrete sense for a range of monsters which aroused awe, amazement, and often fear. The specific name *rhombopteryx* is a combination of the Greek *rhombos*, a diamond or lozenge shape, and the Greek *pteryx*, meaning a fin or wing. Thus the species is the Ness monster with diamond fin."*

From there, Scott and Rines tried to narrow the taxonomic field as best they could, while admitting their evidence was, to put it mildly, scant. The two took it as a given that Nessie was a vertebrate—the paddle fin seemed to confirm that much—but they felt it did not look like a the limb of a cetacean, "and the inclination is to view it as reptilian." Of course, reptiles breathe air, which posed a problem for the pro-monster folks, since Nessie was at best rarely seen on the surface, but Scott and Rines noted that some turtles can survive a year of constant submersion, and suggested that the monster

> would not be detected easily if the nostrils were at the topmost point to break the surface. Many accounts of head sightings speak of 'horns' or 'ears' which might be extensions of breathing tubes. Indeed, the ancient name 'water-horse' suggests the appearance of horses' ears. With any ripple on the water it would not be difficult for a Nessie to breathe undetected. In flat calm conditions, the surface is constantly dimpled by rising fish, and again the animal would be likely to go unnoticed.

Scott supplied two line drawings to round out the paper, showing an "impression of possible appearance of *Nessiteras rhombopteryx*." Based on pictures from the "surgeon's photo" onward, as well as eyewitness accounts and the new underwater images, Scott depicted Nessie as a plesiosaur-like reptile, with a double-humped back, a fairly short and thickened tail, and a thin neck and small head. One drawing showed a pair chasing salmon, but Scott also painted a very different scene—a pair of nuzzling, courting Nessies in the peat-stained water. Nessie had not only a name but a love life.

As technology advanced, so did the hunt for the monster. In the 1980s, Operation Deepscan outfitted a fleet of twenty boats with state-

---

*The name may have made good nomenclatural sense, but if you rearrange the letters—as did Nicholas Fairbairn, a Scottish Member of Parliament and a fan of anagrams—you get "Monster hoax by Sir Peter S." Rines, however, shot back with an alternate version: "Yes, both pix are Monsters R."

of-the-art sonar and deployed them in a picket line, sweeping the loch from end to end; several suspiciously large sonar contacts were made, but nothing conclusive was found, such as a herd of *Nessiteras rhombopteryx*. In recent years, as the chance of finding a large vertebrate shrinks, the explanations have become a good deal more prosaic—among them the phenomenon known as seiche waves.

At both Loch Ness and Lake Champlain, for instance, the dramatic seasonal temperature changes cause the formation of a thermocline—a layer of warmer, more buoyant water that lies like oil on top of a dense, cold bottom layer. Strong winds, blowing along the narrow, deep lakes, cause the surface layer to build up at the leeward end, pushing the colder, deeper layer to the windward end, almost like one side of a seesaw being pushed down. When the wind stops, the warm surface layer surges back, while the deep layer flows in rapidly below it, like the end of the seesaw rising. The result is a seiche wave—a wave that moves along the boundary between the temperature layers, often huge and violent but usually betraying little of its presence on the surface.

Seiche waves in Champlain are commonly 30 feet high, but have been known to reach 300 feet, while those in Loch Ness have been recorded at 130 feet, yet there may be no more than a ripple on the surface. Seiche waves may slosh back and forth for days, and can create large, phantom sonar contacts—but more important, they can carry tree trunks and other debris along with them, forcing them to the top and dragging them along against the wind and surface currents, often at remarkable speed. The long, narrow shape of many glacial lakes, their great depth and northern locations (which produce strong thermoclines)—all features once considered suggestive of a biological explanation for lake monsters—also promote the formation of seiche waves.

Seismic activity can also cause seiche waves, and the Great Glen lies over a geologic fault that rattles with significant earthquakes three or four times a century. In the summer of 2001, Italian researchers—who noted that most of the nearly three thousand Nessie sightings report only odd waves or strange disturbances in the water, not an actual beast—suggested that seiche waves and the sudden release of gas trapped in lake sediments might account for many of the reports.

Even that bastion of Loch Ness evidence, Dr. Wilson's famous surgeon's photo, eventually proved to be much less than it appeared. Sixty years after the picture was published, two friends with an interest in the Nessie phenomenon, Alastair Boyd and David Martin, pieced together clues that the photo was a hoax whose target was the London newspaper the *Daily Mail*—the same paper that had sent Marmaduke Wetherell, he of the hippo-track incident, to the loch in 1934. Boyd and Martin, relying on information from Wetherell's son Ian and Ian's dying stepbrother, reconstructed the scenario: The elder Wetherell, angered by the *Mail*'s treatment of him over the track fiasco, decided to get his revenge. He took a 14-inch toy submarine and, with plastic wood, built the curving neck and head, adding lead to the bottom of the sub for balance. He and Ian actually took the photo—the original of which shows a sweeping view of the loch and surrounding landscape, though the cropped version is always reproduced—then persuaded Dr. Wilson, through the mutual friend in Scotland whom the doctor was visiting, to offer the picture to the newspaper as his own.

It is worth noting that not everyone accepts the Boyd-Martin claim that the picture was faked, and even if it was, it doesn't alter the fundamental question of whether something unknown lives in the loch. To many loch experts, seiche waves don't explain everything. In fact, some Nessie researchers who reject the plesiosaur theory were delighted to see this bit of pro-dinosaur evidence crumble. But if not a plesiosaur, then what? For years, Roy Mackal advanced the idea that the monsters could be giant salamanders, or an extraordinarily large, thick-bodied species of eel; the latter, being a fish, has the advantage of not breathing air, which would explain why the animal isn't seen more often on the surface. (Mackal has since altered his view, and now says the monster is a zeuglodon whale that follows salmon runs up the River Ness from the sea.)

Adrian Shine, a naturalist who in 1974 began exploring Loch Morar (a neighboring lake with its own monster tradition) and who eventually headed up investigations at Loch Ness, rejects the idea of a reptile, amphibian, or proto-whale. A fish is more likely, he thinks, but it couldn't be a resident predator, because there simply isn't enough food in the lake to support a large population of giant carnivores. Besides, he argues, the young of any unknown fish would long ago have been netted or caught by the many fishermen on the lake.

The creature that Shine believes best matches the original, prehysteria sightings of an unknown animal in the loch is a sturgeon. Those who find the notion of Nessie as a big fish disappointing should consider just how primal and strange a sturgeon is. The species that enters British rivers to spawn may exceed 11 feet in length and reach 700 pounds. Sturgeon are primitive fish, and they look it—their long bodies are covered in bony plates called scutes, while their shovel-shaped heads end in a long snout with a cluster of barbels dangling below. Because of pollution, overfishing, and (particularly) weirs and dams that block the ascending fish trying to spawn, sturgeon are extremely rare in Britain, but they once migrated up the Ness to breed, and records from the seventeenth century tell of a monstrous 12-footer captured there.

Many of the early reports of the Loch Ness monster, before the dinosaur archetype became ingrained in everyone's mind, simply described a big, sinuous animal or an unknown fish; the 1932 report by a Miss McDonald, who said she saw something plated like a crocodile with a long snout thrashing in the River Ness, sounds a good deal like a sturgeon. The species' very rarity would explain both the long interludes between sightings and the reason most witnesses don't immediately recognize it. In fact, sturgeon make more sense as the root of those Canadian lake monsters than do ancient whales—the white sturgeon of western North America may grow to 20 feet and weigh almost a ton, after all, and landlocked populations exist within the Columbia River basin.

But long before the fake surgeon's photo was revealed, I'd given up my junior-high hopes, knowing that whatever was in Loch Ness, it wasn't something left over from the Age of Dinosaurs. I'd learned too much about the cruel realities of small-population biology, the utter impossibility of a single lake containing a viable community of huge vertebrates for millions—even for mere thousands—of years, especially without one washing up dead on a beach for science to coldly register.

But there's no question that the mystery still has a hold on me. Traveling through Scotland for the first time many years ago, exhausted from jet lag and running late, I made a detour past Inverness, unwilling to pass without catching at least a glimpse of the distant loch, which shimmered in the late-day sun. I felt a chill that had nothing to do with the Caledonian climate.

———

How important is hard physical evidence? The rationalist in me says that evidence is everything; anecdotes, legends, and eyewitness reports make for entertaining reading, but unless you can measure it, it isn't science. Pin it down, scrutinize it, test it, replicate it. Some people pooh-pooh such convictions as the blinkered, Eurocentric mindset that ignores the fuzzy margins of the universe, but it's an approach that has done an admirable job of explaining the world in which we live.

Yet I believe in many things that I cannot see or touch or *personally* verify, whose existence I take on the word of others with greater experience or specialization. I cannot prove that subatomic particles are real, or that light travels at 186,000 miles per second, but I accept the truth of those statements. With unknown animals, one isn't required to blindly accept the reality of their existence, only the possibility—and possibility is often more exciting and intriguing than concrete fact.

We love to speculate; we are a species of compulsive storytellers, fashioners of myth, spinners of yarns. Most of our early literature, religious and secular, is merely a way to explain the visible and the invisible, and so was the oral tradition that preceded it. The auroral lights were Eskimo ghosts playing with the skull of a walrus, and disease was the work of evil spirits. Maybe Champ is just a massive seiche wave pushing logs around Lake Champlain, but the Abenaki didn't know about seiche waves, and so they saw a monster. We do know about seiche waves, but sometimes a proto-whale is a neater explanation, and a lot more diverting. Besides, no one can yet prove you wrong—and the tantalizing whiff of "maybe" can get to anyone, upsetting the ordered fashion in which we view the world.

Many people are content to daydream about unknown animals, but a few take a more active approach, because the lure of finding a lost or undescribed species is a powerful one, and the pull is magnified exponentially if the creature in question is especially exotic. Sometimes even the most experienced scientist can let imagination and wild hope take the reins from common sense. For proof, I offer an instructive tale that involves the little Illinois fossil *Tullimonstrum*, that same skinny-snouted, foot-long invertebrate that F. W. Holiday thought was the animal behind the Loch Ness phenomenon.

Tullimonstrum was discovered in 1958 by an amateur fossil hunter named Francis Tully, who found it embedded in 280-million-year-old rocks along with a lot of other fossils typical of a prehistoric swamp. Tully took the specimen to the Field Museum of Natural History in Chicago, where the eminent paleontologist Dr. Eugene S. Richardson, Jr., and others scratched their heads over the beast for some years. No one knew exactly what it was, so they dubbed it "Tully's monster," and when at length Richardson formally described it in a scientific journal, the name he chose was a Latinized variation of the nickname. Because the animal was so weird, and the name so suggestive, Richardson's announcement was picked up by the wire services and got a lot of play in newspapers around the country.

Let's leave Richardson and his fossil for a moment and jump halfway around the world. That same summer, 1966, a Harvard paleontologist named Bryan Patterson—"Pat" to his friends—was leading an expedition to the western shores of Lake Turkana in northern Kenya, which was in those days an extremely remote, poorly explored region. A few days earlier, one of the graduate students in Patterson's party had had a birthday, and to celebrate, the field crew got thoroughly sloshed on brandy and warm Tusker beer. Stumbling to the latrine the next day, Patterson stubbed his toe, and it became so badly infected he had to be taken to a medical missionary outpost 30 or 40 miles away at Lokori, where he was pumped full of antibiotics and told to stay off his feet for a while.

Patterson was not one to take easily to enforced rest. His old students and colleagues recall him as something of a character, brimming over with energy and talent; his father, Lieutenant Colonel John Henry Patterson, had been the chief engineer building the Uganda Railway in Kenya, who in 1898 shot two man-eating lions that had killed 130 workers and brought construction of the railroad to a standstill. (This famous incident formed the basis of the 1996 movie *The Ghost and the Darkness*.) In 1926, Colonel Patterson arranged for his son to take a job as a fossil preparator at the Field Museum, which had purchased the skins of the man-eaters two years earlier. Although he lacked any formal training, Bryan Patterson quickly worked his way up through the institution's ranks, eventually becoming curator of fossil vertebrates before leaving for Harvard's Museum of Comparative Zoology.

While laid up at the missionary clinic that summer in Kenya, Patterson read his accumulated mail and found that a friend had sent him a clipping and drawing from the Field Museum's *Bulletin* about Richardson's little monster. Richardson had been Pat's mentor at the Field Museum, and Patterson decided to have some fun. As the days dragged by, fretting around camp while his grad students hunted for fossils, he cooked up a doozy of a practical joke to pass the time: the Dancing Worm of Turkana.

Patterson invented a series of fictional people, with plausible names and backgrounds, and he enlisted his graduate students (I am indebted to one of them, Dr. Roger Wood of Stockton College, New Jersey, for this story) as well as a variety of Kenyans, including a government geologist in Nairobi, the doctor at the clinic in Lokori, and a farmer in the Rift Valley. One of the fictional characters was a Lieutenant Colonel R.G.L. Cloudesley, a retired British Army officer in Nairobi. There was also an Indian merchant, Purshottam S. Patel; an African schoolteacher at Lokori named Joseph N. Ngomo; and a little Turkana boy named Akai s/o Ekechalon. Patterson drafted letters from each of these people, written in very different styles, then had different members of the field crew copy the letters—one student, for example, had spidery handwriting that seemed to fit an elderly British colonel.

"Colonel Cloudesley" 's letter went out first, sent airmail from Nairobi with help from the geologist there. In it, the colonel explained that he had seen a wire-service story and photo of *Tullimonstrum* in the *East African Standard* (the leading paper of the day), and it recalled to him something he'd heard forty years earlier from A. M. Champion, the district commissioner in Turkana, of "a remarkable worm reputed to live in the swamp country to the southeast. The local tribesmen told fantastic stories about its dancing and giving milk, if I remember correctly." The colonel stressed that he put little stock in the story, but the descriptions of the worm and the drawing of the Tully Monster in the newspaper were rather similar. "I hardly dare to suggest that a relative of your extinct 'monster' still survives in one of the remotest parts of East Africa, but it might just be worthwhile to pursue the matter," the letter concluded.

A week later, from a different part of Kenya, "Purshottam Patel" 's letter arrived in Chicago, one with a very different tenor altogether, full of "dear honoured Sirs" and other rhetorical flourishes. Patel said he was a merchant whose family ran a chain of *dukas*, or general stores, in northwest Kenya, and he, too, had heard stories of the dancing worm—and he told Richardson that, honoured Sir, it would be a pleasure for his family to obtain a specimen for the museum. ("With their help I, even I, might catch one for you. The price would be very cheap. But, honoured Sir, tell me how I catch it as it lives in a great swamp. This is a new thing for me. Do I keep it, do I kill it? I await eagerly your orders and instructions.")

Richardson got the Cloudesley letter first, and the great paleontologist was intrigued, but also suspicious of a prank. But then, a week or two later, the Patel letter arrived, postmarked from a completely different part of Kenya. The details that could be checked out were—there really was a Turkana district in northern Kenya, for example, with swamps to the southeast, a fellow named Champion had been district commissioner, and there are many Indian merchants named Patel working in Kenya, "Patel" being the equivalent of Smith or Jones.

Then came the final touch—a letter, sent surface mail so that it took months to arrive, purporting to be from one Joseph N. Ngomo, who introduced himself as a teacher at the mission school in Lokori (which, if anyone bothered to check, would of course prove to be a real place, run by a doctor who was prepared to assure them that he had just such a person working for him). Ngomo's letter, written in a stilted, overly formal manner, apologized for bothering Dr. Richardson, but Ngomo said one of his students had seen an article in the *East African Standard* and would not let him rest until he'd written to the scientist about a story common among the Turkana tribe. "As regards the subject of the letter I can say nothing," Ngomo wrote. "Most Turkana are very primitive people and have many tales in which sometimes is a grain of truth."

Enclosed, on a scrap of white paper in what appeared to be childish block handwriting (but was actually Patterson's own left-handed scrawl), was the following short note: "Today techer show us paper and there is anmal my pepels knows. I not know name Tuly moster but call ekrurut loedonkakini. It live Ayangyangi [Swamp]. In rains at moon fill all dance wave hands give milk. Ekurut loedonkakini very dangery anmal. Bite, man die. [Signed] Akai s/o Ekechalon." (If Richardson had spoken Turkana, he would have realized it was a joke. "Akai s/o Ekechalon means 'House, son of Stool,' which were practically the only two words in Turkana that we knew," Roger Wood recalled recently.)

Naturally, letters went flying back across the Atlantic, but the field season was over and the Americans had all gone home. No matter; Richardson's letters were collected by the various Kenyan conspirators and forwarded to Harvard, where Patterson drafted replies, had his grad students again copy them out, mailed them *back* to Africa, and then had them posted from the correct parts of Kenya to be sent to Richardson. It was an elaborate scam, aided by the slow pace of international mail, and one that took more than a year and a half to play itself out. Richardson and his colleagues even grilled Patterson in person that Christmas, when he was in Chicago for a visit. Did he know a Lokori Mission? Was there such a place as Ayangyangi Swamp? What about an Indian merchant named Patel? Patterson confirmed just enough to keep them interested, and somehow managed to keep a straight face.

The summer of 1967 found the Harvard field crew back in Kenya, and heavy rains meant everyone had more time than usual on their hands. One of the grad students made a papier-mâché model of the "Dancing Worm of Turkana," and they photographed Patterson—bandoliers of cartridges slung across his shoulder, a shotgun under one arm, and his face concealed by a big safari hat—holding the thing by its neck.

But the joke had worked almost too well. Before the picture could be mailed, word came that the Field Museum was preparing to mount a major expedition to Lake Turkana to ferret out the mysterious worm, which would eclipse even the coelacanth as the greatest living-fossil discovery of all. Dozens of scientists were clamoring to join the trek, and it was time to pull the plug before careers were damaged. So Patterson turned the photograph into a Christmas card, signed by all the fictional characters, with a border of little dancing *Tullimonstrums* around the inside, and had it mailed to Richardson from Kenya. The jig was up.

Richardson was apparently a very good sport about it all—the elder scientist, who dabbled in printing as a hobby, even compiled all the correspondence in a little book he produced on his basement printing press (and from which I have excerpted the letters), and a version of the story appeared in the bulletin of the Field Museum.

"But he was completely fooled, no doubt about it," Roger Wood said. "The reality is, every so often something like this is found, and it happens just often enough that you never know."

If cryptozoologists ever choose a motto, perhaps that should be it: You never know. Simply because Nessie's head turns out to be a sunken log, or the Dancing Worm a friendly hoax, there's no saying that the next report won't lead to one of those miraculous discoveries that set the world on its ear; it's happened before. So it pays to keep an open mind—but sometimes cryptozoology can stretch even an optimist's credulity to the breaking point.

A couple of years ago, I'd given a lecture on the natural history of the Appalachians, and afterward, as usually happens, a small group of people gathered to ask follow-up questions. There was one fellow, tall and bearded, who hung back, obviously waiting until everyone else was gone. This didn't strike me as odd; some folks are shy about asking questions in front of a crowd. When he finally had me alone, he asked if I'd ever encountered any stories of the supernatural in my travels.

Oh yes, I said, warming instantly to the topic—the Appalachians have a wonderful folk tradition of haints, spooks, and ghost stories of every sort, and I love collecting them as I travel. I started telling him about an old tale I'd just heard in the Black Mountains of North Carolina, about the ghost of an early frontiersman, but he cut me off, firmly but politely.

"No," he said, "that's not exactly what we meant." I realized with a start that he was referring to himself in the plural. "We were wondering specifically if you ever come across reports of giant vultures—birds with, say, a 50-foot wingspan?"

I could feel my smile slipping. I had to admit that I hadn't, and that I found the idea pretty far-fetched. True, during the last ice age there were giant condors known as teratorns, some of which had a 25-foot wingspan, but they're all extinct. If there really were vultures that large, I said, someone would surely have gotten a picture of one by now. It's not as though condors hide in the woods.

"Oh, don't be so sure. They exist, but in a different dimension, one that overlaps ours occasionally, so one or two slip through for a little while." With that, he handed me a business card with his name and something about investigating cases of spontaneous human combustion. "We do the same thing that Mulder and Scully do on *The X-Files*, only we do it for real. We are really after the same thing you are—the difference is, we're looking for *multidimensional* organisms."

This is a facet of cryptozoology on which I'm not going to dwell, but neither can I let it pass without mention. Interest in plausible unknown animals becomes weirder and weirder the further you penetrate this culture, eventually merging with the realm of UFOs, alien abduction, and the paranormal, just as some people in Britain see a connection between flying saucers, crop circles, and big-cat sightings. While the association makes a lot of serious, biologically trained cryptozoologists cringe, Mothman and El Chupacabra are just as much a part of this world as undescribed bears in Siberia.

Mothman, for the uninitiated, is a monster that first appeared in 1961, described as gray, the size of a man, with glowing red eyes and enormous wings, and which was most often seen around an abandoned munitions factory at Point Pleasant, West Virginia, often in the company of UFOs. After disappearing for a decade, Mothman resurfaced in 1976 in south Texas. El Chupacabra, the "goatsucker," is the current darling of monster-hunters, though it was until recently very much an ethnic phenomenon—a 4-foot-high hairy monster with the kind of round head and huge eyes described by "alien abduction" victims, a row of spines protruding from its back, and fangs. Stories about it first appeared in Puerto Rico in the mid-1990s, linking it with livestock deaths and mutilations, and spread rapidly through the Caribbean basin and Latin America, and thence through Hispanic communities in the United States, thanks in large measure to the Internet.

I don't want to convey a false impression about cryptozoology. It would be tempting to dismiss the Mothman aficionados and UFO kooks as merely the colorful fringe, but the reverse is true; they appear to be in the considerable majority, while the scientists and lay workers who take a more rational, methodical approach are, numerically speaking, very much second fiddle. But that's where the really interesting work is being done, much of it by biologists, paleontologists, or anthropologists with lots of academic initials after their names.

Many of them are associated with the International Society of Cryptozoology, which was founded in 1982 by Mackal and J. Richard Greenwell, an ecologist at the University of Arizona with a special interest in Bigfoot. Bernard Heuvelmans, the Belgian zoologist who coined the term "cryptozoology" in the 1950s, became and remains the group's president. Its self-described goal is to to "apply logic, objectivity and scientific methodology to cryptozoological issues," and while many scientists look askance at ISC's work and its sometimes uncritical acceptance of debatable evidence, in the flaky world of cryptids, it stands as the sweet voice of reason.

You'll hunt in vain through the board of the ISC for the kind of loopy amateurs that make up the bulk of crypto's ardent fans. Among its recent members were the mammalogist Colin P. Groves of Australian National University, an expert on mammalian evolution; Zhou Guoxing, head of the anthropology department at the Chinese Academy of Sciences, who has hunted for evidence of the Yeren, a Bigfoot-like Chinese hominid; and Eric Buffetaut, a vertebrate paleontologist at the University of Paris whose interest in ancient marine crocodiles led him to study sea serpent reports. The late Grover Krantz, a retired physical anthropologist from Washington State University, was a founding ISC board member and is the person who first suggested Sasquatch and other alleged hairy "wild men" could be surviving *Gigantopithecus*, a huge ape species known from Asian fossils. Perhaps the most famous name associated with ISC has been that of Dr. Eugenie Clark of the University of Maryland, known for decades as "Shark Lady" for her groundbreaking work with shark behavior and ecology. These folks have respected careers in fields outside cryptozoology, and their interest in unknown animals often pains their professional colleagues, who frequently treat the crypto work with a mix of embarrassment and infuriating condescension.

Indeed, it must be said that serious cryptozoologists have relatively little in the way of concrete results to show for their work. Much of their evidence is, in the jargon of research, soft—anecdote and eyewitness testimony. Cryptozoologists often stress the ubiquity of unknown animal reports as a point in favor of their accuracy, especially since many accounts share similarities of habitat or physical description, and were often firmly ensconced in local folklore well before global communication made it possible for stories to spread around the planet at light speed.

But the very pervasiveness of cryptid sightings—and the continued absence of conclusive proof—also forces you to at least consider that this may be less of a zoological phenomenon than a reflection of certain universal traits of human imagination and culture: alien big-cat reports writ large. For example, a great deal of cryptozoological attention has been focused on what devotees call "hominology," the investigation of large, hairy near-humans, or hominids. Everyone's familiar with the Big Two of hominology, the Sasquatch in the Pacific Northwest and the yeti, or Abominable Snowman, in the Himalayas. Well, okay, you say; it's a big world, and maybe we humans aren't as all-knowing, all-seeing as we'd like to think we are. Maybe there's room for a few monsters—or if not monsters, at least perfectly normal animals that don't fit the conventional mold. An open-minded person could accept the possibility that a population of large, fairly intelligent primates—perhaps even a relict group of Neanderthals—might be able to evade notice and capture in a place as remote as Tibet or the damp forests of the Cascade Mountains.

"The objections to a second North American hominid are many, and my scientific skepticism counsels caution," writes entomologist Robert Michael Pyle in *Where Bigfoot Walks*, a thoughtful exploration of the monster and its grip on us. "But the long litany of belief and tradition courts fair consideration, as do the numerous clear tracks found in disparate wilds and the many sightings by seemingly reliable folk. To dismiss the unknown out of hand is even more foolish than to accept it unquestioned, more foolhardy than to fear it."

It would be easier for me to accept that premise if Bigfoot and the yeti were the only two such hominids that are regularly reported. But there are dozens—an abbreviated list includes the Almas in the Altai Mountains of Mongolia, Barmanu in Pakistan, the Yeren in China, Nguoi Rung in Vietnam, and Chuchunaa in western Siberia; the Yowie in southern Australia and the Bondegezou in neighboring Irian Jaya; and Sisemite in Guatemala. South America is said to have at least three Bigfoot-like hominids—Ucumar in the Andes, Didi in the Guyanan Shield, and the mapinguari in Amazonia. Nor does this list touch on what crypto-hunters call "true giants," which are similar in build but tower 10 to 20 feet tall and are said to be cannibalistic.

For almost every regional legend of a hairy giant, there is also at least one tradition of small, furry bipeds, often called "proto-pygmies" by cryptozoologists. They are known as *agogwe* in eastern Africa, *sehite* in the Ivory Coast, *nittaewo* in Sri Lanka, and *teh-lma* or *pyar-them* in Nepal,

Bhutan, and Tibet. Depending on whom you believe, they are either un-described primates, surviving early humans (perhaps *Homo erectus*), or even, in the case of African sightings, the ancient hominid *Australopithe-cus*, which lingered millions of years after it was thought to have become extinct.

Bigfoot isn't the only North American version, either. As with lake and river monsters, almost every corner of the United States and Canada has a local legend or two, like the Skunk Ape of Florida, which is said to be 7 feet tall, hairy, have glowing eyes and a horrible smell, and has purportedly been photographed stealing fruit from backyards or running away through the saw palmettos. The Pearl River basin in Louisiana, of ivory-billed woodpecker fame, enjoyed earlier notoriety for the Honey Island Swamp monster, a three-toed biped 7 to 10 feet tall, with lank gray hair, a horrible smell, and a horrifying shriek, which was sighted in the 1970s. Momo—short for "Missouri Monster"—has supposedly been killing dogs and attacking women and children since the 1940s around Louisiana, Missouri; it is one of many reports usually lumped together as "eastern Bigfoots," including Old Yellow Top in On-tario, Fluorescent Freddie in Indiana, and Peg Leg in Georgia (this last, like the bespectacled monkey-man of New Delhi, is an unusually sophis-ticated hominid, since it managed to replace a missing leg with a wooden prosthesis).

During the summer of 1969, the area around Lake Worth, Texas, was gripped with hominid hysteria when a huge, hairy beast reportedly at-tacked three couples in a car, parked at night in a secluded spot—though the Lake Worth Monster broke with the usual mold in that it had a white beard, glowing yellow eyes, scaly hands, and the lower body of what was politely described as "a large and virile goat." Parties of armed vigilantes combed the woods for it, though the only casualty was a teenager wear-ing white overalls, who was shot through the shoulder by mistake. That fall, a man who was camping in the back of his truck said he was grabbed by the monster, which released him only when the victim shoved a bag of chicken in its mouth. Poultry: Don't leave home without it.

Many of these big, hairy creatures seem to have such a propensity for scaring the willies out of young couples making out in lonely spots that they constitute a subgroup, known in the trade as "lover's lane mon-sters." One such is Orange Eyes, an 11-foot-tall orange ape-man with the requisite glowing orbs, a tradition in the Cleveland area dating to at least the 1940s. Those who suspect the legend, and others like it, were concocted by horny teenaged boys trying to scare their dates into snuggling a bit closer are obviously callous cynics and should be ashamed of themselves.

As is the case elsewhere in the world, the ape tales don't stop with Bigfoot-like monsters. There are claims for huge, bloodthirsty baboons (a.k.a. "devil monkeys"), like those said to have killed livestock in Kentucky in 1973, as well as chimplike animals that have been reported from so many places across the South, lower Mississippi basin, and southern Great Plains that cryptozoologists usually lump them together as "Napes," for "North American apes."

The difficulty with cryptozoology is balancing credulity and incredulity—Mothman, no; but the possibility of an undiscovered form of orangutan in Asia, yes. The late astronomer Carl Sagan (who once, for fun, used kinetic theory equations on the movement of atoms to calculate how many monsters might inhabit Loch Ness) spoke to this inevitable tension in his final book, *The Demon-Haunted World*. "[A]t the heart of science is an essential balance between two seemingly contradictory attitudes—an openness to new ideas, no matter how bizarre or counterintuitive, and the most ruthlessly skeptical scrutiny of all ideas, old and new. This is how deep truths are winnowed from deep nonsense. The collective enterprise of creative thinking *and* skeptical thinking, working together, keeps the field on track."

I find myself forever zigzagging across that line, swinging like a pendulum between a desire to embrace a fundamentally weird world that encompasses all manner of oddball beasties and creepy monsters—one that is admittedly a lot more fun than the gray and clinical opposite to which I then lurch when the silliness of it all becomes too much. Sagan's right; neither extreme is healthy, since both are the function of a closed and shuttered mind. The only solution is to mix equal parts healthy skepticism with wide-eyed wonder.

What makes for healthy skepticism? In his book, a biting treatise on pseudo-science and the gullibility of modern society, Sagan lays out what he calls a "baloney detection kit"—useful tools for separating truth from fiction. Among them are independent confirmation of the facts; creation of multiple hypotheses to explain a situation (not just a single pet notion), and then the rigorous testing of all those hypotheses to see which one fits best; quantification wherever possible, so you have some means of discriminating between competing theories; and an avoidance of hypotheses that cannot be falsified—in other words, those that cannot be tested in some way. He also stresses that in a chain of argument, every link must hold up to scrutiny, not just most of them—the failing of many a cryptozoological framework.

A key tool in Sagan's kit is Occam's Razor, the philosophical rule of thumb that says when you have two competing explanations that fit the facts equally well, choose the simpler one. So I ask myself, Which of the following is more likely? That North America is inhabited, for example, by several species of hominids and primates, ranging from violent chimps and huge devil monkeys to smelly ape-men and 20-foot-tall hairy giants, all of which have managed to coexist (in almost every state of the union) with 280 million human beings and yet have avoided leaving any incontrovertible evidence of themselves behind, like a carcass (or that what evidence there is has been covered up as part of a wide-ranging conspiracy)? Or is it more probable that Bigfoot and his ilk are the product of purely human imagination, longing and wishful thinking, spiced with an uncritical acceptance of shaky (sometimes manufactured) evidence?

While skepticism in such matters makes logical sense, it's not very much fun. I can feel the world contracting around me. Come on, I often find myself asking quietly, as I pore through the literature of cryptozoology, throw me a crumb. I want to believe—but I need something plausible to believe *in*, something besides interdimensional vampires and mermaids and plesiosaurs. Give me an animal I can accept, a cryptid that marries legend, place, and biology into a sensible, rational whole, without the kind of special pleadings and suspension of disbelief usually required. Is there anything in the cryptozoo that passes that test?

In fact, there are a few. And I can feel the margins of the world opening up a little, for the spirit of discovery is not yet dead on this old and infinitely surprising planet.

It's worth recalling here that finding an unknown species of plant or animal is not hard. Depending on the estimate, the roughly 1 million species that scientists have named and catalogued may represent only a tenth to a thirtieth of the planet's total biota. But what remains is mostly the small stuff—insects, fungi, spiders, crustaceans, and the like. If you're an entomologist, mycologist, or arachnologist, this is great news, and if you're a myrmecologist—someone who studies ants—well, these days are hog heaven, as long as you're willing to spend time crawling through tropical rain forests. One scientist, working in Madagascar, found more than six hundred new ant species in less than a decade, including one he playfully named the Dracula ant, for the queen's gruesome habit of sucking the blood of her own larvae.

These discoveries are important, both for improving our understanding of the interdependency of the planet's ecological systems and for deepening our wonder at our rich and diverse world. But it's fair to say that most people don't get in a lather when they learn that several new species of bat fleas have been uncovered. It's the small stuff that makes the world work, but big vertebrates grab the headlines.

We've had a fairly complete picture of the world's large, terrestrial mammalian fauna, for example, since before World War I, though new species of rodents, bats, and insectivores continue to be discovered. New bird species keep coming out of the tropics at the rate of a dozen or two a year, but that's small change compared with the nine thousand-plus species already on the books, and most are small, cryptic, or nocturnal; when an undescribed species of antpitta was found in Ecuador a few years ago, it was hailed as one of the largest new birds of the past half-century, even though it was only the size of a quail. The hot discipline for land vertebrates is herpetology, since there are many new species of frogs, toads, lizards, and snakes turning up in Latin America, Asia, and Africa—but none of them, almost by definition, is large.

For big, truly eye-popping revelations, the world's oceans undoubtedly have the most to offer—and to conceal. One would think that something as large as whales, for instance, would all have been catalogued long ago, but the ranks of the beaked whales have expanded several times in just the past decade. This strange group of cetaceans, averaging from 15 to 30 feet in length, tend to inhabit deep water far from shore, which makes studying them—and sometimes just noticing them—difficult.

One species, Longman's (Indo-Pacific) beaked whale, is known only from two weathered skulls picked up on beaches since 1882, and has never been seen in life. The lesser beaked whale was first identified in 1976 from a skull found in a fish market in Peru and not formally described until 1991, while Hubb's beaked whale, described in 1963, is still almost unknown but believed to inhabit deep, cold waters in the Pacific off North America and Japan. The most recent addition to the list is Bahamonde's beaked whale, described in 1996 from a skull found ten years earlier in the Juan Fernández archipelago off Chile. No one knows what it looks like, so it might be the same unidentified beaked whale (known for the moment simply as "*Mesoplodon* species A") seen on about thirty occasions along the Pacific coast of Central and South America; it is a dramatic animal about 18 feet long, with some individuals—presumably adult males—having a wide white band around the middle of the body.

Whales, being air-breathing mammals, must surface regularly—so how much more difficult is it to know what creatures are under the surface, in either open-ocean or deep-water environments where access is difficult? In 1976, a U.S. research vessel off Hawaii hauled in its sea anchor and found a bizarre fish entangled in the cable. It was 15 feet long and weighed nearly a ton, with a sharklike body but a grotesquely enlarged head, like some aberrant tadpole, with a vast maw suited for straining plankton from the water like a swimming seine net. Prolonged study proved that the fish—named megamouth—was, indeed, a shark, though it was so different from known species that it was placed in its own genus and family. In the years since then, only another dozen or so specimens have been found.

If cryptozoology is ever going to hit pay dirt, the jackpot is most likely to be marine. Even inshore waters are largely a mystery, and we know so little of the open ocean that it is the height of hubris to think we've uncovered all the big surprises. In December 2001, scientists announced the discovery of a large and unusual species of squid, with spidery arms stretching 20 feet, that appears to be widespread in the depths of the world's oceans. Nor is it by any means the biggest. Giant squid reach lengths of at least 60 or 70 feet, and scars on sperm whales (which kill and eat the huge cephalopods) suggest they may grow even larger. It's certainly conceivable—perhaps not likely, but conceivable—that one or more large unknown species that fit the old "sea serpent" mold are hiding out there, too, ready to shock and delight us one of these days.

On land, the pickings are much slimmer. The Congo is best known, in cryptozoological circles, as the putative home of Mokele-mbembe, an unknown animal usually described as an elephant-sized, long-necked dinosaur. Mokele-mbembe is said to inhabit the remote Likouala River and swamp, and has been the subject of many a fruitless search, including several expeditions by Roy Mackal. I am not holding my breath for a Congolese sauropod, but central Africa is also the home of another cryptid—and if one can judge the likelihood of discovering an unknown species by the caliber of scientists who look for it, then the Bili ape must rank near the top.

There are, as far as scientists know, four species of great apes in the world—the gorilla (divided into two lowland subspecies and the mountain gorilla); the chimpanzee; the bonobo, or pygmy chimp, which was recognized as a distinct form only in 1929; and the orangutan of Sumatra and Borneo. (Humans are usually accorded their own family, the Hominidae, though we are sometimes folded in with the great apes.)

Cryptozoologists have long held that other, undescribed apes still remain to be found—not necessarily Bigfoot-like giants such as *Gigantopithecus*, but more conventional apes that would nevertheless be revolutionary finds. They often point to reports, never substantiated, of a small bipedal ape in Sumatra, known locally as the orang-pendek, or "short man," which some people think might be a terrestrial relative of the orangutan. Debate has also raged for years over the existence of an extremely large kind of chimpanzee, known as *koolokamba*, from western Africa. Although it is sometimes given official status as a subspecies, molecular biologist Brian T. Shea has argued that the reports were based on local folklore and odd specimens that proved to be either large chimps or small female gorillas, and most scientists consider the subspecies invalid.

But quite apart from *koolokamba*, reports have been coming out of the Bili Forest of the Congo for decades about a weird ape roughly midway in size between a chimpanzee and a lowland gorilla. The descriptions and specimens, including an extraordinarily robust skull found a century ago from a part of eastern Congo where gorillas have never been known to live, were persuasive enough to lure a team of the world's leading primatologists to respond to the invitation of wildlife photographer Karl Amman, who has been hearing about the Bili ape for years.

The expedition entered the Democratic Republic of the Congo (formerly Zaire) in January 2001, dodging rebel armies and battling harsh field conditions. Joining Amman were Harvard animal behaviorist Dr. Richard Wrangham, a protégé of Jane Goodall's who has studied chimps in the wild since the 1970s, and Dr. George Schaller, who in the 1960s was the first scientist to study mountain gorillas and is today one of the world's most respected wildlife biologists. Also taking part were chimp expert Dr. Christophe Boesch of the Max Planck Institute and Dr. Esteban Sarmiento of the American Museum of Natural History. Yet while members of the team found primate beds that looked like gorilla nests, the droppings and tracks they found, and the vocalizations they heard, strongly suggested that the Bili ape is a chimp—perhaps a new form, or perhaps not. The old skull, as well as large ape tracks found more recently, may just have come from unusually large male chimps, since wild animals, like people, exhibit a lot of individual variation.

The Bili expedition also points up a difference between cryptozoology and more traditional branches of research and exploration. Cryptid hunters often start with a pet theory they're seeking to prove—and in this, they aren't much different from scientists of any stripe, who are human and thus may fall prey to tunnel vision that blinds them to other explanations. But because cryptozoology is a field dominated by nonprofessionals, preconceptions and sloppy investigation are rampant. The Bili expedition members, by all reports, approached the question of an unknown ape with open but skeptical minds, and let the evidence, however disappointing, shape their conclusions.

Regardless of the inconclusive result of the Bili ape expedition, cryptid fans are correct when they point out that science is still finding new, undescribed species, some of which were rumored—and dismissed by scientists—for years before their existence was proven. We've come a long way from Georges Cuvier's statement in 1812 that there was "little hope of discovering new species of large quadrupeds." Baron Cuvier was the leading zoologist of his day, but he did not foresee the deluge of nineteenth-century discoveries from Africa, Asia, and Latin America, including the giant panda, Baird's and Indian tapirs, Père David's deer, lowland gorilla, and Przewalski's horse, among hundreds of others.

Henry Morton Stanley, the Anglo-American explorer, wrote in 1860 that Ituri pygmies knew of a strange "donkey" in the rain forests of central Africa, but for nearly forty years its existence was rejected by scientists, because everyone knows that horses live in open grasslands. It wasn't until 1899 that the English governor of Uganda, Sir Harry Johnston, started questioning pygmies about the mystery animal, which they said was "like" a donkey, but with stripes. Johnston assumed they meant one of the striped antelope like bongo or kudu that inhabit the African forests, but in 1900 he obtained the first skin and skulls, and realized the pygmies had been describing an unknown animal related to the giraffe. Now known as the okapi, it is a weird and delightful creature—slim-legged, with a slender but short neck, a long tapered face, and a dark-rust body with white stripes on the legs and hindquarters. It is restricted to the forests of Congo and possibly western Uganda, and more than a century after its discovery by science, we still know precious little about its status or ecology.

Cryptozoologists love the story of the okapi—the ISC even uses it as the organization's symbol—and the similar tale of the mountain gorilla, which was discovered in 1902. The idea that such large mammals could have evaded detection for so long, they say, is a strong argument for the continued existence of other, undescribed species. But the twentieth century was pretty hard on this line of reasoning, and after the spate of spectacular mammals from the rain forests of Africa in the early 1900s, relatively few large, terrestrial species were discovered. The exceptions are interesting, however. In 1937, biologists realized that a calf shipped from Saigon to a Paris zoo wasn't a guar, a fairly common wild cow, but a new species subsequently named the kouprey. The ill-fated young animal starved to death three years later when the German Army overran France, and wild kouprey weren't seen by Western scientists until 1951. (Today, the kouprey is considered one of the most critically endangered mammals in the world, due in large measure to the warfare that has ripped its home for decades.)

Likewise, the Chacoan peccary, a wild pig from the Gran Chaco region of South America weighing 60 to 100 pounds, wasn't recognized by science until 1975, even though fossils of the animal from Pleistocene trash middens had long before been unearthed. What makes the peccary discovery equally unusual is that the pigs live not in deep rain forest, the home of many a newly described species, but in the arid thorn-scrub forests and grasslands of the Chaco, and they are largely active by day. Although native hunters always distinguished the Chaco peccary from the smaller and more widespread white-lipped peccary, its desolate and sparsely inhabited home kept it out of scientific sight long after the rest of South America's larger mammals had been catalogued.

For nearly twenty years, the peccary was the last good-sized land mammal to have been found by scientists, and many experts, like Cuvier a century and a half earlier, considered the book closed—while new species of small mammals, reptiles, amphibians, fishes, and birds would continue to be discovered, everyone assumed the big, spectacular land species were all known. But in the 1990s, that changed in an extraordinary way. War-ravaged Southeast Asia, the same region from which the kouprey had come, at last fell into a state of uneasy quiet, and scientists began trickling into remote areas of Laos, Cambodia, Vietnam, Thailand, and Myanmar (Burma).

In the spring of 1992, a team made up of scientists from the Vietnamese Ministry of Forestry and the World Wide Fund for Nature entered the remote Vu Quang Nature Reserve in the Annamite Mountains between Laos and Vietnam. Thickly forested and relatively untouched by war, the Vu Quang was known to be biologically rich, but the team was still stunned to find, in the homes of hunters living near the reserve, three remarkable skulls—skulls that appeared to belong to an unknown species of bovine, with long, thin, and extremely sharp horns. The hunters called the animal *saola*, meaning "spindlehorns," and said it lived in the forest, feeding on the leaves of fig trees. The following year, the scientists published a description of the "Vu Quang ox," as they initially called it, in the journal *Nature*, based solely on the skulls; it wasn't until 1994 that the first living saola, a calf, was captured. The animal is just as lovely as its horns—dark brown, with white stripes on the face and throat.

But the saola, as shocking a find as it might have been, was only the first in a flood of new species to come from Asia. The 8,000-foot-high Annamite Range also produced a giant muntjac—a species of barking deer the size of a dog—while two other new species of muntjac have subsequently been found elsewhere in the mountains of Vietnam. A warty pig known only from two skulls found in 1892, but never seen in life, was finally located in the Annamites in 1996, while Roosevelt's muntjac, first described in 1929 by one of Teddy Roosevelt's sons but since considered extinct, was rediscovered. Automatic cameras there have also captured the image of an unknown species of rabbit, whose reddish rump is boldly striped in black like war paint. Farther afield, in northern Myanmar, Dr. Alan Rabinowitz of the Wildlife Conservation Society encountered native hunters with what they called "leaf deer," which proved to be the world's smallest species—a deer so tiny (it stands less than 2 feet at the shoulder and weighs barely 25 pounds) that the men wrap the body in a single large leaf to carry it home.

The discoveries seem certain to continue, for scientists know that undescribed species still remain in the deep jungle. For instance, the Cardamom Mountains of western Cambodia are home to a strange ungulate known as the *khiting vor*, or "snake-eating cow," a species whose spiraled horns have been examined by biologists but which has never been seen alive by a Westerner. Everything known about it comes from indigenous hunters, and it's hard to separate fact from folklore; for example, the tribesmen say the fur has a peculiar oiliness that comes off on their hands when they stroke the pelt. The *khiting vor* is described as dark reddish-brown, taller but more gracile in its build than the banteng, another wild Asian ox, and is said to be able to leap over a man—which would make it a very unusual cow indeed. Surveys of hunters across Cambodia suggest that it has disappeared from many areas where it was found through the 1960s and 1970s, and there is even a chance that this strange forest ox may already be extinct.

While all these newly revealed species certainly bolster the cryptozoological argument that the world still holds many mysteries, they also point up one of its greatest weaknesses—the fact that, while new species of animals continue to be found, none have been associated with the kind of long-standing legends toward which most of cryptozoology's efforts have been directed. No one has come up with a giant eel in Loch Ness, or a large, undescribed ape in the Pacific Northwest or Asia, or a proto-whale off Vancouver Island. As beautiful as the saola may be, or as intriguing as the *khiting vor* are, they aren't the kind of radically unexpected beasts that would be required to fill the shoes of most cryptids.

Take, as a final example, the legend of the mapinguari, one of the many hairy hominids the world supposedly holds. Traveling in the western Amazon over the years, I've heard many campfire stories of this monster, said to be taller than a person, covered with long reddish-brown fur, its hands wickedly clawed and its feet turned backward so hunters who follow it go the wrong way. It roars like an approaching storm, its odor (which comes from a "second mouth" on the stomach) is so strong and foul that a whiff renders a man unable to think clearly, and the creature is always surrounded by a swarm of insects. You can't kill it; arrows and bullets just bounce off its hide. The mapinguari is the protector of the forest, and rubber-tappers and Indians believe that the mapinguari attacks those who wastefully kill wild animals, twisting off the offender's head with a quick snap. The first time I heard that—knowing how beset the Amazon basin is by ravenous, destructive outsiders—I couldn't help but think that the monster needed some backup.

David C. Oren isn't so sure that the mapinguari is a myth, though. Dr. Oren, a graduate of Yale and Harvard who has worked for more than a quarter-century in the Amazon, is a respected ornithologist, and now heads the zoology department of the Emilio Goeldi Museum in Brazil. When he first came to the Amazon, he also dismissed the mapinguari as an entertaining bit of local color, simply the Brazilian version of the ubiquitous "hairy man" stories found in almost every corner of the world. But with time, he was struck by how consistent the descriptions were, even over long distances of jungle, and between groups of people with no direct contact with each other. What's more, Oren felt there was a logical explanation for the monster—a real animal that almost perfectly fit the description that Indians and others gave. There was only one problem: that animal is thought to have died out more than 8,000 years ago.

It was the giant ground sloth, a very different beast from the small tree sloths found today in the rain forests of Latin America. Some species, like *Megatherium* of South America, were nearly 20 feet long and weighed several tons, though other species were smaller. All were heavily built, with powerful front legs tipped with curving claws—used not to attack other animals but to rip down small trees, for the sloths were herbivores. They often stood on their hind legs to feed, and like their distant cousin, the giant anteater, the backward-facing claws on a ground sloth's front feet would have left tracks that looked as though its feet were attached the wrong way. As for the mapinguari's impenetrable hide, even that has a parallel with the extinct sloth *Mylodon*, which is known to have had "dermal ossicles," heavily calcified nodules embedded in the skin for protection.

Oren wasn't the first to wonder if ground sloths had survived to modern times. Thomas Jefferson hoped Western exploration would reveal sloths and other Pleistocene animals, and while Lewis and Clark failed to find any, explorers in South America in the late nineteenth century thought they'd stumbled on undeniable evidence—ground sloth dung and even pieces of its skin, complete with reddish-brown fur (just like the mapinguari's) and dermal ossicles, which were found in a cave in Argentina in 1888. One explorer, Ramon Lista, even claimed to have seen and shot at an unknown animal that matched a crude description of a ground sloth, and when the flap of skin turned up, the sloth species from which it came was named *Neomylodon listai* ("Lista's new Mylodon") in his honor. In the 1950s, Bernard Heuvelmans published a seminal book on cryptozoology, and wrote that the ground sloth was one of the more likely lost species to be found. It was only later that scientists realized the cold, arid climate of Patagonia preserves all sorts of biological material for ages; the skin was carbon-dated, and the hide was found to be roughly 13,500 years old and is now believed to have come from one of the extinct *Mylodon* sloths.

Despite the disappointing results of the carbon-14 tests, Heuvelmans's book whetted Oren's appetite for the mapinguari legends he was encountering in the field. The area of western Amazonia where the stories are most prevalent is both the least-explored part of the region and an area where fossils of eight genera of ground sloths have been found. Even some of the unlikeliest parts of the legend make sense from a biological perspective, Oren believes. The odor described as coming from a "second mouth" could be a powerful scent gland on the abdomen, he argues, while the cloud of insects that are said to follow mapinguari might be dung beetles, eager to lay their eggs in the large, round sloth droppings. Although he is criticized by some paleontologists (and even by some of his ornithological colleagues, who admire his bird work but shake their heads over the mapinguari obsession), Oren has mounted half a dozen expeditions to look for the monster, mimicking the cry that dozens of eyewitnesses have described to him, trying to elicit a response. Along the way, he has collected suggestive plaster track casts, videotape of trees that appeared to have been ripped by claws, and even hair and large bags of feces that he was convinced were those of a ground sloth. In this, though, he was disappointed—the hair was from an agouti, and the biochemical traces found by a DNA test of the feces were those of giant anteaters. (In the spring of 2001, a Cincinnati-based geneticist and amateur Bigfoot hunter on an expedition to Brazil announced he'd found sloth feces, and said that tests showed a match with DNA taken from an ancient sloth tooth—but his findings have been published only on the Internet, and the scientific community isn't exactly waiting with bated breath for more formal publication.)

There is one other explanation for the close match between the legends of the mapinguari and the Pleistocene ground sloth. The legends could, in fact, be based on the sloths, yet have their roots not in contemporary sightings but in an oral tradition that dates back eight or nine millennia, to a time when Indians and sloths shared the post–ice age environment. Stories have a remarkable tenacity in pre-literate cultures, and an animal like *Megatherium* or *Mylodon* would make a powerful impression on anyone. Here in North America, some Northeastern Indian tribes preserve stories of "stone giants," great gray monsters that preyed upon people and couldn't be killed with spears or arrows—stories that may harken to the days, 12,000 years ago, when Paleo-Indians had to dodge the huge and undoubtedly dangerous short-faced bear, a behemoth considerably larger than a modern grizzly.

I'll admit, ascribing mapinguari to the tribal memory of Amazonian Indians doesn't have the same sizzle as thinking that there might still be living sloths, walking on their backward feet, in the forests of Brazil or Peru. But there is a power to the tale, regardless of its origins. Sitting around a flickering oil lamp in a thatched Indian village, hearing an old man talk about the screaming monster while the frogs croaked and night monkeys called, I felt the tickle of gooseflesh. The ice age was the crowning moment for mammals, when some of the biggest, most ferocious, most magnificent species roamed the world.

I'm not alone in my craving to touch that time. In Europe between the wars, several men decided to take their obsession with the great megafauna of the Pleistocene and do something no one had ever tried—actually to re-create two species that profoundly changed the course of human civilization.

SEVEN

The Brothers and the Bull

The valley of the Ardèche River, in the south of France, is dry limestone country: rocky gray hillsides studded with junipers and olives, and seared with Mediterranean sunshine. Chestnut trees, some of them a thousand years old, droop heavily with their prized nuts outside villages of pale stone and orange roof tiles, alongside Roman-era ruins.

But there is another Ardèche, one hidden literally under the surface. The limestone dissolves easily beneath the slightly acidic nibble of rainwater percolating down through the bedrock and creating networks of caves in the rugged hills and gorges. Hundreds have been discovered, from narrow, corkscrew channels barely wide enough to admit a slim person, to immense grottos full of sparkling stalactites. The trick is finding an opening, since most caves are all but sealed off from the outside world, often with just the tiniest chink in the rocks to hint at the wonders belowground. But when the last rubble is cleared from a sinkhole, and a cave explorer gets the first breath of damp, chilly air from deep belowground—that, spelunkers say, is the moment that drives them.

For three Ardèche residents, seeking out new caverns is an obsession. Over the years, the trio—experienced speleologist Jean-Marie Chauvet, winemaker and amateur archaeologist Éliette Brunel Deschamps, and cave explorer Christian Hillaire—have become remarkably adept at combing the Ardèche for hidden entrances. They have developed a highly methodical approach, checking every ledge and cliff, poking into every crevice and indentation in the rock face, even those scoured in the past by other cavers. As they work, they do not look for black, gaping holes—those entrances would have been discovered long before by others—but instead they are aware of the slightest breath of moving air, which may indicate a hidden channel that was closed off eons ago by a rockfall or landslide. They may use a smoldering smoke coil, or just the sensitive skin on the backs of their hands or faces, and with time, they have honed what they call a "sense of drafts," an almost uncanny instinct that tells them where an unknown cave may be lurking.

They discovered countless caves and sinkholes, many of them with the rich, flowing limestone formations that cavers love, but most barren of any sign of human habitation. In 1990, however, the trio discovered a fox burrow from which a strong draft was blowing; carefully opening it, they found a narrow tunnel that led to the roof of a large cavern, accessible only down a hundred-foot shaft. Inside were the perfectly preserved remains of campsites and hearths dating back to the Copper Age, nearly 4,000 years ago. (The original opening to the cave had since closed.) Experienced amateur archaeologists, they take exquisite care at such sites, preserving them intact for later study.

Chauvet and his colleagues also uncovered several so-called decorated caves, those with the distinctive rock-wall art of the Pleistocene— nothing like the extravagantly painted halls of Lascaux or Altamira in northern France and Spain, but important finds nevertheless. The best was Grotte aux Points, where the walls were polka-dotted with clusters of large red ocher spots, as well as sketchy depictions of animals; they found the cave in 1993, the same year Chauvet was appointed custodian of the decorated Ardèche caves.

He, Deschamps, and Hillaire continued searching for more. One chilly Sunday afternoon, a week before Christmas in 1994, they were exploring a series of sheepfolds near the entrance to the Ardèche gorges. Near the back of a shallow depression in the cliff, they felt the tiniest of drafts and began clearing away the rocks that blocked it. The soil around the opening was dry; they thought it would prove to be a dead end rather than a connection to a deep, moisture-filled cavern, but they kept digging. Eventually they cleared enough of a passageway for Deschamps to wriggle in headfirst, far enough to see a yawning drop below her that opened into a chamber. Fetching a ladder from their van, they climbed down, finding themselves in a vast room. Walking in careful single file, placing their stockinged feet exactly in the footprints of the leader to avoid disturbing more than was necessary, they moved ahead.

> It was at this moment that we discovered multitudes of bear bones and teeth strewn over the floor, which was calcified here and there . . . All around us were dozens of depressions dug into the earth, as if the ground had been bombed. We recognized them as the "nests" in which bears must have hibernated.

Soon they encountered the first signs of rock art—lines of red ocher on the wall and the simple drawing of a mammoth. Moving farther into the cave, they saw larger and increasingly elaborate paintings—a woolly rhinoceros, a cave bear, another mammoth, a trio of cave-lion heads, stenciled hand outlines, in all a frieze more than 30 feet long.

> During those moments there were only shouts and exclamations; the emotion that gripped us made us incapable of uttering a single word. Alone in that vastness, lit by the feeble beams of our lamps, we were seized by a strange feeling. Everything was so beautiful, so fresh, almost too much so. Time was abolished, as if the tens of thousands of years that separated us from the producers of these paintings no longer existed. It seemed as if they had just created these masterpieces. Suddenly we felt like intruders. Deeply impressed, we were weighted down by the feeling that we were not alone; the artists' souls and spirits surrounded us. We thought we could feel their presence; we were disturbing them.

The Chauvet Cave, as it is now known, proved to be one of the greatest treasuries of Paleolithic art ever found. In the years that followed, the team and other archaeologists found hundreds of paintings and engravings on its walls, depicting an incredible range of ice age fauna, from lumbering cave bears to graceful reindeer. What's more, carbon dating showed them to be 35,000 years old, twice the age of the more famous art in Lascaux. The Chauvet paintings are a window on the birth of human artistry.

When the Chauvet art was created, the Ardèche was a very different place. Glaciers capped northern Europe, swallowing Britain and northern Germany in sheets of ice, while other glaciers chewed down out of the Alps and Pyrenees. South of the glacial front lay expanses of frigid, windswept tundra, though below that, near the shores of the Mediterranean, the climate was tempered enough by the sea to support thick forests. In those forests and meadows lived an array of mammals, spellbinding in their size and diversity, which provided sustenance and inspiration to the early Cro-Magnon hunters.

As someone who is thrilled by large and dangerous wildlife, I've always been drawn to the ice age mammals; if I had just one shot at a time machine, I wouldn't hesitate to set the dial for about twenty thousand years in the past. The ice ages provide a bewitching mix of the familiar and the bizarre—the tundra steppes of North America, during the last glaciation, had such recognizable species as moose and musk oxen, badgers and gray wolves, but also such strange animals as shrub-oxen, with curled horns like a bighorn sheep's, or saber-toothed cats, giant American lions, several species of American cheetahs, and giant ground sloths. There were mammoths and mastodons—and to prey upon them, the immense short-faced bear, a long-limbed, bulldog-faced terror that appears to have evolved to grab elephants by the throat. For a naturalist, what's not to love?

The cast of characters was much different in Europe, where the same recent expansion of ice is known as the Weichselian, or Würm, glaciation. There were mammoths but no mastodons, woolly rhinoceroses but no ground sloths. The huge bear of Pleistocene Europe was the cave bear, *Ursus spelaeus*, a 1,000-pound herbivore and scavenger. There were maneless cave lions, hyenas, leopards, bison, ibex, and reindeer, as well as the giant deer, or Irish elk, doubtless the most impressive ungulate to ever live—a magnificent beast that stood 7 or 8 feet at the shoulder, as big as a moose but built like a robust elk, with palmate antlers weighing 90 pounds that spanned more than 11 feet. We know all these creatures, most now extinct, from the dull bones excavated by paleontologists—but we also know them in all their stunning vitality, thanks to cave art like that in Chauvet. Whatever their motivation, the people who lived in intimate association with the great mammals left us a record that is at once moving and meticulous, blending a surprisingly mature artistic vi-

sion with the sort of detailed behavioral and physical information paleontologists crave but rarely find.

Among the most gripping of the cave-painted animals was the aurochs—the wild bull of Eurasia. Aurochsen (the plural of the German
name) rampage famously across the Great Hall of Lascaux Cave, limbs
flailing, wide horns curved and unmistakably deadly; in Chauvet, they
crowd the edge of one panel, shown in sparse gesture drawings that convey the frenzy of a charging herd, heads and horns tossing. This was no
tame ox but a solid wall of muscle and indomitable spirit; the bulls stood
almost 6 feet at the shoulder and weighed more than a ton, with massive
forequarters, a brawny neck, and trim hindquarters—a combination
that speaks equally of speed and power.

The absence of fossil aurochsen in Europe and Africa from the early
stages of the ice age suggests that the species evolved in Asia, spreading
west and south in the interglacials, the warm spells between expansions
of glacial ice. By the Weichselian glaciation, the animal had split into
three subspecies: *Bos primigenius primigenius* in Europe, *B.p. opisthonomus*
(or *africanus*) in northern Africa, and *B.p. namadicus* in Asia. We know,
thanks to the careful and consistent renditions of ancient artists, that the
aurochs of Africa was reddish, while the European bull was dark brown,
becoming coal-black with age, with white around the muzzle and in a
stripe down the spine, while the cow was somewhat rustier in color and
the calf brown. But there was also quite a bit of variation, with some individuals showing a lighter saddle on the back or a white body speckled
with black; these last, some scholars believe, were odd or albinistic individuals, revered in much the same way that Plains Indians honor the rare
white bison. (The colors of the Asian beast are a mystery, absent any surviving Paleolithic depictions.)

The close of the ice age 12,000 years ago meant doom for many of
the megafauna. Mammoths disappeared everywhere but on Wrangel Island in Siberia, where they hung on until 4,000 years ago; Irish elk
made a final stand in the boggy lands of the British Isles, but became extinct 9,200 years ago. Cave bears, cave lions, woolly rhinos, all lost out
to climate and habitat change, and perhaps to growing predation by humans. The Asian and African races of aurochs died out 2,000 years ago,
too—but in the deep, cold forests of Europe, the bull survived.

Julius Caesar knew the wild aurochs as *urus*, which he hunted during his campaigns in Gaul in the first century B.C. Of it he wrote (with some hyperbole): "In size they are a trifle smaller than elephants; in kind, color and shape they are bulls. Great is their strength and great is their speed" (*magna vis et magna velocitas*). Caesar was also struck by the aurochs's unquenchable wild spirit. "It is not possible to accustom the Uri to men or to tame them, not even though they be caught young."

But in this, however, the general was wrong; it *was* possible to tame the mighty aurochs, and for evidence (had he but known) Caesar need have looked no farther than the placid, castrated oxen pulling his wagons—for all modern cattle are the domesticated progeny of the great ice age bull.

The domestication of wild animals and plants marks one of the great pivot points in the development of modern culture. The earliest domesticate was the dog, which developed from wolves (as far as anyone can tell) about 10,000 to 12,000 years ago in the Near East around Iraq, with other possible domestication sites in North America and China. Sheep, pigs, and goats were tamed about 8,000 years ago, horses and water buffalo around 4,000 years ago. Wheat, peas, and other plant crops were being cultivated by 8500 B.C., making the formation of settlements, and eventually city life, possible. So profound was the effect of domestication of plants and animals on human society that it is referred to as the Neolithic Revolution.

Cattle were among the last animals to be domesticated in the Old World, and given the explosive quality of the aurochsen portraits in cave art, which carries potently across thirty-five millennia, and Caesar's awestruck description, it's easy to understand why: who, in his right mind, would try to harness an elemental power of nature? Yet someone—brave, persistent, foolhardy, or visionary—did.

"It is rather difficult to imagine how or why the change from hunting of wild cattle to husbanding of tame ones began," wrote Juliet Clutton-Brock, now retired from the Natural History Museum in London but still one of the world authorities on the history of domestication.

A large bovid, standing at least 1.5 m at the shoulder, would not make an easy captive, nor would the animal be easy to restrain unless it wished to remain close to human habitation. Again, it is difficult to surmise what the humans could use the captive bovids for in the early stages of domestication. It is very unlikely that a tamed aurochs cow would allow herself to be milked, because considerable effort and guile has to be put into persuading a cow of an unimproved breed to let down her milk . . . Perhaps the earliest taming of cattle occurred by the encouragement of free-ranging animals to remain near a human settlement. This could be done by keeping supplies of salt and water available at fixed places with which the animals could become familiar.

Why go to such trouble? Clutton-Brock points to the mithan, the domestic form of the guar, a wild ox of India. To this day they are lured from the Assam Hills with offerings of salt; they are never eaten or milked but are objects of sacrifice and worship. Perhaps, she wonders, it was the same with the aurochs.

We are not sure why the Cro-Magnon hunters of Chauvet painted aurochsen and other large mammals in the deepest, least accessible caves; hunting magic, fertility rites, and a host of other explanations have been suggested. But there is no question that these great beasts, the aurochs in particular, led humanity on its first, unsteady steps to worship and veneration. Nor is there any question that the wild bull was a deity to many later cultures. At Çatal Hüyük in Turkey, one of the oldest towns ever uncovered, bull worship was firmly established nearly 8,500 years ago—houses contained shrines made of rows of aurochs horns and small effigies of the wild bulls, which may by that time have been brought into at least partial domestication. Bull worship, often associated with fertility gods, was a common theme in early Mediterranean religion—the sacred Apis bulls of Egypt that embodied that god's earthly form, the bull cults of the island cultures on Sardinia, Crete, and Cyprus.

Crete took the cult of the bull to perhaps its highest level. The ruler of Knossos was considered to be the descendant of a sacred bull, and one of the central acts of devotion was the famous "bull-jumping" spectacle, in which young athletes vaulted between the horns and over the backs of the charging animals. It seems that by this time, the aurochs had become domesticated—many of the murals in Knossos show bulls with spotted or piebald coats, the hallmark of a domestic beast, and it seems likely that cattle were brought to the island by Neolithic farmers, rather than tamed on the spot. But their size, speed, and evident ferocity—at least of those used for bull-jumping—remained obviously undiminished. Those used in the rite may, in fact, have been feral; golden cups from the same period show a cow being used to lure a bull from the forest, which is then roped by a man.

The process of domestication has a series of predictable effects on a once-wild species. The size of the brain shrinks, horns take on weird and unusual shapes, and the skull and jaws shorten, often assuming a juvenile or even, in extreme cases, a fetal appearance. One of the most dramatic changes is a reduction in overall size from wild progenitor to domesticate. Why this should be so has been the subject of much scholarly debate over the years. Biologists and archaeozoologists traditionally believed that it was the result of selective breeding by humans—choosing the smaller, and thus more manageable, individuals for mating. In the case of large, potentially dangerous animals like the aurochs, this makes a lot of sense—but size reduction cuts across the board in almost all domestic mammals, from cattle and swine to dogs, goats, sheep, even guinea pigs. (There are obviously some breeds that are larger than their wild ancestors, but averaged across all forms, smaller is the rule.)

What's more, selective breeding seems a poor explanation for the other, equally consistent changes in domesticated pets and livestock. Scholars tried to explain the retention of juvenile characteristics as the innate appeal of a "babylike" appearance, thus affecting which individuals were chosen for breeding; likewise, the near-universality of white, piebald, or unicolored markings (unlike the countershaded pelage common in wild animals) was put down to simple aesthetics. Not everyone was convinced. A Canadian archaeozoologist named Susan J. Crockford, who has studied the domestication of dogs, has proposed a novel hypothesis—that domestication itself alters levels of thyroid hormone, which is critical to an animal's reaction to stress. Those best able to handle the stress of being around humans, thanks to their level of thyroid hormone, would be the ones that would breed most successfully and thus pass on both hormonal and behavioral traits to their offspring in a self-reinforcing cycle. Thyroid hormone, Crockford points out, controls a whole host of developmental characteristics as well—and they, in turn, produce precisely the sort of physical changes in size, shape, and color seen in domestic animals. For proof, she points to an unintentional experiment conducted at Siberian fur farms in the 1950s, when captive Arctic foxes were selectively bred for their ease around people—a trait controlled by thyroid hormones. Within just twenty generations their descendants had developed drooping ears, piebald coats, and the other typical attributes of domestic canines.

By whatever avenue—deliberate breeding, hormonal accidents, or a combination of the two—domestic cattle soon scarcely resembled wild aurochsen. Hundreds of breeds arose in Europe, Asia, and Africa, of two main types—the humpless taurine cattle of Europe and the zebu cattle of Asia, marked by a pronounced shoulder hump and a fleshy dewlap beneath the throat. It was once thought that taurine cattle were the original domesticates and that zebus arose from taurine stock at a later date. DNA studies, however, now strongly suggest that cattle were domesticated at least twice—taurines rising from the European subspecies of aurochs, *B.p. primigenius*, in the Fertile Crescent 8,000 years ago, and zebus from the Asian race, *B.p. namadicus*, about 7,000 years ago, perhaps in the Baluchistan region of Pakistan. (There is some shaky evidence that African cattle may bear the lineage of the African aurochs, though this is unclear; some genetic studies indicate African breeds arose from taurine stock but got their zebu-like appearance from an infusion of Asian blood, likely from travelers bringing zebu bulls west with them.)

By Neolithic times, the farmers of Europe had even created strains of dwarf cattle, barely half the height of their progenitors and infinitely easier to herd, castrate, and butcher. Humans, well-fed and fecund with the products of their agricultural revolution, began converting the great forests of Europe into farmsteads, a process that gained momentum through the Middle Ages. And what of the wild aurochs? Deity of the Pleistocene, majestic *urus* of the Romans, it could only retreat to the shadows as its dull-witted progeny, harnessed to wagon and plow, helped their masters shred the wild landscape on which the last of the ice age bulls depended.

There is little historical information by which we can plot the decline and disappearance of aurochsen across western and central Europe.

It seems to have been a fairly swift demise, for by the thirteenth century they were a memory on most of the continent, and reasonably widespread only in and around Poland. By the fifteenth and sixteenth centuries they were rare even there, restricted to the great Jaktorów forest near Warsaw, along with the wisent, or European bison. That the aurochs survived so much longer in Poland than in the rest of Europe may have been due to the large expanses of virgin forest, but some modern historians, like Dr. Mieczyslaw Rokosz at Jagiellonian University in Kraków, are inclined to credit Polish monarchs, who through the centuries jealously guarded their absolute right to hunt the great bulls—an effective, if unintentional, form of conservation.

But even that wasn't enough. In 1564, a royal inspection of the Jaktorów forest turned up a herd of thirty aurochs cows, calves, and young bulls; the inspectors did not see any mature bulls, but accepted the word of local foresters that there were eight left. The government party also noted that the aurochsen looked pretty scrawny and were told that villagers were pasturing their livestock on grassy meadows that were supposed to be for the use of the aurochs. (Thirty years later, another document notes that trespassing stock were seized and their owners ordered to appear in court.)

By 1602, there were only three males and a single cow remaining, the survivors of a disease that had spread from domestic herds and had all but wiped out the aurochsen. The species shrank further, to a single female by 1620, and the horns of one of the last males were sent to the king, as was the custom. The solitary cow lingered until 1627, dying not from a poacher, as legend often claims, but a natural death, according to the report of a royal inspector who noted the event three years after the fact.

The aurochs was extinct; there is no question about that. But among its descendants, those hundreds and hundreds of breeds of cattle, were a few that seemed to have more than a hint of the old forest bull's character—the big Italian draft breed known as the Chianina, which dates back to ancient Rome, the fierce fighting bulls of the Iberian peninsula, or the shaggy Highland cattle of Scotland. In many cases, though, no one knows how old any given breed may be, since records were rarely kept before the eighteenth or nineteenth centuries. One exception are the white park cattle of England, including those at Chillingham, which are descended from wild cattle "emparked" in 1220, when a wall was built around several hundred acres of forest, trapping the herd, which has lived in a fenced but semi-wild state ever since. Though smaller than an aurochs, with smaller horns, park cattle look and act much like the original wild ox; the herd has a single dominant bull, known as a king, which mates with all the available cows. The origin of the animals from which the herd grew is unclear. While those originally captured were probably just feral domestic cattle, some people contend they were among the last British aurochsen.

Everyone knows a farmer can manipulate the breeding of his stock to produce desired traits, like short horns, abundant milk, or, in the case of a belted Galloway cow, a black-and-white pattern that makes the animal look like a giant Oreo cookie. But what if a breeder tried, in essence, to take livestock the *other* way—to breed the most seemingly primitive types, choosing from each generation only those animals that reinforce the ancient form, with the goal of creating an animal that embodies many of the characteristics of its wild ancestor? Would it be possible— and if it succeeded, what, exactly, would you have? As far back as the early nineteenth century, at least one naturalist in Poland suggested putting primitive cattle into wild forests and seeing what would happen—but a directed breeding project might produce results in much less time.

Such a process is known as "backcrossing," "topcrossing," or "breeding back," and it usually involves mating a hybrid offspring with one of its parents, or an animal of the same type as its parents. In ordinary circumstances, it can cement certain traits in the bloodline or introduce desirable new genes, and it works equally well for plants.

This is an ancient technique of animal husbandry, and so it's not surprising that people had long talked about trying to backcross cattle to see if they could come up with something that resembled an aurochs. The experiment, however, would require years and years of patient effort, more, apparently, than most people were willing to tackle—until the Heck brothers came along.

Lutz and Heinz Heck were born in the early 1890s in Berlin, the sons of Ludwig Heck, the director of the Berlin Zoo. Animals were in

their blood from an early age; both boys studied zoology and animal be-
havior at the university, and then entered their father's profession—
Lutz, the elder by two years, becoming first the assistant director of the
Berlin Zoo and in 1931 (on his father's retirement) its director, while
Heinz took the reins of Tierpark Hellabrunn, the Munich zoo.

The brothers pursued somewhat similar courses at both their respective institutions, abandoning the then-prevalent notion of sticking one
or two specimens of each species in a sterile cage and replacing that approach with more naturalistic enclosures that mimicked the species'
native environment. Heinz in particular was starting from scratch, the
Hellabrunn zoo having been run into the ground financially before his
arrival; on this shaky foundation he created what he called a "geo-zoo,"
exhibiting animals based on global regions, with species from the same
area exhibited together in large, outdoor settings. This strategy paid off
quickly. Hellabrunn enjoyed a remarkable degree of success, for its
time, in breeding exotic animals, including great apes and the first
African elephant ever born in captivity—this last a feat few modern
zoos can claim, even today.

Lutz and Heinz shared a particular interest in large herbivores, especially (in part because they were enthusiastic hunters) the big-game
species of Europe like the wisent, or European bison. But their interest
stretched back further; both men had a passion for the aurochs, and as
the directors of large and thriving zoos, they were for the first time in a
position to implement the kind of backcross experiments that others
had only talked about. In 1921, Heinz decided to try.

"No animal . . . is entirely exterminated as long as some of its hered-
itary factors remain," he wrote.

> The fact that these qualities may not be visible is shown by the
> laws of heredity to be unimportant, for what is hidden may be
> brought to light again and, by cross-breeding, the original com-
> ponent parts may again be isolated. In the case of the Aurochs
> conditions are favourable since all its physical characteristics are
> still present and to be seen. They are, of course, divided between
> many different breeds of cattle, one having preserved a good au-
> rochs horn, another its build, while a third has the characteristic
> coloring, and so on.

Not everyone was so certain. When the Hecks outlined their plan to a noted expert on livestock breeding, he told them, "Of course you can breed back the aurochs, but it has taken more than six thousand years to breed our present-day cattle from it, and it will take you just as long to breed back to them. If that is what you propose to do, I quite agree that your plan is sound!"

Working, he admitted, "in a way that would have horrified a pedigree breeder," Heinz picked stock that showed the various qualities he was hoping to reunite. For size and immense horns, he chose Hungarian and Podolian steppe (or gray) cattle, brawny draft breeds that are among the largest cattle in Europe. These, along with Scottish Highland cattle, were mated with brown-and-gray Alpines, Corsicans, and even Holstein-like Fresians, a dairy breed from the Netherlands.

His brother Lutz, beginning a few years later in Berlin, took a different tack, focusing largely on the cattle of southwest Europe. He later recalled that the idea of backcrossing an aurochs hit him while looking for wild sheep on the island of Corsica, also home to a feral and primitive breed of cattle.

> We climbed up into the haunts of the wild mouflon, and there, in the valley of a rivulet, I saw standing by some bushes a reddish-brown ox. I cannot describe the regular shock it gave me to see that animal in its environment: that was my aurochs! . . . It occurred to me at once that that must make it possible to re-breed the aurochs. I bought three calves, one of them a bull calf that later became the ancestor of all the primeval bulls bred and used for breeding. The main contribution these Corsican cattle made to the breeding was the colour and form of the hair of the aurochs.

Over the course of a year, Lutz traveled to the Carmague in the south of France, where he purchased five of the black cattle that run wild there, and to Spain, where after much wrangling he acquired Spanish fighting bulls, which he felt captured the spirit of the aurochs; later he added white English park cattle like those from Chillingham.

Although the aurochs had, by then, been extinct for three centuries, the Hecks felt they had a good sense of their target animal. They were guided by fossil remains, cave paintings, and at least one contemporary rendition—done from life—of the last wild specimen; it was found by a biologist in the 1820s in a shop in Augsburg, and while the original was subsequently lost, reproductions had been made. Based on all these sources, the Hecks concluded that an aurochs had longer legs and horns than modern cattle, and was even larger than the biggest steppe bull. Males were black with a yellowish-white stripe running down the back, while cows were reddish and calves were brown; the summer coat was short and glossy, the winter pelage shaggy, and there was a curl of hair, often white, between the horns.

Heinz Heck was prepared for a long, tedious breeding process, but he was stunned by how soon his backcrossing showed results. "Success came incredibly quickly: by the spring of 1932 the first good specimens of the Aurochs of modern times, one of each sex, were born of this mixed breeding. Concentrated in them were the desired characteristics that in their grandparents' and great-grandparents' generations had been divided between so many breeds. It was like a miracle. The first Aurochs for 300 years could be seen alive." To his even greater surprise, the newly reconstituted aurochsen bred true to type. "I expected piebalds and all kinds of curious beasts to succeed them," he wrote in 1951. "But up to this day—and a great number of calves have been born—this has not happened, and there has not been one throw-back to any of the domestic breeds used. The calves are all as alike as slices of bread from one loaf." Like the ancient aurochs, calves of either sex were born brown and took on their distinctive sexual coloring as they aged.

Yet the Hecks' near-aurochs (as they were often called) differed from the ancestral cattle in significant ways, particularly their overall size and the size and shape of their horns, both of which were noticeably smaller in the modern version than in the ice age fossils that have been unearthed. Heinz's animals tended to be a bit heavier in the body than a true aurochs, and the bulls often grew a dewlap, a fleshy flap beneath the throat.

Probably because he started with breeds that were closer in appearance to the original aurochsen, Lutz Heck in Berlin got results in an even shorter time than Heinz, and in certain ways, his animals more closely resembled the aurochs of ancient cave paintings, lithe in the hindquarters like a fighting bull, with sweeping horns. But both strains shared a common resistance to deadly livestock diseases—when epidemics of foot-and-mouth and rheumatic fever decimated the domestic cattle at Munich's zoo, the new aurochsen seemed slightly ill for three days, then shook off the ailments completely, to Heinz Heck's shock.

Among the Hecks' criteria for a new aurochs was a return of the wild spirit they imagined the original had possessed, and in this they also felt they succeeded. The beasts had a peppery temperament, quick to attack with little or no provocation, and Heinz said that the cows were "positively dangerous" when they had calves. When given their freedom (as some eventually were in Poland during the war), they developed a wariness around people said to exceed that of wild red deer. While aggression is not uncommon in feral cattle of any sort, there is something especially imposing about such an attitude in one of these beasts. There's a photograph by Lutz from those days, showing a bull charging across its enclosure at the Berlin Zoo, dust exploding from beneath its hooves, while a young man in suspenders and lederhosen ducks behind a tree for cover.

Given the fact that both Hecks started with different breed mixtures but ended up with remarkably similar results, it might seem logical to suppose that all domestic animals carry, within the varied breeds that comprise each species, a genetic template for their wild ancestor. And yet, if you take a diverse mix of dogs—for instance, Chihuahuas, sheepdogs, collies, Labs, poodles, Pyrenees, elkhounds, whatever you like— and allow them to breed in a random, undirected fashion, after a time you do not end up with a pseudo-wolf. Don't take my word for it; all over the world, people have conducted this experiment over and over again without meaning to, simply by letting their dogs run loose. While you don't get a wolf, you do get a pretty standard-issue creature, whether it's in the slums of Lagos or the suburban fringe of an American city—a short-haired, ginger-yellow canine with upright ears and a curled fishhook tail, the sort known as a pariah dog in parts of the Old World. Many ancient breeds, including dingoes in Australia, New Guinea singing dogs, and African basenjis, also fit this model. To some biologists, this suggests that canine bloodlines have been muddled and tampered with for so long that the distance to wolves is simply too great to bridge. (To others, however, it is evidence that dogs arose not from northern gray wolf stock at all, as is commonly believed, but from the nearly extinct Simien jackal of northern Africa, which looks a fair bit like a pariah dog.)

But while the cattle that the Hecks created bred true to type, they were the result of a specific, highly directional breeding program, no different in that regard than black Angus or any other modern type of livestock, and their appearance was a careful construct due to rigorous artificial selection, not a relaxation to some genetically archetypal form. What the Hecks created was a facsimile, not an aurochs; that beast died a lonely death in 1627, and nothing anyone can do changes that fact a tiddle. When you go to your family reunion, maiden aunts may tell you you're the spitting image of your grandfather or grandmother, but at best it is a family resemblance—a long face, a quirky nose, small ears, or even, God forbid, a Hapsburg lip that keeps bubbling up through the generations. You are your own genetic stewpot, representing bloodlines not of your grandparents' making. Likewise with the neo-aurochs. Yes, it looks a good bit like *Bos primigenius*, and that in itself is an interesting accomplishment, but these were not aurochsen. From the beginning, zoologists drew a fine distinction, referring to the beasts as "reconstituted" aurochs, near- or neo-aurochs, or, perhaps most accurately, Heck's cattle. Heinz Heck might have called his animals "the first Aurochs for 300 years," but his colleagues generally saw that as forgivable hyperbole.

Not everyone is so generous. Seventy years after the first neo-aurochs calf was born, the Hecks and their reconstituted ice age mammals are to some people a symbol, not of a creative approach to restoring an extinct species, but rather of the hateful excesses of the Third Reich's brutality and pseudo-science.

Although Lutz and Heinz Heck were, in their day, among the most recognized experts on large herbivores, you'd have a hard time finding more than a bare-bones account of their work today, with little or no biographical information at all. Their father, Ludwig, handed down not only a love of wildlife but a German ultranationalism that intersected in the aurochs. The bull wasn't just a link to the ice ages; to the Hecks, it was a token of German power and culture, a role the animal played as far back as the epic medieval poem *Nibelungenlied*, which sparked their interest as boys. The aurochs, Lutz Heck wrote, was an authentic symbol of German force and courage. What better way to crown Germany's ascendant power than by restoring this larger-than-life image from its past?

Not long after he took over the Berlin Zoo, Lutz began to remake the institution on ideological as well as ecological grounds. To mark the opening of the Berlin Olympic Games in 1936, he unveiled a "German zoo," one newly devoted to the nation's wildlife, with a central "Wolf Rock" display surrounded by enclosures with lynx, otter, bears, and other species from primal German forests, including the newly refashioned aurochs. Such a themed approach to zookeeping is innocent enough, and can even be seen as a laudable attempt to show the public the wonders at its own doorstep, instead of focusing on glitzy and exotic animals from overseas. But Heck kept some unfortunate company, which casts an ominous light on the changes at the Berlin Zoo. Nazi propaganda minister Joseph Goebbels was a frequent houseguest, and Heck had for years been a close friend of Reichsmarshal Hermann Göring, who shared Lutz's passion for big game and hunting. There is a photograph of Heck and Göring sitting on a fence at Schorfheide, a hunting reserve where aurochsen were released along with wisent and other game; the photo was taken in 1936, the year before Lutz joined the Nazi Party.

The Nazi occupation of eastern Europe was, to Lutz Heck's way of thinking, a golden opportunity for wildlife conservation—with an Aryan twist. He was given broad responsibility to craft nature policies for the occupied lands, which he wanted to reshape in a mythically German mold—complete with mythic German animals like the new aurochs. No sooner had the Wehrmacht moved into eastern Poland than Göring seized the great virgin forest reserve of Bialowieza, allowing Lutz to take control of its tiny, critically imperiled population of wisent. Heck had already earned the enmity of other conservationists by hybridizing his zoo wisent with North American bison in an attempt to increase the European species' fertility, a move that, in their opinion, rendered the Berlin animals permanently tainted from a breeding perspective.

But the Nazi occupation also gave Lutz the chance to hijack an attempt to re-create another ice age mammal he and his brother had long admired—the European forest horse. Like the aurochs, the horse was a frequent subject of Paleolithic cave art—not because early humans rode it, but because they ate it. After the last ice age ended and forests covered most of Europe, however, horses shifted their range farther east, into the open steppes of Asia, though some populations of forest horses appear to have survived the climate change. These wild horses were stockily built, with large, blocky heads, luxuriant tails, and stiff, upright manes; in winter they grew shaggy and pale, all features that can be seen in the cave paintings.

The wild stock were hunted and hybridized almost out of existence, so that by the early nineteenth century, when scientists began to study horse taxonomy, there were few truly wild herds still in existence—the ginger-brown Przewalski's horse of Mongolia, and the south Russian tarpan, a small gray horse that some specialists consider a hybrid between domestic and wild animals but that others believe was a legitimate subspecies. Scientific attention came just in time. The last Russian tarpan died in the Ukraine in 1880, while Przewalski's horse was narrowly saved from extinction when some were captured around the turn of the last century; though the subspecies is now secure in captivity, none have been seen in the wild since 1968.

The fate of the forest horse is much less clear. It seems to have disappeared from most of its range by the Middle Ages, supplanted by domestic horses, though there is a good possibility it provided the originating stock for the konik, an ancient Polish breed. Some accounts say the forest horse was extinct by 1800, while others claim that one managed to linger in captivity until 1918. Just to make all this a bit more confusing, the name "tarpan" has been applied to all three of these forms of wild horse, especially the south Russian and European equines, the "steppe tarpan" and "forest tarpan," respectively.

The idea of backcrossing primitive horses in an attempt to re-create an even older form had been kicking around for a while. In 1904, a Scottish professor and horse expert named J. Cossar Ewart tried crossing a black Welsh pony with a dun-colored Shetland, and produced "as typical a tarpan as ever roamed the Russian steppes"—a result, incidentally, that Ewart felt confirmed his belief that the steppe tarpan had merely been a hybrid. But Tadeusz Vetulani, a Polish zoologist at Poznan University, took the experiment much more seriously, and much further. Vetulani knew that the forest tarpan had survived longest in the great woodlands of Poland, and the konik, the tough little horse that Polish peasants used to work their farms and pull their carts, was the product of hybridization with the tarpan, perhaps as recently as 1820. Polish koniks, like the original tarpan, are mouse-gray, with a dark stripe running down the spine, and some of them grew a pale, almost white winter coat, though their legs, head, tail, and mane stayed dark—a pattern seen in Paleolithic cave art.

So in the 1920s, Vetulani combed the countryside, collecting the most primitive-looking koniks he could find, and brought them to Bialowieza, the largest tract of virgin woodland left in central Europe—and the former home of the last free-ranging tarpans. He began precisely the kind of backcrossing work that the Hecks were doing at the same time with cattle. With each generation, Vetulani chose his breeding stock based on primitive, tarpanlike characteristics, and success was swift; by the mid-1930s, he had re-created an animal that looked and acted much like a cave painting come to life, though the mane lay flat instead of erect and the animal was a touch larger than the original forest horse.

At almost the same time as Vetulani's work began, Heinz Heck also started backcrossing to create a new tarpan in Munich, though his raw material was quite different from the Pole's. "I was, of necessity, obliged to proceed by a somewhat different method from that used for the aurochs," he wrote, noting that with cattle, all the characteristics of the aurochs were represented among various breeds. "But looking at the characteristics of the tarpan, I realized there was a gap, since there appear to be no primitive domesticated horses of the tarpan type that have preserved one of the most important points of their wild ancestors, namely the short, upright mane." So starting with pony mares from Iceland and Gotland, Heinz crossed them with a stiff-maned Przewalski's stallion from Asia, an animal that he believed was ancestral to domestic horses (in this, apparently, he erred; modern DNA work suggests Przewalski's split off from European horses long before domestication took place). Later, Celtic, Scandinavian, and other small horse breeds, including a German form similar to the konik, were added to the mix. By 1933, Heinz Heck was getting foals that fit his conception of a tarpan, and in the years just before World War II, the Heck brothers even re-

leased some neo-tarpans in the Schorfheide game park to join the aurochsen.

At the end of the 1930s, then, there were two distinct strains of
tarpanlike horse, each with different lineages. The Heck horses in
Germany may have, in some superficial respects, more closely resembled the original tarpan's physical appearance, given its more upright,
Przewalski-like mane, but they were nothing more than an imitation,
even less authentic than the neo-aurochs. On the other hand, the Polish
horses, despite their lax manes, retained a good deal of true forest
tarpan blood, thanks to their hybrid konik ancestry—they were, in
a slim but a real sense, the genetic heirs of the Pleistocene forest
horse.

Unfortunately, the war radically altered the course of both tarpan
projects. With the Nazi occupation of Poland, Vetulani's work was appropriated by the Germans at Lutz's behest—the best of the Polish
breeding stock, numbering more than thirty head, were shipped back to
Germany, and Bialowieza became a German hunting preserve. Adding
insult to injury, Lutz sent Berlin-bred near-aurochsen to Bialowieza,
where they were released to see how they would fare in the wild. (In his
1954 memoir, *Animals—My Adventure*, Heck blandly refers to this period
as "five years under German administration.")

But control over the tarpan was short-lived. The Allied assault in the
final days of World War II destroyed the animals at the Berlin Zoo, including the tarpans and all of Lutz Heck's near-aurochsen (though, ironically, those sent to Bialowieza survived). Lutz fled west from the
advancing Soviet Army, which was anxious to interrogate him about the
theft of animals from eastern European zoos, and he did not return to
the divided city, living out his life in Weisbaden writing books and making animal-collecting trips abroad. Munich's zoo fared better; though air
raids damaged the zoo and killed many of its animals, some of the near-
aurochsen and tarpan survived, and after the war Heinz rebuilt both the
facility and the stock of both reconstituted breeds. (He continued as director of Hellabrunn until his retirement in 1969, and died in 1982, a
year before Lutz.)

The war also killed many of the near-tarpans taken from Poland, the
especially valuable animals descended from koniks. Fewer than half
the horses stolen by the Nazis were recovered following the war, but the

survivors were patiently reassembled and returned to Bialowieza, where the Poles again resumed their backcrossing work. In the decades since then, the focus of the breeding work has shifted from Bialowieza to the Popielno forest reserve in the north, where the Polish Academy of Sciences has expanded the herd to such an extent that neo-tarpans are being sold abroad. (Bialowieza is now a UNESCO World Heritage site with the adjoining Belovezhskaya Pushcha forest in Belarus, and a small tarpan herd is kept there for display.) Because they are hardy under the worst weather conditions, requiring little care, impervious to many livestock diseases, and able to thrive in wet, cold environments that would kill many other horses, tarpans are proving ideal for some ecological restoration projects, and are being purchased by land managers in parts of Europe. For example, the Redgrave and Lopham Fen National Nature Reserve in Suffolk, England, was looking for grazing animals to maintain its grassy wetlands and found the modern tarpans from Pipielno to be well suited to the task. (A small number of neo-tarpans also exist in the United States, largely in private hands, the descendants of animals from the Munich strain that were exhibited in American zoos following the war.)

Despite the passage of years, both the neo-aurochs and the tarpan remain sore subjects. Poles, understandably, resent both the way Lutz Heck and the Nazis plundered their breeding program and the way they managed to get most of the credit for backcrossing the ancient horse, despite Vetulani's arguably more legitimate efforts, and in the postwar years, rebuilding the tarpan project became a matter of national pride. Though long ignored, Lutz Heck's deep involvement with the Nazi Party has been brought to light recently, including the shameful way that Berlin Jews, who had contributed much of the capital used to found the zoo in the late nineteenth century, were stripped of their stock in the institution during the Nazi era—a wrong that some of their children are fighting to correct.

Less predictably, the near-aurochs has become something of a flashpoint in France, where a group named SIERDAH (the French acronym for the International Syndicate for the Breeding, Reintroduction and Development of Heck's Aurochs, based at the national veterinary school at Nantes) has been pushing the animal's use by farmers and landowners. Because of the connections between the Hecks, Nazism's focus on "master races" and genetic superiority, and the aurochs' symbolism in German nationalism, SIERDAH's actions recently drew a sharp rebuke from the French national commission on human rights. Polish-born historian Piotr Daszkiewicz and French writer Jean Aikhenbaum have even formed a small Paris-based society that they call History, Sciences, Totalitarianism and Ethics Co., which in the late 1990s published a booklet the pair wrote about Lutz Heck and the near-aurochs. The pair (who have also co-authored, among other things, a guide to herbal remedies) were motivated, they said, by a groundswell of aurochs-mania among livestock breeders, range managers, and government officials in France and elsewhere in Europe, fueled by an uncritical acceptance of the reconstituted cattle and a whitewashing of the Hecks' background.

For good or ill, the Heck brothers are still closely associated with the technique of "breeding-back." But what is less well known is Heinz Heck's suggestion of another way to manipulate bloodlines to re-create an extinct species, a technique he called "new-breeding"—the idea of starting with one group of animals and selectively breeding them *forward* to approximate a vanished species to which they were related but from which they did not descend.

"Let us consider an example," Heck wrote. "The African steppe zebra [his term for the plains, or Burchell's, zebra] used to extend from Cape Colony northwards through the East African plains to the mountainous country of Abyssinia. Over this wide distribution the steppe zebras developed into a number of varieties with different striping." These races of zebra form, he said, "a fine series of animals in which one kind merges into the next with two termini of development and in which it is purely a matter of taste whether they are called species, sub-species, geographical varieties, or anything else."

One of those races, which, as Heck indicated, was often considered a distinct species, was the quagga—an animal with stripes on the head, neck, and shoulders, but with a chestnut-brown body and white legs. The Afrikaans term "quagga," pronounced *quah-ha*, was an onomatopoeic version of the horse's coughing alarm bark, derived from such native names as *khoua khoua*, *iqwaha*, or *quoha*. Quaggas were extraordinarily common on the Karoo and other arid plains of South

Africa. "I could not estimate the accumulated number at less than fifteen thousand, a great extent of the country being actually chequered black and white with their congregated masses," wrote one observer in 1811. But because they competed with livestock for forage, the quaggas were exterminated in the wild by the 1870s, and the last captive died in Europe in 1883.

To re-create it, Heck proposed selecting Burchell's zebras with minimal stripes, like those from the populations just north of the quagga's original range, and selectively breeding them for even more reduced striping. "This would be a repetition of a process that had already taken place in nature and would probably be achieved fairly quickly . . . I know it would be possible because in 1940, when I was breeding this way from lightly striped zebras, I obtained a foal that had no stripes on the hind quarters. Unfortunately, this experiment was undone by the war."

For years, no one pursued the idea of crossbreeding zebras, but the notion stuck in the head of Reinhold E. Rau, a German native who was hired as chief taxidermist for the South African Museum in Cape Town. Rau's interest in the quagga was sparked by a mounted foal in the museum's collection, a poor specimen stuffed with straw and much the worse for nearly a century of wear. One of Rau's tasks was to remount the quagga, and he later said he was moved by the pathetic baby and the species' sad history. He became hooked on quaggas, obsessed with the animal to such an extent that he traveled back to Europe, examining twenty-two of the twenty-three quagga specimens in existence. In doing so, he was struck by how widely they differed in their colors and patterns.

As Heck had noted, there was a geographic cline in Burchell's zebra populations, from the boldly marked animals in the north of its range to those in southern Africa with much narrower, weaker stripes, often with pale brownish markings ("shadow stripes") in between on the white base color. What hit Rau was how variable the quagga skins were—some, like a mounted skin in Frankfurt, were striped all the way to the hindquarters, and the most heavily marked quaggas weren't too different from the most lightly striped Burchell's zebras. But when, in 1975, he tried to interest others in a crossbreeding experiment, he ran into almost universal apathy, if not outright hostility. The quagga, the experts informed him, was a distinct species, and tinkering with a completely different type of zebra was therefore a waste of time.

In the 1980s, however, that view changed dramatically. Rau, who was working in Germany remounting several quagga skins at the time, was contacted by scientists in California interested in using genetics to sort out the confusing taxonomy of zebras. Rau supplied them with well-preserved tissue from one of the quagga specimens, and they compared the mitochondrial DNA from it with that of other zebras. Mitochondrial DNA (mtDNA for short) is remarkably stable stuff, passed down virtually unchanged from mother to daughter, and it has been widely used as a sort of molecular clock for determining relationships between closely related species and estimating how long ago they diverged.

The group, headed by Russell Higuchi of the University of California at Berkeley, found that quaggas and domestic horses were quite different (shooting down a once-fashionable notion that the quagga was more closely related to horses than to other zebras), and they also found substantial differences between it and the mountain zebra, another southern African species. But the mtDNA from quaggas and Burchell's zebra was, for all intents and purposes, identical. Far from being a separate species, the quagga was, as Heck and others had contended, simply a race of the plains zebra.

And if that was the case, Rau reasoned, then the quagga's genes were still roiling around out there—diluted to be sure, spread among zebra populations just to the north of its historic range with which the quagga once interbred—but available as raw material for a directed breeding program like the one Heinz Heck had tried.

Armed with the new research findings, Rau was able to line up private supporters, and in 1986 the Quagga Project was born. Rau examined more than 2,500 Burchell's zebras at national parks in KwaZulu Natal and Namibia, choosing nine with markedly reduced striping on the legs and flanks; later, additional lightly marked zebras were added to the captive herd. Rau and his associates worked on sweat equity and the donations of private organizations, individuals, and companies, since the South African government initially offered no support.

With time the herd has grown, but the process is slow, because it takes zebras up to five years to attain sexual maturity. Now, more than thirteen years into the process, Rau's group has half a dozen breeding sites, with zebras from the second hybrid generation reaching maturity. Many of the foals they have produced have greatly reduced stripes or a light brown tinge to the body, though none as yet combines these two crucial aspects of the original quagga. Although Rau and his supporters say that achieving the goal of a neo-quagga may take more than thirty years, some of the rebred animals have already been transferred to Karoo National Park, a newly established unit on old, overgrazed pastureland, to which rhinos, Burchell's zebras, and other animals have been reintroduced.

As was the case with the aurochs and tarpan, there is a mingling of excited interest and cautious criticism surrounding the quagga. While stories in the general press have been almost universally positive ("Brave Quest of Africa Hunt: Bringing Back Extinct Quagga," the normally sedate *New York Times* trumpeted), scientists have been much more circumspect, even some of those who conducted the mtDNA analysis that provided the Quagga Project with its biggest boost. Although the undertaking is not burdened by backcrossing's association with the Hecks (probably because Lutz's Nazi ties do not appear to be widely known), critics have challenged it on other grounds. They point out that we know little about the quagga beyond its appearance, and that is a slim thread on which to hang any claims of resurrection; for instance, no one knows what behavioral or ecological adaptations the quagga may have evolved for its semidesert home, and which may or may not be shared by other races of Burchell's zebra. We don't even know what its bark sounded like, except for those old tribal names with their huffing syllables.

This is not helped by the take-no-prisoners attitude that Rau and the Quagga Project hold on the subject. "Since there is no direct evidence for such characters and since it would be impossible now to demonstrate such characters were they to exist, the argument is spurious," the project's Web site states flatly. "The definition of the quagga can only rest on its well-described morphological characteristics and, if an animal is obtained that possesses these characters, then by definition, it will be a quagga." Or, as Rau bluntly told an interviewer a few years ago, "The quagga is a quagga because of the way it looked, and if you produce animals that look that way, then they are quaggas. Finished."

Maybe. The original quagga was a unique end point that cannot ever be truly replicated; it possessed, if you will, an indefinable "quaggaish-ness" that stemmed from millions of years of evolutionary history, fil-tered through the demands of habitat and environmental conditions that no longer exist. To think that a few decades of selective breeding can bridge that chasm is the height of hubris.

That does not necessarily rob the Quagga Project of its legitimacy. There are criteria that stretch beyond morphology, taxonomy, and ge-netics, judgments that must be viewed through the prism of human ac-tions. Investing the time and effort to create a faux-quagga is a potent admission that we, as a species, screwed up, and we're doing the best we know how to make amends. It's not full restitution, but even if we can't pull the great herds back from oblivion, so that the veldt is again "che-quered black and white" with them, we can offer our pale approxima-tion as a living, barking symbol of what we lost.

For the same reason, I'm reluctant to dismiss the Hecks' neo-aurochs and backbred horses, and still less the Polish tarpans, too quickly. If you strip away the vicious politics that cloud their story, you have at its core a very human desire to touch a glorious and ancient past, one whose history intertwines with ours as far back as we dare call our-selves fully human. I feel it myself, looking at those vivid paintings from Chauvet Cave—the urge to see, smell, and hear the beasts that inspired our first, wobbling steps to art, to worship, and to civilization. The great bull. The wild horse. And humanity, poised to move out of the shadows and harness them both.

Some years after the war, Heinz Heck wrote two short articles for the nature journal *Oryx* about his experiences with the neo-aurochs and tarpan. He started the work, Heck wrote, from curiosity, but there was, he said, a deeper motive—"the thought that if man cannot be halted in his mad destruction of himself and all other creatures, it is at least a con-solation if some of those kinds of animals he has already exterminated can be brought to life again."

If Heck believed this, then he was deluding himself; theirs was a neatly done counterfeit, but not a resurrection. The only way to truly restore an extinct animal is by reconstructing its very genome, the unique DNA sequences that lie, trapped and inert, within the preserved tissues of musty museum specimens. Only by breathing life into that DNA could the dead walk.

And that was, until recently, the stuff of science fiction. Many molecular biologists argue it still is. But headlong advances in genetic science, coupled with great sums of money being funneled into several high-profile projects, have made the prospects for cloning an extinct species seem tantalizingly possible—raising the dead in the most literal sense imaginable.

EIGHT

Test-tube Babies

What the Heck brothers accomplished was, despite their personal failings, a remarkable feat of historical replication, but in 1990 Michael Crichton raised the bar considerably. Despite cardboard characters and stiff dialogue, *Jurassic Park* sold like hotcakes, thanks to its believable technojargon and a grabber of a premise—that scientists could extract DNA from the guts of fossilized bugs and clone dinosaurs from it. Forget about creating facsimiles of ice age cattle; Crichton's book made it sound plausible for science to raise the ultimate in charismatic megafauna from the grave.

I like mentioning *Jurassic Park* around molecular biologists, geneticists, and other specialists who play with DNA on a daily basis, because the inevitable reaction is so satisfying: a heavenward rolling of the eyes and a quiet, long-suffering sigh. They know how fragile those twisted helixes of amino acids really are—how quickly DNA begins to degrade after death, how positively loony is the idea of extracting dino-DNA from the guts of mosquitoes that had blundered into tree sap, which then fossilized into amber, which then sat buried for tens of millions of years. "The only reason that book sold so well is that nobody who read it knows jack-shit about DNA," one blunt-spoken scientist told me.

The subsequent Spielberg movie adaptation really whipped up the dino-cloning frenzy. (If that geneticist thought he was speaking to deaf ears then, his frustration must be even greater today, with Dolly the sheep a household name and renegade scientists publicly announcing plans to clone a human being.) The result is that almost the only people who know how impossible it would be to clone a dinosaur are the ones who would be in a position to actually try.

The only method that molecular biologists credit with any chance for success—and this will require an understanding of DNA and techniques to handle it that far surpass what we now have, or are likely to possess anytime soon—would be to comb through the complete genetic library of a variety of birds, which many scientists now believe descended from agile, carnivorous dinosaurs known as theropods, the group that included *Tyrannosaurus*. First, they'd identify all the areas of genetic similarity between such widely divergent modern birds as ostriches and kiwis (at the primitive end of the scale) and highly specialized songbirds, waterfowl, raptors, and others. Then they'd dig even deeper, looking at the so-called junk DNA, the stuff that no longer plays an active role in coding the physiology and behavior of the living bird. Buried here, scientists suspect, are obsolete sequences that date back to the dinosaurian age in bird evolution—genes that are no longer expressed but that haven't been jettisoned from the library, like old books shoved to the back of a shelf, unread and unremarked for millions of years.

Because vertebrates of all stripes, from fish to mammals, share so many genes, the number separating a modern red-tailed hawk from a late Cretaceous dinosaur might not be all that many; chimps and humans, after all, differ by just 2.4 percent of their genetic code. Through trial and error, scientists might learn which old genes code for which ancient features, until after enough false starts they'd have a recipe for a dinosaur—not a particular species, since that exact genetic mix would be lost to the ages, but a generalized beast in the theropod mold, a composite picture, in a sense, of the many reptilian ancestors of modern birds.

(And all *this*, skeptics point out, hinges on an important and still-unproven assumption—that birds really are direct lineal descendants of theropod dinosaurs. While widely accepted by paleontologists, it's a contention hotly disputed by some ornithologists, who hold to the older view that birds and dinosaurs share a more ancient common ancestor. Strip-mine the avian genome for old DNA, they say, and you'll most likely wind up with a small arboreal reptile with a knack for gliding between trees, not a flashy *Velociraptor*. Interesting, but hardly *Jurassic Park* material.)

So let's forget about dinosaurs for a moment. Instead of reconstruct-ing the genome of an extinct animal from scratch, why not try to locate a source of DNA that's still usable? Here's where science fiction and sci-ence fact begin to overlap in strange and exciting ways, with recent ad-vances in molecular science suggesting, for the first time, that the idea of literal resurrection of an extinct animal is not so far-fetched after all.

Although I count myself among the skeptics who question the dinosaur-bird link, I'm always a little bemused by the sight of a ratite—the order of large, flightless birds that look so much like dinosaurs it's hard to dis-believe the evidence of your eyes. The group is scattered across the Southern Hemisphere, a distribution that harkens back 120 million years to the days of Gondwana, the southern supercontinent that united South America, Africa, India, Antarctica, Australia, and New Guinea. When the landmass broke up, the ancestors of the ratites were ma-rooned on many of the pieces, where their descendants remain today—ostriches in Africa, rheas in South America, and emus and cassowaries in Australia and New Guinea. All these are big, dramatic birds; ostriches can weigh nearly 300 pounds, while the northern cassowary, with its blue head and horny "casque" poking up like a tall, conical hat, is not only big but cranky and has been known to eviscerate people with a well-aimed kick.

The ratites on two island groups evolved in especially spectacular ways. On Madagascar, seven species of elephantbirds had developed by the Pleistocene—some about the size of a cassowary and weighing about 100 pounds, but one behemoth that probably tipped the scale at half a ton and clumped around on thick, trunklike legs. On New Zealand, ratite evolution went in opposite directions. In the absence of mammals (which aside from bats never reached the isolated archipelago), one branch of ratites evolved to fill a normally mammalian niche—the ki-wis, with their furlike plumage, burrowing habits, and long, worm-probing bills. The other branch took the more typical ratite route and went big—the moas, which radiated into about a dozen species, ranging from the size of a turkey to *Dinornis maximus*, the giant moa of the South Island, which stood up to 12 feet tall and weighed more than 500 pounds.

In Africa, with its host of mammalian predators and increasing numbers of tool-wielding hominids, ostriches survived by staying alert and
running fast, talents (and cautions) shared by rheas, emus, and cassowaries. The ratites of Madagascar and New Zealand had it a bit easier.
Both islands had large eagles that preyed on them (Haast's eagle of New
Zealand, which may have weighed 30 pounds, is generally considered
the largest and certainly the most formidable modern raptor), but they
lacked large ground predators, and the ratites probably evolved the kind
of gentle naïveté often seen in island species.

This was rough luck for them, since people eventually sniffed them
out. Human beings rafted across the narrow Mozambique Channel from
Africa to Madagascar about 2 million years ago, and began a steady assault on the elephantbirds they found. It took a long time to kill them
off; the largest species was apparently still alive in the thirteenth century, when Marco Polo pinpointed Madagascar as the home of the legendary giant bird the roc, and perhaps still later, judging from the nearly
three dozen intact eggs that have been found on the island, including
some that were valued heirlooms among high-ranking Malagasy tribesmen. It may be that the last elephantbird survived as late as the seventeenth century, for European explorers were told that a few still lived in
the deep forests, though no white man ever claimed to have seen one.

The moas enjoyed an even longer respite, for according to the latest
radiocarbon dating of old campfires, Polynesians didn't reach New
Zealand until the thirteenth century. But when they did, they made up
for lost time and tucked in with gusto. Archaeologists have uncovered
many moa butchering and cooking sites, some of them with the remains
of up to ninety thousand moas scattered around in heaps of bone. What's
striking, as Australian mammalogist Tim Flannery has pointed out in his
book *The Future Eaters*, about humanity's impact on Australasia, is the
staggering waste that these moa sites represent. Like nineteenth-century
bison hunters taking only the rump meat or tongues, the Maori apparently (judging from the position and condition of the disinterred bones)
often cooked only the haunches, leaving the rest of the meaty carcass for
the flies.

And like the bison hunters, the Maori butchered themselves out of a
resource, no doubt aided by the passivity of the birds—the absence of
any specialized weapons suggests the Maori may simply have walked up

to the moas and clubbed them over the head, or strangled them in snares. However they managed it, they wiped out the moas in a flash. The conventional wisdom is that the extinction took three or four centuries, but a recent analysis of those old butchering sites, coupled with the assumption that a pair raised just one chick a year (typical for large animals with few predators), suggests that the Maori probably wiped out the moa in no more than 160 years, and probably much less than that— perhaps only a single human lifetime. It's entirely possible that the first human to lay eyes on a moa was also among the last to see one alive. By the time Europeans made landfall on what they sometimes called the "Islands of Birds" (not realizing that a substantial chunk of New Zealand's avifauna, large and small, had already been eaten out of existence), the moas had been gone for centuries and the burgeoning Maori population, hungry for protein, was gripped by ferocious intertribal war in which the bodies of enemies were routinely consumed for food.

As with many large, exotic, and recently extinct species, there have been reports from time to time of live moas being sighted in the mountains of New Zealand, but only the cryptozoological fringe gives them any credence; it's hard to imagine a population of 12-foot birds being overlooked for so long. One reason for the stray hope is that very well preserved moa eggs, mummies, and even feathers have been found in caves; one such feather was bright purple, which makes me imagine moas not as the stolid gray reconstructions usually seen in museums but more like ostriches decked out for Mardi Gras. But while we didn't miss them by much, we definitely did miss them; "there ain't no moa," as the old Kiwi joke goes.

But with advances in molecular technology, a few people began to wonder if it might not be possible to bring the moa back—or at least something vaguely hinting of a moa. In 1996, scientists at the University of Otago in New Zealand supplied several grams of ground-up moa leg bone to Dr. Yasuyuki Shirota of Hirosaki University in Japan; Shirota planned to replicate large quantities of the DNA and inject it into chicken embryos, in the hope of isolating moa genes that controlled features like size, color, and behavior.

This would not re-create the moa, not by a long shot; the very best they could hope for was a weird bird with an amalgam of chicken and ratite features. In fact, judging from their comments at the time, it appears that one of the scientists' main goals was the discovery of the moa genes that controlled size, with an eye toward inserting those genes into farm-reared ostriches to make them larger and plumper for the meat market. The anticipated hybrid was (inevitably) referred to as a "mostrich."

By 1998, however, the moa project was on hold; funding was a problem, and the Ngi Tahu Maori of the South Island were disputing ownership of the bone specimen from which the DNA had been extracted. But while moas were the most famous of New Zealand's extinct birds, they were not the only ones, or the most recently lost. With the moa work at an impasse, interest shifted to the huia, a crowlike bird with a strange beak and a tragic history.

Huias were wattlebirds, a small family of New Zealand endemics related to the honeyeaters of Australasia. Black and shiny, with bright orange skin hanging from the corners of their mouths, the male and female huia were similar but for their bills, which were so different they were at first assumed to belong to separate species—the male's was short and stoutly conical, the female's long, thin, and sickle-shaped. Both sexes fed on the wood-boring larvae of large beetles, the males hammering them out of solid wood, the females probing down the bugs' tunnels and pulling them free; mated pairs were said to cooperate in their hunting.

Huias managed to survive the first wave of human-induced extinctions after Polynesian settlement, though because of widespread burning and clearing for agriculture, their range contracted from the whole of the country to a small part of the North Island. The odd sexual dimorphism in the beak made huia specimens a hot museum commodity when Europeans came to New Zealand, and collecting for the scientific trade took a further toll on the birds in the late 1800s. A bizarre twist, however, sealed the huia's fate. In 1901, the Prince of Wales (soon to become King George V) toured New Zealand, where an elderly Maori woman presented him with a white-tipped huia feather—a symbol of royalty among some Maori—which he wore in his hatband. When photos of the prince hit the streets in London, everyone who was anyone felt they had to have a huia feather, too. Demand soared, and with the feathers selling for the astronomical price of £5 each, the final huias came under the gun, most falling to Maori hunters interested in a quick

buck. The last credible sighting came in 1907, though the species may
have lingered until the 1920s.

Fast-forward to 1999, when some of the same biochemists from the
University of Otago who had been pursuing the moa project struck up
an unlikely partnership with a group of students at Hasting Boys' High
School, a New Zealand academy whose symbol was the huia, and with
Cyberuni, a California-based Internet company whose founder is a
Hasting alum. Collectively, they announced their intention to clone the
huia using DNA extracted from old stuffed specimens.

The New Zealand huia, a type of wattlebird, was uniquely specialized—the males had
short, chisel-shaped bills, while the female's beak was long and curved. (American
Museum of Natural History Special Collection)

At a conference convened at the school in July 1999, the ethics of such an undertaking were debated; while the moa project had a distinctly commercial flavor, the goals outlined for the huia were couched in much nobler terms—"restorative justice," for example, the notion that since humanity was responsible for the species' extinction, it should bear responsibility for its revival. Significantly, unlike the moa project, this one had the blessing of the Ngati Huia tribe, representatives of which said re-creation of the once-sacred bird could be considered an obligation of the *pakeha*, or Europeans, under the 1840 Treaty of Waitangi—which, among other things, "guarantees to the Chiefs and Tribes of New Zealand and to the respective families and individuals thereof the full exclusive and undisturbed possession of their Lands and Estates, Forests Fisheries and other properties."

Armed with Cyberuni's $100,000 start-up grant, University of Otago scientists led by Dr. Diana Hill took tissue from a stuffed huia, a female whose plumage had been attacked by bugs and whose tail feathers were broken, while junior-high students at Hasting helped extract nuclear DNA from the old samples and assisted scientists as they began to sequence the strings of amino acids that made it up. The project certainly garnered a lot of good press for the school, even though headline writers couldn't resist a raft of clone-related puns. (My favorite, from a New Zealand newspaper: "Jurassic Lark.")

The cloning process that most people are familiar with, the one used to create Dolly the sheep, is known as nuclear transfer. In it, a fine needle is inserted into the donor egg, and the chromosomes—an organism's basic blueprint, stored in the cell's nucleus—are withdrawn. Next, a whole skin cell from the animal to be cloned is inserted into the cell, which is zapped with an electrical shock that fuses the new skin cell with the remaining cytoplasm of the donor egg. If all goes well, within a few hours the merged cell begins to divide. Eventually, the egg is implanted into a ewe that serves as surrogate mother, where it grows to maturity.

For a variety of technical reasons, this is a difficult enough process; Dr. Ian Wilmut and his colleagues at the Roslin Institute in Scotland tried 277 times before they succeeded with the single live birth that produced Dolly. And that was with live skin cells, freshly plucked from the animal being cloned. In the case of the huia, the cells have been dead for more than ninety years, shriveled and desiccated. But Hill and her colleagues see that as an opportunity; they posit that the prolonged "starvation" and drying might force the cell to lose its differentiated status—the chemical instructions that occur as an embryo develops, forcing one cell to become bone and another skin or liver.

The hope is that old huia DNA will have reverted to an undifferentiated state, so that when it is inserted into the egg cell of another bird, fused with an electrical charge, and placed in a nutrient medium, it will sputter back to life and begin dividing—not forming clusters of bone or wattle (or whatever tissue the sample originally came from), but starting from square one and building a whole huia embryo from scratch. Once the egg is growing, it would be inserted into the oviduct of a host bird, probably one of the two surviving species of wattlebirds—because tissue rejection is a major concern in this kind of cloning, the closer the relative, the better.

Cyberuni's Web site lays out a seven-step process for cloning the huia, and makes it all sound simple enough for, well, schoolkids. ("7. Incubate the egg. Hatch a huia.") The company refers to cloning as "an established technology now," though, in fact, no one has ever brought back to life cells that have been dead for so long, much less successfully cloned them. And so they have a backup plan if the seven-step method fails—use the DNA from a living bird as a template, identify areas of difference between its genome and that of the huia, then tinker with the blueprint until what comes out looks and acts like a huia.

If the idea of teenagers cooking up a clone seems a bit far-fetched, not everyone is laughing. Most geneticists dismiss the idea, usually citing the fragile nature of DNA and the near-impossibility of finding an undamaged nucleus, while others complain that the diversion of time and attention from endangered species is a disservice to conservation. Still others fret that the sudden chatter about cloning might lead the public to believe it is a realistic means of saving extinct animals—and thus blunt their concern for highly endangered species while there is still time to save them. For now, most of these arguments are academic, since only a small bit of huia DNA has been sequenced, never mind any attempt at cloning.

Some skeptics have noted that, even if the techniques were sound, the cost would be prohibitive despite funding from the high-tech sector.

But there is one segment of society with money to burn, even on quixotic ideas like cloning extinct species: the entertainment industry. And so it was that even while the uniformed lads of Hasting Boys' High School debated the ethics of playing God with the huia, Hollywood—which made the notion of cloning extinct species so sexy in the first place—was going for the biggest prize of all in Siberia.

Nomadic reindeer herders in Russia's far north have been finding woolly mammoth carcasses for millennia, preserved in the permanently frozen soil since their deaths tens of thousands of years ago. Knowing nothing of elephants, the herders ascribed them to a giant race of molelike monsters that are killed by sunlight. The mammoths reached the attention of the outside world in 1806, when the skeletal remains of one that had weathered out of the ground two years previously were shipped off to St. Petersburg. Several more came to light over the next two centuries, including one that was carted back in chunks to show the czar. Most were in a fairly poor state of preservation, but "Baby Dima," a small calf found in 1977 at a gold mine along the Kolyma River, was in such good condition scientists were able to extract intact blood cells from it. (Folklore holds that the beasts are so well preserved that explorers are able to slice off mammoth steaks for supper. In truth, while some expeditions did occasionally feed mammoth meat to their sled dogs, the remains were usually so ripe they robbed even the hungriest explorer of his appetite.)

The notion of reviving ancient beasts (or ancient humans) frozen in Arctic ice is a much-worn plot device in science fiction, but it was never taken seriously until the 1980s, when cloning technology began to improve. Scientists had already extracted fragmentary DNA from a mammoth in 1978, and as the techniques for cloning became more sophisticated, several people in the 1990s decided to re-create a mammoth using frozen tissue.

Mammoths put the "mega" into the term "ice age megafauna." Standing 8 to 10 feet tall and weighing about 7 tons, woolly mammoths towered over the other huge mammals of the Russian Pleistocene, including woolly rhinos, Irish elk, cave bears, and saber-toothed cats. Their world was the flat, grassy tundra, brutally cold in winter and no picnic even in summer, when (as now) the soggy land exploded with swarms of mosquitoes. Like most animals living in cold climates, the mammoth showed significant adaptations compared to its warm-weather relatives—a thick undercoat of dense fur, covered by long reddish-brown guard hairs, relatively small ears (which were, like the trunk, completely furred), and extraordinarily long, curving tusks, which, judging from the scratches and wear on their lower surfaces, were used to scrape aside snow to expose food. Large as the woolly mammoth was, it wasn't the biggest of the lot; the Columbian mammoth of western North America stood up to 14 feet high at the shoulder and weighed as much as 10 tons.

From their heyday during the depths of the Pleistocene glaciation, mammoths made a rapid descent into oblivion at the end of the ice age, disappearing from most of their range by 9,000 or 10,000 years ago—although a dwarf race lingered on Wrangel Island in the Siberian Arctic until just 4,000 years ago, about the time the Pyramids were going up. Exactly why they, and dozens of other species of large mammals, vanished is a matter of hot debate—some scientists blame climate change, while others pin the cause on human overhunting, especially in newly colonized North America. A few paleontologists have proposed what they call the "hyperdisease hypothesis," suggesting that pathogens carried into the mammoth's range by expanding humans or their domestic animals wiped out the megafauna.

Before their extinction, however, the conditions peculiar to the Arctic preserved a snapshot of the ice age, in the form of carcasses buried in the perpetually frozen soil known as permafrost—and while mammoths attract the most attention, they are by no means the only frozen fauna to be found. Gold miners and others have uncovered the remains of long-horned bison, woolly rhinos, ice age horses, and many other species. But the notion of finding an elephant in the Arctic has an undeniable cachet for even the most unlikely people.

In the early 1990s, for instance, a Japanese businessman named Kazutoshi Kobayashi was traveling in the Russian Arctic, looking for inventions whose sale abroad he could license. Instead, he became fascinated with mammoths, so much so that a few years later he teamed up with reproductive scientist Kazufumi Goto and the Mammoth Museum in Siberia, and announced their joint intention to find a frozen male mammoth; their plan was to either extract frozen sperm, which they hoped to inject into the egg of an Asian elephant to produce a hybrid, or—assuming the DNA was intact—create a pure clone.

In 1997, a thirty-three-man Japanese-Russian-British team, funded in part by Kobayashi's Creation of Mammoth Association, trekked into the Siberian bush looking for a suitable carcass. All they found were bones, but when they returned the following year, they located a scrap of hide sticking out of the permafrost, which they identified as that of a mammoth that had died 30,000 years ago. The tissue was returned to Japan in a glare of media attention—but after further analysis, its finders were forced to admit it was really a piece of skin from a woolly rhino.

But even before this embarrassing admission, the Japanese project had been eclipsed by news that another mammoth had been found, this

one said to be almost completely intact, frozen in the soil of Siberia's remote Taimyr Peninsula—coincidentally, the same empty quarter the
Japanese had been searching. In the brief Arctic summer of 1997, a Dolgan reindeer herder named Ganady Jarkov had come across the tusks,
gracefully curved and the color of cherrywood, protruding from permafrost along the banks of a river, and the next year he and his family
cut them free and hauled them to town to sell. There's nothing odd
about that; tusks and tusk fragments are common as sin in the Russian
Arctic, and the sale of mammoth ivory is big business, with several tons
a year entering the market. But then the Dolgan herder encountered
Bernard Buigues, a colorful French polar explorer, who realized the
tusks meant that a frozen carcass was probably still buried in the permafrost, too.

Buigues visited the site, saw the partially exposed mammoth—its
head had largely decomposed—and hatched an audacious plan. Until
then, the standard method for freeing frozen ice age mammals like
mammoths or bison was to use jets of hot water, followed by baths in
harsh preservatives; while this was quick, it ruined much of the specimen's scientific value. Buigues decided to excavate the elephant intact
and still frozen, move it 200 miles to an ice cave in the city of Khatanga,
where it could be kept at a constant temperature, and then slowly and
carefully thaw it bit by bit, cataloguing even the pollen grains, skin par-
asites, and tiny fragments of vegetation clinging to its pelt, which might
answer questions about the ice age environment.

It would be an extraordinarily costly undertaking; Buigues later said
he spent $1.2 million of his own money just getting the project started.
But by the summer of 1999, when the Jarkov mammoth's existence was
announced to the world, Buigues had lined up partners with deep pockets—the French magazine *Paris Match* and, significantly, cable television's Discovery Channel, which paid an undisclosed sum for exclusive
television rights.

It was a savvy investment; the subsequent two-hour documentary on
the mammoth's disinterment was the highest-rated show in the network's history, capped by dramatic scenes of a 33-ton block of icy soil
the size of a delivery van slung beneath a military helicopter. Buigues,
evidencing a flair for showmanship, reattached the tusks so they curved
out the front of the huge, squared-off block. But it wasn't the mere ex-

citement of unearthing an ice age giant that generated so much attention—it was the assertion that one goal of the project was to clone the
Jarkov mammoth.

The point man for the cloning proposal was Dr. Larry D. Agenbroad,
a geologist at Northern Arizona University with a special interest in
mammoths, and the sole American on the international team of French,
Dutch, and Russian scientists. The plan Agenbroad outlined was similar,
in fact, to what the Japanese team had already proposed. One avenue
would be to remove frozen sperm from the testes of the male mammoth, which tooth analysis showed to be forty-seven years old when he
fell into a hole 23,000 years ago and died. The sperm would be injected
into a donor egg from an Asian elephant, the surviving species considered closest to the mammoth, then implanted in a female elephant to
develop. There were big questions about whether this would work, including how well sperm would survive the long freeze and the degree of
genetic compatibility between mammoths and elephants. Failing that,
Agenbroad told the press, the team would try to isolate intact DNA and
attempt standard nuclear transfer cloning with a stripped elephant egg,
which would produce a nearly pure mammoth calf instead of a hybrid.
Asked why scientists were going to all this trouble to clone an extinct
animal, Agenbroad said, "Why not? I'd rather have a cloned mammoth
than another sheep."

By the fall of 1999, when the crew assembled in Siberia and began
hacking at the rock-hard soil with picks and jackhammers, the mammoth was big news, in a way that moas and huias never were. Ground-
penetrating radar showed what scientists assumed to be the massive
body of the mammoth, and they carefully dug wide of it, removing
plenty of soil on all sides. They ran into a glitch when the block was de-
livered to Khatanga and they realized it was too big to slide through
the mouth of the ice cave; they had to leave it sitting outside until modifications could be made in the spring. This was no problem from a
preservation perspective—winter temperatures of −70° F would keep
the mammoth just fine—but the lack of security was an issue, and by
spring, residents had plucked away most of the long, exposed fur as
keepsakes.

It also became clear that the Jarkov mammoth wasn't in quite the
pristine condition its discoverers had expected. As the scientists began

thawing the animal in the spring of 2000 (using that most sophisticated of technical implements, the hair dryer), bones and flesh showed around the edges of the excavated block. The condition of the mammoth reinforced what a lot of molecular biologists had been saying from the start—that even assuming it was frozen quickly after its death, there was no way its DNA would be in any condition for cloning. Almost from the instant of death, DNA starts to degrade, broken up by decomposing microbes, oxidation, hydrolysis, and other forces. Nor is freezing a particularly good way to keep DNA intact—unless the tissue is treated with a chemical agent, the process shatters the cell nucleus and the membrane surrounding it. And freezing is also rough on sperm, unless the semen is treated with chemicals like dimethylsulfoxide to prevent cell damage.

One of the most prominent naysayers was Dr. Alex Greenwood, a molecular biologist at the American Museum of Natural History in New York, who is part of a team extracting DNA from mammoth remains on Wrangel Island to test the idea that disease wiped out the great beasts. The best he's been able to retrieve from mammoth bones was highly fragmented DNA, in pieces containing just a few hundred base pairs—the amino acid "rungs" on the twisted ladder of a DNA molecule. To put that in perspective, the genetic code of a mammoth probably contains billions and billions of base pairs, all of which would have to be reassembled in exactly their correct order just to read its genome, never mind reanimating it for cloning.

Although the possibility of cloning or hybridizing a mammoth is what excited most of the world's attention, Buigues and many of the scientists on the project seemed to back away from that angle once the animal was moved to the ice cave and the thawing process started, saying that the focus was on who and what killed off the mammoths, not resurrecting one. Still, they said, they would cooperate with scientists who wanted samples for cloning research. And despite Agenbroad's earlier comments, they specifically dismissed the idea of using mammoth sperm to create a hybrid with an Asian elephant, saying it was "unrelated to the goals of this project."

Even assuming a clone could be created, critics said, then what? The world has changed since the last mammoths died; even the Arctic tundra, which seems a timeless place, is very different ecologically than it was during the Pleistocene, when it was dominated by grasslands instead of the shrub communities found there today. There may be no place for a mammoth to live, although Agenbroad suggested the grasslands of the central Plains might work. Nor did that stop the administrator of Pleistocene Park, an experimental wildlife preserve in Siberia, from offering to give any mammoth clones a good home, where they could roam with his reintroduced horses and bison.

Home or no home, no matter how many clones of the Jarkov mammoth might be churned out, they would all be copies of the same individual male, which points up the biggest problem with cloning—even after all that expense, you have only a carbon copy of what you started with. Perhaps the most poignant comment on the mammoth was something I read from David Wildt, a cryopreservationist at the National Zoo in Washington known for his work in helping to breed critically endangered species. Cloning, Wildt pointed out, is the ultimate case of inbreeding.

But what if someone with the experience, the technology, and the funding thought they could bring back not just one male elephant, but an actual population of an extinct animal—many individuals, enough for substantial genetic variation? Then, might it not be worth the effort and the expense? That's why, of all the cloning efforts being bruited around the world these days, the one that's received some of the most serious scrutiny—and generated some of the most acrimonious debate—doesn't involve the mammoth in Siberia. It's Down Under in Australia, and it involves a most peculiar predator, the thylacine.

The first Europeans who saw the thylacine didn't know quite what to make of it—which isn't a surprise, since they were at a loss when it came to most of Australia's unique, marsupial-dominated mammalian fauna. Many species had evolved into rough physical analogs of the placental mammals found in the rest of the world, from marsupial "mice" like the ningaui and dunnart (which, despite appearances, are not placid seed-eaters but, rather, aggressive little predators) to three species of gliders, which sail between trees like the flying squirrels of North America. Other marsupials, like kangaroos, were ecologically analogous to grazing ungulates like deer, but so wholly different in appearance that they baffled the Europeans.

Such a parallel between unrelated groups of organisms is known as convergent evolution, and the thylacine, *Thylacinus cynocephalus*, is one of the textbook examples. A trim, short-haired predator with roughly the build of a large dog, the thylacine weighed about 65 pounds, with a long muzzle and a straight, tapered tail also covered in short fur. The coat was sandy brown, with about fifteen dark stripes beginning just behind the shoulder and continuing down over the rump.

That combination—doglike body but a zebra's stripes—spawned a host of common names for the thylacine. Though not even remotely cat-like, it is most widely known as the Tasmanian "tiger," a name whose origin dates to the initial European landfall on the island of Tasmania in 1642, when Abel Tasman's Dutch crew reported that they "saw the footing [tracks] of wild beasts having claws like a Tyger." (Cat tracks do not, of course, show claw marks, and some people believe Tasman's crew actually found the prints of the large, slow-moving wombat, but the notion of tigers was planted.) The French d'Entrecasteaux expedition, which touched on Tasmania in 1792, reported seeing a "big dog" that was probably a thylacine, while English settlers a decade later referred to it variously as a native cat, native tiger, tiger-cat, native hyena, and, less often, as the marsupial wolf. (The odd word "thylacine" derives from the Greek word *thylakos*, meaning a leather pouch, coupled with a derivation of *kuon*, "dog.")

By the time Tasman's ship arrived, the thylacine had already fallen far from the apex of its fortunes. Fossil evidence suggests it evolved at least 30 million years ago, during the Miocene, a period of great mammalian radiation. During the peak of the last ice age, when Tasmania, mainland Australia, and New Guinea were linked by lower sea levels, the thylacine was found right across this unified landmass known as Meganesia. It shared the stage with an incredible assortment of megafaunal species; among the mammals were huge "tree-fellers" similar to the giant ground sloths of the Americas, short-faced kangaroos that weighed 450 pounds, rhino-sized marsupials known as diprotodons, and marsupial "lions" of the genus *Thylacoleo*, while the reptiles included a giant land tortoise with a clubbed tail and horns like a longhorn cow's, a 200-pound python, and—perhaps most spine-tingling of all—a fast, predatory lizard similar to the Komodo dragon, but exceeding 21 feet in length.

All these species vanished about 40,000 years ago, at roughly the time that humans boated across the narrow Banda Sea and colonized

Australia and New Guinea. To many experts, the timing is a little too neat to be a coincidence; the rapid extinction of large mammals, birds, and reptiles in several parts of the world conveniently dovetails with the arrival of people, suggesting a correlation—the so-called blitzkrieg hypothesis, which blames overhunting, ecosystem changes, and other fallouts of humanity for mass extinctions. (The moa's extinction is the best-documented example, and the extinction of ice age mammals in North America is a strong second.) Tim Flannery has suggested that the ancestors of the Aborigines, besides overhunting Australia, also wreaked wholesale change through the use of fire, creating a much drier, more blaze-dependent landscape than existed before. The result, he contends, was a domino effect that directly and indirectly forced many species into rapid oblivion.

Whatever the reason—and some paleontologists blame the extinctions on more mundane causes like climate change—many of Australia's largest and most spectacular species died out roughly forty millennia ago, leaving the thylacine as the top predator across Meganesia. There is no doubt that humans coexisted on the Australian mainland with the tiger (I'll dispense here with those annoying quotation marks; we all know by this point that it's not a cat), and there are some beautifully rendered examples of Aboriginal rock art that depict thylacines. But humans also eventually imported dogs from Asia, including the feral dingo, which may have been a potent competitor with the thylacine. The best guess by archaeologists is that placental dogs appeared in Australia between 8,600 and 3,000 years ago—and the tigers vanish from the archaeological record toward the end of that same period. It's another coincidence that seems a little too tidy to dismiss.

Dingoes never made it across Bass Strait to Tasmania, however, and the sparse Aboriginal population—an estimated five thousand people in an area the size of West Virginia—kept human impact on the environment to a minimum. A number of species that became extinct in the rest of Australia survived here, including the squat Tasmanian devil, a black, bulldog-jawed scavenger built like a miniature bear, and a large, flightless rail known as the Tasmanian native hen. Tasmania was also the final redoubt for the thylacine, which hunted wallabies and other grazing marsupials in the open gum forests and coastal heaths of the island, avoiding only the dense rain forests of the western mountains.

A pair of thylacines pause in their enclosure at the National Zoo in Washington, D.C., in 1906, barely thirty years before the species was declared extinct in its native Tasmania. (Smithsonian Institution Archives)

Thus, when the first British settlers arrived in what was then known as Van Diemen's Land in 1803, they found the thylacine sitting at the summit of the terrestrial food chain—and did everything they could to dethrone it. Encouraged by the climate and vegetation, wool-growing operations like the vast Van Dieman's Land Company sprang up, converting gum forests to pastures and moving large numbers of sheep into the meadows of native buttongrass and silver tussock in the mountains. The thylacine, in both its wolflike appearance and its predatory habits, was seen as a threat.

Whether or not the tiger really was a hazard to sheep is, like much about this enigmatic creature, open to dispute. The long-held gospel is that Tasmanian tigers ate a lot of mutton, ripping the sheep's throats and drinking their blood like vampires, and the wool growers (and later the state government) reacted with bounties that eventually led to the tiger's extinction. By the 1920s, thylacines were rarely encountered in the wild, and zoos were offering substantial sums for living specimens. The last documented tiger was, in fact, a captive, which died in a small private zoo in the Tasmanian capital of Hobart, in 1936—ironically, less than two months after the Tasmanian government belatedly extended legal protection to the species.

This is a neat, sensible story—predator threatens colonists' livelihood, colonists react with righteous violence, predator vanishes under the onslaught—and it is the one promulgated over the years by most of the authors who have written about the tiger. It is being challenged by a new, revisionist view that suggests that neither was the thylacine the livestock menace it was portrayed as being nor were persecuting humans the sole agent of destruction they were assumed to be. That's a controversial change in tiger circles, but more on that later. For now, it is enough to say that the thylacine has been officially extinct for nearly seven decades, and the only remnants of it are old photographs and museum specimens—one of which in particular drew me to Australia.

Wrinkled and gray, its forelegs curled against its chest in an inadvertently protective position and a long, open incision running the length of its stomach, the small animal in the clear jar of alcohol hardly looks like the stuff of high-tech science and acrimonious debate. Taken from its mother's pouch in 1866, this young thylacine was at first a curiosity from a weird and newly settled land, and later a pitiable relic of a species driven recklessly to extinction. But now, more than 135 years after its death, the preserved baby sits at the junction of modern molecular biology, conservation ethics, and endangered-species politics—and also at the locus of humanity's guilt and hopes in dealing with the natural world. That's a lot to pin on a dead creature you could easily cup in two hands.

The baby thylacine resides these days in the Australian Museum in Sydney, which in 1999 grabbed headlines around the world when its director, Michael Archer, announced an ambitious plan to sequence the tiger's DNA, use as-yet-unperfected techniques to construct artificial chromosomes, and eventually clone a living thylacine. Although hardly the first ancient-DNA cloning project to hit the papers, reaction to the museum's plan was surprisingly fierce. Critics have lambasted it as science fiction that will drain money from more important work; its proponents see it as a way to mitigate a grievous wrong committed against the planet, while burnishing Australia's languishing scientific reputation.

The Australian Museum is housed in a solid old sandstone building in the heart of Sydney, next to Hyde Park, which is lovely even on a dreary day like the one on which I arrived. There is, of course, a distinctly British air to the formal walkways and monuments of the park, which I crossed in a spitting rain shower, but the wildlife is unmistakably Australian—colonies of flying foxes roost upside down in the huge trees, and the birds mooching handouts are as likely to be white ibises and sulphur-crested cockatoos as pigeons.

I'd given myself a couple of hours before my appointment, so I shook the rain off my jacket and strolled through the exhibits, which include a fine dinosaur display and reconstructions of Australia's ice age megafauna. But what really caught my interest was a minute-long film loop playing in one corner—grainy footage of the last captive thylacine, pacing around its concrete-and-wire cage in the Hobart Zoo in 1933.

The motion pictures were shot by naturalist David Fleay, who went on to mount an unsuccessful search for wild tigers in the 1940s. Though the thylacine was said to be stiff and awkward in its movements, this one seemed as graceful as its cramped, artificial surroundings would permit; the film showed a lithe, tapered animal, but to an eye used to a dog or wolf, the proportions seemed a bit off—the head looked too long and conical, the ears too small, the almost tubular tail too straight and stiff. At one point the tiger yawned, and the narrowness of the long, toothy lower jaw, which gaped unusually wide, seemed distinctly strange. This "yawning" behavior, incidentally, is a common threat display among marsupial carnivores, but was ignored by Fleay—at his peril, as it transpired, since he was shortly thereafter bitten on the buttocks by the animal. He thereby became the last human victim of a thylacine attack, however provoked.

It's apt that the museum shows this endless, ghostly image of a living thylacine, given the institution's push to bring the animal back from the dead, a proposal that quickly drew a small seed grant of $10,000 from the government of New South Wales and the backing of a private foundation set up by two brothers specifically for the purpose. Negative reaction was equally swift. Some Australian scientists attacked it on much the same technical grounds as other such endeavors, while conservationists bewailed the expense at a time of meager funding for many rare native species teetering on the brink. It didn't help when, early on, Professor Archer suggested that thylacine clones might make trendy pets.

Though Archer was the lightning rod, I was actually at the museum to meet Dr. Don Colgan, the evolutionary biologist he'd tapped to head up the cloning project. Colgan proved to be a big, dark-haired fellow, cordial but so soft-spoken and hesitant that at times I had to strain to hear him. This may have been natural reticence and the trait, common among thoughtful scientists, of choosing his words carefully. But it may also have been a reflection of outside constraints. Like the mammoth researchers in Siberia, the Australian Museum had just signed an agreement with the Discovery Channel, granting the entertainment giant exclusive rights to the project; simply getting this interview had entailed weeks of transpacific E-mails and phone calls with the museum's publicity office, and when I arrived in Sydney I still wasn't sure Colgan would be allowed to meet with me. Even so, he explained apologetically as he led me through the cluttered corridors of the museum's research wing, he was permitted to discuss only aspects of the project that were already public knowledge.

The thylacine project is a big departure from Colgan's usual work, which focuses on the relationships between major groups of arthropods. In fact, he originally dismissed the idea of cloning the tiger, which Archer had proposed in off-the-cuff remarks to the press.

"So I sent him an E-mail saying how it wasn't possible at this stage for this reason and that reason, and he E-mailed back: 'Thanks for your support, I'm glad you're on board.' That'll teach me," Colgan said with a rueful smile. But in the two years since that careless remark, he's obviously warmed to the idea—and the fact that his team has had some notable success certainly helps. In May 2000, Colgan and his colleagues announced that they had extracted high-quality DNA from minute samples of heart, liver, muscle, and bone marrow removed from the preserved pup, and were confident they would be able to fully sequence the thylacine's entire genetic code.

In this, they started with a piece of good luck. While most of the thylacine specimens in museums are skins or bones, there are a fair number of preserved "pouch babies," the nearly hairless neonates too young to be out on their own. The usual method for preserving such a soft-tissue specimen is to submerge it in a solution of formaldehyde, but the Australian Museum's tiger joey was pickled in alcohol, a medium much gentler on DNA's double helix of amino acids, pairs of which form the base, or rungs, on the twisted ladder of the DNA molecule.

Colgan pulled a large X-ray film from a file and held it up to the light, showing me five lines a couple of inches long and heavily cross-barred with light and dark bands—the DNA, treated with radioactive nucleotides and photographed. With his index finger, he indicated one of the blurry streaks.

"The DNA represented on this line would be about forty copies of every gene in the thylacine genome," Colgan said. "That doesn't sound like a lot, but it was extracted from probably a matchhead-sized piece of tissue." The DNA is in pieces containing between twelve hundred and two thousand base pairs of amino acids—badly fragmented when compared to samples from living organisms, but ten times better than is normal with ancient DNA. Encouraged by the surprising results, the museum's team has moved on to the lengthy and expensive task of sequencing the genes—the same process recently completed in a preliminary fashion with the human genome, in which the genetic code is "read" in its proper order, like gluing together torn pages from a book.

In the near term, Colgan said, the genomic sequencing promises several scientific payoffs. One is the creation of a thylacine "genetic library," in which the extracted DNA is inserted into bacteria or yeast cells, which replicate it (and thus preserve it) indefinitely, allowing the production and distribution of large quantities of tiger DNA. Once finished, the sequenced genome would also allow comparisons of the thylacine to its fellow marsupials, clarifying its relationship with other mammals and perhaps answering such intriguing questions as whether an inherent susceptibility to disease contributed to the thylacine's extinction.

But it is the prospect of cloning—creating a living, breathing thylacine—that raises the greatest expectations and presents the most serious challenges, not only technically, but philosophically. Because each clone is an exact genetic copy of the parent specimen, one must have multiple specimens of both sexes and a variety of family lineages to create a reproducing population; Colgan notes that there are hundreds of thylacine specimens in the world's museums, many of which may provide equally usable DNA. The trouble is that with ancient DNA from any source there is no living cell to serve as a starting point. Buigues and his mammoth researchers had hoped to find a frozen but still viable nucleus, but Colgan admits that's almost certainly impossible with the thylacine. So they must use what he calls "the brute force approach." This entails first sequencing the entire thylacine genome—filling in any gaps with DNA from closely related marsupials—then creating artificial chromosomes, packaging them in synthetic membranes, inserting them into a host egg of a closely related species from which the nucleus has been removed, and finally implanting the egg in a surrogate mother. (The Tasmanian devil and the numbat, the latter a small, striped termite hunter, are prime candidates for supplying missing DNA and a host egg, as well as serving as surrogates.)

If that sounds a bit like science fiction, you're close. To create each of a thylacine's thirty to eighty chromosomes would require assembling roughly fifty thousand pieces of DNA, each containing about two thousand base pairs, in exactly the correct order—a task currently beyond anyone's capability and likely to remain so for the foreseeable future. But the surprisingly good condition of the DNA extracted from the preserved pup makes at least the sequencing part of that job easier.

"It's like putting a jigsaw together—if you have large pieces covering the same area as a number of very small pieces, obviously it's a lot easier with large pieces," Colgan said. He is confident that sequencing the tiger's genome is simply a matter of time, though his lab's single, small sequencer can run through only a few thousand base pairs each day, and the genome probably contains 3.5 billion of them. But if, as he hopes, one of the world's large sequencing companies takes on the thylacine on a pro bono basis—armed with banks of sophisticated sequencers that dwarf Colgan's—that phase could be completed in a few years.

One of the trickiest hoops to jump through in the sequencing phase of the project may be dealing with that so-called junk DNA, the long strings of highly repetitive base pairs that make up as much as 90 percent of the genetic code. Unlike genes that regulate the functioning and development of an organism, junk DNA seems to play no direct role, though it might serve as "packing material" to shield the crucial segments from infiltration by retroviruses and other hazards. Because it's so repetitive, reassembling the fragments of these strings in their proper length and order is a real challenge. To use the jigsaw-puzzle analogy again, it's like doing a massive puzzle made up mostly of tiny, largely identical pieces that form a cloudless blue sky.

Does it even matter if they get the junk DNA right? Colgan isn't sure. "You've got the possibility that these highly repeating sequences do vary between themselves a little bit," he said, and perhaps the number of times the sequence repeats itself, or the overall length of the chromosome it forms, has some unknown function. "This is probably going to be the most technically difficult aspect of reconstructing a chromosome, but I would anticipate that we do have some degree of slop in the system."

Colgan stressed several times that the thylacine project is in the very early stages of what promises to be a long and expensive process. He pegs their chance of cloning a live thylacine at only 6 to 8 percent over a twenty-year span, with an enormous price tag—although initial work has been relatively inexpensive, it could cost $15 million each just to sequence the genome of the tiger and any surrogate candidates. Even if they construct a complete genetic library, he gives only even odds over the long haul. "If the project ever does come to fruition, and we have a bounding thylacine joey, it'll be because of advances we simply can't conceive of at the moment," he said.

And in the fast-changing world of molecular biology, it can be hard to say what's inconceivable from one year to the next—or even week to week. When the thylacine project was first announced, Dr. Ian Wilmut, the Scottish scientist who cloned Dolly the sheep in 1996, told a newspaper that cloning the tiger was "extraordinarily unlikely"—but then, people had until recently dismissed the chance of cloning a sheep, too. But Dr. Alan Trounson, who is using cloning technology to help an endangered marsupial, says the roadblocks facing the Australian Museum are almost insurmountable.

Trounson heads a small team at the Monash Institute for Reproduction and Development in Melbourne working to clone the critically endangered northern hairy-nosed wombat, a species with fewer than eighty individuals left in a single tract of sandy forest in Queensland. Like its more widespread cousin, the common wombat, the hairy-nosed is a big, bulky herbivore weighing more than 50 pounds—think of a bearlike animal with the build of a woodchuck but the heft of a Labrador retreiver, which despite its size digs elaborate tunnel systems and spends much of its life belowground. It's endangered, Trounson told me, because its forest habitat was converted to pasture for cattle and water buffalo, which step on the burrows and, in the sandy soil, collapse them and crush the marsupials within.

Trounson has collected samples from roughly half the surviving wombats—tiny plugs of ear tissue that are removed when the animals are tagged for monitoring studies. He is working now with the common wombat to perfect techniques for harvesting eggs and manipulating the reproductive cycle; once that is complete, he can begin the actual cloning work.

So Trounson is in a better position to evaluate the thylacine project than most folks, and he believes it faces two barriers, one technical and the other biological. One is the enormous strides required for synthesizing artificial chromosomes. The alcohol that preserved the DNA so well for sequencing also negates, in his view, the chance of ever using those cells directly for cloning, as there is no way to rehydrate them once the alcohol is removed and the cellular structure collapses.

"I am very supportive of them looking at the DNA sequence, and perhaps comparing it to the DNA of existing Australian mammals—I think that could be very valuable," he told me. "But if they're talking about cloning a living animal, there's no way they can use cells that have been fixed in alcohol. I know what alcohol does to cells, and I can't for the life of me see how they think they're going to do it."

And even if they progress beyond that, there's a bigger hurdle remaining: finding a suitable surrogate.

"If it were technically feasible, and we had cells that were theoretically alive, that is, the nucleus was whole and functional, then what do you put it in?" Trounson's own project is possible, he said, because he has a very close relative of his study animal to serve as a surrogate mother when it comes time to implant a cloned egg; without a close match, the mother's body will reject the egg as foreign. Because the thylacine split off from other marsupials, like the Tasmanian devil, approximately 30 million years ago, there simply are no suitable surrogates, he believes.

"That stops the opportunity for [cloning] the Tasmanian tiger, in my mind, because there's nothing close to them," Trounson said.

Others in the Australian conservation community look askance at the

thylacine project, not on scientific grounds, but for reasons of priority
and ethics. Several days after my meeting with Colgan, I boarded a small
jet for the 600-mile flight from Sydney to Hobart, the Tasmanian capital,
to meet with some of them. The weather had remained overcast and
poor in Sydney, but Tasmania was bathed in uncharacteristic sunshine. As
the plane banked for a landing, I could see, west of the city, rank after
rank of high, jagged mountains, while the lowlands to the east were
golden with rolling pastures and deeply indented by scenic, beach-
rimmed bays.

The very first thing I saw as I walked off the plane and across the tar-
mac was a thylacine—a stylized Tassie tiger on a large sign by the termi-
nal entrance that said WELCOME TO YOUR NATURAL STATE. (The same logo
graces the state's license plates, I was soon to discover.) Inside the ter-
minal, waiting for a cart to pull up with our luggage, the other passen-
gers and I stood beneath a wall-sized billboard for locally brewed
Cascade lager, with a realistic painting of a thylacine peering from the
foliage.

I was itching to get out into the bush, to visit some of the places
where thylacines once roamed. But first I had an appointment with
Michael Lynch, the executive director of the Tasmanian Conservation
Trust, who had been a harsh critic of the cloning project when it was
first announced. I was curious to learn if time, and news of the museum's initial successes, had altered his opinion. It had not.

"It just seems so loopy," said Lynch—a bluff, open-faced guy with a
full head of curly gray-white hair and an expression that seemed to still
register bafflement at the notion of cloning tigers. "I said at the time,
and the more I think about it, I still believe it—it's a bit like boys with
their toys, like men with their big guns and their bulldozers. It's about
science for the sake of science.

"Like the United States, we've got thousands of species that are on
the endangered list, and we are just so poor in terms of the ability of the
commonwealth and the states to fund threatened species recovery programs," Lynch said. "If somebody gave the Tasmanian Conservation Trust
that amount of money, I could run fifty recovery programs, and with the
people I could have at my disposal, I could guarantee a bloody good success rate. And these are species that are here now, that are being threatened."

It was only later, when we were talking about the motives that drive cloning attempts, that his position seemed to soften a bit. The subject of "restorative justice" had come up, the concept articulated by those trying to clone the huia in New Zealand, which says that humanity has an obligation to bring back that which it has destroyed.

"It seems to me that one of the things in play here is a recognition that we, the human race, caused these animals to go to extinction," Lynch said. "And at some level we're saying, if we can find one out there in the wild, or if we can clone one, we're assuaging that guilt somehow. I think that's the kindest spin one can put on it, as opposed to lots of money and lots of fancy science."

Finding one in the wild—that brings up another fascinating aspect to the story of the thylacine, one that has been overshadowed by all the cloning hoopla of late. The official extinction date of September 7, 1936, has never washed with some folks, who believe the beast is still out there.

"We probably get two or three calls a year from people who say they've seen one, and they're absolutely positive," Lynch said. "I got a call just a few weeks ago, from a guy—and I didn't write his name down or anything—who said he had the remains of one. And I said, Well, you come up with the carcass and we'll have a discussion—and he never got back to me." He shrugged and shook his head; Michael Lynch is as skeptical of the notion of live thylacines in the Tassie wilderness as he is of the chances of cloning one in a Sydney lab. When he learned I'd been searching for black panthers in Cornwall—an area he knows well—he couldn't help but draw some parallels between the big cats and the thylacines, and about the eternal nature of hope in the absence of evidence.

"But the difference between a black panther on Bodmin Moor and a thylacine in Tasmania is the habitat," he said, leaning forward. "If you flew in a helicopter over Devon and Cornwall, you wouldn't find an area more than a square mile that wasn't covered in bloody houses or sheep. The idea of a panther there, that's just stupid. Whereas, it's vaguely likely—*vaguely* likely—and only from a habitat point of view, that there could be areas in Tasmania that could still support a population of thylacines. And that's a very different matter from saying that the species actually exists. That's simply saying that the degree of human interference in the landscape of Tasmania has been much, much less than in the southwest of England. So if thylacines were out there, there is habitat that they could exist in.

"But that in no way gives any credence to the notion that they're there. If they were there, there'd be whole lots of interaction with people. Which there isn't," he said with an air of finality.

Me, I wasn't so sure. Maybe it was just the kind of blind optimism that Lynch was talking about, but those mountains I'd seen looked awfully big, and the map of Tasmania has a lot of empty space on it. Besides, I'd been talking a lot in the preceding weeks with Dr. Eric Guiler, a retired zoologist who has studied the beast *in absentia* for more than four decades. Guiler is Mr. Thylacine; he organized several major expeditions to the Tasmanian bush in the 1950s, '60s, and '70s, and as a member of the state Fauna Board in the early 1960s, he oversaw the acquisition of land for Maria Island National Park, in part so that the government would have an isolated breeding area to place any wild thylacines they might catch. Now in his eighties, Guiler remains an active field researcher, and I found it hard to discount the fact that the man who arguably knows more about the thylacine than anyone else remains convinced the animal is out there, albeit in low and probably declining numbers.

Guiler once called the cloning proponents "bloody idiots," but today he just shrugs off the question, saying he doesn't know enough about cloning to evaluate the project. Nor does he seem to care that much— to him, the thylacine isn't an abstract concept or a matter of high-tech research but a flesh-and-blood predator, still haunting the mossy mountains and deep green fern gullies of Tasmania. As I walked down the stairs from the TCT office and climbed into my car, I checked the notebook in which I'd scribbled a list of Guiler's suggestions, places where thylacines were still, in his view, being credibly reported. I rolled down the windows and sped out of Hobart, heading at last for the bush. It was time to go tiger hunting.

NINE

The Tiger That Isn't

⤳⤳

If the official view is correct and the last thylacine on Earth died in the Hobart Zoo on September 7, 1936, then it's hard to explain what Hans Naarding saw in March 1982. Naarding, who was working as a ranger near Togari, in the Arthur River country of northwest Tasmania, had fallen asleep in his truck, waking about 2:00 a.m. in a downpour; out of habit, he flicked on his truck's spotlight to see what animals were prowling around.

What Naarding saw, he swears, was a male thylacine. The people who worked with him considered him a highly credible witness, and he certainly wasn't a city slicker who couldn't tell a house cat from a kangaroo. His sighting, meticulously described (even to the color of the animal's eyeshine, which he said was yellow), set off a two-year official investigation. We'll return to Naarding's claim and what came of it; for now, I mention it merely to explain why this trip to the bush felt different for me. Over the years in which I traveled the world looking for lost species, I often felt as though I was giving myself over to make-believe—looking for ivory-billed woodpeckers within earshot of busy interstates in Louisiana, or seeking the Black Beast of Inkberrow in pantherless England. Looking for animals in such altered landscapes, it was sometimes hard for me to suspend disbelief long enough to catch the thrill of the hunt.

That wasn't the case in Tasmania. As in the mountains of St. Lucia looking for Semper's warbler, I had the feeling that there was a chance—not that I would stumble across a thylacine myself, perhaps, because even with Eric Guiler's guidance and several weeks to spend camping and hiking in the backcountry, that would be the longest of long shots. Rather, it was a sense that this time I wasn't just going through the motions. The human dimension—why the ghosts of lost species resonate with us and haunt our dreams—was accompanied by the possibility that the animal itself still waited out there somewhere.

Naarding's sighting was by no means the first thylacine report to come in—almost from the moment of the species' putative extinction, people had been claiming they still saw tigers in the bush, and even now, the parks and wildlife folks get a couple of alleged sightings each month. Most of them are demonstrably mistaken, prompted by an overactive imagination and a questionable glimpse of some other large animal, often an oddly marked dog or a big feral cat. Some are the products of fraud or a self-aggrandizing quest for attention, and a case can be made for a correlation between the not-insignificant local consumption of alcohol and the frequency of tiger reports. But much of my guarded optimism about the tiger grew out of Tasmania itself.

On a map, Tasmania looks like an arrowhead sitting at the southeastern corner of Australia, its point aimed at Antarctica. In comparison to the mainland it looks like a tiny tag end, but it covers an area about the size of Ireland. Virtually all of it is hilly or mountainous, much of the eastern and central portions now bucolic pastureland or dry gum forest, while the western half is ruggedly mountainous, particularly the Tasmania Wilderness World Heritage Area, a U.N.–designated preserve which, at more than 3 million acres, accounts for roughly 20 percent of the island.

Which is to say, there is a lot of empty land in Tasmania, a fact important to the question of the thylacine and its possible survival. It's also spectacularly beautiful—and not in a sporadically pretty way, with all the good bits swept up in a few especially scenic parks. The whole damned island is gorgeous and varied, from rocky coastlines to deep gum forests, deeply cleft bays with deserted white sand beaches that run for mile after empty mile, to glacier-carved lakes on the central plateau and the rugged majesty of its high western mountain ranges.

The spirit of any natural landscape dwells in its wildlife, and here Tasmania also shines. It boasts close to two hundred species of birds, and nearly three dozen species of native mammals, from the egg-laying

platypus and echidna to wallabies and kangaroos, the Tasmanian devil
(a fierce little scavenger), several charming possums, and a bestiary of
other marsupials whose names fall oddly on an American ear—potoroos, bettongs, quolls, bandicoots, dunnarts, and antechinuses among
them. Coupled with this diversity is sheer abundance—the number of
grazing marsupials like wallabies and pandemelons, as well as ringtail
and brushtail possums, is staggering. It is something any visitor immediately recognizes in a straightforward but fairly macabre way—through
roadkill. The two-lane country roads that are the rule through most of
the island, and along which the Tassies drive with breakneck speed and
abandon, are littered with astounding numbers of dead animals. Living
in the central Appalachians, I am no stranger to roadkill, but nothing I'd
seen in a lifetime of driving prepared me for the level of highway carnage I encountered in Tasmania. Before I'd left home, I'd been warned
repeatedly by friends who'd driven there to avoid going anywhere after
dark if I could help it, and I quickly realized they weren't kidding—my
very first day I counted seven or eight species of large and mid-sized
marsupials, including the threatened barred bandicoot, all of them
freshly dead from the night before. Driving east of Hobart for an hour, I
lost count of the number of dead possums somewhere beyond 185, and
the big wallabies, which would put a dandy dent in my rental car, lay
every hundred yards or so, their enormous feet splayed skyward. Not
for nothing are most of the vehicles in rural areas of the state fitted with
protective metal "roo bars" over the grille to absorb the inevitable impact with big mammals.

The large-scale clearance of forest for pastureland has benefited the
grazing marsupials like wallabies, while the cessation of the once-
lucrative possum and kangaroo fur industries also allowed numbers to
soar. Wallabies are still culled for meat (I had delicious wallaby tender-
loins one night for dinner, though I disappointed the waitress by not re-
acting visibly when she joked, "Oh, you want the roadkill?"), but the
take is strictly controlled, and by one estimate there are more than 10
million wallabies on the island. That's a lot of food on the hoof—and
coupled with its remote and thinly traveled land, Tasmania certainly has
the two most critical requirements for the survival of a large predator
like the thylacine, a solid prey base and good habitat.

There is one further cause for hope on the thylacine's behalf. Aus-

tralasia—that is, Australia, New Zealand, New Guinea, and the neighboring Pacific islands—has been a hot spot in recent years for the
rediscovery of species long thought extinct, like that mummified night
parrot that Walter Boles almost stepped on in the Outback desert. There
are several reasons for this: the region is ecologically diverse, so there
are many range-restricted plants and animals endemic only to certain regions, and it is big, rugged, and sparsely settled, so it's easy to overlook
the more cryptic or secretive animals. In 1994, for example, a couple of
university students studying the small wallabies known as quokkas set
live traps in Two Peoples Bay Nature Reserve in western Australia and
instead captured three Gilbert's potoroos, a rabbit-sized marsupial presumed to be gone since 1866. Solitary and strongly nocturnal, the potoroos were the fourth "extinct" mammal to be found by scientists in
that part of Australia in recent years.

Most of the newly found species of flora and fauna are small and not,
to the average eye, terribly exciting, like clubmoss everlasting, an odd
member of the daisy family last collected in Tasmania in 1840 but relocated by a sharp-eyed botanist a couple of years ago on a nature preserve
just east of Hobart. Likewise the Lord Howe Island stick insect, also
known as a land lobster—a rather imposing bug the length of a man's
hand that had been AWOL for eighty years until three females were
found in 2001 on a small rock island known as Ball's Pyramid, which
pokes 2,000 feet out of the sea like a wizard's hat. (Scientists believe the
bug's near-brush with extinction forced it to become an all-female
species, with unfertilized eggs developing into daughters without the
benefit of males.) But the ranks of the refound include some of the
largest animals in the world; in 1997, scientists doing a DNA analysis of
southern right whales off the Aukland Islands realized the cetaceans
were not from Australia, as had been assumed, but were a remnant of
the New Zealand population, which had been thought extinct since the
1830s. That the slow-moving coastal species survived the intense whal-
ing of the nineteenth century at all is miraculous, though the fact that
the population still numbers only 100 to 150, scientists said, is an indication of how long it may take whales to recover from overhunting.

But probably the strangest story of loss and rediscovery to come out
of this part of the world involves Bulmer's fruit bat, a New Guinea
species first described in 1975 after twelve-thousand-year-old bones

were excavated from a cave. The scientists who found and named the bat assumed, naturally enough, that it had vanished in the waves of post–ice age extinctions, but just two years later an anthropologist living with the newly contacted Wopkaimin people sent a curious package to the University of Papua New Guinea. In it was the unmistakable skull of a Bulmer's fruit bat, which unlike other species lacked front teeth—a bat killed just a short time before in an area about 250 miles from the cave where the fossilized remains had been found.

As it developed, native hunters in that area had just acquired their first shotgun and a long length of rope, and one of them had availed himself of this new technology to descend the 300-foot vertical shaft into a vast cave known as Luplupwintem, previously inaccessible to people, where tens of thousands of bats roosted. He proceeded to blast the hell out of them, going through five boxes of shotgun shells—about a hundred rounds—in that first visit alone, and killing thousands and thousands of the tightly packed bats. The skull and jaws saved by the anthropologist were leftovers from the huge feast that followed. Although the cave was once considered sacred by local villagers, word spread through other highland communities of this newly available resource, and hunters flocked to the cave—so that by the time the scientists got there, hoping to see a live Bulmer's fruit bat, the colony had been exterminated.

Australian mammalogist Tim Flannery, whose fieldwork in New Guinea is legendary, spent years checking caves in that part of the country, hoping to find another relict population of the mysterious fruit bat. He had no success—but then, in 1990, by pure chance he discovered the unmistakable skull of a Bulmer's fruit bat in a jumble of unidentified specimens at the Australian Museum, where he worked; more remarkably, the tag showed it came from a joint expedition he and a colleague had made to New Guinea six years earlier. Apparently his friend, working alone, had misidentified it as a common species, and once in Australia, the skin and skull (which could have cleared up the confusion) became separated.

Now Flannery had something to go on, because the specimen tag bore the name of the village where the bat had been collected. Returning to New Guinea, he learned that the bat had been shot by a local man in a tree behind his house, about 20 miles from the cave where the species once roosted. With New Guinea scientist Lester Seri, he went back to Luplupwintem cave, convinced that at least a few fruit bats had survived the massacre. In *Throwim Way Leg*, Flannery's immensely entertaining account of his adventures in New Guinea, he wrote:

> We found ourselves standing on the very lip of a vast, roughly circular shaft, perhaps four hundred metres across, its walls plunging vertically for hundreds of metres. Looking across the chasm to its southern face, I saw that we stood on the lowest point of the entrance. All around, the cliff-like sides of the doline [sinkhole] soared hundreds of metres overhead, as well as below. It was by now early afternoon, and a shaft of sunlight pierced down into the gloomy depths. I could see that the doline opened into a cathedral-sized cavern, across the mouth of which flowed a fine, almost mist-like waterfall. The height of the south wall appeared to be the best part of a kilometre, if not more.

They could hear and see fruit bats down in the cave mouth, but had no way of knowing if they were Bulmer's or a more common species that had moved in later. For four nights, Flannery and Seri tried stringing mist nets across the opening, but without success; only after climbing out over the yawning cave mouth on a couple of mossy trees and maneuvering long, unbalanced net poles into place—a dangerous, last-chance attempt—did they finally catch the first living Bulmer's fruit bat seen by a scientist. At most, Flannery believes, only ten or twenty bats out of the tens of thousands that once lived in the cave escaped the carnage in 1977, and given their extremely low reproductive rate, they have been slow to recover, with the population up to only 160 or so by the early 1990s. But local villagers, to whom the cave and its bats are sacred, are once again protecting Luplupwintem from outside hunters, so with time Bulmer's fruit bat may make at least a partial recovery.

While Flannery had a bat specimen to go on, modern thylacine hunters have little more than stories—many of them, it is true, but anecdotes nevertheless. Eric Guiler, the retired zoologist who spent his life studying thylacines, had told me that in recent years most sightings he con-

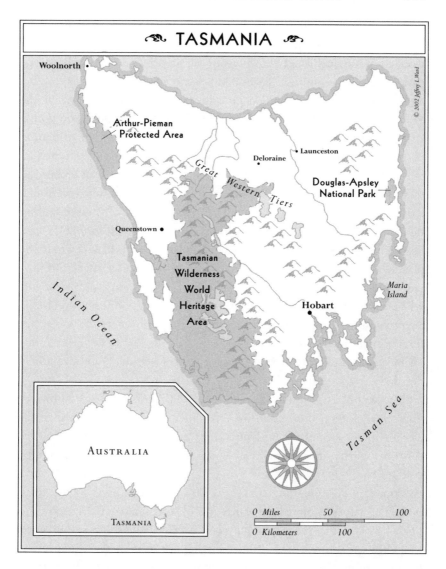

sidered legitimate had come from the northwestern and northeastern corners of the island. I had almost three weeks to hike and camp my way around Tasmania, and so I decided to focus much of my attention on the flared prongs of the Tasmanian arrowhead.

Douglas-Apsley National Park is along the northeast coast, just beyond the little resort town of Bicheno, with its headlands of orange-flecked granite and crashing white-topped combers. But once I moved in from the rocky shore, the landscape reminded me sharply of the Cumberland Plateau of eastern Kentucky, a maze of crumpled, heavily wooded mountains laced with twisting dirt roads and tiny hamlets. The park is fairly new and not developed beyond a few hiking trails; the big attraction is a deep blue-green pool in the Apsley River known as the Waterhole, a crystalline basin several hundred yards long cupped within a steep gorge, where locals like to picnic and snorkel with the minnows.

It was a brutally hot day, and the water looked inviting as I crossed the outflow on an erratic line of stepping-stones, a couple of bikini-clad teenaged girls squealing in the shallows and a family with several small kids playing on the pebble beach. Then I moved out of earshot and up the steep wall of the river gorge, topping out on a plateau that lay embraced by a huge loop of the river. The gum trees that covered the plateau were big enough to block any breeze, but too scattered to provide more than fitful shade. Tasmania was in the midst of a drought, which made the east coast—warmer and drier than the rest of the island anyway—a real oven much of the time. Little moved in the forest but for a host of small, iridescent blue skinks that seemed to be forever skittering out of my path; I tried to calculate their spacing and eventually decided I was seeing one lizard every 9 feet or so.

The woodland, typical of northeastern Tasmania, is a type known as sclerophyll forest, dominated by drought- and fire-resistant plants, including many species of eucalyptus, or gum trees. The gums, which are Australia's signature tree, have an airy beauty, with their peeling, multicolored bark; they are tall and gangly, loose-limbed, with heavy trunks and open, wide-spreading branches, but to an eye used to the thick crown of a maple or oak, the leaves look too sparse, the canopy too open—as if you've caught the gum half-dressed. There's a curious smell to a eucalyptus forest, too—not the cough-drop odor you'd expect, at least not to my nose, but a subtle tang with a hint of citrus that catches at the back of the throat in a strangely pleasant way.

The botanical diversity was supposed to be high in this park, but as a newcomer, I could identify only a few species: some of the eucalypts and the *Banksia* that formed much of the understory. *Banksia* is a genus of flowering tree unique to Australia and New Guinea, named for Joseph Banks, the pioneering botanist who accompanied Captain Cook's expedition of discovery in 1770. A *Banksia* flower is unmistakable, starting out like a knobby, vertical pinecone a few inches high, then erupting into a thick yellow bottlebrush the size of a juice glass. Rich with nectar, the flowers attract a host of birds like honeyeaters and wattlebirds during the day and marsupials like sugar gliders at night.

After several miles of fairly monotonous walking, during which I cut across the narrow neck of a sweeping oxbow in the river, the path suddenly dropped over the edge of the gorge and tumbled down several hundred feet to the riverbed again. In winter, the Apsley is big, muscular water, full of rapids and waterfalls, but with summer and the drought, it had retreated to a series of quiet pools, connected by water that mostly flowed, heard but unseen, below the rocky riverbed. Thus, it was possible for me to loop back downstream by an alternate route, following the deeply cut gorge, where shadows already lay dark and cool. Gray currawongs, black, crowlike birds with heavy bills, called hoarsely from the branches of the gum trees, then flew off on swishing, white-marked wings. In the undergrowth, tiny fairy-wrens hopped around like windup toys. These were among the most common birds in Tasmania, but I never tired of watching them—little golf ball–sized things, their ridiculously long tails pointing straight up in the air, and the males with powder-blue heads so shiny and metallic that the color looked enameled.

The air within the gorge was still and damp, completely silent. The cliff walls were sheer and dull orangish, made of dolerite, a type of basalt that weathers in characteristic "organ pipe" columns and that lent the gorge the feeling of an immeasurably ancient man-made structure. There was no trail; I had to pick my way slowly over the boulder-strewn riverbed for miles, and stopped twice when I ran into deep pools that stretched from cliff to cliff with no apparent way around. The first time I eventually skirted the water on a narrow ledge, figuring that the worst that would happen was I'd fall and get wet. The second time, with darkness starting to close in, I'd just about decided to strip down and ferry my clothes, pack, and boots across to the other side when I spotted a small game trail that ascended the gorge about halfway and wrapped around the far side of the bend, out of sight. It proved to be a double gamble, for not only couldn't I see where the trail ended, but once I was on it, I realized it was even more precarious than it had looked, and I found myself inching along with my face and arms plastered to the cliff

and my heels hanging over a 50-foot drop, loose gravel treacherous beneath my feet. But my shaky luck held, for on the other side of the bend
the trail vanished into a series of shelving rock ledges that brought me
easily back to the river.

I was moving slowly because of the rough, uncertain footing, and because I didn't fancy stepping on some of the native fauna. I'd already had
several close encounters with tiger snakes, including one I'd nearly trod-
den on earlier in the day—a thickset serpent about 3½ feet long and
glossy black like obsidian, curled up in a patch of sunlight. I froze, but it
saw me and bunched, raising its short, chunky head and cocking its
neck.

There are only three species of snakes in Tasmania, but all are venomous. The tiger snake is usually ranked among the world's most toxic
species and has a reputation for being unusually aggressive. Aussies had
warned me, in dead earnestness, never to run over a tiger snake in a car,
because it would wrap itself around the axle and bite me later, when I
stepped out. That's obvious nonsense, but the tiger snake is reputed to
be one of the few species that will, at least on rare occasions, press an attack against a human, even when there is an escape route open to it. As
someone who's been hooked on snakes since childhood, seeing a tiger
snake in the wild was a dream come true. But suddenly the gap between
us looked uncomfortably short, and I found myself doing something I'd
never done in a lifetime of messing around with snakes—checking over
my shoulder to make sure my *own* escape route was clear. But I needn't
have worried; the snake hadn't read its own press, and it bolted the
other way, sliding down a nearby hole between two rocks. (It's worth
mentioning that every one of the dozens of snakes I saw during my time
in Tasmania acted exactly the same way.)

Even for someone used to traveling in the tropics, Australia's array of
venomous creatures—not merely annoyingly venomous but dangerously
so—is sobering. Unlike any other place on Earth, where nonpoisonous
snakes outnumber venomous ones, the ratio is reversed in Oz, and
though many are at best mildly toxic, the taipan of northern Australia is
often called the world's most dangerous snake. Australia has the world's
most venomous spider (the Sydney funnelweb), octopus (the blue-
ringed), jellyfish (the sea wasp or box jelly), shellfish (the textile cone
and a host of near relatives), and mammal (the otherwise cuddly duck-

billed platypus, whose males are armed with poison leg spurs, for reasons no one can fathom). It also has the paralysis tick, whose saliva may
induce a potentially fatal paralytic condition that makes Lyme disease
look like a vacation. I came to realize that hazards like tiger snakes and
annoyances like land leeches, which are ubiquitous in damp forests, are
simply the price of enjoying Tasmania's beauty.

Night comes on slowly in the long austral summer. At 8:30 p.m., the
tops of the gum trees rimming the canyon were still glowing in low
light, but it was dim and murky down where I was along the riverbed
and I had to be especially careful not to miss my footing on the boulders.
More and more wildlife was emerging. At first I heard only unidentified
crashings in the brush, but as I was moving silently over rock, I soon began to startle animals coming out to feed or drink. Most were Tasmanian
pandemelons, small kangaroos with bodies about the size of spaniels,
though once I saw a Bennett's wallaby, nearly twice as big, which
bounded away in powerful leaps.

Such marsupials were the original prey of the thylacine, which inhabited all but the dense, rain forest–clad mountains of western Tasmania when the first European settlers arrived in 1803. Early accounts
suggest they were frequently seen in the coastal forests of the northeast,
but the tigers can't have been terribly common; while a French expedition in 1792 reported seeing a "big dog" when it stopped in Tasmania, it
took English settlers more than two years before they encountered the
first one. (Tasmania, like the rest of Australia, was initially settled as an
English penal colony, and the first "tyger" was reported by a party of
convicts that tried to escape into the bush.) A description published in
1810 of the newly discovered "Hyæna Opossum" said, "It flies at the approach of Man, and has not been known to do any Mischief, though [is]
apparently well formed to be the destroyer of Weaker Animals."

The little we know about the thylacine comes mostly from the reports of trappers, sheep-growers, and the very few naturalists who had
firsthand contact with it in the nineteenth and early twentieth centuries,
and a good deal of that is contradictory. Some who lived in tiger country
even swore there were really two kinds—"bulldogs," with stout, heavily
muscled jaws, and "greyhounds," which were slimmer and had more tapered muzzles. One scientist went so far as to describe them as separate
species, but it appears to have been a sexual difference, with the females

having the shorter, heavier heads—though adding to the confusion was the fact that male thylacines had a "pseudo-pouch" that protected the testes, similar in appearance to the one a female used for carrying her young. About the only thing everyone agreed on was that it was a decidedly odd beast.

Thylacine biology and ecology is a laundry list of unknowns. It is unclear whether they used a permanent den (most old trappers thought not), or if they established a home range—most bushmen believed the tigers were faithful to one place, refusing to move even when hunted, while others thought they were nomadic, drifting across the land on a seasonal basis in search of game. Still others argued that the thylacines made altitudinal migrations, up into the mountains during the summer months and retreating to the lowlands during the cold and often snowy winters.

No one ever recorded seeing thylacine courtship or mating behavior, though we know they could raise up to four young, since this was both the maximum number of nipples available to the babies and because females with one to four young in the pouch were often snared. Based on old bounty records (which noted the age of the dead tigers), breeding must have occurred year-round, though a midsummer peak is presumed, and while the gestation period is unknown, it seems probable a female would have had only one litter per year. Judging from development rates in other marsupial carnivores, the young would likely have remained in the pouch for four months or more, with several additional months during which they were dependent on the female.

One of the central questions about thylacines is their hunting behavior. They have always been assumed to have eaten mid-sized and large marsupials like wallabies and kangaroos, though one scientist, examining the shape and arrangement of a thylacine's teeth, recently concluded they were in large measure insectivorous. Guiler just snorts at that: "For Christ's sake, there must have been some bloody big insects around." Most of the early records suggest the tiger was a solitary hunter, though some accounts describe a female and her half-grown young hunting together, with one tiger spooking the prey and the rest trailing after it, or a mated pair working together to make a kill. Most observers felt the tigers hunted mainly by sight, not scent (a conclusion backed up by the small olfactory lobes in the brain), and they may have risen up on their

hind legs while hunting to periscope over tall grass. Thylacines were often described as being slow and rather stiff in their movements, which if
true is a fairly unusual trait for the predator of large and unquestionably
agile prey. One way the thylacine may have gotten its food was to take
advantage of a wallaby's tendency to run in a large circle when chased;
the tiger, trappers said, cut across the inside of the circle and waylaid its
prey. Others said the slower but more dogged tiger simply kept after the
other animal until it flagged from exhaustion.

Much has been made of the thylacine's extremely wide jaw gape, and
what role it might play in hunting and feeding. Guiler, like most of the
older experts on Tasmanian tigers, accepts the contention voiced by
some early-twentieth-century trappers that thylacines were, in a sense,
predatory vampires. "Tasmanian tigers would kill sheep in a very characteristic way," Guiler wrote in 1991. "They used their huge gape to bite
out the throat and then they drank the blood. They ate the vascular nasal
tissues followed by the liver, kidneys and some of the other meat . . .
Tigers killed kangaroos by biting the throat and then ripping open the
the rib cage, eating the heart, lungs and liver while lapping up the
blood." If the thylacine was primarily or even largely a blood-feeding
predator, it would make it virtually unique among mammals. But in recent years, as part of a wider rethinking of the thylacine's ecology and
history, this belief has come under ferocious attack.

Another facet of the thylacine's biology that was long held as dogma,
but that is now open to question, is its intelligence—or lack thereof.
The notion of dim-witted thylacines entered the historical record right
from the start, in the original description of the species published in
1807. Though noting that the animal on which the description was based
received "some internal hurt in securing it," and died a short while later,
the author concluded that "it appeared exceedingly inactive and stupid."
For the next century, many authors wrote of the tiger's stupidity, though
often from little or no personal experience. In large measure, the thylacine was simply tarred with the same brush as the rest of Australia's
marsupial fauna, which were held to be inherently inferior to the animals of Europe (as Australian Aborigines were considered culturally and
physically inferior to Europeans).

Almost everything we know—or think we know—about the thylacine comes from observations of snared specimens and the recollec-

tions of those who spent their time in the bush trying to catch and kill them. Scientific observations were primarily limited to captive animals held in highly unnatural conditions, like concrete-and-wire zoo cages. They were uncommon enough that even those naturalists who spent a significant amount of time in the bush rarely saw them, and as time went on, those sightings came less and less frequently. As early as 1842, one author described the tiger as a "species whose term of existence seems to be fast waning to its close." Twenty years later, the naturalist and artist John Gould—having just completed a beautiful painting of a pair of thylacines—said, "The numbers of this singular animal will speedily diminish, extermination will have its full sway, and it will then, like the Wolf in England and Scotland, be recorded as an animal of the past." By the end of the nineteenth century, those predictions seemed on the verge of coming true.

That's because the very first English ship to make landfall on Tasmania all those years before had, along with colonists, prison officers, and convicts, also brought another immigrant, one that would profoundly shape the economy and landscape of the island, and with it the fate of the thylacine: sheep.

It's hard to overestimate the importance of sheep in the European history of Tasmania. The first settlement along the Derwent River had just thirty rams and ewes, but more followed, and the climate and vegetation proved so nearly perfect for sheep—especially once the forests were widely cleared for pasture—that much of Tasmania soon echoed with bleats. Barely fifteen years after the first colonists arrived, sheep numbered 172,000, and by the 1880s the total had climbed to 1.5 million. Any person (or animal) who so much as looked sideways at all that mutton was open to suspicion and persecution.

The bounty system that is popularly credited with wiping out the thylacine was a wool industry invention; the first cash rewards for dead tigers were offered by the Van Dieman's Land Company, starting in the 1830s and continuing for almost ninety years. But stockmen were unwilling to go it alone, and in the 1880s they began to bring political pressure to bear forcing the government to fund its own bounty scheme. The evidence to support such a move was shaky and of the loosest sort;

some wool ranchers asserted that a single adult thylacine would kill a hundred sheep per year, while others claimed thylacines would stampede whole flocks over the edge of cliffs. One especially strident member of the House of Assembly, John Lyne, was paraphrased by the local newspaper as telling his colleagues that "these dreadful animals may be seen in hundreds, stealthily sneaking along, seeking whom they may devour, and it is estimated that they will have swallowed up every sheep and bullock in Glamorgan," on the east coast. Lyne, who spearheaded the drive for a bounty, went on to claim that tigers killed 50,000 sheep per year on the east coast—quite an accomplishment, since this constituted half the total number of sheep then in the district.

Not everyone joined the hysterical chorus. Many naturalists (and more than a few ranchers) said the thylacine was at worst an occasional killer of sheep, and an examination of early records supports this—thylacine predation was rarely noted in wool station diaries, even in the first decades of colonization when the number of sheep was increasing exponentially and tigers were presumably still the most common. Feral dogs were often the culprits in livestock deaths, and many of the sheep whose disappearances were ascribed to tigers were probably stolen, since rustling was (and remains) a significant problem. All in all, there is no real evidence for the kind of widespread sheep killing that bounty proponents described. But the wool industry carried the day, and in 1887 the government decreed that "a reward of One Pound shall be payable . . . for the destruction of every full-grown Native Tiger (*Thylacinus cyanocephalus*), and the sum of Ten Shillings for every half-grown or young Native Tiger." That was a lot of money, the equivalent to an average month's pay, and it ratcheted up the pressure on thylacines almost immediately.

The government bounty remained in effect until 1909, with up to 168 turned over for cash in a single year. In all, payments were made on more than 2,200 thylacines, including more than 230 caught in one small area of the Central Plateau by essentially three families of trappers working the edge of the Great Western Tiers, a rugged mountain range south of Deloraine. The region has also spawned more than its share of modern thylacine sightings; a tiger was said to have been struck and killed by a car near Deloraine in 1952, though if so, the body was never given to anyone in authority. The Western Tiers are really an escarpment, great turreted mountains that rim the north edge of the plateau, bisected by waterfalls, underlain with caves (including one that is famously lit by millions of bioluminescent fly larvae), and covered with a mix of dry gum woods and, at higher elevations, dense temperate rain forest. Much of the forest is state-owned and managed for timber, and you have to stay on your toes when driving the dirt roads, because fast-moving, heavily laden logging trucks trailing curtains of yellowish dust will suddenly fill the curve ahead of you, leaving you scant moments to swerve out of the way.

The logging trucks are gone at night, which is when the marsupials are out in force, and if a driver is slow and careful not to smack into a wallaby, poking around the back roads after dark is a great way to see the native fauna. So one night, as a full moon rose, I left my tent and drove back a dirt track into the Tiers. In the lowlands, where sheep pastures lap against the mountains, wallabies exploded from the grassy margins like coveys of quail taking flight, animals the size of collies bouncing in every direction; I learned to come to a full stop until they were gone, because you never knew when one would panic from the headlights and hurtle straight back at the car. Once, I saw a large, squat beast up ahead in the lights, lumbering along like a furry tank—my only glimpse of a live wombat, at 50 pounds one of the biggest burrowing mammals in the world, whose large tracks I found almost everywhere I hiked in Tasmania.

Opossums abounded, mostly brushtail possums, each the size of a fat house cat, with glossy brown-black fur, a long, bushy tail, and an ineffably sweet face set off by large ears and a small pink mouth. Most waddled unhurriedly off the road when I'd coast to a stop, but one animal, a male with a bad eye, climbed head-high in a tree and began to nonchalantly lap nectar from flowers as I stood a few yards away playing a flashlight on it. It reached out a soft-fingered paw and pulled the branch closer, its little tongue quickly lapping and dabbing in the open flowers, and I couldn't help but wonder why, of all the possums in the world, we in the States ended up with one that looks like a grinning rat.

Possums, wallabies, wombats—all these animals belong to the marsupial order Diprotodonta, related to the extinct, rhino-like giant diprotodons of the ice age. But the carnivores are a different matter. The thylacine was merely the largest of the dasyurids, a remarkably diverse order ranging from the tiny white-footed dunnart, which at less than an ounce weighs about as much as a sparrow, to the infamous Tasmanian devil, an admittedly irascible scavenger whose cartoon reputation for gluttony is badly overdone—though with its powerful jaws it usually consumes everything in a carcass, including the bones, which end up in large, jagged white chunks in its scat.

I wandered away from the nectaring possum, holding my flashlight at the tip of my nose to get the maximum reflection from any distant shining eyes. Somewhere off to my right, a Tasmanian owl known as a boobook called its name monotonously. Twin flashes of purple eyeshine, tiny but vivid, distracted me from mammals; they were neighboring trapdoor spiders, their clusters of turreted eyes glowing violet as they perched at the entrances to their silk-lined tunnels, trapdoors hanging open like the hatches of submarines.

I was looking at them closely when I heard a scuffle not far away and glanced up to see an eastern quoll. About 2 feet long, it was gray with large white spots, a narrow face, and a long, furred tail. The old-timers called the quoll "native cat," for though it is a dasyurid, it has a certain felineness about it—or perhaps, I thought after a few moments of watching, a dash of weasel, as it went back to the business of finding dinner, leaping and pouncing and poking with gusto, crunching on some large bug it snagged in the grass.

Quolls are common almost everywhere in Tasmania, but that wasn't always the case; early in the twentieth century they were quite scarce, as were several other carnivores, including the Tasmanian devil. This may have been due to hunting and trapping pressure, but there is evidence that an epidemic swept through Tasmania's marsupial predators around the beginning of the twentieth century, decimating quolls, devils, and other species. It may have been a naturally occurring pathogen that cycled regularly through game populations, or it might have been a newly introduced disease brought in by accident by the many species of foreign pets, livestock, and game animals that the Tasmanians were importing with great abandon. There is no question that an epidemic affected tigers, which were often found in snares with skin lesions and mangy pelts, though we cannot be sure it was the same disease that hit the quolls. In fact, no one knows exactly what the disease was, though it is most often described in contemporary writings as either distemper or mange.

"I can take a good guess," Eric Guiler told me when we finally met.

"Viral pneumonia. In 1952, a disease went through the ringtail possums, and when you went bushwalking you were nearly killed by possums falling out of the trees on top of you. I managed to get hold of one which was doing poorly and shipped it back to the animal health lab for tests." He thinks the epidemic that hit a century ago was the same thing.

"People have been misquoting me for years, saying the tigers had distemper—they did not have distemper, which is a canine disease. This was a disease *like* distemper. Well, pneumonia is like distemper," he said.

To Guiler's thinking, the epidemic was the last straw. He doesn't believe that snaring and hunting alone, even buoyed by bounty payments, would have been enough to virtually exterminate the thylacine over such a large and rugged landscape as Tasmania; instead, he thinks the epidemic pushed the thylacine population to near-extinction—to levels from which it could not easily recover. It is a view shared by other zoologists and writers who have looked at the thylacine's death spiral—the difference being that Eric Guiler thinks the tiger managed to squeak through the keyhole. Hampered by a low reproduction rate, killed by possum snarers who never told anyone for fear of prosecution, the thylacine's numbers never rebounded the way the small, more fecund quolls and devils did—but neither, he is convinced, did they go extinct, all the history books to the contrary.

My dealings with Eric Guiler did not start quite the way I expected them to. I called him long before I left for Australia, wanting to introduce myself and arrange a meeting once I arrived in Hobart. But no sooner had I explained that I was writing about Tasmanian tigers than he cut me off in mid-sentence.

"Thylacines? I wish I'd never heard of the wretched animals," he said. This was a shock, coming from Dr. Thylacine himself, but I sallied on with a halting explanation of my work. After a while the frost seemed to thaw a bit, and he agreed, though with thinly concealed reluctance, to meet.

Once I got to Australia and called from Sydney, though, Guiler became a good deal more evasive; he wasn't sure about his schedule, he would be in the field doing research or going bushwalking with friends, and perhaps other people would be better for me to interview. "What did you say you were again? Television? Radio?" he asked at one point. No, I assured him, I was a writer, one who specializes in natural science. It wasn't until my third or fourth phone call that the topic of my own wildlife research came up; I was commiserating with him about the difficulties of fieldwork and happened to mention the modest bird-banding and radiotelemetry I do back home in Pennsylvania. That proved to be the key, and his reticence began to evaporate. When we finally met, on a sunny morning in Hobart, he explained his initial reluctance.

"Don't get this wrong," he said at one point. "I'm enjoying talking to you, because you're a biologist and we have common interests, but normally you get some crack-headed bloody idiot who knows nothing about science and asks the most stupid goddamned questions. I just got sick of it. That's why I don't have E-mail—I'd be flooded with stupid thylacine questions."

Guiler's relationship with "the wretched animal" has clearly been a two-edged sword. He is, of course, best known for his interest in thylacines, an obsession that started fifty years ago, culminating in several major expeditions to search—he believes successfully—for evidence of its survival, and which he has documented in a number of popular books. But while the thylacine has given him international recognition, there is a lot more to Eric Guiler than Tassie tigers. A native of Belfast, he served in Africa during World War II, then fled Ireland's draconian postwar rationing to take a position at the University of Tasmania, where he got a doctorate in marine biology. Even though he retired from teaching in 1982, the eighty-year-old continues to do research on the rare Cape Barrens goose, among other topics. A bit below average height, with a square, lined face and a fringe of white hair, he is a charming man, given to sly jokes and a blunt, colorful turn of phrase.

When Guiler arrived in Tasmania, the thylacine had been officially extinct for just eleven years, and many of the old trappers and hunters who had pursued it for bounty were still alive, their minds sharp and their recollections fresh. This, he understandably believes, gives him an unparalleled grasp on a vanished species, and he bristled a little when I asked about some of the newer theories about the thylacine that have gained credence in recent years, such as skepticism about the tiger's supposed taste for blood.

Perhaps the strongest challenge to Guiler's traditional view has come from Robert Paddle, an animal behaviorist who teaches psychology at Australian Catholic University. Paddle's interest in the thylacine led him first to a doctoral dissertation on its extinction and then to a dense and rigorously documented book, *The Last Tasmanian Tiger*, based primarily on nineteenth-century sources, like wool-station archives, which he believes have been overlooked or misinterpreted by previous researchers. Paddle disputes almost everything held in common wisdom about the thylacine—its propensity for eating sheep, the stories of it drinking blood (the index lists "blood-feeding: *see* myths, vampirism"), the impact of the bounty schemes on its population, and even the gender and name of the last captive tiger, a creature that has, with time, become a symbol of lost species in general.

In a way, Paddle and the old guard, represented by Guiler, are engaged in a battle for the soul of the thylacine—one side casting it in the traditional role of the stupid and ill-adapted marsupial that survived only where placental mammals did not live, addicted to an easy meal of stolen mutton and incapable of surviving in the face of modern human society. Paddle and his supporters, which include Tim Flannery, take a much different approach, one that aims directly at what they see as a Eurocentric, anti-marsupial bias coloring the perception of not only the thylacine but all of Australia's natural heritage—an extension of the racist and condescending attitude most Europeans also had toward Aboriginal culture. Anything Australian was, they charge, held to be fundamentally inferior to its European equivalent. One benefit of such a belief is that it conveniently absolves Europeans of blame for losses and extinctions, be they natural or cultural, since the losses were obviously the result of inferiority.

While acknowledging the great store of material Paddle combed through, Guiler dismissed the most controversial aspects of the new book: "Bob and I had it out over the phone the other night—he said the *Mercury* [the Hobart newspaper] is trying to stir up a row between the two of us, and he said I'm not in it. I said, I'm not interested in having a row with you, Bob, but I did tell him, You did make some wild statements, completely unsubstantiated."

For example, Paddle—seeking in part to dismantle the old notion that thylacines were stupid and untrainable—mentions a number of cases in which people claimed to have kept them as pets. "But he doesn't substantiate keeping them as a household pet. He does quote some people, but it's obviously wrong—everyone I interviewed said nobody would ever keep them as a pet. And he also says they didn't feed on blood. Well, all the old-timers—you see," he said, leaning forward and tapping a finger on the table for emphasis, "I'm in a privileged position inasmuch as I could interview the old-timers who actually caught the animals and knew something about them. They're all dead now, and at best the stories you get now are thirdhand. I prefer to believe the guys who actually knew something about the animal."

Guiler and Paddle agree that the epidemic had a serious impact on the thylacine, though Paddle believes a significant upsurge in the number of tigers killed for bounty around World War I was a sign that the disease had altered their behavior, making them less wary and easier to catch, a view Guiler rejects. But without question, by the 1920s the beasts had become profoundly rare, and increasingly worried conservationists were agitating for their full protection. It was too little, too late. The last thylacine to be killed, at least so far as the official record goes, was one shot in 1930 near Mawbanna in the northwest. There's an oft-reproduced photo of the lean animal, propped up next to a fence beside the chap who killed it, a smiling, handsome young man named Wilf Batty, posing with his obviously nervous sheepdog and an old hammer shotgun. The tiger had been hanging around the neighborhood for some time before Batty encountered it at his henhouse, and it showed no fear of him, even when he tried to catch it by the tail; only when he missed the grab and the thylacine ran for the fence did he shoot.

Three years later, in 1933, a timber cutter and trapper named Elias Churchill captured a live thylacine somewhere in the Florentine valley, on the fringe of the southwestern mountains. Churchill had snared seven other tigers in the preceding decade, though only two of them were in good enough condition to sell to zoos—snaring is hard on an animal, and most were dead when found, or had to be destroyed. But this last animal, a young female, wasn't hurt badly, so Churchill contacted the Beaumaris Zoo, a small collection of native and exotic wildlife in Hobart, and they agreed on a price. Eventually the tiger was tied up, strapped to the back of a horse, and hauled to the nearest railway line, where it was caged and shipped to Hobart.

Catching thylacines for zoos was a bit of a local industry in the Tasmanian bush in the late nineteenth and early twentieth centuries. The species was kept in captivity as early as the 1840s, and by the Victorian era there was a small but brisk trade in live thylacines—the Melbourne Zoo acquired seventeen of them between 1875 and 1925, and thylacines were exported to zoos as far afield as Berlin, Antwerp, Paris, and New York. The London Zoo exhibited thylacines almost continuously from the 1860s until the last one died in 1931, while the National Zoo in Washington was notable for its acquisition, in 1902, of a female with three pouch babies—the only such family ever studied in captivity.

As the only zoo in Tasmania in the early decades of the twentieth century, the Beaumaris Zoo figures prominently in the story of the thylacine's twilight. Founded privately in the 1890s, the zoo was transferred to the city of Hobart in the 1920s, when the original owner died. It may have been a way station for many of the thylacines shipped overseas, perhaps in a swap for other animals the Hobart Zoo needed. Eventually, the tiger's scarcity put an end to this trade; in fact, one of the underlying motives for the first (and failed) attempt to grant the thylacine legal protection, in 1928, was the fact that Tasmanian institutions were miffed at being priced out of the market for their own rarity.

The city of Hobart took over operation of the Beaumaris Zoo but seems to have had little real interest in maintaining it, though a well-qualified naturalist and gamebird breeder, Arthur Reid, was hired to act as curator. But after he was severely beaten by a man whom he'd caught trying to steal birds from the zoo, Reid's health began to decline, and eventually his thirty-one-year-old daughter, Alison, took over care of the animals. So it was Alison Reid who was in charge of animal care after the last thylacine, the one snared by Elias Churchill, reached Hobart; shortly after its arrival, David Fleay filmed it in its spartan cage and received his infamous bite on the rear.

By all reports (and I rely here primarily on Paddle's excellent account), Alison Reid was highly competent at her job, but she was a woman in a man's world, and after her father's death in 1935 the zoo withdrew any salary, requiring her to work as unpaid curator in return for free housing for herself and her mother in a small zoo cottage—conditions she later recalled, with understandable bitterness, as being little more than slavery. Nor was she entrusted with a set of keys for the zoo, which meant she was unable to tend the animals before the facility opened in the morning or closed in the afternoon, and was unable to deal with emergencies that arose after hours. This often meant that animals were left out in their exposed runs overnight, instead of being returned to their shelters. Cutbacks in zoo staff brought on by the Depression further reduced the level of animal care, as did replacement of trained workers with those from the local welfare rolls.

All this was a catastrophe for the Hobart Zoo's animals, which began to die from neglect despite Reid's best efforts and increasingly frantic pleas. She was particularly concerned about the last thylacine, which was often forced to spend the night in its open concrete run because she couldn't get back into the zoo after hours to open its sleeping cage. She went over the head of the zoo manager to the town clerk with her complaints, and was rewarded by being evicted from the cottage she shared with her mother.

As this was transpiring, Tasmania was experiencing strangely extreme weather—the winter had been particularly frigid, and with the arrival of spring in September 1936, the mercury rocketed to nearly 100 degrees, though it plunged below freezing at night. Exposed to the sun and (when its sleeping cage was left unopened) the cold nights, the thylacine was in serious trouble, and Alison Reid was unable to do much to help it. "Thus, unprotected and exposed, the last known thylacine whimpered away during the night of 7 September 1936, as much a victim of sexual as species chauvinism," Paddle noted, accurately if a bit portentously.

But this question of sexism and the Tasmanian tiger takes an even weirder turn. Open virtually any book or article on thylacines published in the last thirty years and you'll probably see the last tiger referred to as a male named Benjamin. Giving the last survivor of a vanished species a personal name somehow makes the tragedy more immediate, as with Martha, the last passenger pigeon, and few authors miss a chance to pin a name on the last thylacine. But as already noted, the animal that died in the Hobart Zoo was a young adult female—a fact confirmed by Alison Reid before her death in 1997. So why the switch in gender?

The false story was spread in later years by a fellow named Frank Darby, who claimed—absent any evidence—that he worked for the zoo and cared for the tiger. His colorful stories about caring for "Benjy" were published by a mainland Australian newspaper columnist and have been circulating in both the scientific and popular press ever since. It's representative, Paddle argues, of the mythology and misinformation surrounding the thylacine, and larger social issues between the sexes, that Darby's statements on everything from thylacine behavior to vocalization (he claimed they were mute, when in fact they could be quite noisy) have entered the canon on the species, while the experiences of the woman who actually had the most contact with the last known thylacine were completely ignored.

The death of the Hobart Zoo's thylacine was not immediately recognized as the end of the species. The very next year, the first of what would become a long string of hunts and searches for the beast were mounted, and initially, most people thought a few more tigers would certainly turn up. Sightings were still being reported, but from unofficial sources and without the kind of physical evidence, like a corpse or a live tiger, that would be incontrovertible. Only with time did the realization sink in that the thylacine was extinct.

But Tasmania remains reluctant to let go of its tiger. As I noticed from my first moments at the Hobart airport, the beast has become an icon—stylized on automobile license plates, gracing the label of the state's best-selling beer, adopted as the symbol of everything from a regional television network to local sports teams. In the weeks that I wandered around Tasmania, I started collecting pictures and notes of the various thylacine incarnations I encountered, like the Tiger Bar in the little hamlet of Mole Creek up by the Western Tiers (also home to the "Tassie Tiger Research Centre," which appeared deserted, even though I rapped on its storefront window, which was decorated with a hand-painted thylacine), or the bronze effigy of a thylacine family in a wildlife sculpture garden that sits, unexpectedly, in the middle of nowhere along a dirt road on the Central Plateau. In northwestern Tassie, I found signs along the "Tasmanian Tiger Trail," a recent promotional idea hatched by the local government council as a way of attracting tourists. (The sign in the town of Waratah, for example, noted that, in 1933, two thylacines captured near there were sent to the Launceston Zoo.) There are tigers everywhere on the bookshelves, too, not only serious adult works like Guiler's and Paddle's, but many children's books—and I find it interesting that every kid's book I saw took it for granted that the tigers still exist. Some were nonfiction, but most were illustrated storybooks in which kids spot a thylacine; in one, they tell a Parks and Wildlife ranger, who counsels them to keep it a secret to protect the tigers.

The most surprising and affecting memorial I saw, though, was a piece of what can only be described as roadside folk art. Driving along a lonely track in central Tasmania, I found a crude painting rendered on the flat rock wall of a shallow road cut. It was maybe 6 feet long and 3 feet high, showing a pair of tigers against a simple background of brown earth and blue sky. There was no signature, no legend or title— no explanation at all for why the anonymous artist chose this subject, or this spot, though the old bounty records suggest that this part of Tassie was once a stronghold for thylacines.

In 1952, Eric Guiler was appointed to the Animal and Birds Protection Board, the government wildlife agency commonly referred to as the Fauna Board. "Reports kept coming in of thylacine sightings, and nobody was doing anything about it, so I decided I'd just start writing them down—and that's really how I became interested," he said.

It had been the Fauna Board that, with the Tasmanian Museum, pulled together a three-man contingent in 1937 that scoured the hinterlands, finding what they believed to be tracks and droppings, and collecting eyewitness accounts from trappers who agreed that yes, there were still a few thylacines about. The police officer who led the venture recommended the government create a thylacine sanctuary on the Arthur and Pieman Rivers in northwestern Tasmania, but no action was taken. Later that same year, a follow-up search in an especially remote section of the western mountains turned up signs of what the trackers believed were at least four individual tigers. David Fleay, he of the thylacine bite, spent months in the field in 1945–46 with several colleagues, lugging heavy metal live traps deep into the bush, baiting them with raw meat and live chickens. They failed to catch a thylacine, though Fleay did claim that one had narrowly escaped a trap, leaving some of its hair snagged in the door.

With a mounting number of sightings—and with concern about expeditions specifically intending to catch a tiger for zoo exhibition—the Fauna Board clamped down on permits for privately funded parties at the same time Guiler began what would prove to be several decades of periodic searching for the elusive animal. Much of this fieldwork was conducted with the help of two police officers—"wardens really," Guiler told me, "and one of these two police sergeants, George Hanlon, was an extremely good bushman, very competent. He was tops, and I learned a helluva lot of bushcraft from him. We were walking through the bush, and he says to me, 'Doc, how many possum trees have we passed?' And I say I don't know, and he says, 'Well, Doc, you should keep your bloody eyes open.' Another time we were down in a deep rain-forest area and he asked me where was north. I bumbled and pointed and said, 'That way, George.' And he said, 'Doc, you're 2 degrees out.' He was a remarkable man."

Hanlon was also a master of the arcane craft of snaring, a technique that Tasmanian bushmen had been using for centuries to catch game, especially brushtail possums, whose thick, glossy pelts were valuable. A limber sapling was bent down to the ground, rigged with rope to a complex arrangement of carved wooden stakes and pegs so that an animal stepping into it and jarring the treadle peg would find itself suddenly yanked into the air. Snaring had also been the method of choice in bounty days for catching thylacines, and with some modifications—using leg-hold sets instead of "neckers" designed to kill the animal—Hanlon and Guiler set many in the hopes of catching a live tiger. The amount of physical work involved was staggering; over the course of one six-month stretch they set 72,000 snares.

"George was a brilliant snarer. He once caught a kangaroo by its back toe—the kangaroo was a bit cross, of course—and another time he set a snare outside the hut and caught me in it! We caught everything else in the bush that creeps or moves, but we didn't catch a thylacine," Guiler said. Often, the game they caught became food for the expedition, since they were usually a long way from the nearest store, and some of the black-and-white photos from those days show Hanlon and Guiler working over a makeshift plank table in their tent camp, skinning wallabies, the muscular hindquarters hanging from the limb of a tree with canvas covers to keep away the flies.

Though they never succeeded in catching a thylacine, they did find what Guiler considers convincing physical evidence. From 1959 to 1961, he and Hanlon mounted expeditions to the northwestern tip of Tasmania to survey Woolnorth, the last remaining parcel of the old Van Dieman's Land Company, and to this day a sprawling sheep and cattle operation that has changed little with the centuries. They were drawn to Woolnorth, from which many thylacines had been turned in for bounty, by continuing sightings by the station personnel. On their very first visit, Guiler and Hanlon found a line of what appeared to be thylacine footprints along a section of muddy dirt track.

"They were in firm mud, which is the best medium for footprints," said Dr. Guiler, who quickly mixed up plaster and created casts of the long line of tracks. The tracks had all the characteristics of a thylacine print, including a deeply cleft rear footpad and toes that were significantly less bunched than on a dog's foot. Tellingly, while they'd been scouting in the same area the previous night with lights, the hunters noticed that the other wildlife was very skittish, sticking close to cover— behavior they'd never encountered before. The tracks convinced them that they'd come within a whisker of seeing a live thylacine.

On other occasions at Woolnorth, the expedition found scat, several inches long and containing calf hair, which could have been from a thylacine—or, he concedes, from a Tasmanian devil or a dog, since their droppings are all rather similar. In 1965, also at Woolnorth, they found an animal's lair in a rocky cave, with indistinct tracks and piles of old scat—intriguing, but again not as conclusive as their first set of tracks. Once, Guiler's party actually saw a large, striped animal they were certain was a thylacine—until they got binoculars on it and realized it was an enormous house cat, so large that the ranch personnel said it had attacked some of their dogs.

By Guiler's reckoning, there were more than thirty thylacine-hunting expeditions between 1937 and the mid-1990s, ranging from poorly planned private undertakings to large, well-heeled affairs with official imprimatur, like the Woolnorth search. Some were meticulously organized, using then-cutting-edge equipment like automatic cameras set along game trails. But whether it's the Loch Ness monster or ivory-billed woodpeckers, the notion of lost species also brings out the silly in people. Over the years, the folks clamoring to look for the thylacine included filmmakers from Walt Disney Studios (who quickly abandoned the idea when they realized how limited their chances of success would be) and French actress and animal activist Brigitte Bardot, whose much-hyped proposal to conduct a search died a rapid death as well. Media mogul Ted Turner once offered a $100,000 reward for evidence of a thylacine, setting off such a stampede of interest that the government had to mount a publicity campaign to remind folks that it was still a crime to kill a tiger. It wasn't the first time press hype got caught up in the thylacine's tale—when Sir Edmund Hillary arrived in Tasmania a few years after climbing Mt. Everest, the papers were full of reports that he, too, was seeking the legendary tiger, when in truth, all Sir Edmund was looking for was some peaceful hiking.

As a result of all his fieldwork, Guiler is certain that the thylacine survived its putative extinction. In a book he co-authored a few years ago with Philippe Godard, Guiler lists thylacines said to have been caught or killed after the last captive died in 1936. They include one caught in 1948 by possum trapper Ray Blizzard, who admitted clubbing to death what he described as an old and mangy tiger, known to have been in the area for years. Another was said to have been "killed and buried in a fowlyard" in 1950, and two years later a tiger was allegedly run over by a car near Deloraine. The last killing Guiler lists came in 1977, a thylacine said to have been shot somewhere on the northwest Tasmania coast.

In none of these cases, however, was a body produced for the authorities—the one undeniable bit of evidence that would have cinched the tiger's survival. Skeptics consider this proof that all the talk about living thylacines is so much wishful thinking, but Guiler thinks those who found themselves possessing a dead thylacine took the "shoot, shovel, and shut up" approach.

"This is one of the problems of the legislation [protecting thylacines]—when I was running the Fauna Board I made it quite clear to people that biological information brought into me would have nothing whatsoever to do with prosecutions, so that if somebody ran over a Tasmanian tiger and brought the body in, there would be no prosecution," he said. "You'd never make it stick in court anyway. In those days there was a big snaring industry in Tasmania, and there was something like 250,000 brushtail possums taken a year. And incidental to that, some tigers must have been snared, but nobody ever told anyone about it. I've heard of them being snared, but nothing official."

Not everyone would consider wandering around the Tasmanian bush at night looking for a large carnivore to be a prudent thing to do. Though old-timers often expressed a fear of thylacines, it's hard to say whether they posed any significant danger to humans—some folks called them man-killers, while one naturalist in the 1850s who had kept

them in captivity said the thylacine "seems far from being a vicious animal at its worst, and the name tiger or hyena gives a most unjust idea of
its fierceness." Here again, contradiction is the order of the day, and as
an indication of the level of uncertainty and conflicting information
that's been published on the thylacine, I offer the case of Miss P. Murray,
who appears to have been attacked by a Tassie tiger around—well, you'll
understand in a moment. This, as Robert Paddle pointed out in his
book, is the most frequently cited case of a thylacine attack on a person,
but almost every detail about it is up for grabs, as his recitation of the
various versions makes clear. (For ease of reading, I have omitted Paddle's dozens of parenthetical sources.)

> Miss Patricia, Pricilla, Priscilla or Prucilla Murray; either as a
> young girl in the 1860s, young girl in 1900 or mature woman in
> 1900; was outside, in the winter, or in the summer; either doing
> the laundry—by washing clothes at a bench, washing clothes in a
> river, or hanging clothes out to dry—or alternatively, peeling po-
> tatoes; either at Springfield, near Scottsdale, in a suburb of Ho-
> bart, or at a west coast creek; when she was bitten, either on an
> arm, the right arm and left hand, shoulder, or leg; by a one-eyed
> thylacine that was either toothless (apparently as suggested in the
> original newspaper report), or well-fanged (as suggested by the
> permanent scar left from several teeth). With the thylacine at-
> tached to a part of her anatomy Miss Murray tried to protect her-
> self by reaching for a garden hoe, hose or rake. In doing so she
> trod on the thylacine's tail and the thylacine let go. Threatened
> with the hoe/hose/rake the animal either successfully 'slunk
> away,' or ran and fled or unsuccessfully retreated, before being
> killed.

"From the above, it would appear not unreasonable to suggest that a
Miss Murray did exist, who, at some point in her life was bitten by a
thylacine," Paddle concluded—with a relatively straight face.

For many lost species, there is one canonical moment that defines the
hope for its survival—one incident that even the greatest skeptic must
admit carries the weight of credibility. In the case of the thylacine, that

moment was Hans Naarding's purported 1982 sighting, which I mentioned earlier. The official report submitted by the Tasmanian Parks and Wildlife ranger read as follows:

> As I swept the beam around, it came to rest on a large thylacine, standing side-on [in profile] some six to seven metres distant. My camera bag was out of immediate reach so I decided to examine the animal carefully before risking movement. It was an adult male in excellent condition with 12 black stripes on a sandy coat. Eye reflection was pale yellow. It moved only once, opening its mouth and showing its teeth. After several minutes of observation I attempted to reach my camera bag but in doing so I disturbed the animal and it moved away into the undergrowth. Leaving the vehicle and moving to where the animal disappeared I noted a strong scent. Despite an intensive search no further trace of the animal could be found.

When a farmer says he saw a thylacine scurry across the road in the wavering headlights of his truck, it's easy to dismiss the sighting as a misidentification, but Naarding was an experienced wildlife professional, and the sighting occurred at close range. What's more, there had been a spate of tiger reports in the area—a second-growth stand of gum forest near Togari, close to the northwestern tip of the island—over the preceding two years. Certainly, his superiors took the report very seriously. They kept the claim strictly quiet, so as not to attract hordes of thrill seekers or, God forbid, someone who might want to shoot a tiger, and they assigned one of their research officers, Nick Mooney, to the case. Mooney mounted an intensive search of the Togari area over the next two years, monitoring hundreds of sections of trails for tracks, some baited with road-killed wallabies and kept artificially muddy for the best tracking conditions. He set automatic cameras along game runs, located more than fifty potential den sites, and regularly monitored several of the most promising ones. Some prints and scat were found, though nothing that Mooney considered at all conclusive, and the investigation ended without proof.

Naarding's sighting is as good as an eyewitness account alone can get—and yet, to my surprise, I found that Eric Guiler doesn't believe it.

In part because Mooney did such a thorough job with such meager results, Guiler wonders whether Naarding experienced a sort of waking
dream—jarred awake from a nap alone, in the middle of the night, in
the midst of a storm, he may have been groggy enough to think he saw a
thylacine when in fact he was still half-asleep.

The Togari incident was on my mind one dawn as I hiked along a high
ridge near the Collingwood River in western Tasmania, with honeyeaters crowding the yellow flowers of *Banksia* trees and low clouds
sweeping their chill, foggy undersides through the woods. Unlike the
dry hills along the Apsley River in the island's northeast, the western
mountains stand jagged and thousands of feet high, wringing a lot of
moisture from the air, so the forests along the Collingwood's headwaters
are mostly temperate rain forest. Thick bright-green mosses grew chest-
high on the tree trunks, and the understory was crowded with tree ferns
that rose well above my head. Whenever the forest opened, I could see
the precipitous drop on either side of me, and the low yellow light striking the eastern flanks of imposing mountains. I was near the rugged
heart of the enormous Tasmanian Wilderness World Heritage Area,
which encompasses three major national parks—Cradle Mountain,
Franklin-Gordon Wild Rivers, and Southwest, as well as several smaller
units. Together they account for more than 5,000 square miles of
quartzite peaks, beech and gum forests, and fast-flowing, rapids-strewn
rivers, an area more than a third larger than Yellowstone.

This is good country, the kind of place where you see and feel little
of humanity. The World Heritage Area protects one of just three major
temperate rain forests in the Southern Hemisphere, a wonderland of giant trees, buttongrass meadows, and silent, mossy shadows. Tree ferns
with spreading umbrellas of fronds like ostrich feathers grow beneath
tall, conical myrtles of the genus *Nothofagus*—one of many Australian
plants with hand-me-down English names, for this attractive tree is actually related to the Northern Hemisphere beeches. It was once the
dominant player in the forests of old Gondwana, the ancient southern
supercontinent that also included South America, where *Nothofagus* is
still found in the southernmost Andes.

Myrtle is a graceful tree, with tiny, fingernail-sized leaves that give
it an airy quality, but the real monarchs here were the gum-topped
stringybarks that towered above them, a species of eucalyptus that may

exceed 100 feet, with heavy trunks as much as 8 or 10 feet through the base. They rose above the canopy of dark beeches, their branches drooping with slender silvery leaves that danced in the boisterous mountain wind, which cooled my sweaty shirt when I stopped and unslung my pack for a breather.

The trail I was following, in the northern fringe of the Franklin-Gordon, had emerged again from the trees to run along a narrow saddle, dropping off steep and sheer on one side toward the foaming Collingwood hundreds of feet below. The view was arresting, with the pale quartzite peaks of several high ranges to the south, including the tilted, triangular hulk of Frenchman's Cap, at nearly 4,800 feet the highest point on the horizon. The river, tannin-brown with white rapids, flowed through a tangled gorge thickly forested in myrtle and gum that opened up to one side to a wide, flat expanse of buttongrass meadow fringed with ranks of tall eucalypts. Everywhere I looked there were mountains, and if they were not as high as, say, the Rockies or the Sierras, they certainly rivaled them for utter beauty—which is a biased way of putting it. It would be as true to say that the Tetons or Sierras rival anything in western Tasmania.

Almost from the moment of its purported extinction, thylacine reports have come from this region, including sightings along the Collingwood River that attracted an expedition in the 1940s. With the exception of the paved Lyell Highway, which now bisects the World Heritage Area, very little has changed here since the 1940s—or the 1840s, for that matter, when Sir John Franklin and his wife struggled through here with a surveying party, a few years before his famous disappearance in the Arctic. Looking out over this small slice of what I know to be an extraordinary reach of wild land, I find myself wondering, How can anyone *not* believe there are still thylacines here? More than any lost species I've chased, this one would seem to have its context intact and unbroken, both a sanctuary and a hiding place, here in this fortress of alpine forest. Who could ever hope to penetrate these mountains and their dense forests carefully enough to ferret out the existence of a few shy and lingering marsupial wolves?

And yet that hope ignores the history of the thylacine itself, for the animal that now embodies Tasmania's wild, pre-European past was never a creature of the high mountains and rain forests. Using bounty payments, trappers' accounts, and other records, Eric Guiler has mapped the thylacine's range in Tasmania, and while it was found in most areas of the state, it was especially common along the coast and in scrub, and on the eastern slope of the central mountains—not in the rugged, wet ranges that make up most of the wilderness heritage area, where the thick cover wasn't suitable for the large, grazing marsupials like wallabies on which the thylacine most heavily preyed. Old trappers told Guiler they never caught a tiger west of King William Saddle, the pass that divides the more arid east from the rain-soaked mountains of the west.

There is wilderness that would make good thylacine habitat—Guiler especially wonders about parts of the southwestern coast, protected within national parks and the heritage area. "It's good tiger country, because you've got consolidated sand dunes with little watery ponds behind them, nice green grass, everything's nice and shiny and bright, and tigers could sneak around there at night and nail a wallaby," he said. "One night I was walking along the beach down there, about one o'-clock in the morning, and the game was behaving in a most peculiar fashion. It was a full moon that night, and the kangaroo and wallaby were the most scared I've ever seen in my life, feeding right close to the edge of the scrub, and the minute you appeared—*whoosh*—right into the scrub. I think a tiger went through there ahead of us. I have no evidence for it, but I had that hunch that something had gone through there."

He still feels fairly confident about northwestern Tasmania, too, but in the northeast, fewer and fewer tiger sightings are being claimed. I find this a telling clue that is, oddly enough, perhaps stronger evidence for the continued survival of thylacines than the more consistent reports out of the northwest. If the reports were all moonshine and twaddle, then you'd expect them to be rather evenly spread out in time and place, since imagination is not limited by geography. The fact that in one region they are declining, while in another they remain steady, makes me suspect there is a living creature at their core.

That belief wars with what I know about small-population biology—the dangers faced by any tiny community of animals. If thylacines have survived the nearly seventy years since their assumed extinction, they must be in extraordinarily meager numbers and spread thinly over a huge landscape. It seems likely they would be fiercely inbred, with all the reproductive and genetic problems that flow from that. They would be prey to what scientists call stochastic factors, random, unpredictable events like droughts, fires, storms, horrific winters, disease; the list is long, and each of these occurrences has an effect on animal populations. Those species that are widespread and abundant can absorb stochastic events, while those that are exceedingly rare, as the thylacine would have to have been to have evaded us for so long, often cannot, and thus they become extinct.

The rule of thumb biologists have come up with for the viability of mammalian populations is that you generally need about five hundred individuals to maintain long-term genetic variation and health. Not even Eric Guiler thinks there are anywhere near five hundred thylacines hiding in the Tasmanian wilds, and he suspects that even in their heyday they were still pretty rare critters. "I did some very simple calculations once which suggest that at the time of maximum abundance, around about 1900, there were between two thousand and four thousand thylacines in Tasmania. So they were never a common animal. In the early 1900s, the father of a friend of mine who lives up at Ringarooma rode 20 miles on a horse to see one that had been caught. Now, you're not going to ride 20 miles to see a common animal—so it always was rare. And I theorize they were on their way out and we just kicked them over the edge."

Over the edge? Such past-tense slips are understandable when the subject is a lost species, but in fact I was surprised that Dr. Guiler argued as forcefully and convincingly as he did for the continued existence of the thylacine. In his last book on the species, the one he co-authored in 1998 with Philippe Godard, they wrote: "In all honesty, the authors must admit to being of those who no longer really believe—an attitude that certainly earns them no compliments—in the survival of the Tasmanian tiger, when others continue to nurture the hope of seeing the animal reappear one day."

Yet as we wrapped up our long conversation about tigers that day in Hobart, I asked him the simple question that had been on my mind for weeks: Does the Tassie tiger still live? For the first time, his direct gaze wandered, and he was quiet for so long I wondered if I'd somehow offended him.

"I know I said in that last book that I thought they'd finally gone ex-

tinct," he said at last, "but now, I'm not so sure. Nick Mooney's still getting reports, and some of them are pretty good, especially from the
northwest. Perhaps I'm just reluctant to let it go, too. I don't know," he
said, shaking his head and lapsing into silence, looking out the window.
"I just don't know."

"So what should be done to save them, if there are any left to save?" I
asked.

"There's nothing you *can* do," Guiler said flatly. "You've got an animal
about whose behavior we know virtually nothing, about whose movements we know nothing, about whose general physiology we know
nothing. We know so little about it, it's impossible to devise a management plan. We don't even know where the damned things are living.
How do you devise a management plan for something like that?" In the
end, although he remains defiantly hopeful, even Eric Guiler can't be
sure if the Tasmanian tiger still moves, wraithlike, in the shade of the
swamp gums and stringybarks, sending the wallabies scattering in fear as
it did for millions of years.

That image, of a lissome, wolflike shape moving through a rich and dap-
pled forest, was on my mind one morning when I rose in the darkness in
the Western Tiers, the waterfall-scoured mountains that rim the Central
Plateau. The hiking track to one of those falls is a long, rugged climb
skirting the edge of a valley, originally cut by glacial ice in a wide-
mouthed U, but eroded further by the large stream it carries into a
steep-sided defile. Well-watered and shaded by tall beeches and eucalypts, the forest is a mossy, dimly lit place, broken at higher elevations
by wide fields of boulders, cracked loose over the eons from the high
cliffs and now covered in orange and gray lichen.

I started up the mountain shortly after sunrise, and by late morning I
was high on the escarpment, moving across talus slopes that reached
down like gray tongues from the peaks. As the trail reentered the trees,
something big crashed through the undergrowth, and a pandemelon
leaped onto the trail, saw me, and froze for a long moment, then
bounded away; I couldn't imagine how anything could move with such
speed through such thickets. But I had no time to wonder, because up
ahead, it sounded as though someone was rhythmically working a badly

oiled pump handle—then many pump handles. I found a tall beech tree full of squawking, flapping parrots the size and color of crows—yellow-tailed black-cockatoos, their inky body feathers edged with yellow, big canary patches on their cheeks and their long, square tails. As I watched, more and more flew in, to the accompaniment of still more caterwauling, until two dozen of the big birds scrambled around the slender branches of the *Nothofagus*, nibbling at the tiny nuts borne in small greenish capsules on the twigs. Standing beneath the loud, gluttonous flock, I felt and heard a steady rain of empty seed cones and severed twigs, and the methodical clatter of big, thick beaks.

Another half hour brought me to the falls. The small river I'd been paralleling crashed down a sheer 400-foot cliff, broken in the middle of its drop by a single ledge, onto which, with a little careful climbing, I was able to scramble to sit beside the rushing waterfall. The view down the valley was breathtaking; bare fields of orangish dolerite rock littered the sides of the high peaks, below which grew a solid blanket of eucalyptus and beech forest. The long, wide valley faded to blue in the distance, with rank after rank of mountains, hazy and indistinct, on either hand.

Once, this had been tiger country—and perhaps still is, if Dr. Guiler and the other diehard optimists are right. But let us say for the moment that the thylacine exists only in museum specimens, like that pickled pouch baby in Sydney. If, by a miracle of molecular science, Don Colgan and his colleagues at the Australian Museum succeed in creating a living, breathing animal, what will they have? One individual does not a species make, and even with many old specimens to mine for DNA, building a population of a few dozen unique tigers would be the labor of decades and many more millions of dollars.

Today, the thylacine is a phantom, a warning, and an icon, all clad in a striped coat. Clone one, the skeptics say, and it becomes a mere novelty; clone a couple dozen, and they become a conservation headache—a population that needs a home, and managing, and oversight, just another endangered species in a world already parceling out limited resources to husband so many others. And it may serve to deaden the public's worry over critically rare organisms by planting the comfortable but incorrect notion that there's a scientific quick fix even for something as permanent as extinction.

And there is an even less tangible question, but one that struck me hard, as I sat in the bright sun and looked out over Tassie's beautiful mountains, a wedge-tailed eagle riding on cocked wings over the high peaks. How much of what made a thylacine a thylacine—the way it moved, the way it hunted, the way it integrated itself with its prey and its environment—was a matter of hard-wiring in the genes, and how much was a matter of cultural transmission from parent to offspring, in links that spanned 30 million years but now are irrevocably broken? How much came from within—how much can be reconstituted from strings of synthesized amino acids wrapped in an artificial membrane— and how much came from without, from the tiger's connection with the land itself? What relation would a cloned tiger have to the animal that met the first Aborigines forty thousand years ago, or watched with hungry eyes as the tall sailing ships unloaded their bleating cargo?

Yet despite the doubts, the roadblocks, the uncertainties, and the astronomical price tag, it's hard to argue with another feeling I had that day, and on many days in the forests of Tasmania—the almost visceral absence of a capstone predator, which even the project's critics acknowledge may provide the noblest motive for the drive to resurrect the thylacine. It made me think of what Michael Lynch, the fellow at the Tasmanian Conservation Trust, had said about cloning a tiger to wipe away the stain of guilt for our role in its extinction. Perhaps we need the thylacine more than the thylacine—sleeping in its jars of alcohol, stuffed in museum display cases, or, just maybe, still running in the nighttime woods—needs us.

TEN

Sweat Bees Ate Our Earwax

There was nothing subtle about the smell. When the breeze shifted, pushing the damp morning air into our faces, the stench walloped us like a physical blow—the reek of rotting meat and decay.

"Whew, *man*," Doug Wechsler said, wincing. "Smells like something died."

"Lots of somethings," I agreed, trying to breathe through my mouth.

We stood along a narrow, packed-dirt road in the hinterlands of Mato Grosso, in western Brazil, less than a hundred miles from the Bolivian border. On either side of us, low forest covered the rolling hills, with a wide band of tall grass fringing the road for a hundred yards or so. It was obvious the grass was hiding something very large and very ripe; just ahead, several yellow-headed vultures formed a mourning party on the road, and as we walked closer, they flapped languorously into the air.

Now we could hear the buzz of flies, and realized the smell was coming from a dump beside the road full of old cow hides, entrails, heads, and partial skeletons—apparently the offal of a butchering operation at one of the ranches we'd passed a few miles back. Unfortunately, the trail we needed to take was almost buried by the stinking heap—but it was either that or push through the waist-high grass, which in tropical pastureland is an invitation to a miserable number of chiggers and ticks. We held our breath and took the path, flies rising in clouds as we edged by.

Upwind of the dump, we gasped clean air and walked gratefully away from the mess. At the edge of the woods, Fabiano Olivera, a young biology student from the university in Cuiabá, paused and nudged a white object with his foot—the shoulder blade of a cow, one of hundreds of bleached bones lying in great piles; this had been a slaughterhouse dump for a long time, obviously.

"Looks like we've found the legendary Bovine Graveyard, where the cows of Brazil come to die," Doug said. Fabiano looked at him with some bewilderment. We'd hired the young man, slim, with a long brown ponytail hanging behind his head, as our guide and driver—something he often does between semesters, but he was slowly coming to realize we were not his typical ecotourists, interested in watching pretty sunsets from the verandah of a comfortable lodge in the Pantanal.

The three of us were starting an expedition that would, over the course of several weeks, carry us across nearly a thousand miles of bad road, forest, highland savanna, degraded farming land, and lush river valleys, searching for an enigmatic bird that had been seen only once, more than sixty years ago, in a place no one today can pinpoint. There were times when I felt it might make more sense to stand in the dark with a burlap sack, yelling, "Here, snipe snipe snipe!" But that came later.

While it might have felt like a snipe hunt, we were looking for a very real creature, a songbird that is one of the most famous lost species of South America. In the 1930s, a doctor traveling through Mato Grosso made a small collection of birds typical to the region, shooting and stuffing a few dozen species he encountered; later he showed his skins to a prominent French ornithologist, who realized that one of them— black with a white belly and an unusually pronounced beak—was a new species. This he named the cone-billed tanager, *Rhynchopthraupis mesoleuca*; scientists later decided it was similar to another, better-known bird, the black-and-white tanager of Peru and Ecuador, and shifted the cone-billed to the black-and-white's genus, *Conothraupis*, where it remains today.

That is all we know about it—the physical description of a single male specimen, and nothing else. No one has ever seen a cone-billed tanager again, and given the passage of time, it is generally considered to be extinct. Large areas of Mato Grosso have been wrecked ecologically—the dry forest slashed and scorched into small, isolated fragments; the native *cerrado* savanna plowed up for crops or converted to cattle pastures. It is entirely possible that the cone-billed tanager was a rare or local species even in the 1930s, and before anyone could find it again, its habitat was destroyed and it was driven to extinction. But Brazil is a huge country, and Mato Grosso is a vast state, almost a million square kilometers, one and a half times the size of Texas. Large areas of it have rarely if ever been visited by ornithologists or birders, and a 6-inch bird would be easy to overlook.

Moving in single file, we followed a sandy trail through the forest, Doug hauling a voluminous blue backpack from whose top protruded a telephoto lens the size of a kitchen waste can. Doug has what is arguably one of the world's cooler jobs; a trained ornithologist and a respected wildlife photographer, he directs VIREO (Visual Resources for Ornithology), an ambitious photo archive at the Academy of Natural Sciences in Philadelphia that plans to document all of the world's nine thousand or so species of birds photographically. That means he spends a lot of time overseas, in places like Borneo and Guyana, and today he was wearing his usual field uniform: a long-sleeved Oxford dress shirt well past its prime, sleeves flapping unbuttoned; a green Academy of Natural Sciences cap; and high-topped leather boots against the risk of snakes and thorns. Tall and lanky, with a boyishness that belies his forty-nine years, Doug's red hair is going sandy, but his beard is still orange; when he was a young man in the 1970s, studying antbirds in the Brazilian Amazon, the locals nicknamed him *guariba*, the Portuguese name for the red howler monkey.

I had my heavy tape recorder slung over one shoulder, and a shotgun microphone, an 18-inch-long wand with a foam cover, hanging in a leather holster at my belt. While Doug played a tape of the black-and-white tanager (we hoped the sound of its closest relative might entice a cone-billed tanager into view), I was recording unidentified bird songs and playing them back, usually luring the singer into view as it hunted for what it assumed was an intruder. Besides helping us in our search for the tanager, it gave me an opportunity to record the vocalizations of many species of birds that have rarely, if ever, been taped.

I was crouching in the middle of the trail, the microphone aimed at a thicket where a nameless antbird was warbling, when a most remarkable fly buzzed close. At first I was annoyed; the loud drone of its wings ruined the recording, but the bug was so beautiful—bright, metallic green and more than an inch long—that my disappointment vanished. It hovered a few feet away as though nailed in place, drifted closer and paused, then zoomed almost to my extended hand holding the microphone.

A second later it landed gently on my thumb; I was charmed, wishing I could get a picture of it. But the peaceful spell was broken when Fabiano glanced over, shouted something in Portuguese, and lunged at me, smacking at the fly with his hat.

"What the hell was that all about?" I asked, baffled and a bit angry.

"You do not know that fly?" Fabiano was incredulous. "It was a botfly, wanting to lay egg," he said.

I was no longer mad, or feeling especially charmed by the local insects; botflies present the traveler with a highly personal opportunity to become one with the tropical ecosystem. The adult female deposits her egg on the skin of a mammalian host, where the maggot hatches, burrows under, and begins to eat, eventually reaching the size of a peanut. I was familiar with the species common in Central America, which uses a mosquito as an intermediary—catching one, gluing an egg to its body, and releasing it like a guided missile to deliver its cargo (the body heat of a warm-blooded host prompts the egg to hatch, and the maggot squirms in the minute wound left by the mosquito). But this was the first time I'd encountered this species, which takes a more direct approach to offspring placement. For the rest of the day, I unconsciously kept rubbing at the spot on my thumb where the fly had landed, sure I could feel something prickling beneath the skin, and energetically swatted away the green flies whenever they became too bold.

We were about 50 kilometers north of the town of Jauru, which is itself about 300 kilometers west of Cuiabá, the capital of Mato Grosso. Jauru is pretty much the end of the line, a place of a few thousand souls where the asphalt runs out; beyond it is a rough dirt road that serves the ranches to the north, up toward the Rio Juruena—a river that would figure significantly in our search.

We'd left Jauru an hour before daybreak, driving our white VW van past the 50-foot-tall portrait of the Virgin that crowned the end of the main street, then out the washboard road, a plume of dust glowing red in our taillights. This road, we knew, used to lead to the river, but we had been warned in Jauru that 40 or 50 kilometers from town it was largely impassable. Such Third World travel updates, I've found, are no-

MATO GROSSO, BRAZIL

toriously unreliable, but this time our informants were right on the mark—at 44 km, just past two prosperous *estancias*, or ranches, the road became an eroded gully that promised to chew us up and spit us out if we continued.

On the horizon a couple of miles away, though, we could see the beginnings of forest. The tanager, as near as anyone can tell, is a creature of the forest edge, and we'd been looking for several days for just this kind of habitat—low, dry forest on sandy soil. We parked the van, gathered up our equipment, and Doug, Fabiano, and I set out on foot, passing the cow dump along the way.

I've known Doug Wechsler professionally for more than a decade, and after I'd returned from my search for Semper's warbler in St. Lucia—a species he'd looked for himself in the past—we started talking about collaborating on a hunt in South America. Doug had asked Dr. Robert Ridgely, a colleague of his at the academy and perhaps the leading authority on Neotropical birds, about the white-masked antbird, a mysterious species known from a single skin, collected near the Ecuador-Peru border in the late 1930s; because Doug's first research experience had been with antbird ecology, it seemed an enticing target. But Bob pointed out that the "type locality" for the antbird—the place where it had originally been collected—was known to within a couple of miles and had been scoured repeatedly by birders staying at a new ecotour lodge right in the area. No one had seen a trace of the antbird, which he considered a lost cause.

Instead, Ridgely suggested we make a run after the cone-billed tanager, which he thought a much more likely candidate for rediscovery. Over the years I'd read several times of the tanager—a bird somewhat larger than a sparrow, glossy black on its head, back, wings, and tail, with a small patch of white on each wing that, when at rest, looks like the corner of a handkerchief poking out of the breast pocket of a man's dark suit. In its general appearance, the cone-billed was very similar to its closest relative, the black-and-white tanager of Ecuador and Peru, but the two were separated by nearly 1,500 miles.

This description applies only to the male cone-billed tanager, because the female remains unseen and undescribed—the species is known from the single specimen collected by Dr. A. Vellard in Mato Grosso on August 25, 1938. In this, the tanager is unusual but by no means unique. There are, in fact, a number of South American birds that turned up in specimen collections in the nineteenth and early twentieth centuries, never to be seen again—like the buff-cheeked tody-flycatcher, a tiny bird with a name longer than itself, collected just once, in 1830 in Brazil. Yet despite the long stretch since their original discovery, some birds have recently been relocated; they include the Tumaco seedeater, first collected in 1912 on a tiny island off the Colombian coast and not found there again until the mid-1990s. A case that gave us particular hope was that of the cherry-throated tanager from eastern Brazil—first recorded in the mid-nineteenth century, it vanished for nearly a hundred years, was briefly sighted in 1941, and then dropped from sight again for almost six decades before it resurfaced in 1998.

Several of the most intriguing examples of South America's lost avifauna are hummingbirds. These are the so-called Bogotá skins, referring to the lively commerce in stuffed birds of all kinds flowing in and out of that Colombian city in the early 1800s, bound not for museum collections but for the then-thriving millinery industry in Europe. Traders purchased the birds from a variety of sources, mostly Indians who had been given rudimentary training in skin preparation, and because they were destined for ladies' hats, there was generally no attempt made to pinpoint their source—most were simply labeled *Bogotá*.

The Bogotá skins provide a glimpse of a newly tapped continent, before the wholesale habitat destruction that quickly followed European settlement. Because many Andean birds have small, highly restricted ranges—some are found only in a single valley—it's assumed that a fair number were driven to extinction before they could be discovered and catalogued by scientists. (This is a state of affairs which, tragically, continues with living things of all stripes in the tropics to this day, and at a much accelerated pace.) For that reason, the Bogotá skins are, in a way, a snapshot of a lost world.

There is, for example, the tiny hummingbird known as the coppery thorntail, a bronzy-green creature 3½ inches long, with a white bar across its rump and two long, sharp tail feathers. Known only from three trade skins purchased by collectors in the 1850s (of which only one can now be found in a museum), the thorntail has at times been dismissed as a possible hybrid, explaining why it has never been found again in the wild. Yet more recent examination has convinced scientists that it is a full, valid species. Nothing at all about its range is known— there is speculation that it came from the Amazonian lowlands of northern Bolivia, but that is based only on the habitat preferences of other thorntails.

Even less certain is the status of the Bogotá sunangel. Bought from a trader in that city in 1909, the sole skin (which is thought to have come from the eastern or central Colombian Andes) languished for more than eighty years before it was finally described as a new hummingbird species in 1993. Opinions differ on the validity of the sunangel's designation; some experts believe it is a hybrid between the long-tailed sylph and the fork-tailed woodnymph, among other possible contenders for parentage. If it is a true species, and if the broad assumptions about its type locality are correct—and those are big ifs—then there is a good chance the sunangel is extinct, because most of that region of the Andes has been cleared for crops. If it is truly extinct, it would be the first of the more than 310 species of mainland hummingbirds to vanish—a dubious honor indeed. (One of the eighteen island species, Brace's emerald of the Bahamas, is known from just a single 1877 specimen and is without question gone.)

Another of the Bogotá specimens is the turquoise-throated puffleg from northern Ecuador and perhaps neighboring Colombia. As the name suggests, this minute bird, emerald with a touch of cobalt at the throat, has fluffy white "pantaloons" at either leg. It was collected at least six times, though only in one case was the location recorded—a male shot in 1850 in the arid ravines along the Rio Guaillabamba, 7,000 feet up in the Andes. Throughout the twentieth century there were no reports of the species, and although an unconfirmed sighting was claimed in 1976 near Quito, an exhaustive search near the type locality several years later failed to turn up any sign of the bird. "The forest of this area has been almost wholly cleared so unless new populations are found, perhaps in quite different habitats or even in southern Colombia, then the outlook for this species looks decidedly bleak," concluded a recent work on hummingbird conservation. Yet a related species of hummer, the colorful puffleg, was rediscovered in Colombia in 1997 after thirty years of fruitless searching. You just never know what's waiting out there.

All this was at once hopeful and discouraging through the months that we planned an expedition to Mato Grosso. The biggest hurdle we faced was a simple lack of knowledge; as with the Bogotá skins, exactly where the cone-billed tanager had been found was pretty much anyone's guess.

The entire canon on the cone-billed tanager consists of two scientific journal articles, both by French ornithologist Jacques Berlioz, the chap who examined Dr. Vellard's collection of Brazilian birds, now in the

A male cone-billed tanager, based on Dr. Vellard's 1938 specimen; the female and juvenile plumages have never been described, and after more than sixty years without a sighting, the bird is generally considered extinct. (Scott Weidensaul)

Paris Museum. In 1939, Berlioz published a brief, seven-paragraph note in the *Bulletin of the British Ornithology Club* announcing the discovery of a new species of tanager in central Brazil; after the war, he followed this up with a somewhat longer description of the specimen, and a list of the other birds Vellard had collected on the same trip, in a French publication.

Both papers indicate that Dr. Vellard shot the bird "at Juruena, northeast of Cuyaba, Matto Gross (Central Brazil)." This is less straightforward than it may appear. "Juruena" could refer to either the 500-mile-long river by that name or to a city on its lower reaches, near the northern border of Mato Grosso. But both are several hundred miles northwest of Cuiabá (as it is now spelled)—not north*east*, as both papers state. No one knows if the error was made by Vellard (perhaps through poor record-keeping or unfamiliarity with the region) or by Berlioz, but attempts over the years to clarify the issue failed. Berlioz himself later told the great Brazilian ornithologist Helmut Sick that the location probably did not refer to the river, yet Sick concluded that it couldn't have meant the city, either, for it is located deep in Amazonian rain forest, while Vellard said he collected the tanager in dry forest. But if not there, then where had Vellard pulled the trigger on his puzzling little bird?

Before we left for Brazil, Doug contacted the Paris Museum, hoping that Vellard's original specimen tag might have more details, but he got nowhere. That left us with Berlioz's journal articles, especially the 1946 paper describing the rest of the birds collected on that same expedition. Vellard shot and stuffed more than thirty other species of birds on his trip, all of them well known to ornithologists today; the habitat affinities of those species might prove useful in guiding where we should look.

Most of the birds the doctor collected are associated with open *cerrado*—chalk-browed mockingbirds, vermilion flycatchers, gray monjitas and blue-black grassquits, and several hummingbirds, including the glittering-bellied emerald, horned sungem, and blue-tufted starthroat. But Vellard also had some forest birds in the mix, species like brown and bronzy jacamars, masked tityras, and several kinds of manakins, warblers, and honeycreepers. What's telling is that these species prefer forests on the margins—gallery forests along rivers running through open land, small pockets of trees scattered across the *cerrado*, or larger patches of low, dry forest.

Taken together, the species that made up Vellard's small collection point to the intersection of Brazil's three great ecosystems, which link hands in western Mato Grosso—the seasonally flooded Pantanal marshes to the south of Cuiabá, the great Amazonian rain forests to the north, and the belt of *cerrado* grassland stretching across the midriff of the state, mostly at higher elevations. Putting our heads together with birders and ornithologists in Brazil and the United States, we decided to aim for the western fringe of Mato Grosso, beyond the Rio Paraguay and close to Bolivia, where several large *chapadas*, or plateaus, meet the upper Juruena, Guaporé, and other rivers. This region, we felt, offered the best chance for the right habitat—low, scrubby, dry forest at the edge of the *cerrado*.

So why, despite all the reasons why the Rio Juruena could not be the type locality for the tanager, were we trying so hard to get there? We'd been talking to a group of men hanging around our small hotel in Jauru the night before, asking them about the roads north, trying to figure out where to head in the morning. The road, they told us, went all the way to the river . . . and to an old settlement called Juruena. Our ears pricked up at that; the maps gave no hint of a town by that name anywhere in this region, on the headwaters of the river (the city of Juruena being a good 400 kilometers to the north). We eventually learned that the area had long since been abandoned, but it had been a thriving community in the 1930s, when Vellard had passed through Mato Grosso. Here was a fresh possibility for the type locality, one that made perfect sense from both geographic and ecological perspectives—the kind of accidental clue that sometimes leads to pay dirt.

The problem was, we couldn't get there from here—not from Jauru, anyway, since, as we found out the next day, the road petered out long before it got close to the Rio Juruena. We finished the morning there in the dry forest without seeing anything close to the cone-billed tanager, backtracked past the rotting cow carcasses, and mulled over our options. We decided to head west first, to explore some areas in the Serra de Ricardo Franco, a range of mountains astride the Bolivian border, then to swing north again and try to find a way to the Rio Juruena—and the site of the abandoned town—from the west.

By this point, we'd settled into a routine—up at 4:30 in the morning, we'd load the van in the dark, wash down some crackers or granola bars with packaged fruit juice, and arrive in the field as it was getting light, to take advantage of the dawn frenzy of bird activity. We spent several days exploring the mountains and the floodplain of the Rio Guaporé; it was rugged, beautiful country, the *serra* a green wall edged with orange cliffs like castle ramparts, above which flew flocks of scarlet macaws. One memorable morning we hiked back into the mountains, visiting several stunning waterfalls that thundered over the high cliffs, where squadrons of swifts flew through the skirts of falling water to their nests on the slick rocks behind the falls. But it was much too lush and wet a forest for the tanager, and so at length we turned north, hunting for a way to the Juruena.

The federal highway, a paved two-lane road that runs from Cuiabá and Cáceres west to the state of Rodônia, was a weird shock after days on slow-motion dirt tracks, and the long-haul truckers roared past us in clouds of diesel fumes. We drove north for hours, watching the land to our right—an impressive plateau, Chapada dos Parecis, which separated the Rio Guaporé drainage from the Rio Juruena. Our maps, which were (like most maps of this region) at best only modestly accurate, showed no roads crossing the highlands, so we decided to push on to the town of Commodoro, where the map hinted at a way over the *chapada*.

We needed to stop for fuel, so Fabiano pulled into a service station. We slouched in our seats, tired and sticky with sweat and road dust, while Fabiano unlimbered himself, stretched, and drifted off to chat up the service station attendants, as had become his custom, about any small roads into the mountains. A few minutes later, he was back with a big smile on his face. Just ahead, at the little hamlet of Nova Lacerda, there was a road into the hills—and it went, so the men insisted, all the way to the Rio Juruena, more than 70 kilometers across the narrow waist of the *chapada*.

It was good news, certainly, but all three of us knew better than to get too hopeful. For one thing, the attendants warned us that the road just outside town was nearly unusable, having become badly eroded; we might not even get into the mountains, much less across the highlands. To our surprise and pleasure, though, we found that the road had just been roughly graded with some heavy equipment a day or two before—a crude job, but it smoothed out the worst of the crevasses, even where small waterfalls tumbled down beside the dirt track, and we climbed the couple of thousand feet to the summit without undue strain on our weary van.

The *serra* was wrapped in thick, wet forest. We saw toucanets and heard the hoot of a motmot, both birds of the deep jungle, and halfway up, we flushed a white hawk, which looked like a perfect ivory carving until it opened its black-tipped wings and soared up through a gap in the forest, shimmering against the pocket of blue sky. In fact, the forest was so luxuriant that we were getting worried, but once we reached the top and began to cross the plateau, the trees became noticeably shrubbier, and our interest piqued even more.

We had suspected from the very beginning, judging from the sketchy details recorded sixty years ago by Vellard, that the cone-billed tanager was most likely a creature of the ecotone—a dressed-up word for the edge of two major habitats, like grassland and forest. The Chapada dos Parecis, like many of the tablelands in Mato Grosso, is covered by hundreds of square kilometers of *cerrado* grassland, but the ragged, mountainous edges and bordering rivers are lined with forest. It was along the intergrade between these two ecosystems that we felt we had the best chance of finding the tanager.

The road was wide, scraped from orange-brown soil that had hardened to rock and dust, except in low-lying spots where turgid puddles lay. The going was slow but fairly easy, though at times we were forced to detour around especially large water holes, following the tire tracks of others who had also skirted the edge rather than risk flooding their engine or miring in the mud. Within half an hour, the forest was visibly dwindling, many of the trees showing blackened, scorched bark and dead trunks, and it quickly disappeared into true *cerrado*, a plant community maintained by lightning and the sweeping range fires it sparks.

After spending a week in forested landscapes, it was liberating and exhilarating to rumble along beneath an open prairie sky. The *cerrado* extended to the horizon in all directions—not a waving grassland like the American Plains or the Argentine pampas, but a shrubbier place more akin to the savanna of Africa, with an even scattering of head-high trees and bushes, many of them bearing colorful flowers. Agaves with serrated, succulent leaves grew among wastebasket-sized termite mounds of hardened soil, and a few large trees punctuated the skyline at infrequent intervals, usually with hawks or caracaras perched like sentinels at the highest point. Several times, we encountered groups of rheas, the South American ostrich, one of them a male tending a convoy of new chicks the size of terriers. The babes were doubtless all his, but produced by perhaps as many females, each of which would have laid an egg or two in his nest—a parade of girlfriends but no helpmates, since the polyandrous females leave him sole responsibility for incubating and guarding their offspring through the six months it will take the chicks to reach independence.

The *chapada* undulated, but its hills and swales were gentle, and those who had bulldozed this road ignored them while maintaining the shortest route between points—for hours we bumped and rattled along a straight, unvarying line to the northeast, a rule drawn in orange dust across the brown and green of the *cerrado*. The sun crested the zenith and arched down; we stopped from time to time to wander the grassland for pictures, or to allow me to tape-record curl-crested jays harassing a falcon or the gentle song of a seedeater. A brocket deer, gray and sleek, its muscles bunching as it ran, rocketed out of a thicket as we chugged past, and later we saw a larger species, the campo deer. The road stayed almost unswervingly straight. We passed no other vehicles, but could see that large trucks passed this way regularly, presumably from the soybean farms we'd been told lay at the far edge of the plateau.

It was getting late in the day when we finally met the farmland, and we weren't prepared for the incongruity of the sight. For hours we'd been passing through virtual wilderness, but as we crested an unusually sharp hill and started down the other side, we saw that the *cerrado* had been wholly replaced by lime-green fields of staggering dimensions— individual fields that must have encompassed tens of thousands of acres, fading to milky haze in the distance without ever showing sign of a break in the furrows.

"That's a helluva lot of soybeans," Doug said, his voice thin with disbelief, as Fabiano let the van roll to a stop.

I grew up in farm country where the fields are usually a few dozen acres each, stitched with fencerows and creating a patchwork quilt of colors and textures; that's the mental template that means "farm" to me, but of course I've seen industrial agricultural landscapes before, in places like the Central Valley of California. Yet nothing I'd seen compared with the sheer scale of these fields, coupled with the improbability of their existence in the middle of the vast *cerrado* wilderness. From our high vantage point, it looked as though someone had decided to paint an entire county bright green, and I later learned that the oddly geometric shapes of the fields are easily visible on satellite photos—and not the spy satellites that can photograph your license plate from orbit, either, but the kind that snap pictures encompassing a couple of hundred thousand square miles in a single exposure. It was, as Doug said, a helluva lot of soybeans.

The *chapadas* of Mato Grosso have the rough luck to be nearly ideal for soybean culture, with the right rainfall, climate, and soil conditions, and increasing chunks of the *cerrado* have been converted to such immense monocultures, mammoth farms under the control of a very few enormously wealthy men. Fabiano claimed (and I had no way to check the truth of this) that one family alone controls 1.5 million square kilometers of soybean farms in Brazil. If he had told me this earlier in the day, I would have thought it a wild exaggeration; now it seemed not only plausible but maybe an understatement.

Beyond the soybean fields, and a down-in-the-mouth government processing plant that turns much of the crop into fuel-grade alcohol, the road's condition took a serious turn for the worse. *Sim, sim*, the few field-workers we saw assured us, yes, the road continued on to the Juruena, 10 kilometers that way—their hands waving vaguely to the east—maybe 20 kilometers or 30, certainly no more than 40; no one was really sure. They all agreed that the road ended near the river, and on the other side was land set aside for the Parecis Indians; if we kept going we'd find it.

Long, low shadows lay across the *cerrado*, and the western sky was tinged with lemon, fading to indigo in the east, where the planet's shadow gathered itself. The road still ran in a straight line, but it was now a thin, anemic scratch hardly visible in the distance, more of a streambed than a thoroughfare, uneven and deeply gullied where the bed was clay, loose and treacherous where it was sand. We lurched from side to side, brush scraping the metal body, as the rented van listed drunkenly first one way, then the other, Fabiano fighting to keep it both under control and moving ahead in the deep, soft sand. We'd been unable to rent a four-wheel-drive vehicle for the trip, and so we had to be more careful than we would have liked. Several times we bogged down for a few seconds, but Fabiano pumped the accelerator and eased us out, fishtailing uphill.

Finally, driving up a long, gentle rise, we reached a place where water had cut away the road, creating what would have been a waist-high waterfall in the rainy season. There was no question of the van scaling this, and Fabiano's suggestion—that we simply edge along the steep side of the gully to get around it—struck both Doug and me as foolhardy.

"Look at the angle," I said, pointing through the evening gloom as we stood by the vehicle. The van was top-heavy, and if we tried to drive it farther, I was certain we'd roll it.

"Let's go back down that way," Doug said, pointing the way we'd come. "It's flat down there, and the soil's harder. We can find a place to pull off and spend the night." We'd known we'd have to bivouac out on the *cerrado* anyway; the river, as best we could judge, was probably another 5 or 6 miles farther on, and we could hike the rest of the way at daybreak.

Fabiano shook his head emphatically at the suggestion of retreat, gesturing ahead with quick, stabbing movements of his arm. "We go forward. We must go forward!" he said several times, and his insistence was starting to get on my nerves.

The truth was, we'd been fighting a communications barrier the entire trip. Fabiano's English was fairly good, and Doug could squeak by with the Portuguese he'd picked up living in Brazil twenty-five years earlier, which led us all to believe the other knew what we meant—but subtleties were often lost. We thought Fabiano was being muleheaded and a bit macho, wanting to rush forward regardless of the risk, and so for the first time on the trip we pulled rank and insisted he put the vehicle in reverse and back down to the base of the hill.

What Fabiano knew, but couldn't express in English, was that while the van might have enough juice to muscle us forward through the sand, it simply lacked the horsepower when in reverse. He looked at me, gave a long sigh, and worked the gears. The bright backup lights lit the *cerrado*, and we started racing backward as fast as Fabiano could move us. But within thirty seconds we were axle-deep in loose sand, stuck but good.

I looked over at our guide, smiled a rueful smile, and said, "This is where you say, 'I told you so.' " To his eternal credit, Fabiano did not, but as he climbed out, he gave another sigh that spoke volumes.

For a long time, no one said much; three guys stood staring at a white van that tipped unpleasantly toward its left rear corner. Doug and I shouldered the back of the VW while Fabiano gave it some gas, but the tires just splattered a rooster tail of damp sand against our legs, and the car settled farther. So we did what anyone stuck in the middle of nowhere would do. We went for a hike.

It was an odd time to take a walk, I now realize—the sun had set, our only transportation was mired a very long way from help, and we were unsure of even where we'd camp for the night. We walked, I think, because we'd been on the go all day and we just couldn't quit. We walked because we sensed the end of the road was close, and after weeks of scheming to get here, we wanted to see it. Finally, we walked because the crest of the hill was just ahead—and peeking over the crests of hills is what human beings have been doing for hundreds of thousands of years.

Over the last rise, in the dim twilight, the land dropped off in a series of mile-wide steps to the valley of the Rio Juruena, vague in the hazy distance. Not far away, like a line drawn across the *chapada*, lapped a low, scrubby forest that could not have looked more ideal as potential tanager habitat. We were stuck, but we were obviously stuck in the right place.

Getting the van out took an hour or so, and entailed a lot of digging in the damp, cool sand, scavenging dead branches in the dark, jamming them under the wheels for traction, and then straining as hard as we could while Fabiano tried to coax the VW out of its trench. He had, finally, made us understand the folly in going back, and when the van at last broke free, on the seventh or eighth attempt, we watched with our hearts in our throats as he careened up the uneven edge of the gullied road, twice coming (I was sure) within a hairbreadth of rolling the van on its side. But it remained upright, defying gravity, and when the taillights disappeared over the crest, we wearily climbed up to meet him on firmer ground.

We found a wide, flat spot with hard soil on which to park and turned to making ourselves comfortable for the night. There had been plenty of mosquitoes at the edge of the forest, and as it grew dark, I expected them to move the mile or so to our camp and make for a miserable night, since only Fabiano had brought a tent. (A sore subject for me, since against my better judgment I'd removed a backpacking tent from my gear the night before we left, after Doug had urged me to economize on weight. He said I should do as he planned—buy a hammock with a mosquito net once we reached Cuiabá. However, we arrived in Cuiabá on a Saturday, when the stores were all closed for the weekend, and instead of wasting two days in town, we reluctantly set off without the hammocks, knowing our camping options were thus limited.)

Fortunately, the mosquitoes never materialized. Instead, as the darkness deepened and a cooling breeze began to blow, hundreds of moths gathered around us, from tiny micros barely a quarter of an inch long to the chocolate-colored giants known as black witches, which were the size of my palm. Soon there were thousands, drawn by the salt and moisture on our dirty clothes and skin—indeed, on anything we touched. We had left the van doors standing open, and I found that the steering wheel was completely covered with moths of all sizes and descriptions, as were Fabiano's binoculars sitting on the dash. They flew at our faces and bare arms, landing with tickling feet and uncurling tongues that flickered gingerly over our skin, greedily lapping. It was obviously not painful or even particularly unpleasant, but the sensation was decidedly odd and a little disconcerting.

We opened one of the tripods to head height, and from its center post I hung a candle lamp, which created a pool of yellow light beneath the wide, dark sky. We dug through our box of supplies and assembled a makeshift meal from what remained—sardines and crackers for Doug and Fabiano, a tin of fruit cocktail and a tangerine for me, followed by salty banana chips passed around until the bag was empty, and washed down with lukewarm water, since the ice in our cooler had long since melted.

We were in high spirits, laughing and joking, the exhaustion and scraped nerves of the day forgotten; it felt good to be on the very edge of things, a long way from anywhere, with nothing but ourselves in this bubble of companionable light. I was in a poetic frame of mind, trying out possible chapter titles that fit the auspicious mood; the one that seemed to work best was "Hope Starts Where the Road Ends," and I knew that if this were Hollywood, tomorrow would be the day of discovery, with the tanager waiting for us at dawn. Fabiano eventually retreated to his little tent, and Doug simply wrapped himself in his mosquito net and lay on a poncho spread on the ground. I gave a thought to the likelihood of snakes and scorpions, dug a sheet out of my gear, and curled up on the reclined driver's seat of the van with the doors cocked open, too tired to mind the multitude of moths that settled on me.

Yet I didn't fall asleep immediately. I could see a triangular piece of the sky overhead; the thick stars of the Milky Way smeared with strands of hazy clouds and the absence of any familiar constellations made me acutely aware of how far from home I was. This wasn't a melancholy feeling by any means, but it hit me with a pang of a different sort. I'd been following the faint track of lost animals for nearly two years, immersing myself in many exotic landscapes like this one—a pursuit that forced me to look at the world in a new and more auspicious way, alive to hope, however tentative, in the face of great and grievous biological loss. As I drifted off to sleep, the sound of a nightjar calling in lonely whoops across the *cerrado*, I was grateful to the tanager and the thylacine and all the other members of this ark of loss and expectation for that gift.

We woke at 5:00 a.m., chirped awake by watch alarms, shrugging off the stiffness and the chill; the moths, I noticed, had largely gone, perhaps chased away by the cool air, or maybe their craving for salt had at last been satisfied. We said little, assembling our gear, filling our water bottles, and slogging up the soft sand of the road in a single-file line toward the Juruena. Our flashlights showed that while we'd slept, the residents of the *cerrado* had come to call on us—the sand, damp with dew, held the perfect footprints of beetles and large toads, snakes and lizards. Just a few yards from where Doug had slept, a tapir had left its three-toed tracks; Fabiano told us the huge, semiaquatic mammals, which may weigh 600 pounds, often come up from the gallery forests along rivers to feast on the abundant fruit of the savanna.

I was puzzled at first by a long line of tracks that looked as though something had been walking on its knuckles, until I realized that was, indeed, the case—they were the prints of a giant anteater, which has such huge, curving claws on its front feet that it must turn its paws inward, pigeon-toed, and walk on the outsides of its feet. I thought about those Brazilian legends of mapinguari, the monster with the backward feet, and smiled. The anteater's claws left deep, C-shaped impressions in the sand, smudged a little by the swish of the beast's long, shaggy tail. But perhaps the most exciting prints we found were those of what we at first dismissed as a couple of domestic dogs, but that we eventually concluded must have been maned wolves—a weird, little-known predator of the South American grasslands that looks like a giant red fox on stilts, for its black legs are almost ridiculously long. Maned wolves are endan-

gered across most of their range, shy and so seldom seen that they are almost mythical; not even the tracks of a jaguar could have been more exciting to me.

At the edge of the forest the trail forked, and we chose the one that
speared directly east toward the river valley, even though it was less
heavily used. We were torn by twin impulses to move on to our destina-
tion and to amble slowly in this bird-rich environment, in case we might
stumble across the tanager. Ambling won out—there was simply too
much to see and hear to move quickly. Flocks of blue-and-yellow
macaws flew silhouetted against the sky, big wings rowing gracefully,
their long tails dragging behind them like rudders. We heard and occasionally saw groups of red-legged seriemas, peculiar birds vaguely related to cranes but looking like the secretary-birds of Africa—3 feet
long, with skinny scarlet legs, scrawny necks, and floppy crests of sparse
feathers that rise from the base of the bill.

Doug was laboring beneath the weight of his heavy tripod, a pack full
of camera gear, and the enormous, 600mm telephoto lens, which with
its hood was nearly 3½ feet long. While Doug eased into position to photograph the macaws, I drifted off, tape recorder ready, listening through
my headphones to the awakening birdlife.

I make a lousy field recordist, frankly, because I have bad hearing.
Whatever the reason (in part, I blame a high school job at a shotgun
range without adequate ear protection), my hearing is fairly limited, especially at the upper register, and while birding with sharp-eared people
like Doug and Fabiano, I realize how very much I miss. But my handicap
goes further. I have a terrible time remembering any but the most distinctive bird songs, while all the rest form a pleasing but confusing cacophony of chirps and twitters and flutings. I may know I know a song,
but damned if I can recall, half the time, what species it is from; this is
one reason that my own research focuses on hawks and owls, a group
with a very basic vocal array.

It is said that Ted Parker, the legendary young ornithologist who died
a few years ago in a plane crash while doing fieldwork in Ecuador, was
able to identify more than four thousand species of birds by song alone. I
suppose I am the anti-Ted, but despite my shortcomings, I have found I
love making field recordings of bird songs. With the headphones on and
the directional mike powered up, at least my physical limitations are

negated; as my binoculars give me the vision of a hawk, the microphone grants me the hearing of a wolf, aware of even the tiniest rustle of a bird's wings. An auditory world, usually blank to me, suddenly opens wide.

I am playing a copy of that morning's tape as I write this, in the depths of a Pennsylvania winter. There is sleet and snow outside, but with the headphones over my ears I am instantly back in the dry forest of the Juruena. The microphone, indiscriminate as an ear, picked up all the ambient sound; I can hear the crackle of dead grass and brush underfoot as I shifted position slightly, the quiet murmur of my companions talking many yards away, unaware that I was recording, the occasional drone of a bee flying past, and the hiss of the day's first breeze, which I quickly blocked with my body.

A seriema begins to call, a braying laugh that rises—*hah-hAH-HAAH-HAAH*—cracks like an adolescent's unsteady voice, and then drops off; another answers it, and another, until a chorus of maniacs is barking unseen from the thickets. There are low growls from a flock of young turquoise-fronted parrots squabbling in a fruit tree, the metronomic peep of a collared crescentchest in the bushes below them, and the staccato rattle of a scolding antwren. Suddenly I flinch in real pain and turn down the volume, as a flock of macaws screams nearby—a fingernails-on-blackboard sound that dissolves into a contented chatter and the rattle of wings as the great birds settle into the tree to feed. I can even hear the faint scrabble of their claws on the rough bark, and a series of hollow thunks as one uses its bill like a third hand to climb from branch to branch.

With such distractions, we made slow progress through the forest, made slower by the ever-fainter trail, which eventually dissolved entirely into featureless scrub, leaving us to backtrack to the edge of the *cerrado* and try a different route to the river. By now the sun was well up, and it was getting hot; the bird activity was slackening visibly. We played our tapes of the black-and-white tanager and a pygmy-owl (a predator whose call often gets a rise out of smaller birds)—but while we saw tanagers of half a dozen other species, including one or two rarities, we saw nothing that even hinted at a cone-billed. Eventually, we just put our heads down and trudged on through the loose sand, trying to get to the Rio Juruena.

The land between the *cerrado* and the river was, as I've said, a series of wide, descending steps. The evening before, from the high ground near camp, we had guessed the river was 4 or 5 miles away, but because of the lay of the land, we couldn't actually see where the undulations dropped at last to the Juruena. Now we realized we'd underestimated how long it would take to reach the river, even if we hadn't spent half the morning birding. Except for a few small hummingbirds, we'd seen no birds for more than an hour. We were tired and thirsty; each of us had brought several quarts of water, but in the dry air and ferocious sun, that was nearly gone. Hot and dehydrated as we were, we were reluctant to quit. In the low forest, where our heads were as high as most of the trees, there was no real shade to speak of, but we could see a tall copse at the edge of the next drop-off, perhaps a mile ahead, that promised some shelter. We would go at least that far before making a decision about pushing on.

Reaching the shade, we dropped our packs with relief and dug out breakfast, which amounted to little more than a few handfuls of granola cereal and a tangerine each. The mosquitoes and sand flies that had plagued us all morning were gone, but now that we were sitting down, we noticed a new player—tiny sweat bees, not much bigger than gnats. Because they do not sting, the bees were at first a mild annoyance, crawling around our faces and burrowing into our hair, but after we'd sat just a few minutes, the swarms became thick enough to become a real bother, and we were constantly wiping them away from our eyes and noses, where they crowded for moisture.

Even with the bees harassing us, it was hard to get ourselves moving again, in either direction. We reluctantly decided to turn back to camp, much to the frustration of Fabiano, who'd had his heart set on a swim. Doug and I agreed, though, that there was little point in pushing on in the hottest part of the day, when the chance of finding any birds at all was nil. Better, we decided, to regroup. We would hike back to the van and return to Nova Lacerda, which would give us a chance to clean up, rest for a night, and resupply. Then, with a fresh start, we'd drive straight back to our camp here near the river, get a little sleep, and hike through the night, reaching Juruena before dawn, when the greatest bird activity could be expected. Even Fabiano, his disappointment fading, agreed it made the most sense.

The return hike to the van was excruciating. The high sun reflected off the light ground and broiled us, wicking moisture out of our bodies that our empty water bottles could not replace, even as the soft, sugary sand sucked at our feet with every step. No one said much, and our rest stops were short and infrequent, because the only thing keeping the sweat bees at bay was constant movement; slow our pace even fractionally and they cloaked us immediately.

"Well, this is our Death March," Doug said. "Can't have an expedition without a Death March." He said this brightly, almost cheerfully, but I was worried about him; the color in his cheeks and forehead was high and flushed, but there was a pinched whiteness around his eyes and mouth that didn't look good. We stopped while he dug out his water bottle and had the last swallow, waving his free arm as our inevitable shadow of sweat bees caught up with us and bore right in on business. He recounted other places, other death marches, with an evident fondness some people reserve for beach holidays—a dry peninsula in Panama where the water ran out, for example, or a three-day slog through the jungles of Borneo which he completed despite a wrenched knee.

But when we arrived in Nova Lacerda late in the day, the weather finally turned against us. The air grew thick and stagnant, presaging the first heavy downpours of the rainy season, which rattled the roof of the small, shabby hotel where we spent the night, grateful for the battered air conditioner. While the Brazilians have adopted the words "hotel" and "motel" from English, they are not at all interchangeable. A hotel is for overnight accommodation, while motels rent their rooms by the hour. Even fairly small towns usually have one or two motels on the outskirts, screened by high walls and with concealed parking areas for privacy. The names, often in English, leave little doubt as to their purpose—one day we passed the Alibi Motel, the Feelings Motel, and—I'm not making this up—the Stiffness Motel.

We waited for the rain to abate, hoping to make another run at the Rio Juruena, taking our meals in the restaurant attached to the hotel, where a constantly blaring television was always tuned to soccer and they served the essentially unchanging menu universal to rural Brazil: beans, rice, heavily salted beef, potatoes, and a few limp vegetables. We passed the wet, sultry afternoons reading and catching up on our notes, and every morning we drove up into the *serra*, where the forest and *cerrado* blended, to look for the tanager—for although we felt the Juruena offered our best hope of relocating the bird, there was no particular reason the species might not be found in similar habitat on this side of the Chapada dos Parecis.

One sodden morning we had a teaser, the first time in the trip when our hopes really soared and our hearts started pounding. It was sometime after sunrise, though the gray overcast sky had a twilight feel at odds with the hour, and we were in a mix of pasture and brushy forest, listening to a very different suite of birds than we'd encountered thus far—channel-billed toucans, turkey-like Spix's guans, moustached wrens. Many of the birds, like brown jacamars, were species that Vellard had collected on the same expedition as the cone-billed tanager, giving us hope that we might have stumbled at last on the right mix of habitat and locality.

I was recording a wren singing in the trees when Doug spun around, pointing, and said with quiet but unmistakable excitement, "A black bird just flew across the road!" My adrenaline surged even more a moment later, when I spotted it perched in a solitary tree draped with vines—it was clearly a tanager, almost entirely black, with a spot of white on its wing. I remembered the drawings I'd seen of the cone-billed, with its fleck of white that had reminded me of a pocket handkerchief.

But then I noticed two things. This bird was black clear to its belly, with none of the white underparts that a cone-billed tanager would have, and the white on its wing was a thin silver at the shoulder, not a square spot on the folded flight feathers.

"Where is it? Do you have it?" Doug asked, binoculars poised; then, before I could say anything, he saw the bird move and snapped his glasses to his eyes. "Oh," he said, his voice flat. "That's a white-lined tanager. It's a good bird to find, but . . ." He didn't need to finish the thought.

So the next day, when we shifted to an open area with more *cerrado* than forest, I wasn't expecting much. Perhaps after a couple of fruitless weeks in the field, I was growing a little jaded about our chances. Whatever the reason, I was content to putter around with my tape recorder and microphone, concentrating on the solid, substantial birds of the *chapada* instead of chasing after mirages. Doug and I parted company, he to photograph some small species of spinetail he'd spotted, me to wander off along the dirt road, stopping here and there to tape a new species.

It was midmorning, and the insect changing-of-the-guard was begin-

ning; with the mosquitoes abating, I rolled up my shirtsleeves against
the heat, since the sun, though barely visible through the thick clouds,
was growing noticeably hotter. The first few sweat bees were starting to
appear, and I knew that within half an hour we'd be smothered beneath
them. It was probably time to head back to the van, half a mile up the
track, where Fabiano was taking a nap.

I turned to retrace my route, which is the only reason I saw the flock
of birds flit across the road, about a dozen of them in a ragged line, landing in a fruit tree about 20 feet high. Even that quick glance showed there
were several sizes and colors—tropical birds often move in mixed-species
flocks like this. I scanned the tree, still not particularly hopeful, and
quickly recognized a couple of cinnamon tanagers and black-faced tanagers, two of the more common species we'd been seeing. These are
distinctive-looking birds—the cinnamon tanager is pale chestnut on the
head and breast, with a black face and gray back; the black-faced is overall
gray, but with a black bib and mask. In both cases, the sexes are identical.

Then one more bird flew into the outside edge of the tree—a tanager similar in size and shape to the others, but olive, with a more intense lime-green on the upper parts and upper breast, with a fair bit of
streaking. The beak was typical of a tanager, somewhat conical and powerful, light at the base and dark toward the tip. My first thought was,
Oh, a female tanager.

I will not be melodramatic and say that my heart stopped; the embarrassing truth is that for the first few seconds I couldn't recall where
I'd seen the bird before. But then I remembered the field-guide illustra-
tions I'd studied of a female black-and-white tanager, the cone-billed's
closest relative—a bird that was a dead ringer for this one but not found
within a thousand miles of us. No one knows what a female cone-billed
tanager looks like, but given the similarity of the male to its black-and-
white cousin (and the general propensity among female birds of many
genera to resemble one another), what I was seeing is exactly what one
would expect if a female cone-billed were to materialize.

Unfortunately, I had only a few seconds more to stare before the
flock, perhaps spooked by a passing hawk, broke into flight and disappeared into the *cerrado*. I dug out my notebook, furiously scribbling
down every detail that I could remember, then found myself unsure
what to do next. My inclination was to charge off after the flock, but

Doug and Fabiano had no idea where I'd gone; besides, if the tanager *was* the undescribed female plumage of a long-lost species, I'd need all the witnesses I could get.

My indecision lasted only a minute or two, because Doug appeared at the crest of a low hill several hundred yards away, and my frantic gestures brought him at a trot. Fabiano, by another stroke of luck, followed moments later in the van, wondering what was keeping us. Grabbing gear, tapes, fresh film—and slathering ourselves with bug repellent, for the sweat bees were now bearing down in force—we sketched a hurried plan. Doug and I would make a beeline in the direction the flock had been heading, while Fabiano stayed at the van and watched the clock; the thickets in this part of the *chapada* were dense, and visibility was only a few yards, so getting turned around and lost was a real concern, since we didn't have a compass with us. If we didn't return in an hour, Fabiano was to start blowing the horn to guide us back to the road.

Heading into the brush, I felt the same keen edge as I have when tracking a buck during deer season—the heightened awareness of my surroundings, the way movement and sound were amplified, the reaching beyond oneself to connect with another animal. There were a few birds in the low trees, mostly sparrows and spinetails, flickers of movement catalogued and ignored. We moved quickly, trying to stay on a straight course, but the undergrowth was so thick—vines, sharp-spined agaves, stunted trees with soot-blackened bark from the last brushfire— that our progress slowed and our path meandered. I tried to keep the sun over my left shoulder, but the clouds, which had shown some breaks earlier in the morning, thickened almost as soon as we entered the *cerrado*, and I was forced to rely on instinct to stay on course.

All the while, we were battling ferocious clouds of sweat bees, far worse than anything we'd yet experienced. More seemed to rise from the brush with every step. My eyes were red and watering from bees that crawled under the lids; they didn't sting, but the little bastards bit like tiny ants, and so many of them clogged my nose that I was finding it hard to breathe without choking on them. They packed into my ears, crawled by the dozens under my hat and down to my scalp, and crept with abandon into my clothes so that my skin twitched with them. At one point, I twisted my watch, felt a weird slickness that wasn't perspiration, and realized I'd mashed thirty or forty of them under the band.

Doug crashed through a dense patch, his tripod over his shoulder and one arm flailing around his head like a windmill, to no apparent effect. He had a slightly lunatic look in his bleary, watering eyes, and I'm sure he saw the same thing on my face.

"You want a chapter title?" he asked through clenched teeth. "Okay, I have a chapter title for you: 'Sweat Bees Ate My Earwax!' How does that grab you?"

There is a reason lost species are lost in the first place. Sometimes the reasons are weighty and formidable, like civil unrest, impenetrable mountains, or bandit warlords who use visitors for target practice. Sometimes they are more prosaic, like bad roads and worse information. And sometimes the reason is sweat bees—too many sweat bees. We staggered out of the brush, eyes streaming and our faces speckled with dead, smeared bugs, just as Fabiano started blowing the horn. We never did find the tanager flock.

So, had I seen a female cone-billed tanager? I'll never know, but I later learned something that casts a fair bit of doubt on it. Like any birder, I'd pored over the field guides for months before going to Brazil, and had memorized most of the common species illustrated in the color plates. But I'd fallen into the trap of mostly looking at the pictures and paying scant attention to the text. When I later sat down with Bob Ridgely's *Birds of South America*, I read something I'd overlooked until then, hidden in the account of the black-faced tanager, one of the species that made up the flock that day: "Sexes alike, but immature entirely different (and may not even be recognized as the same species): olive above, more yellowish on the head and with yellow eye-ring; paler yellowish-olive below." That's a rough description of what I saw, but it's not precisely the same; for instance, my tanager was brighter green than this description indicates, nor did I see a yellow eye ring—the sort of basic field mark birders usually notice quickly. Yet if I were to apply Occam's razor to the problem, it seems far more likely that my greenish mystery bird was a young black-faced tanager traveling with its parents, rather than a never-before-seen cone-billed female.

Although the weather remained wet—at most we had just a few hours without rain—we were stir-crazy enough after a couple of days in Nova Lacerda to chance the drive back to the Juruena anyway, realizing we might not get another opportunity. We loaded up the van with fresh water and supplies, and as the clouds began to break over the *serra* in late afternoon, we churned and slid our way up the road, which was in considerably worse shape than when we'd arrived the week before.

The road into the mountains almost stopped us, but each time we began to spin and skid, Fabiano managed to find some traction and get us moving again. The weather was looking better than it had in days, however. Thick wraiths of mist rose from the forested hollows of the *serra*, and here and there in the lowlands to the west, shafts of diffuse sunlight streamed through the clouds. Our spirits rose, but we soon learned that a favorable change down on the plains means nothing in the mountains and on the plateaus. Within an hour, we had to stop because of torrential, frog-choking rain, which turned the road into a shallow whitewater stream and forced us to wait out the worst of the storm. And once we got under way again, we found that the dirt road across the tableland was a morass, with huge sheets of water blocking it again and again. Some of these we eased through, water lapping at the undercarriage, or edged around as best we could through the brushy *cerrado*, but we finally encountered one that halted us cold.

Twenty or thirty yards of the road vanished beneath deep, silty water. There was no question of driving through—we'd barely squeaked across this mudhole days before, when everything else had been dry—but Doug noticed a side track going around to the right. It was flooded, too (much of the surrounding *cerrado* had turned into a miles-wide pond), but the water looked shallow enough that we might not have a problem.

Nor would we have, if the subsurface had been solid. But days of rain had turned the soil into something close to the consistency of cake batter, and we got less than halfway through the flooded area before the van lurched, spun its wheels impotently a few times, and settled firmly into place.

Digging a van out of loose sand on a cool and breezy evening is a lark; doing the same job in pelting rain, standing in half a foot of cold water and red mud, is a chore, and an unpleasant one at that. Every tropical traveler who gets off the beaten track has had the experience, usually many times, and it doesn't improve with repetition. I will not belabor the hours it took us to extricate ourselves, first waiting for the rain to finally stop and the water to recede a bit, then Fabiano digging at the slurry of mud with a hoe he pulled out of the nether reaches of the van, while Doug and I scavenged the *cerrado* for dead sticks and branches to jam beneath the tires.

I was walking back with a large armload of dead wood on my shoulder, my right arm curled around it, sloshing through the standing water, when something fell from the sticks and landed by my feet with a splash. It was a pale, sand-colored scorpion maybe an inch and a half long, which had obviously been hiding beneath the bark of the old wood I carried. Fabiano grinned when he saw it, dropped the muddy hoe, and dug an empty film canister out of the van, his green poncho flapping as he ran back to me.

"It is the genus *Tityus*!" he said excitedly, scooping up the arthropod before it could skitter away. "My girlfriend will want to see this!" (If this seems odd, understand that Fabiano's girlfriend is also a wildlife biologist.)

As a naturalist, I know I shouldn't harbor grudges against any wild creature, but I will confess to a deep and abiding distaste for scorpions. I have shaken them out of my boots too many times, seen their wickedly curved tails, stingers poised, poke out from the thatch of a jungle hut above my face too often, watched them scramble on madly dancing legs from beneath my cot too frequently, to view them with much equanimity. Knowing that I'd been cradling this one next to my head was not a pleasant thought.

"Just out of curiosity, Fabiano, are there any—you know, *dangerously* venomous scorpions in this part of Brazil?" I asked, keeping my voice carefully nonchalant.

"Oh yes," he said, "there is one species that might not kill a man, but a child, yes, it kill many children."

"Which one is that?"

"This one," he said, smiling down admiringly at his captive.

When, after much pushing and digging and swearing, the van finally pulled free of the sucking mud and slewed back to firmer ground, we knew the rainy season had beaten us, where sweat bees and heat and sand could not. To push on for the Juruena, even if we could have gotten past this immediate hurdle, would have been foolish, and the road beyond the soybean farms would no doubt be impassable for months, until the dry season baked it hard again. We limped down off the *chapada*, back through the dirty streets of Nova Lacerda, and turned east on the highway.

We didn't give up, exactly; we spent several more days exploring the flanks of the Serra dos Araras north of Cáceres, but while the region was rich in birds, we knew that the habitat was wrong for the cone-billed tanager, and we were just marking time until we headed home. But our failure to find the tanager did not diminish our belief that the bird was still out there somewhere—if anything, it reinforced it, by the simple experience of showing us how huge the bird's potential world is. We had looked hard for the tanager, but when we plotted our route on the map, it was a squiggle in an immensity of space. There was another wrinkle to consider as well—the possibility that the unlucky tanager Vellard shot in 1938 wasn't on its breeding grounds but in migration, just passing through Mato Grosso on its way, perhaps, to the poorly explored mountains along the Bolivian frontier. This is the case with the black-and-white tanager, its closest relative and a bird that is both rare and nomadic within its range. Even within the areas we had visited, there are many places where few but the Indians have gone, valleys and drainages that have changed not at all with the coming of the Europeans. There were times when I felt you could easily hide not just a small bird out there but the whole ark of cryptozoology—mapinguari, Sasquatch, and the entire hoary crew of mythical beasts.

Though the world is shrinking daily, much of it is still unknown; the blank spots are disappearing beneath the unblinking eyes of satellites and the probing fingers of chainsaws, bulldozers, and the farmer's hoe, but great swaths of the planet remain a mystery to polite society, fit habitat for myths and monsters, a place where dreams can live. One of those dreams is 6 inches long, has a white spot on each wing, and has kindled an obsession within me.

Even before we were down off the *chapada*, we were hatching plans to come back to Mato Grosso again, someday soon—with a better vehicle, a better sense of where and when to go, ready to do things differently so that we could explore the area around the Rio Juruena that we'd barely penetrated. Far from being discouraged, we were energized by our failure, convinced—in the absence of proof—that we were on the right track.

Who cares if the cone-billed tanager is alive, or if it, like tens of billions of organisms since life first arose, is now extinct? What does one tanager, more or less, matter when weighed against more than nine thousand living species of birds? You're asking the wrong person. Leaving aside the fundamental worth of every species, representing the unique harvest of more than 3.5 billion years of natural selection—forgetting the value of a salvaged treasure in the face of global extinction—Dr. Vellard's small black bird has come to matter a very great deal to me, out of all proportion to its size and ecological role, or even its place in a sixty-year-old ornithological mystery. Obsession doesn't need reason or rationale, it simply requires an object of desire, the less attainable the better. I lie awake some nights, thinking back to the hot breeze on the *chapada*, hawks wheeling overhead and tinamous hooting mournfully in the thickets, the hazy line of forest along the river we never reached, and I am certain the tanager is still there. I am certain I am the one who can find it.

And, in the final analysis, perhaps that is the greatest gift these lost creatures give this too-fast, too-small, too-modern world: an opportunity for hope. I'd felt it that first night near the Juruena, sitting beneath the spectacular sky as tapirs and anteaters prowled beyond our lamplight. I'd felt it again in the *cerrado*, with the memory of that green bird fresh and the scent of the hunt in my nose—felt it more surely than I felt the humid Brazilian heat, the salt crusting my filthy hat brim, and the legions of sweat bees crawling into every opening they could find.

In fact—and this did not occur to me until days later, when we were packing up our gear for the flight home—it may be that the best thing that can happen is for the tanager to remain unfound. What makes the cone-billed tanager special is its mystery; should it ever reappear, it would become just another rare bird in a world already saddled with too many threatened organisms. It may be that we need icons of faith and aspiration, objects of great quixotic quests, more than we need the reality.

Or this may be the worst kind of rationalistic bull. If we'd found the tanager, no doubt I'd be writing an equally eloquent denouement on the joys of dreams realized, instead of dreams deferred. Maybe the only benefit to failure is that is makes the victory that much sweeter, when it finally comes.

I don't know where the truth lies between these two poles, but I do know one thing. I'm going back to Mato Grosso to look for that bird again. Soon.

Notes and Bibliography

ONE

Citations

12 "You must have the bird": John Burroughs, "The Art of Seeing Things," in *Birch Browsings: A John Burroughs Reader*, Bill McKibben, ed. (New York: Penguin, 1992), p. 133. (Originally published in *Leaf and Tendril*, Boston: Houghton Mifflin, 1908.)

15 "Though the voice": Allan R. Keith, *The Birds of St. Lucia, West Indies* (London: British Ornithologists' Union, 1997), p. 62.

18 "any detailed observations": Paul B. Hamel, "Bachman's Warbler (*Vermivora bachmani*)," in *The Birds of North America*, no. 150, A. Poole and F. Gill, eds. (Philadelphia: The Academy of Natural Sciences, and Washington, D.C.: The American Ornithologists' Union, 1995), p. 13.

21 "I sent them off": Peter Zahler, "The flap over the woolly flying squirrel," *Wildlife Conservation* (September/October 1998), 56.

22 "a webbe-footed Fowle": W. Strachy, 1609; quoted in Arthur Cleveland Bent, *Life Histories of North American Petrels and Pelicans and Their Allies* (Washington, D.C.: Smithsonian Institution, 1922), p. 116.

34 "Human activity has increased extinction": Edward O. Wilson, *The Diversity of Life* (Cambridge, Mass.: Harvard University Press, 1992), p. 280.

Bibliography

Bond, James. *Birds of the West Indies*, 5th ed. Boston: Houghton Mifflin Co., 1993.

Cokinos, Christopher. *Hope Is the Thing with Feathers*. New York: Jeremy P. Tarcher/Putnam, 2000.

Collar, N. J., et al. *Threatened Birds of the Americas*, 3rd ed. Washington, D.C.: Smithsonian Institution Press and International Council for Bird Preservation, 1992.

del Hoyo, Josep, Andrew Elliott, and Jordi Sargantal, eds. *Handbook of Birds of the World*, vol. 4. Barcelona: Lynx Ediciones, 1997.

Feduccia, Alan. *The Origin and Evolution of Birds.* New Haven, Conn.: Yale University Press, 1996.

Hedges, S. Blair. "Historical Biogeography of West Indian Vertebrates," *Annual Review of Ecology and Systematics,* vol. 27 (1996), 163–96.

Leakey, Richard, and Roger Lewin. *The Sixth Extinction.* New York: Doubleday, 1995.

Raffaele, Herbert, et al. *A Guide to the Birds of the West Indies.* Princeton, N.J.: Princeton University Press, 1998.

Ward, Peter. *The End of Evolution.* New York: Bantam Books, 1994.

Yoon, Carol Kaesuk. "Watching as Species Fall into Extinction," *The New York Times,* March 16, 1999.

TWO

Citations

45 "Actually, I kind of believe": Rick Bass, *The Lost Grizzlies* (Boston: Houghton Mifflin, 1995), p. 5.

46 "Would that I could describe": John James Audubon, *The Birds of America,* vol. IV (Philadelphia: J. B. Chevalier, 1842).

50 "I have seen entire belts": Ibid.

51 "To-day it must be numbered": T. Gilbert Pearson, *Birds of America* (Garden City, N.Y.: Garden City Publishing Co., 1936), p. 139.

52 "We are just money grubbers": Quote in Christopher Cokinos, *Hope Is the Thing with Feathers.* (New York: Jeremy P. Tarcher/Putnam, 2000), p. 101.

54 "I found these bottoms": James T. Tanner, *The Ivory-Billed Woodpecker* (New York: National Audubon Society Research Report No. 1, 1942), p. 25.

54 "We wondered, as we took a parting look": Roger Tory Peterson and James Fisher, *Wild America* (Boston: Houghton Mifflin Co., 1955), p. 157.

57 "Victor couldn't bring himself": George Plimpton, "Un gran pedazo de carne," *Audubon,* vol. 79 (November 1977), 21.

57 "In short, a few Imperial Woodpeckers": J. M. Lammertink, J. A. Rojas-Tome, F. M. Casillas-Orona, and R. L. Otto, *Status and Conservation of Old-growth Forests and Endemic Birds in the Pine-Oak Zone of the Sierra Madre Occidental, Mexico* (Institute for Systematics and Population Biology, University of Amsterdam, 1996), p. 67.

58 "by pounding with the bill": Tanner, p. 62.

Bibliography

Bent, Arthur Cleveland. *Life Histories of North American Woodpeckers.* Washington, D.C.: Smithsonian Institution, 1939.

Berger, L., et al. "Chytridiomycosis Causes Amphibian Mortality Associated with Population Declines in the Rain Forests of Australia and Central America," *Proceedings of the National Academy of Sciences,* vol. 95 (July 15, 1998), 9031–36.

Brown, David E. *The Grizzly in the Southwest.* Norman: University of Oklahoma Press, 1985.

Brown, Gary. *The Great Bear Almanac*. New York: Lyons and Burford, 1993.

Hodges, Sam. "Seeing Is Believing" [ivory-billed woodpecker sighting], *Mobile Register*, July 9, 2000.

Howell, Steve N. G., and Sophie Webb. *A Guide to the Birds of Mexico and Northern Central America*. New York: Oxford University Press, 1995.

Lammertink, Martjan. "No More Hope for the Ivory-billed Woodpecker," *Cotinga*, vol. 3 (February 1995), 45–47.

LeFranc, Maurice N., Jr., et al., eds. *Grizzly Bear Compendium*. Washington, D.C.: National Wildlife Federation for the Interagency Grizzly Bear Committee, 1987.

Phillips, Kathryn. *Tracking the Vanishing Frogs*. New York: St. Martin's Press, 1994.

Reid, Bruce. "Glimpse of Ivory Stirs Up Woods," *Clarion-Ledger*, January 30, 2000. http://www.clarionledger.com/news/0001/30/30woodpecker.html.xw

Tanner, James T. "A Postscript on Ivorybills," *Bird Watcher's Digest*, vol. 23 (July/August 2000), 52–59.

Winkler, Hans, David A. Christie, and David Nurney. *Woodpeckers*. Boston: Houghton Mifflin Co., 1995.

Zickefoose, Julie. "Ivory-billed Woodpecker," *Bird Watcher's Digest*, vol. 21 (May/June 1999), 28–43.

THREE

Citations

74 "April 30th, 1984, was the type of day": Dick Watling, "Ratu Filipe and MacGillivray's Petrel," *Journey*, vol. 8 (December 1986), 81.

76 "There is little to record": Gregory Mathews, *The Birds of Australia* (1910–1927), quoted in Walter Boles, Wayne Longmore, and Max Thompson, "The Fly-by-Night Parrrot," *Australian Natural History*, vol. 23 (Winter 1991), 691.

82 "sort of a nightmare composite": Peter Hathaway Capstick, *Warrior* (New York: St. Martin's Press, 1998), p. 85.

85 "I can say *upon my oath*": Charles Vaurie, quoted in Alan G. Knox, "Richard Meinertzhagen—a Case of Fraud Examined," *Ibis*, vol. 135 (1993), 320.

Bibliography

Abbott, David F. "Mystery, Intrigue, Confusion: Searching for India's Least-known Endemic," *Birding*, vol. 30 (October 1998), 392–404.

Allen, Thomas B. *Vanishing Wildlife of North America*. Washington, D.C.: National Geographic Society, 1974.

Associated Press. "He Thought He Caught a Blue Pike. He Didn't," *The New York Times*, May 26, 1999.

Belluck, Pam. "In Angler's Freezer Since '62, Fish May Refute 'Extinction'." *The New York Times*, March 15, 1999.

Blythe, J., A. Burbidge, and W. Boles. "Another Night Parrot Search," *Western Australian Bird Notes*, vol. 81 (1996), 13.

Blythe, John. *Night Parrot* (Pezoporus occidentalis). *Interim Recovery Plan for Western Australia.* Wanneroo, Australia: Department of Conservation and Land Management, 1996.

Blythe, John, and Walter Boles. "An Expedition to the Murchison, Gascoyne and East Pilbara Areas to Search for Night Parrots, November 1997," *Eclectus*, vol. 6 (1999), 12–16.

Boles, Walter, Wayne Longmore, and Max Thompson. "A Recent Specimen of the Night Parrot, *Geopsittacus occidentalis*," *Emu*, vol. 94 (1994), 37–40.

Busch, Dieter, Carol Stepien, Betsy Trometer, Mary Burnham-Curtis, and Cathy Dayon. *Reassessment of the Existence and Taxonomic Classification of the Blue Pike (Percidae: Stizostedion vitreum glaucum).* Amherst, N.Y.: U.S. Fish and Wildlife Service, Lower Great Lakes Fishery Resource Office, 1998.

Collar, Nigel J., M. J. Crosy, and A. J. Stattersfield. *Birds to Watch 2.* Cambridge: BirdLife International, 1994.

del Hoyo, Josep, Andrew Elliott, and Jordi Sargantal, eds. *Handbook of Birds of the World*, vol. 1. Barcelona: Lynx Ediciones, 1992.

———. *Handbook of Birds of the World*, vol. 5. Barcelona: Lynx Ediciones, 1999.

Gerhart, Ann. "The Rat's Tale," *The Washington Post*, March 29, 2000.

Higgins, P. J., senior ed. *Handbook of Australian, New Zealand and Antarctic Birds.* London: Oxford University Press, 1999.

Madge, Steve, and Hilary Burn. *Waterfowl.* Boston: Houghton Mifflin Co., 1988.

Milius, Susan. "Second Group of Living Fossils Reported," *Science News*, vol. 154 (September 26, 1998), 196.

———. "A Second Living-Fossil Species?" *Science News*, vol. 155 (April 24, 1999), 267.

Nowak, Ronald M. *Walker's Mammals of the World*, vol. 2, 5th ed. Baltimore: Johns Hopkins University Press, 1991.

Nugent, Rory. *Search for the Pink-headed Duck.* Boston: Houghton Mifflin Co., 1991.

Perkins, Sid. "The Latest Pieces of an Evolutionary Puzzle," *Science News*, vol. 159 (May 5, 2001), 282–84.

Schodde, Richard and Ian J. Mason. *Nocturnal Birds of Australia.* Melbourne, Australia: Lansdowne Editions, 1980.

Simons, Elwyn L. "Lemurs: Old and New," in *Natural Change and Human Impact in Madagascar*, Steven M. Goodman and Bruce D. Patterson, eds. Washington, D.C.: Smithsonian Institution Press, 1997.

Voous, Karel H. *Owls of the Northern Hemisphere.* London: William Collins Sons & Co., 1988.

Watling, Dick. "Rediscovery of a Petrel and New Faunal Records on Gau Island," *Oryx*, vol. 20 (January 1986), 31–34.

Watling, Dick, and Ratu Filipe Lewanavanua. "A Note to Record the Continuing Survival of the Fiji (MacGillvray's) Petrel *Psuedobulweria macgillivrayi,*" *Ibis*, vol. 127 (1985), 230–33.

FOUR

Citations

93 " . . . There is / One great society": William Wordsworth, "The Prelude," Book XI, line 393. *The Complete Poetical Works* (London: Macmillan and Co., 1888).

108 "This very evening": Peter Matthiessen, *Wildlife in America*, rev. ed. (New York: Viking, 1987), pp. 280–81.

Bibliography

DeBlieu, Jan. *Meant to Be Wild*. Golden, Colo.: Fulcrum Publishing, 1991.

Deer, Mark. "Setbacks Raise Doubts about Captive Breeding," *The New York Times*, January 19, 1999.

Long, Michael E. "The Vanishing Prairie Dog," *National Geographic*, vol. 193 (April 1998), 116–31.

Matthews, Mark. "Standing Up for the Underdog," *High Country News*, vol. 31 (August 16, 1999).

Miller, Brian, Richard P. Reading, and Steve Forrest, *Prairie Night: Black-footed Ferrets and the Recovery of Endangered Species.* (Washington, D.C.: Smithsonian Institution, 1996), p. 25.

Nowak, Ronald M. *Walker's Mammals of the World*, vols. 1 and 2, 5th ed. Baltimore: Johns Hopkins University Press, 1991.

U.S. Fish and Wildlife Service. *Black-footed Ferret Recovery Plan.* Denver, Colo.: U.S. Fish and Wildlife Service, 1988.

Van Pelt, William E. "The Black-tailed Prairie Dog Conservation Assessment and Strategy," fifth draft. Phoenix, Ariz.: Arizona Game and Fish Department, 1999.

Williams, Ted. "The Final Ferret Fiasco," *Audubon*, vol. 88 (May 1986), 110–19.

FIVE

Citations

125 "In view of the poor tracking conditions": Robert L. Downing, "Investigation to Determine the Status of the Cougar in the Southern Appalachians," in *Proceedings of the Eastern Cougar Conference, 1994*, Jay W. Tischendorf and Steve J. Ropski, eds. (American Ecological Research Institute, Fort Collins, Colo., 1996) pp. 46–49.

128 "Animals as metaphysically important as tigers": John Seidensticker, "Bearing Witness: Observations on the Extinction of *Panthera tigris balica* and *Panthera tigris sondaica*," in *Tigers of the World*, Ronald L. Tilson and Ulysses S. Seal, eds. (Park Ridge, N.J.: Noyes Publications, 1987), p. 1.

145 "The conclusion is that this particular leopard skull": Daphne M. Hills, internal specimen identification report, August 7, 1995, Natural History Museum of London.

Bibliography

Anon. "Eastern Cougar (*Felis concolor cougar*)" species account. U.S. Fish and Wildlife Service Division of Endangered Species. http://endangered.fws.gov/i/a/saa48.html

Baker, Simon. "Big Cats in the British Countryside: Can We Always Believe Our Eyes?" *Mammalaction News*, no. 90 (Summer 2000), 3–4.

Baker, S. J., and C. J. Wilson. *The Evidence for the Presence of Large Exotic Cats in the Bodmin Area and Their Possible Impact on Livestock*. Cambridge: ADAS Cambridge; and London: Ministry of Agriculture, Fisheries and Food Publications, 1995.

Corbet, Gordon, and Denys Ovenden. *The Mammals of Britain and Europe*. London: William Collins & Sons, 1980.

Downing, Robert L. "The Cougar in the East," in *Proceedings of the Eastern Cougar Conference, 1994*, Jay W. Tischendorf and Steve J. Ropski, eds. American Ecological Research Institute, Fort Collins, Colo., 1996, pp. 163–66.

Lutz, John, and Linda Lutz. "The Eastern Puma," in *Proceedings of the Eastern Cougar Conference, 1994*, Jay W. Tischendorf and Steve J. Ropski, eds. American Ecological Research Institute, Fort Collins, Colo., 1996, pp. 127–38.

Schneck, Marcus. "Pennsylvania's Unseen Predators," *Keystone Conservationist*, vol. 2 (November–December 1999), 28–30.

SIX

Citations

158 "The White River case": Roy P. Mackal, *Searching for Hidden Animals* (New York: Doubleday and Co., 1980), p. 206.

160 "even though the creature's relationship": Peter Scott and Robert Rines, "Naming the Loch Ness Monster," *Nature*, vol. 258 (December 11, 1975), 466.

160 "The generic name *Nessiteras*": Ibid.

161 "would not be detected easily": Ibid, pp. 467–68.

167 "a remarkable worm": Eugene S. Richardson, Jr., *The Dancing Worm of Turkana* (Gurnee: Ill.: The Vanishing Press [self-published imprint], 1969), p. 10.

168 "With their help I, even I": Ibid, p. 11.

168 "As regards the subject": Ibid, p. 12.

168 "Today techer show us paper": Ibid, p. 14.

173 "The objections to a second North American hominid": Robert Michael Pyle, *Where Bigfoot Walks* (Boston: Houghton Mifflin Co., 1995), p. 32.

175 "[A]t the heart of science": Carl Sagan, *The Demon-Haunted World* (New York: Random House, 1996), p. 304.

Bibliography

Blackman, W. Haden. *The Field Guide to North American Monsters*. New York: Three Rivers Press, 1998.

Coleman, Loren, and Jerome Clark. *Cryptozoology A to Z*. New York: Fireside, 1999.

Goering, Laurie. "Biologist on Trail of Sloth Thought to Be Extinct," *Chicago Tribune*, January 9, 1995.

Gugliotta, Guy. "Along Laos-Vietnam Border, a Menagerie," *The Washington Post*, December 17, 1999.

Hendrix, Steve. "Quest for the Kouprey," *International Wildlife* (September/October 1995), 20–23.

Holloway, Marguerite. "Beasts in the Mist," *Discover*, vol. 20 (September 1999), 58–65.

Kimchhay, Heng, et al. *The Distribution of Tiger, Leopard, Elephant and Wild Cattle (Guar, Banteng, Buffalo, Khiting Vor and Kouprey) in Cambodia: Interim Report*. Cambodia Wildlife Protection Office, July 1998. http://www.felidae.org/PROJECTS/Tiger_in_Cambodia/weiler_prelim_report.html

Knippenberg, Jim. "Tristater Searches for Giant Sloth," *Cincinnati Enquirer*, May 31, 2001. http://enquirer.com/editions/2001/05/31/tem_tristater_searches.html

Line, Les. "Alan Rabinowitz: Indiana Jones Meets His Match," *The New York Times*, August 3, 1999.

Mackal, Roy P. *The Monsters of Loch Ness*. Chicago: The Swallow Press, 1976.

Milius, Susan. "And Now There Are Two Striped Rabbits," *Science News*, vol. 156 (August 21, 1999), 116.

Mydans, Seth. "Cambodia's Mountains Hide a Wildlife Refuge, *The New York Times*, April 8, 2000.

Perkins, Sid. "Is Nessie Merely a Bad Case of the Shakes?" *Science News*, vol. 160 (July 7, 2001), 5.

Rajesh, Y. P. "New Dehli in Grips of 'Monkey Man' Panic," *USA Today*, May 17, 2001.

Sagan, Carl. "If There Are Any, Could There Be Many?" *Nature*, vol. 264 (December 9, 1976), 497.

Shine, Adrian J. "Postscript: Surgeon or Sturgeon?" *Scottish Naturalist*, vol. 105 (1993), 271–82.

Shine, Adrian J., and David S. Martin. "Loch Ness Habitats Observed by Sonar and Underwater Television," *Scottish Naturalist*, vol. 105 (1988), 111–99.

Stolzenburg, William. "Bigfoot of the Amazon," *Nature Conservancy*, vol. 44 (July/August 1994), 7.

SEVEN

Citations

189 "It was at this moment": Jean-Marie Chauvet, Éliette Brunel Deschamps, and Christian Hillaire, *Dawn of Art: The Chauvet Cave* (New York: Harry N. Adams, 1996), p. 39.

189 "During those moments": Ibid, p. 41.

192 "In size they are a trifle smaller": Julius Caesar, *Bellum Gallicum VI*, quoted in *Animals in Roman Life and Art*, Joceyln M.C. Toynbee (Ithaca, N.Y.: Cornell University Press, 1973), p. 148.

192 "It is rather difficult to imagine": Juliet Clutton-Brock, *A Natural History of Domesticated Animals*, 2nd ed. (Cambridge: Cambridge University Press, 1999), p. 87.

198 "No animal . . . is entirely exterminated": Heinz Heck, "The Breeding-Back of the Aurochs" (trans. Winifred Felce), *Oryx*, vol. 1, no. 3 (1951), 119.

199 "Of course you can breed": Lutz Heck, *Animals—My Adventure* (trans. E. W. Dickes) (London: Methuen & Co., 1954), p. 142.

199 "We climbed up into the haunts": Ibid, p. 144.

200 "Success came incredibly quickly": Heinz Heck, 120.

204 "as typical a tarpan": J. Cossar Ewart, quoted in David P. Willoughby, *The Empire of Equus* (Cranbury, N.J.: A. S. Barnes and Co., 1974), p. 139.

205 "I was, of necessity": Heinz Heck, "The Breeding-Back of the Tarpan" (trans. Winifred Felce), *Oryx*, vol. 1 (1952), 340.

208 "Let us consider an example": Heinz Heck, p. 117.

209 "I could not estimate": William Burchell, quoted in Robert M. McClung, *Lost Wild Worlds* (New York: William Morrow and Co., 1976), p. 134.

209 "This would be a repetition": Heinz Heck, p. 118.

211 "Since there is no direct evidence": "Criticism of the project," Quagga Project home page, http://www.museums.org.za/sam/quagga/criticis.htm

211 "The quagga is a quagga": Quoted in Don Boroughs, "New Life for a Vanished Zebra?" *International Wildlife*, vol. 29 (March/April 1999), 46–50.

212 "the thought that if man": Heinz Heck, "The Breeding-Back of the Aurochs" (trans. Winifred Felce), *Oryx*, vol. 1, no. 3 (1951), 122.

Bibliography

Anthony, David W., in *Horses Through Time*, Sandra L. Olsen ed., Boulder, Colo.: Roberts Rinehart Publishers (undated).

Artinger, Kai. "Lutz Heck: Der 'Vater der Rominter Ure': Einige Bermerkungen zum wissenschaftlicher Leiter des Berliner Zoos im Nationalsozialismus," *Der Bär von Berlin*, vol. 43 (1994), 125–38.

Attenborough, David. *The First Eden*. Boston: Little, Brown and Co., 1987.

Barnaby, David. "The Karoo Receives Plains Zebras from the Quagga Project," *International Zoo News*, vol. 46 (March 1999), 94–98.

Brisbin, I., Lehr, Jr., and Thomas S. Risch. "Primitive Dogs, Their Ecology and Behavior: Unique Opportunities to Study the Early Development of the Human-Canine Bond," *Journal of the American Veterinary Medical Association*, vol. 210 (1997), 1122–26.

Chelminski, Rudolph. "Polish Forest, a Time Machine," *Smithsonian*, vol. 9 (May 1978), 66–71.

Clottes, Jean. "Chauvet Cave: France's Magical Ice Age Art," *National Geographic*, vol. 200 (August 2001), 104–21.

David, P.D.C., and A. A. Dent. *Animals That Changed the World*. London: Phoenix House, 1966.

Groves, Colin P. "Morphology, Habitat and Taxonomy," in *Przewalski's Horse: History and*

Biology of an Endangered Species, Lee Boyd and Katherine A. Houpt, eds. Albany, N.Y.: SUNY Press, 1994.

Heptner, V. G., A. A. Nasimovich, and A. G. Bannikov. *Mammals of the Soviet Union*, vol. 1. Leiden: E. J. Brill, 1989.

Kurtén, Björn. *The Cave Bear Story.* New York: Columbia University Press, 1995.

Loftus, Ronan T., et al. "Evidence for Two Independent Domestications of Cattle," *Proceedings of the National Academy of Sciences*, vol. 91 (March 1994), 2757–61.

MacHugh, David Evan. *Molecular Biogeography and Genetic Structure of Domesticated Cattle.* Doctoral thesis, University of Dublin, 1996.

McNeil, Donald G., Jr. "Brave Quest of African Hunt: Bringing Back Extinct Quagga," *The New York Times*, September 16, 1997.

Munzinger Archive/Internationales, online biographic files: Heinz Heck, 32/82; Lutz Heck, 32/82. 1998.

Rokosz, M. "History of the Aurochs (*Bos taurus primigenius*) in Poland," *Animal Genetic Resources Information*, no. 16 (1995), 5–14.

Silverberg, Robert. *The Auk, the Dodo and the Oryx.* New York: Thomas Y. Crowell, 1967.

Winstead, Edward R. "In South Africa, the Quagga Project Breeds Success," *Genomic News Network*, October 20, 2000. http://www.celera.com/genomics/news/articles/10_00/Quagga_project.cfm.

Zeuner, Frederick E. *A History of Domesticated Animals.* New York: Harper and Row, 1963.

EIGHT

Citations

221 "guarantees to the Chiefs and Tribes": Treaty of Waitangi, 1840. Article the Second. Online English version, http://www.govt.nz/aboutnz/treaty.php3

Bibliography

Anon. "Briefing Notes on Dolly," Roslin Institute Online, December 12, 1997. http://www.ri.bbsrc.ac.uk/library/research/cloning/dolly.html

————. "Fictional Science," *Nature Genetics*, vol. 23, no. 1 (October 1999), 137.

————. "The Huia—Prospects for Cloning," Cyberuni, 1999. http://www.cyberuni.org/research.html

Associated Press. "Mammoth Sperm Search Fails," September 19, 1997.

————. "Frozen Woolly Mammoth Inspires Cloning Project," *The New York Times*, October 5, 1999.

Flannery, Tim. *The Future Eaters.* Chatswood, Australia: Reed Books, 1994.

Goodheart, Adam. "Bringing Back the Beast," *Outside*, vol. 26, no. 3 (March 2001), 48–54, 116–19.

Kiger, Patrick J. "The Mammoth Waits," Discovery.com, February 4, 2000. http://www.discovery.com/exp/mammoth/20000204dispatch.html

Kloor, Keith. "Back from the Dead," *Audubon*, vol. 101, no. 6 (November–December 1999), 20–21.

Lanza, Robert P., Betsy L. Dresser, and Philip Damiani. "Cloning Noah's Ark," *Scientific American*, November 2000, 84–89.

Matthews, Louise. "Jurassic Lark," *The Listener*, May 20, 2000.

Pielou, E. C. *After the Ice Age*. Chicago: University of Chicago Press, 1991.

Reuters. "Intact Mammoth to Be Carved from Siberian Tundra," *The New York Times*, July 23, 1999.

————. "Scientists Dig Up Near-Intact Woolly Mammoth," *The New York Times*, October 21, 1999.

Rose, Danny. "Tiger Cloning Project Delayed by TV Deal," Hobart *Mercury*, March 30, 2000.

Shaw, Muriel. "Moa Hunting at Chipstead Valley," *Bulletin of the Croydon Natural History and Scientific Society*, vol. 103 (September 1997), 3–4.

Stevens, William K. "Suspects in 'Blitzkrieg' Extinctions: Early Hunters," *The New York Times*, March 28, 2000.

Wade, Nicholas. "Cloning of Intact Siberian Mammoth Is Unlikely, Expert Says, Citing Fragmented DNA in Earlier Finds," *The New York Times*, October 29, 1999.

Whipple, Dan. "The Return of the Siberian Mammoth," Environmental News Network, February 10, 2000. http://www.enn.com/features/2000/02/02102000/mammoth_9461.asp

NINE

Citations

248 "We found ourselves": Tim Flannery, *Throwim Way Leg* (New York: Atlantic Monthly Press, 1998), p. 156.

253 "It flies at the approach of Man": J. Oxley, "Account of the Settlement at Port Dalrymple, 1810; quoted in Eric Guiler and Philippe Godard, *Tasmanian Tiger: A Lesson to Be Learnt* (Perth, Australia: Abrolhos Publishing, 1998), p. 78.

255 "Tasmanian tigers would kill": Eric Guiler, *The Tasmanian Tiger in Pictures* (Hobart, Tasmania: St. David's Park Publishing, 1991), p. 14.

255 "some internal hurt": G. P. Harris, "Description of two new Species of Didelphis from Van Diemen's Land," *Transactions of the Linnean Society of London*, vol. IX (1808), p. 175.

256 "The numbers of this singular animal": John Gould, *The Mammals of Australia*, 1851; quoted in Robert Paddle, *The Last Tasmanian Tiger* (Cambridge: Cambridge University Press, 2000), p. 223.

257 "these dreadful animals": quoted in Paddle, p. 161.

265 "Thus, unprotected and exposed": Paddle, p. 195.

271 "Miss Patricia, Pricilla, Priscilla": Paddle, pp. 92–93.

272 "As I swept the beam around": quoted in Guiler and Godard, ibid., p. 211.

276 "In all honesty": Ibid, p. 8.

Bibliography

Milius, Susan. "Stick Insects: Three Females Remain," *Science News*, vol. 159 (March 3, 2001), 143.

Stackhouse, John. *Australia's Venomous Wildlife*. London: Paul Hamlyn, 1970.

TEN

Citations

287 "The forest of this area": K. L. Schuchmann, "Family TROCHILIDAE (Hummingbirds)," in *Handbook of Birds of the World*, vol. 5, J. del Hoyo, A. Elliott, and J. Sargatal, eds. (Barcelona, Spain: Lynx Ediciones, 1999), p. 531.

306 "Sexes alike": Robert S. Ridgely and Guy Tudor, *The Birds of South America*, vol. 1 (Austin: University of Texas Press, 1989), p. 333.

Bibliography

Berlioz, J. "A New Genus and Species of Tanager from Central Brazil," *Bulletin of the British Ornithological Club*, vol. 59 (1939), 102–3.

————. "Note sur une collection d'oiseaux du Brásil Central," *L'Oiseau et La Revue Française d'Ornithologie*, vol. 16 (1946), 1–6.

Graves, Gary R. "Relic of a Lost World: A New Species of Sunangel (Trochilidae: *Heliangelus*) from 'Bogotá,' " *Auk*, vol. 110 (1993), 1–8

Hilty, Steven L., and William L. Brown. *Birds of Colombia*. Princeton, N.J.: Princeton University Press, 1986.

Ridgely, Robert S., and Guy Tudor. *The Birds of South America*, vol. 2. Austin: University of Texas Press, 1994.

Stotz, Douglas F., John W. Fitzpatrick, Theodore A. Parker III, and Debra K. Moskovits. *Neotropical Birds: Ecology and Conservation*. Chicago: University of Chicago Press, 1996.

Acknowledgments

I am, as usual, indebted to a wide variety of people who helped make this book possible, starting with my family. And once again, I leaned heavily on my friends for support; three whose advice was particularly helpful were Bruce Van Patter, Mike Orlofsky, and Chuck Fergus. Special and deep-felt thanks to Sharon Gaughan, for uncountable other favors, including holding down the fort.

It has again been a great pleasure to work with my editor at FSG/North Point Press, Ethan Nosowsky, and with Peter Matson and Jim Rutman at Sterling Lord Literistic, who smooth out the bumps in this peculiar business of writing.

Portions of Chapter 4 first appeared in *Smithsonian* magazine, where I am grateful, as always, to editors Marlane Liddell, John Ross, Elizabeth Erskine, and Don Moser. Portions of Chapter 8 and Chapter 9 appeared in *Audubon*, where my thanks go to features editor Mary-Powel Thomas.

At the Smithsonian's Conservation and Research Center in Virginia, I'd like to thank director Dr. Chris Wemmer, Linwood C. Williamson, and Dr. JoGayle Howard for the chance to observe the black-footed ferret breeding program at such an intimate level. Dr. Robert S. Ridgely, formerly of the Academy of Natural Sciences of Philadelphia and now at Audubon, was very helpful on a number of fronts, particularly with advice on Semper's warbler and the cone-billed tanager. Appreciation is also due Erik Blom; Dr. Dick Watling in Fiji; Janet Hinshaw of the University of Michigan Museum of Zoology; Professor Werner

Cohn, professor emeritus of the University of British Columbia; Dr. Roger Wood of Stockton College, N.J.; Catherine Levy of Kingston, Jamaica; Steve Shively of the Louisiana Department of Wildlife and Fisheries; Rob Butler of the Canadian Wildlife Service in British Columbia; Dr. Louise Emmons and Dr. Pamela C. Rasmussen of the National Museum of Natural History, Washington, D.C.; Dr. Gary Alt; and Terence Bostic.

Greg Budney of the Library of Natural Sounds, Cornell University, provided invaluable technical assistance and equipment. Thanks also to Dr. I. Lehr Brisbin, Susan Crockford, and Juliet Clutton-Brock for my tutorial in the process of domestication.

In St. Lucia, thanks to chief forest officer Michael Andrew, to chief wildlife officer Donald Anthony, and to biologist Michael Bobb, all of whom aided in my search for Semper's warbler. Also, many thanks to my friend Amy Gaberlein, who took what certainly ranks as one of the more unusual Caribbean vacations to serve as unpaid field assistant. Dr. Herbert A. Raffaele, U.S. Fish and Wildlife Service Office of International Affairs, and Paul Sweet, collections manager of the American Museum of Natural History, were also quite helpful. In England, I am especially grateful to Quentin Rose for his hospitality and time and to Dave Maehr for his patience and diplomacy. Thanks also to Daphne M. Hills, curator of mammals at the Natural History Museum of London; Simon Baker; Dr. John Seidensticker of the National Zoological Park in Washington, D.C., for his insights into ghost cat reports; and Douglas M. Richardson, zoological director of the Rome Zoo.

In Brazil, I'd like to acknowledge Doug Wechsler of the Academy of Natural Sciences in Philadelphia for working so enthusiastically to plan the tanager search, and to our guide, Fabiano Olivera, for an endless supply of good humor. Doug and I also wish to thank a number of people who gave us valuable advice, including Edwin O. Willis and Yoshika Oniki Willis, Kevin Zimmer, Bret Whitney, and Tom J. Ulrich. In Australia, in addition to Dr. Don Colgan and Walter Boles at the Australian Museum, thanks to Heidi DeWald for her assistance. Thanks also to Dr. Alan Trounson of Monash University, Dr. Wayne Longmore of the Queensland Museum, Dr. Eric Guiler, Michael Lynch of the Tasmanian Conservation Trust, and Senator Bob Brown of the Tasmanian Green

Party, as well as Doug Gross, Jerry Hassinger, and Jane Kirkland in the United States for helpful advice.

And finally, I offer a quiet prayer that the lost species that live in our hearts also still live in their own, private corners of the world, making it by their mysterious presence a richer, more vibrant place.

Index

Abbot, David F., 90, 91

Abenaki, 165

Abominable Snowman, *see* yeti

Aborigines, Australian, 231, 255, 262, 279

Academy of Applied Science, 159

Agenbroad, Larry D., 227–29

agoutis, 4–6

Aikhenbaum, Jean, 208

Alkali Lake monster, 159

Allen, Arthur A. "Doc," 51, 52, 55, 58

Allenby, Field Marshal E.H.H., 82

Almas, 173

American Museum of Natural History (New York), 25–26, 55, 85, 90, 180, 228

American Ornithologists' Union, 17

Amerindians, 6, 186

Amman, Karl, 180

Andes, hummingbirds of, 286–87

antbirds, 282, 284

anteaters, 298

antechinuses, 245

Anthony, Donald, 10, 13–15

Anthony, Jim, 70–73

Anthony, Mary Lynn, 72

antpittas, 177

ants, 177

antwrens, 300

anurans, die-offs of, 40–41

apes, 179–80; captive breeding of, 198; giant, 172, 175

Appalachians, 245; cougars in, 10–11, 23, 123–28, 150; cryptozoology in, 170

arachnology, 177

Archer, Michael, 233, 235

Argentina, 159

Arizona, University of, 171

artificial insemination (AI), 112–16

Ashaninka culture, 68

Athene blewitti, 86

Atlas lion, *see* Barbary lion

Audubon, John James, 46–50, 62, 83, 93–95, 103, 122

Audubon, John Woodhouse, 93

Audubon, Victor, 93

Audubon Society, 51, 52, 64

aurochs, 191–97; reconstituted, 197–208, 211, 212

Australia, 21, 35; anuran die-offs in, 40, 41; big-cat sightings in, 132; hominids in, 173; human colonization of, 231; marsupials of, 19, 229, 230, 245, 253, 258–59 (*see also* thylacine); ratites of, 216; rediscovered species

Australia (*cont.*)

    in, 19, 75–81, 246; venomous crea-
    tures of, 252–53; wild dogs of, 201;
    see also Tasmania

Australian Aborigines, 231, 255, 262,
    279

Australian Catholic University, 262

Australian Geographic, 76

Australian Museum (Sydney), 76, 233–
    36, 238, 247, 278

Australian National University, 172

Australian Natural History, 78

Australopithecus, 174

aye-ayes, 69

Bachman, John, 93–95

Bachman's warbler, 11, 17–18

backcrossing, 197–208

background extinction rate, 34

badgers, 129, 130, 149; ice-age, 190

Badlands National Park (South Dakota),
    97

Baird, Spencer Fullerton, 95

Baker, Simon, 144–45, 148

bananaquits, 28–30, 32

bandicoots, 245

Banks, Joseph, 250

Banksia, 250–51

Barbary lion, 109–11

Bardot, Brigitte, 269

Barmanu, 173

basenjis, 201

Basilosaurus, 157

Bass, Rick, 45

bats, 5, 246–48

Batty, Wilf, 263

Bayou Sauvage National Wildlife Refuge
    (Louisiana), 53

beaked whales, 177–78

bears, 39, 42–45, 203; ice-age, 190,
    191, 223; *see also* black bears; brown
    bears; grizzlies

Beast of Bodmin Moor, 12

Beaumaris Zoo (Tasmania), 263, 264

Beebe, William, 35

bee hummingbird, 6

Belize, 124

Bennett's wallaby, 253

Berlin Olympics (1936), 203

Berlin Zoo, 197, 198, 201, 203,
    206

Berlioz, Jacques, 287–89

Bermuda, 22, 74

bettongs, 245

Bhutan, 174

big cats, 127–28, 173; British sightings
    of, 128–50, 152, 171; captive breed-
    ing of, 112; ice-age, 190, 223; *see also*
    specific animals

Bigfoot, 151, 172–76, 179

Bili ape, 152, 179–80

biogeography, 6, 156

Biological Survey, U.S., 96

BIOTA, 103, 105

biotic recovery, 35

birds: discovery of new species of, 177;
    DNA of dinosaurs and, 215; endemic
    species of, 5–7; flightless, 216; songs
    of, 299–300; Tasmanian, 244; *see also*
    specific birds

Birds of South America (Ridgely), 306

Birmingham (England) *Post*, 136

bison: American, 95, 97, 98, 123, 203,
    217; European, 196, 198, 203; ice-
    age, 224

black bears, 44–45, 123, 132, 138;
    giant, 152

black panthers, *see* panthers

black-footed ferret, 22–23, 93–96, 99–
    109, 111–22

Blair, Frank, 151

Blewitt, F. R., 86

"blitzkrieg hypothesis," 231

Blizzard, Ray, 270

blue pike, 70–73, 101

Blythe, John, 79–80
bobcats, 123, 126
Bodmin Moor, Beast of, 129, 142–45, 148, 152, 241
"Bogotá skins," 286–87
Bogotá sunangel, 286–87
Boesche, Christophe, 180
Boles, Walter, 76–81, 246
Bombay Natural History Society, 88–89, 92
Bond, James, 8
Bondegezou, 173
bonobos, 179
boobook owl, 259
Boque Chitto National Wildlife Refuge (Louisiana), 53
Bos primigenius, 191, 195, 202
botflies, 282–83
Bowden, Les and Brian, 140
Boyd, Alastair, 163
Brace's emerald hummingbird, 287
Brazil, 280–310
"breeding back," see backcrossing
British Joint Air Reconnaissance Intelligence Centre, 155
British Ministry of Agriculture, Fisheries and Food, 144
British Museum, 82, 86, 155; see also Natural History Museum
brown bears, 44, 149; see also grizzlies
bubonic plague, 100; see also sylvatic plague
buff-cheeked tody-flycatcher, 285
buffalo, see bison, American
Buffetaut, Eric, 172
Buigues, Bernard, 226, 228, 237
bullfinches, 30–32
Bulmer's fruit bat, 246–48
Burchell's zebra, 208–11
Burma, 112
Burroughs, John, 12
Buru, 19
Bush, Mitch, 114

Caesar, Julius, 191–92
cahows, 22, 23, 74
California, University of: Berkeley, 210; Bodega Marine Reserve, 18
Calliota gomerana, 20
Cambodia, 11–12, 152, 182, 183
Campephilus, 56, 59; C.p. bairdii, 55–56; C.p. principalis, 55
Canada, lake monsters in, 156, 164
Canary Islands, 20
canine distemper, see distemper
Cape lion, 110, 111
captive breeding, 16, 72, 112, 198; of black-footed ferrets, 23, 102–3, 105–8, 111–22
caracal lynx, 134, 137
Caribbean elaenia, 32–33
Carolina parakeet, 16–17
Carpenter, Jim, 102–3
Case Western Reserve University, 72
Cash, Liz, 139–40
cassowaries, 216, 217
Castro, Fidel, 55
cattle, 196–97; backcrossing of, 197–205; domestication of, 192–95
cave paintings, 187–91, 200, 204
Centers for Disease Control and Prevention, 105
cephalopods, 178
cetaceans, 178–79
Chacoan peccary, 181–82
Champlain, Lake, monster, 156–58, 162, 165
Champlain, Samuel de, 157
Chauvet, Jean-Marie, 187–89
Chauvet Cave (France), 188–91, 193, 212
cheetahs, 113, 136; ice-age, 190
Chicago Mill and Lumber Company, 52
chimpanzees, 179, 180
China, hominids in, 172, 173
Chinese Academy of Sciences, 172
Chuchunaa, 173

Chupacabra, El, 153, 171

Churchill, Elias, 263

chytridiomycosis, 41

Cincinnati Zoo, 17

Clark, Eugenie, 172

Clark, Tim, 103, 105

climate change, 34, 231; anuran die-offs
and, 40–41

cloning, 213–29; of birds, 216–23; of
endangered species, 238–39; of
mammoths, 223–29; of thylacines,
229–42, 278–79

clouded leopards, 113

cloud rats, 67, 77

Clutton-Brock, Juliet, 192–93

coccidia, 106

coelacanths, 65–66, 169

Cokinos, Christopher, 51, 52

Cold War, 55

Colgan, Don, 235–38, 240, 278

Collar, Nigel J., 83, 86

collared crescentchest, 300

Colombia, 286–87

Colorado Division of Wildlife, 43

colorful puffleg, 287

Columba, St., 153–54

Columbian mammoth, 224

Comoros Islands, 65, 66

condors, 6; giant, 152, 170

cone-billed tanager, 281, 282, 284–92,
297, 298, 300, 302–6, 309–10

Congo, 152, 179–81

Congo bay owl, 20

Connors, Peter G., 18

Conothraupis, 281

Conservation International, 67

Conservation of Wild Creatures and
Wild Plants Act (U.K., 1975), 160

Convention on International Trade in
Endangered Species of Wild Fauna
and Flora (CITES), 10, 18, 23

convergent evolution, 230

Cook, Captain James, 250

Cooper's hawk, 97–98

Copper Age, 187

coppery thorntail, 286

Cornell University, 51; Library of Natural Sounds, 24; Ornithology Lab, 64

Costa Rica, 23, 38–42

cottonmouth, 60

cougars, 10–11, 23, 101, 123–28, 150;
British sightings of, 132, 137, 142,
144, 147; as pets, 136

cow, snake-eating, 152, 183

coyotes, 123

Creation of Mammoth Association, 225

Cretaceous Period, 11, 33, 35

Crete, ancient, 193–94

Crichton, Michael, 214

Crockford, Susan J., 194

Cro-Magnons, 190, 193

Crump, Martha, 39–41

Crusades, 109

cryptosporidia, 106

cryptozoology, 151–76, 218, 309;
fringe of, 170–71; "hominology" in,
172–76; lake monsters and, 151–65;
and recently discovered species, 178–
83

Cuba, 5–6, 17–18; ivory-billed woodpecker in, 55–56, 64

currawongs, 251

Cuscomys ashaninka, 68

Cuvier, Georges, 180, 182

Cyberuni, 220–22

Cyprus, 193

Dancing Worm of Turkana, 167–69

Dangerous Wild Animals Act (U.K.,
1976), 136, 147

Darby, Frank, 265, 266

Dartmoor Wildlife Park (England), 137

dasyurids, 258–59

Daszkiewics, Piotr, 208

Davidson, James, 87, 90

deer, 112, 113, 123, 180, 183, 293
Demon-Haunted World, The (Sagan), 175
Dennis, John V., 54
d'Entrecasteaux expedition, 230
Deschamps, Éliette Brunel, 187–89
Didi, 173
Dietemann, Chantal, 20
dingoes, 201, 231
Dinornis maximus, 216
dinosaurs, 11, 151, 152; cloning of,
    214–16; cryptozoology and, 179
Dinsdale, Tim, 155
diprotodons, 230, 258
Discovery Channel, 226, 235
diseases: anuran, 41; and extinction of
    ice-age mammals, 224, 228; ferret,
    100, 102, 105–8, 117–18, 121; live-
    stock, 201, 207; marsupial, 259–60,
    263
Disney, Walt, Studios, 269
distemper, 102, 106, 107, 111, 117,
    118, 259, 260
DNA, 19, 124; of bears, 45; for cloning,
    214–16, 218–23, 227, 228, 233,
    235–39, 278; cryptozoology and,
    186; of lions, 110–11; and reconsti-
    tution of extinct species, 195, 205,
    210–12; of whales, 246
dogs, 201–2; domestication of, 192,
    194–95
domestication, 192–95, 204, 205
Douglas-Apsley National Park (Tasma-
    nia), 249–53
Downing, Robert L., 125n
Doyle, Arthur Conan, 11
ducks, 16, 88
dunnarts, 229, 245, 258–59

eagles, 99, 217
earthquakes, 162
Eastern Puma Research Network, 125
Ebedes, Hym, 110

echidnas, 245
ecological restoration projects, 207
ecotourism, 4, 41, 285
Ecuador, 19, 177, 281, 285, 287, 299
Edgerton, Harold, 159
Edmond Forest Reserve (St. Lucia), 12–
    16, 24–33
Edwards, Yvonne, 138
egg-laying mammals, 244–45
Egypt, 109; ancient, 193
elephantbirds, 216, 217
elephants, captive breeding of, 198
elephant seals, 158–59
elk, 123; Irish, 190, 191, 223
El Niño, 41
Emanuel, Victor, 57
Emmons, Louise, 66–68, 77
emus, 216, 217
Endangered Species Act (ESA; 1973),
    10, 23, 97, 99, 101, 126
Endangered Species Preservation Act
    (1966), 101
endemic species, 5–6, 16, 80
England: big-cat sightings in, 128–50,
    152, 171, 241, 243; cattle in, 197,
    199; ecological restoration projects
    in, 207
entomology, 177
Eocene Epoch, 157
eradication campaigns, 96–97, 99, 100,
    102, 118, 122
Erdmann, Arnaz Mehta and Mark, 66
Ethiopia, 110
eucalyptus, 250, 273–74
Eurasian ferrets, 108, 113, 115
evolution, 34–35; convergent, 230
Ewart, J. Cossar, 204
Exmoor, Beast of, 129, 135, 146
Exmoor National Park (England), 146
exotics, escaped, 136, 139
extinctions, 152; of anurans, 40; at-
    tempts at reconstitution of species af-
    ter, 197–212 (*see also* cloning);

extinctions (*cont.*)
  determination of, 17–18; fascination
  with, 10–11; "first contact," 6; local,
  42, 100, 122; on Madagascar, 68;
  mass, 33–35, 231; process of, 16–
  17; in tropics, 286, 287
extirpation, 42
Eyrean grasswren, 76

Fairbairn, Nicholas, 161*n*
fairy-wrens, 251
falcons, 99
Faulkner, William, 60
Federal Bureau of Investigation (FBI),
  87
fer-de-lance, 31
ferrets, *see* black-footed ferret
Field Museum of Natural History
  (Chicago), 166–69
Fiji petrel, 74–75
finches, 8; Arctic, *see* redpolls; rediscovered, 19–20
Fisher, James, 54
fishers, 123
Flannery, Tim, 217, 231, 247–48,
  262
Fleay, David, 234, 267
Fleming, Ian, 8
Florida Game and Fresh Water Fish
  Commission, 132
Florida panthers, 123–24
flycatchers, 19, 32, 285
flying squirrels, 20
foot-and-mouth disease, 201
forest owlet, 86–92, 152
Forest Service, U.S., 97
Forrest, Steve, 107
fossils, 11, 33–35, 165–67, 169, 200,
  247; cryptozoology and, 157, 158,
  172; of ice-age mammals, 190, 191,
  200, 230
foxes, 99, 129, 130, 149, 195

France: aurochs in, 207–8; cave paintings in, 187–90; wild cattle in, 199
Franklin, John, 274
fraud, scientific, 81–87, 89, 95
frogs, 40; *see also* tree frogs
Future Eaters, The (Flannery), 217

galliwasps, 5
genetic studies, 72, 73; *see also* DNA
George V, king of England, 219
Ghost and the Darkness, The (movie),
  166
giant woolly flying squirrel, 20–21
Gigantopithecus, 172, 179
Gilbert's potoroo, 19
glaciations, *see* ice ages
gliders, 229, 251
Gloucester sea serpent, 151
Godard, Philippe, 270, 276
Goebbels, Joseph, 203
Goeldi, Emilio, Museum (Brazil), 184
golden eagle, 99
golden toad, 23, 38–42
Gondwana, 216
Goodall, Jane, 180
gorillas, 179, 180
Göring, Hermann, 203
Goto, Kazufumi, 224
Gould, John, 256
Great Lakes fisheries, 70–73
Greenwell, J. Richard, 171
Greenwood, Alex, 228
grizzlies, 39, 42–45; Mexican, 56
Groves, Colin P., 172
Guam rails, 112
guar ox, 193
Guatemala, 173
Guiler, Eric, 242, 244, 248–49, 254–
  55, 259–63, 266–70, 272–73, 275–
  78
gum trees, 250
Guyana, 173

Haast's eagle, 217
habitat, 241, 245; critical, protection of, 101; destruction of, 34, 79, 122, 239, 281–82, 286 (*see also* logging); fragmentation of, 97
Hamel, Paul, 17–18
Hanlon, George, 268, 269
harlequin frog, 40
Harvard University, 34, 166, 169, 180, 184; Museum of Comparative Zoology, 26, 166
Hasting Boys' High School (New Zealand), 220, 221, 223
hawks, 4, 69, 97–99, 291–92, 299
Heck, Heinz, 197–203, 205–10, 211, 212, 214
Heck, Ludwig, 197, 202
Heck, Lutz, 197–203, 205–8, 211, 212, 214
herons, 52, 61
herpetology, 177
Heuvelmans, Bernard, 171–72, 185
Highland Wildlife Park (Scotland), 137
Higuchi, Russell, 210
Hill, Diana, 221, 222
Hillaire, Christian, 187–89
Hillary, Edmund, 270
Hillman, Conrad, 102–3
Himalayan quail, 88
Himalayas, 20–21, 153, 173
Hirosaki University, 218
Hispaniola, 5
History, Sciences, Totalitarianism and Ethics Co., 208
hoaxes, 155; Beast of Bodmin Moor, 144–45; Dancing Worm of Turkana, 166–69; Loch Ness monster, 155, 163
Hobart Zoo, 234, 243, 264–66
Hoedspruit Research and Breeding Centre for Endangered Species, 110

Hogg, Lucille and John, 104–6, 108
Holiday, F. W., 158, 165
Homer, 160
hominids, 172–76, 183–84
Homo erectus, 174
honeycreepers, 18
honeyeaters, 219, 251
Hoogland, John, 98
Hopkins, Joshua, 132
horses: backcrossing of, 204–7, 212; ice-age, 224; quaggas and, 210
Howard, JoGayle, 113–18, 120
huia, 219–23, 241
hummingbirds, 6, 28–30, 32, 286–87, 301
hutia, 5
Hylochoerus meinertzhageni, 82
Hyophorbe amaricaulis, 16

ice ages, 6, 135, 152, 170, 189–91, 200, 202, 223–24, 226–27, 230–31, 258
iguanas, 20
imperial woodpecker, 56–57, 152
Inca, 66
India, 81–83, 86–92, 152, 193
Indian clover, 18
Indians, American, 6, 186
Indonesia, 66
influenza, 106
International Society of Cryptozoology (ISC), 171–72, 181
International Syndicate for the Breeding, Reintroduction and Development of Heck's Aurochs, 207–8
Internet, 143–44, 220
Irian Jaya, 173
Irish elk, 190, 191, 223
islands, biodiversity of, 5–6
ivory-billed woodpecker, 12, 21, 39, 47–65, 101, 243
Ivory Coast, 173

jackals, 202
Jackson, Jerome, 55
Jagiellonian University, 196
jaguars, 124, 126, 149
Jamaica, 5, 20
Jarkov, Ganady, 226, 227
Java, 128
Javan rhino, 19
Jefferson, Thomas, 11, 185
jellyfish, 252
Jerdon's courser, 88–89
Jet Propulsion Laboratory, 160
Jews, Nazi persecution of, 207
John, Stanley, 9
Johnson, Harry, 181
Journal of Cryptozoology, 152
"junk DNA," 237–38
Jurassic Park (Crichton), 214, 215

kangaroos, 229, 245; ice-age, 230
Karoo National Park (South Africa),
    211
Kauai 'akialoa, 18
Keel, John and Richard, 129–30, 132,
    134
kelpies, 154
Kentucky, University of, 132
Kenya, 166–69
kestrels, 16
keystone species, 99
King, Ben, 90, 91
kingfishers, 112
King Kong (movie), 154
kiwis, 215, 216
Knox, Alan, 82–84
Kobayashi, Kazutoshi, 224, 225
Komodo dragon, 230
koniks, 204–6
kouprey, 181, 182
Krantz, Grover, 172
Kulivan, David, 57–58, 60, 62–64
KwaZulu Natal, 210

lake monsters, 151–65
Lammertink, Martjan, 64
lampreys, 71
"land lobster," *see* Lord Howe Island stick
    insect
Laos, 11, 182
Lascaux Cave (France), 189, 191
Last Tasmanian Tiger, The (Paddle), 262
Lawrence, T. E., 82
Laysan duck, 16
lemurs, 68–69, 135
Leningrad Museum, 85
leopards, 113, 126, 149; black, *see* pan-
    thers
Leopold, Aldo, 125n
Leucopeza, *see* Semper's warbler
Lewanavanua, Ratu Filipe, 74
Lewis and Clark expedition, 11, 93, 185
Libya, 109
Linnaeus, Carolus, 83
lions, 19, 109–11, 137; cave, 135; ice-
    age, 190, 191; marsupial, 230; as
    pets, 136
Lista, Ramon, 185
lizards, endangered, 20
Loch Ness monster, 151–65, 170, 175,
    183
Loch Ness Phenomenon Investigation
    Bureau, 156
logging, 50, 52, 56–57, 62–64
London Daily Mail, 154, 163
London Zoo, 132, 264
Longmore, Wayne, 76–78
Lord Howe Island, 80
Lord Howe Island stick insect, 246
Lost Grizzlies, The (Bass), 45
Lost World, The (Doyle), 11
Louisiana Department of Wildlife and
    Fisheries, 46
Louisiana State University, 57–58
Lower Great Lakes Fisheries Resource
    Office, 73
Lowery, George, Jr., 55

Lynch, Michael, 240–42, 279
Lyne, John, 257
lynx, 123, 134, 139, 149, 203

macaws, 6, 290, 299, 300
Machu Picchu, 66–68
Mackal, Roy, 156–59, 163, 171
Mackay, Aldie, 154
Madagascar, 19, 68–70, 177; ratites of, 216, 217
Madagascar serpent-eagle, 69
Maehr, David S., 132–33, 138–43, 145–48, 150
Maiden, Leslie "One-Eyed Nick," 136
mammals: domestication of, 192–95; egg-laying, 244–45; ice-age, 190–91, 223–24, 231, 258; marsupial, see marsupials; new species of, 11–12; venomous, 252–53; see also specific animals
Mammoth Museum (Siberia), 224
mammoths, 11, 190, 191; cloning of, 223–29, 235, 237
Mandelli, Louis, 85
maned rat, 67
maned wolves, 298–99
Mansi, Sandra, 157
Maori, 217–19, 221
mapinguari, 173, 183–84, 186, 298, 309
Maria Island National Park (Tasmania), 242
marsupials, 229, 230, 245, 253; predatory, 258–59 (see also thylacine); rediscovered, 19
Martin, David, 163
Maryland, University of, 172
Massachusetts Institute of Technology (MIT), 159
mass extinction, 33–35, 231
mastodons, 190
Matthiessen, Peter, 108–9

Mauritius, 16
Max Planck Institute, 180
Meganesia, 230
Megatherium, 184, 186
Meinertzhagen, Colonel Richard, 82–87, 89
Melbourne Zoo, 264
Merriam, C. Hart, 93
Meru-Betiri National Park (Java), 128
Mesoplodon, 178
Mexico, 56–57; prairie dogs in, 95, 118
MGM Studios, 109
Micronesian kingfishers, 112
Middle Ages, 195, 204
Miller, Brian, 107
Miocene Epoch, 230
Mirounga, 158
Mississippi State University, 55
mithan, 193
mitochondrial DNA (mtDNA), 210, 211
moas, 216–21, 231
Mokele-mbembe, 11, 179
Monash Institute for Reproduction and Development, 238
Mongolia, 173, 204
mongooses, 31–32
Monteverde Rain Forest Preserve (Costa Rica), 38–42
Mooney, Nick, 272–73, 277
moose, 190
Moreland, Rachel, 114, 116
Morocco, 109–11
Mothman, 153, 171, 175
moths, 297, 298
motmot, 291
mountain lions, see cougars; pumas
mountain plover, 99
muntjacs, 136–37, 182–83
Murray, P., 271
musk oxen, 190
Mustela nigripes, see black-footed ferret
Myanmar, 182, 183
mycology, 177

Mylodon, 184–86
myrmecology, 177
myrtles, 273

Naarding, Hans, 243, 244, 272
Namibia, 210
National Air and Space Administration (NASA), 159
National Fish and Wildlife Foundation, 73
National Wildlife Federation, 97
National Zoo (Washington, D.C.), 132, 229, 232, 264; Conservation and Research Center (CRC) of, 105, 112–22
Native Fish Conservancy, 73
Natural History Museum (London), 82, 83, 87, 145, 192
natural selection, 34–35
Nature, 160
Nazis, 203, 206, 207, 211
Neanderthals, 173
Neolithic age, 149, 192, 194, 195
Neomylodon listai, 185
Nepal, 173
Nessiteras rhombopteryx, 160–62
"new-breeding," 208–9
New Guinea, 201, 216, 246, 250; human colonization of, 231
New York Times, 92, 122, 211
New Zealand, 216–19, 241; rediscovered species on, 246–48
Nguoi Rung, 173
night parrot, 75–81, 246
ningaui, 229
Noble, Ted, 137
Northern Arizona University, 227
northern hairy-nosed wombat, 238–39
Nothofagus, 273, 278
Nubian lion, *see* Barbary lion
nuclear transfer, 221

Nugent, Rory, 88
numbat, 237

Occam's Razor, 176, 306
ocelots, 137
octopus, blue-ringed, 252
okapi, 180
Olivera, Fabiano, 280–85, 291–309
Operation Deepscan, 161
Operation Last Look, 138
orangutan, 179
Oren, David C., 184–86
oriole, St. Lucian, 8
oryx, 112
Oryx (journal), 212
ostriches, 215–17
Otago, University of, 218, 220–21
otters, 123, 203
owls, 6, 20, 70, 82, 86–92, 259, 299; burrowing, 99; endangered, 101
Oxford University, 110

Paddle, Robert, 262–63, 265–66, 271
Pakistan, 20–21, 173; domestication of cattle in, 195
pale-headed brush-finch, 19–20
Paleocene Era, 35
Paleolithic age, 189, 191, 204, 205
panda: giant, 180; red, 112
pandemelons, 245, 253
Panthera; *P. tigris*, 128; *P.l. leo*, 109; *P.l. melanochaitus*, 110
panthers, 123–24, 126–28; in England, 129–50, 152, 241, 243
Papua New Guinea, University of, 247
paradise parrot, 80–81
parakeets, 16
Paris, University of, 172
Paris Match, 226
Paris Museum, 85, 288, 289
Parker, Ted, 299

Parliament, British, 130, 136
parrots, 4, 35, 278, 300; endangered,
    7–8, 24; extinct, 6; rediscovered,
    75–81, 246
passenger pigeon, 17, 123
Pasteur, Louis, 65, 67
Patterson, Bryan, 166–69
Patterson, Lt. Col. John Henry, 166
Patuxent Wildlife Research Center, 102,
    105, 112
Peacock, Doug, 44
Pearl River Wildlife Management Area
    (Louisiana), 45–47, 52–54, 57–65
Pearson, T. Gilbert, 51–52
peccaries, 181–82
Pennsylvania State University, 123
Peregrine Fund, 69
Permian Period, 33–34
Peterson, Roger Tory, 54
Peru, 66–68, 77, 281, 285
petrels, 22, 74–75
pewee, St. Lucian, 8
Philadelphia Academy of Natural Sci-
    ences, 282
pileated woodpecker, 49, 58, 59, 63
pink-headed duck, 88
plants: backcrossing of, 197; domestica-
    tion of, 192; rediscoveries of, 18–19,
    246
platypus, 245, 252–53
Pleistocene Epoch, 228; birds of, 216;
    cave paintings of, 188; mammals of,
    181, 185, 186, 190, 195, 223 (see also
    specific animals)
Pleistocene Park (Siberia), 229
Plimpton, George, 57
plovers, 99
pneumonia, 260
Poland, 197; aurochs in, 196, 201; back-
    crossing of horses in, 204–7, 212;
    Nazi occupation of, 203, 206
Polo, Marco, 217
possums, 245, 258, 259–60

potoroos, 19, 245, 246
Pounds, J. Alan, 40
Powys Puma, 129
Poznan University, 204
Pradhan, Ranjan Kumar, 90
prairie dogs, 93, 95–100, 102–6, 118–
    22
pratincole, 76–77
protomammals, 33
"proto-pygmies," 173
Prys-Jones, Robert, 83, 85
Przewalski's horse, 180, 204–6
pufflegs, 287
Puma concolor; P.c. coryi, 124; P.c. cougar,
    10, 123, 126
pumas, 129, 134, 138, 140–41, 143,
    144
Pyle, Robert Michael, 173
pythons, 230

quagga, 208–12
Quagga Project, 210–12
Queensland Museum, 76, 78
quokkas, 246
quolls, 245, 259

Rabat Zoo (Morocco), 110
rabbits, 183
Rabinowitz, Alan, 183
rails, 112
raptors, 99; see also eagles; hawks
Rasmussen, Pamela, 81–92
ratites, 216–20; see also specific birds
rats, 31–32, 66–68
rattlesnakes, 99
Rau, Reinhold E., 209, 210
Reading, Richard, 107
red-bellied woodpecker, 52
Redgrave and Lopham Fen National Na-
    ture Reserve (England), 207
red owl, 70

red pandas, 112
redpolls, 82, 84
Reid, Alison, 264–65
Reid, Arthur, 264
religions, ancient, 193
Remsen, J. V. "Van," 58, 63
restorative justice, 241
rheas, 216, 217, 292–93
rheumatic fever, 201
rhinoceros, 19; woolly, 190, 191, 223–25
Rhynchophthraupis mesoleuca, 281
Richardson, Douglas, 132
Richardson, Eugene S., Jr., 166–69
Ridgely, Robert, 285, 306
Rines, Robert, 159–61
roadkill, 245; of cougars, 141
Rockies, grizzlies of, 39, 42–45
Rokosz, Mieczyslaw, 196
Rome, ancient, 109, 110, 136, 149, 191–92, 195, 196
Roosevelt, Theodore, 183
Rose, Quentin, 130, 132–34, 138–42, 147–50
Roslin Institute, 221
Royal Auxiliary Air Force, 138
rufous-throated white-eye, 19
Russia: mammoths of, 223–27; wild horses of, 204; *see also* Siberia
Russian Revolution, 82

saber-toothed cats, 190, 223
Sagan, Carl, 175–76
St. Lucia, 3–10, 12–16, 21, 24–33, 243, 285; Forestry Department, 10, 13
saola, 182
Sardinia, 193
Sarmiento, Esteban, 180
Sasquatch, 12, 151, 173, 309
Savage, Jay M., 38
Schaller, George, 180

scimitar-horned oryx, 112
sclerophyll forest, 250
scorpions, 308
Scotland, 149; big-cat sightings in, 131, 137; cattle of, 196; lake monster in, *see* Loch Ness monster
Scott, Peter, 156, 160–61
Scott, Robert Falcon, 156
Searching for Hidden Animals (Mackal), 157
sea serpents, 152, 157, 172, 178–79
sea wasp, 252
seiche waves, 162, 165
Seidensticker, John, 128, 132
seismic activity, 162
Selassie, Haile, 110
selective breeding, 194, 197, 212; *see also* backcrossing
Semper, John E., 8, 9, 26
Semper's warbler, 8–10, 12, 13, 15, 21, 24–33, 80, 152, 243, 285
Seri, Lester, 248
seriema, 299, 300
Seton, Ernest Thompson, 95, 99
Seychelle Islands, 35–36
sharks, 172
Sharpe, Bowdler, 85–86
Shea, Brian T., 179
sheep: in England, 129, 133, 135–38, 141, 144, 147, 149; in Tasmania, 256–58
shellfish, venomous, 252
Shine, Adrian, 163
Shirota, Yasuyuki, 218
Shively, Steve, 45–47, 53, 58–64
Short, Lester, 55–56
shrews, 5
shrub-oxen, 190
Siberia, 195; giant black bear in, 152; hominids in, 173; mammoths in, 191, 224–29, 235
Siberian ferrets, 102, 108, 113, 115
Sick, Helmut, 289

SIERDAH (Syndicat International pour l'Elevage, la Reintroduction et le Développement de l'Aurochs de Heck), 207–8
sika, 137
Simien jackal, 202
Singer Tract, 51, 52, 54, 55
Sisemite, 173
Sixth Extinction, 34
skin specimens: Bogotá, 286–87; fraudulent, 84–87, 89; preparation of, 83–84
skinks, 250
Skunk Apes, 153, 174
sloths, 5, 6; giant ground, 10, 152, 184–86, 190, 230
small-population biology, 164, 275
Smith, Dick, 76, 78
Smithsonian Institution, 66, 81, 83, 87, 95; National Museum of Natural History, 84; see also National Zoo
snakes, 5, 31–32, 60; venomous, 252, 253
solenodon, 5
South Africa, 110, 111; see also KwaZulu Natal
South African Museum (Cape Town), 209
South Australian Museum, 76, 78
South West Coast Path (England), 146
Southwestern College, 76
Spain, 199
Spence, John, 110
spiders, 259; venomous, 252
Spielberg, Steven, 214
spotted owl, 101
squid, 178
Sri Lanka, 173
Stanley, Henry Morton, 181
Stepien, Carol, 72, 73
stochastic factors, 276
streaky-breasted jungle-flycatcher, 19
sturgeon, 162–63

sugar gliders, 251
sweat bees, 301, 302, 304–6, 308, 310
Sweet, Paul, 25–26
swifts, 291
Sybille Wildlife Research and Conservation Education Center, 107, 112
Sydney funnelweb spider, 252
sylvatic plague, 100, 102, 105–6, 117–19, 122

taipan, 252
Takhtajania perrieri, 19
tanagers, 281, 282, 284–92, 297, 298, 300, 302–6, 309–10
Tanner, James T., 21, 51, 52, 54, 56, 58–59, 62, 63
tape-playback technique, 15
tapirs, 179, 298
tarpan, 204–7, 211, 212
Tasman, Abel, 230
Tasmania, 230–33, 240–45, 249–53, 256–79; Animal and Birds Protection Board (Fauna Board), 242, 267, 270; University of, 261
Tasmanian Conservation Trust, 240, 279
Tasmanian devil, 231, 237, 239, 245, 259
Tasmanian Museum, 267
Tasmanian native hen, 231
Tasmanian "tiger," see thylacine
Tasmanian Wilderness World Heritage Area, 244, 273–74
taurine cattle, 195
teratorns, 170
textile cone, 252
Thailand, 182
Theodore Roosevelt National Park (North Dakota), 97–98
thermoclines, 162
theropods, 215
Thomas, Mike, 142–43
Thompson, Max, 76, 77

thrashers, 29, 31

threatened species, 97, 99, 101, 122; recovery projects for, 240

Throwim Way Leg (Flannery), 248

thylacine (Tasmanian "tiger"), 11, 21, 76, 79, 152, 229–45, 260–79, 298; biology and ecology of, 253–56, 262; in captivity, 256, 262–66, 271; cloning of, 233–42, 278–79; evidence of survival of, 261, 268–70; government bounty on, 256–57, 261–63; habitat for, 245, 275; modern sightings of, 243–44, 248–49, 257, 267, 269, 272–75, 277

Thylacinus cynocephalus, 230

Thylacoleo, 230

thyroid hormones, 194–95

Tibet, 173, 174

ticks, 253

Tierpark Hellabrunn (Munich), 198, 201, 206

tigers, 128, 139, 149

tiger snakes, 252, 253

Times of London, 92

Tityus, 308

toads, golden, 23, 38–42

Today show, 151

topcrossing, *see* backcrossing

tortoises, giant, 36, 230

toucanets, 291

trapdoor spiders, 259

tree frogs, 5

tropical ecosystems, biodiversity of, 5, 68

Trounson, Alan, 238–39

Tullimonstrum gregarium, 158, 165–67, 169

Tully, Francis, 165–66

Tumaco seedeater, 285–86

Tunisia, 109

Turkey, bull worship in, 193

turkeys, wild, 123

Turner, Ted, 269

turquoise-throated puffleg, 287

turtles, giant, 152, 156

Two Peoples Bay Nature Reserve (Australia), 246

Tyrannosaurus, 215

Ucumar, 173

Uganda, 181

Uganda Railway, 166

UNESCO World Heritage Areas, 207, 244

Ursus spelaeus, 190

U.S. Department of Agriculture: Animal Damage Control Division, 97, 102

U.S. Fish and Wildlife Service (USFWS), 55, 96, 97, 101–3, 105, 117, 122, 125n

vaginal cytology, 112

Van Dieman's Land Company, 232, 256, 268

Vaurie, Charles, 85

Vellard, A., 285, 287–90, 292, 303, 309–10

venomous creatures, 252–53, 308

Vetulani, Tadeusz, 204–5

Vietnam, 11, 19, 152, 173, 182; Ministry of Forestry, 182

Visual Resources for Ornithology (VIREO), 282

Viviparous Quadrupeds of North America, The (Audubon and Bachman), 93, 94

Vu Quang Nature Reserve (Vietnam), 182

Waitangi, Treaty of (1840), 221

Wales, big-cat sightings in, 129, 131–32, 134, 135, 138

wallabies, 137, 231, 245, 246, 253, 258, 275

walleyes, 70–73
warblers, 8–11, 17
Ware, Lisa, 113, 115
Washington State University, 172
Watling, Dick, 74–75
wattlebirds, 219, 220, 222, 251
Wayne, A. T., 50
weasels, 96, 121; see also black-footed
  ferret
Wechsler, Doug, 280–85, 291–309
Weichselian (Würm) glaciation, 190,
  191
Western Australian Department of Con-
  servation and Land Management,
  79
Wetherell, Ian, 163
Wetherell, Marmaduke, 154, 163
whales, 157, 163; beaked, 177–78; re-
  discovered, 246
Where Bigfoot Walks (Pyle), 173
whitefish, 70–71
White River monster, 158–59
wildcats, Scottish, 143
Wildlife Conservation Society, 20,
  183
Wildlife in America (Matthiessen), 108–9
Wildt, David, 229
Williamson, Linwood, 119–21
Wilmut, Ian, 221, 238
Wilson, C. J., 144
Wilson, E. O., 34
Wilson, R. Kenneth, 155, 162
Wingate, David, 22
Winteraceae family, 19
Wiseman, Ed, 43
wisent, 196, 198, 203
wolves, 123, 149, 192, 202, 203; ice-

age, 190; maned, 298–99; Mexican,
  56
wombats, 230, 258; see also northern
  hairy-nosed wombat
Wood, Roger, 167–69
woodpeckers, 52; see also imperial wood-
  pecker; ivory-billed woodpecker
Wopkaimin people, 247
World War I, 82, 154, 263
World War II, 43, 52, 88, 132, 181,
  201, 203, 206, 261
World Wide Fund for Nature, 182
World Wildlife Fund, 156; of India,
  88
Wrangham, Richard, 180
Wright, Bruce S., 125n
Würm glaciation, see Weichselian
  (Würm) glaciation
Wyoming Game and Fish Department,
  105–8

Yale University, 184
yellow-bellied water snake, 60–61
Yellowstone National Park, 42
Yeren, 172, 173
yeti, 153, 173
Yowie, 173

Zahler, Peter, 20–21
Zaire, 20
zebras, 208–11
zebu cattle, 195
Zeiss, Carl, Sports Optics, 64
zeuglodons, 157, 163
Zhou Guoxing, 172